… Longman

21st Century Science

Science GCSE Foundation

Series Editor:
Penny Johnson

Peter Ellis
Michele Francis
Sue Kearsey
Penny Marshall
Michael O'Neill
Gary Philpott
Steve Woolley

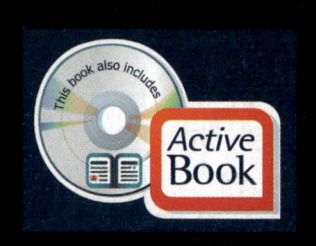

PEARSON
Longman
Edinburgh Gate
Harlow, Essex

Contents

How to use this book   6

B1   You and your genes

B1.1	You and your genes	8
B1.2	Genes and DNA	10
B1.3	One parent or two?	12
B1.4	Specialised cells	14
B1.5	Sex chromosomes	16
B1.6	Alleles	18
B1.7	Inherited diseases	20
B1.8	Healthy children?	22
B1.9	Genetic testing	24
B1.10	Modifying genes	26
B1.11	Cloning and stem cells	28
B1.12	Using embryos	30
B1.13	Gene clinic	32

C1   Air quality

C1.1	Air quality	34
C1.2	Looking at data on air quality	36
C1.3	Air – a mixture	38
C1.4	Checking the pollutants	40
C1.5	Making new compounds	42
C1.6	Burning fuels	44
C1.7	Making pollutants	46
C1.8	Air pollutants and the environment	48
C1.9	Air pollution and health	50
C1.10	Pollution and power stations	52
C1.11	Pollution and transport	54
C1.12	Making choices about air quality	56
C1.13	Looking at air quality	58

P1 The Earth in the Universe

P1.1	The Earth in the Universe	60
P1.2	The face of the Earth	62
P1.3	Continental drift	64
P1.4	Plate tectonics	66
P1.5	Weighing the evidence	68
P1.6	Geohazards 1 – Volcanoes	70
P1.7	Geohazards 2 – Earthquakes	72
P1.8	The Solar System	74
P1.9	Asteroid impact!	76
P1.10	Studying the stars	78
P1.11	The Sun and other stars	80
P1.12	The Milky Way and beyond	82
P1.13	Planet for sale!	84

B2 Keeping healthy

B2.1	Keeping healthy	86
B2.2	Microorganisms and disease	88
B2.3	Body defences	90
B2.4	Fighting off infection	92
B2.5	Helping the immune system	94
B2.6	The good and bad side of vaccination	96
B2.7	Choosing to vaccinate	98
B2.8	Antibiotics	100
B2.9	Testing treatments	102
B2.10	The testing debate	104
B2.11	Heart disease	106
B2.12	Finding the cause	108
B2.13	A doctor's day	110

C2 Material choices

C2.1	Material choices	112
C2.2	Fit for the job	114
C2.3	Comparing properties	116
C2.4	More properties	118

C2.5	Plastics, rubbers and fibres	120
C2.6	Synthetic materials	122
C2.7	Refining oil	124
C2.8	Making polymers	126
C2.9	Inside polymers	128
C2.10	Changing polymers	130
C2.11	Life cycle of a polymer	132
C2.12	Life Cycle Assessments	134
C2.13	A shopping trip	136

P2 Radiation and life

P2.1	Radiation and life	138
P2.2	The electromagnetic spectrum	140
P2.3	Heating with radiation	142
P2.4	Mobile phones and microwaves	144
P2.5	Ionising radiation	146
P2.6	The ozone layer	148
P2.7	Photosynthesis	150
P2.8	The carbon cycle	152
P2.9	The greenhouse effect	154
P2.10	A warmer Earth	156
P2.11	The global warming debate	158
P2.12	The way forward	160
P2.13	Staying safe	162

B3 Life on Earth

B3.1	Life on Earth	164
B3.2	Starting out	166
B3.3	Evolution of life on Earth	168
B3.4	Evolution by natural selection	170
B3.5	Darwin's theory of evolution	172
B3.6	Sensor and effector cells	174
B3.7	Communication systems	176
B3.8	Human evolution	178
B3.9	Food webs	180
B3.10	Extinction	182

B3.11	Humans and extinctions	184
B3.12	Biodiversity	186
B3.13	Earth, life and humans	188

C3 Food matters

C3.1	Food matters	190
C3.2	Producing food	192
C3.3	Intensive farming	194
C3.4	Organic farming	196
C3.5	Food additives	198
C3.6	Additives and safety	200
C3.7	Chemical contaminants 1	202
C3.8	Chemical contaminants 2	204
C3.9	Digestion	206
C3.10	Using food	208
C3.11	Diabetes	210
C3.12	Diet and health	212
C3.13	Food and its uses	214

P3 Radioactive materials

P3.1	Radioactive materials	216
P3.2	Radioactivity	218
P3.3	Three types of radiation	220
P3.4	Activity and half-life	222
P3.5	Ionising effects of radiation	224
P3.6	Exposure to radiation	226
P3.7	Are we safe?	228
P3.8	Fossil fuels and electricity	230
P3.9	Renewable energy resources	232
P3.10	Nuclear power	234
P3.11	Renewable or non-renewable?	236
P3.12	Sustainable development	238
P3.13	Power for the people	240

Glossary	242
Index	250
Acknowledgements	254

How to use this book

Each module starts with a double page that introduces some of the ideas that you will learn more about in the module.

It also has questions that will help you to start thinking about the ideas in the module.

Each module is divided into 12 topics. Each topic is a double page.

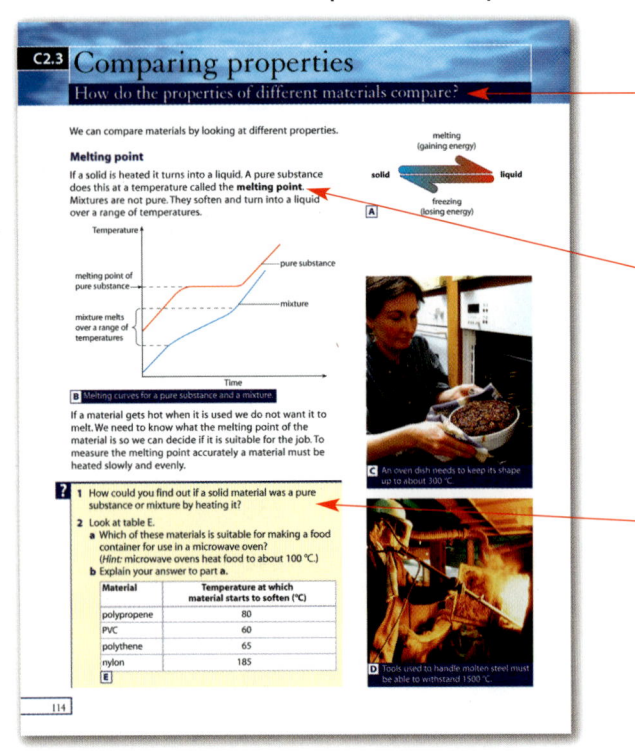

You should be able to answer this question when you have finished this topic.

The words in **bold** are important scientific words. You can check their meanings by looking at the glossary at the end of the book.

The questions will help you to understand what is on the page.

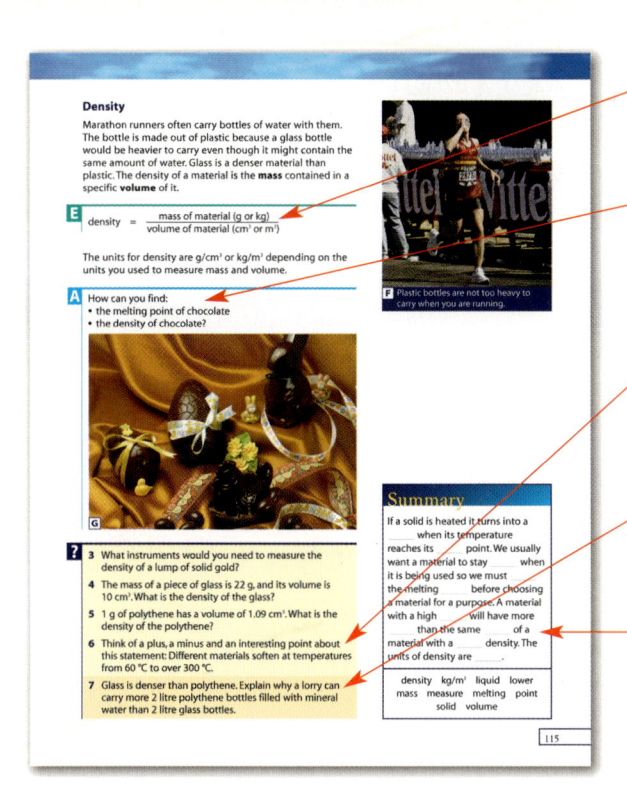

These boxes show important equations that you need to remember.

These boxes give you ideas for practical work or other activities.

Some questions ask you to give more than one answer, to help you think harder about what you are learning.

The last question is more difficult than the others, to see how well you understand the topic.

The summary will help you remember all the ideas you need from this topic. Keep the answers to the summaries for when you are revising for tests or examinations.

The last two pages have revision questions that will help you check how much you have remembered from this module.

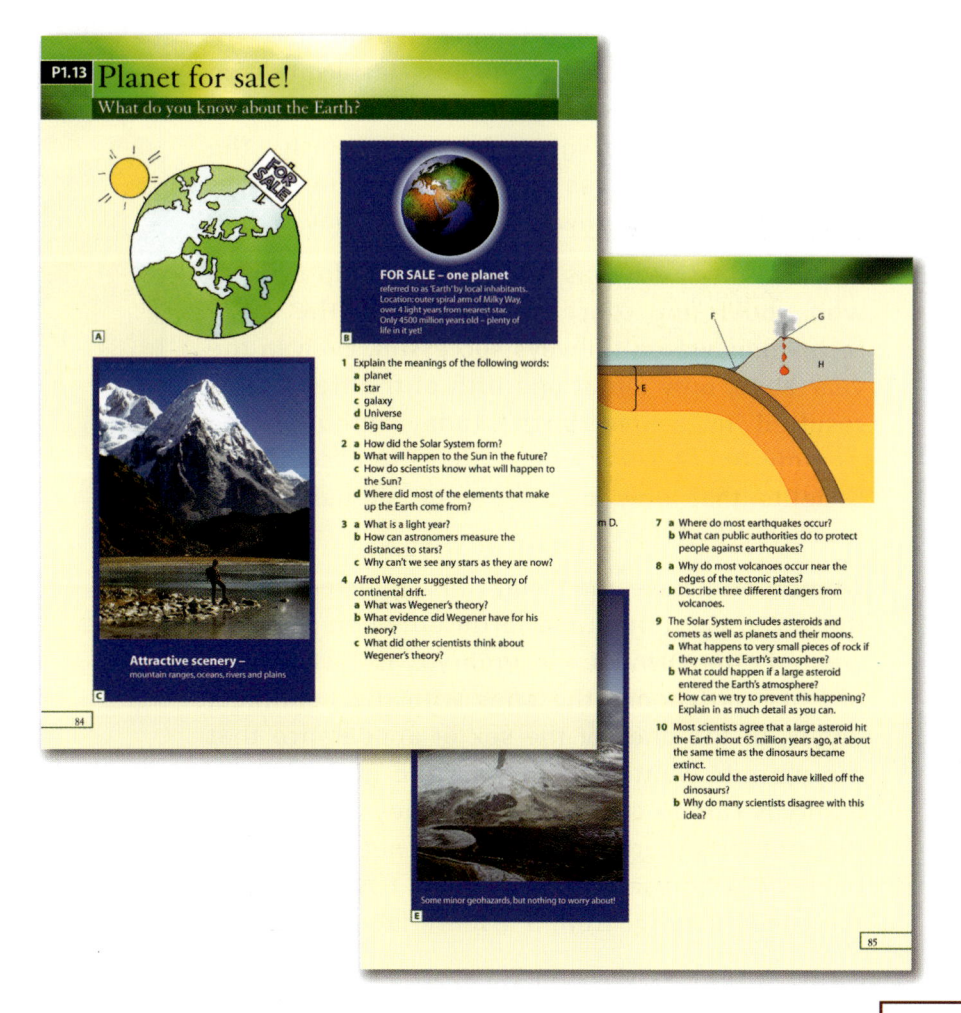

B1.1 You and your genes

How are genes passed on?

Health news, 1 April 2056

Non-IVF to be banned?
Law proposed to ban 'natural' conception

The 'Right to Health' group is campaigning for a new law to ban the old 'natural' method of conception, where a sperm fertilises an egg cell inside the woman's body.

The modern era started back in 1978 with the birth of Louise Brown, the world's first 'test tube baby'. The official name for the treatment is 'In-Vitro Fertilisation', which means 'fertilisation in glass'! Egg cells were taken from Louise's mother and fertilised in a glass laboratory dish. The fertilised egg cell was placed back in her uterus for the embryo to grow in the normal way.

In those days, IVF was only used to help couples who could not conceive 'normally'. The early techniques weren't always successful. Even in the year 2010, only about one fifth of the treatments resulted in a live birth. Today, though, the treatments always work, and offer so many benefits that now over 95% of all babies are conceived by IVF.

Women only have their egg cells collected once – these can be stored, and fertilised when they are wanted. The DNA of the embryos is tested, and parents can choose the ones with the healthiest genes, or the ones of the sex or appearance that the parents want. If necessary, the genes of the embryos can be changed before they are put into the mother's uterus. Any embryos not wanted for babies can be used for spare body tissues in case the children suffer from a disease later in life.

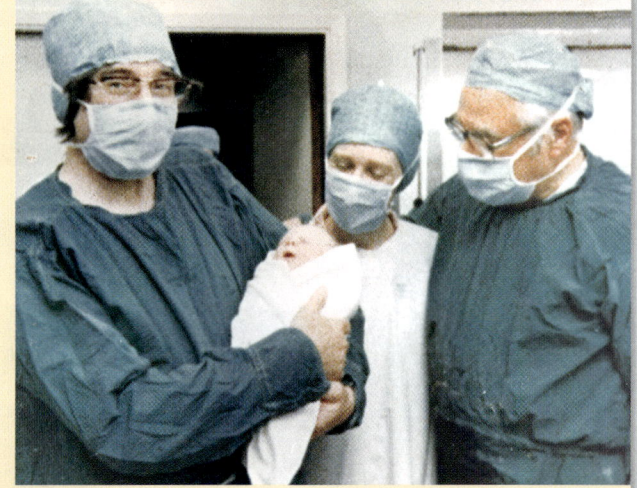

Louise Brown

Some opponents say that this way of reproducing is un-natural, and should not be allowed. Right to Health campaigners point out that there are far fewer cases of inherited diseases today than there were 50 years ago, and future children should not be denied the right to health, good looks and happiness. IVF treatments do cost a lot of money, but the Health Services have saved even more money by not having to care for people with genetic diseases.

We don't know what will happen in the future, but scientists are discovering more about us and our genes all the time. The way of reproducing described in the news report *could* happen at some time in the future.

However, just because something *can* be done, does not mean that it *should* be done. People will have to decide whether genetic testing and cloning are morally right. Decisions like this are called **ethical decisions**. They will need to know something about genes and how they work to help them to decide.

?
1. Describe how humans normally reproduce.
2. a What does IVF mean?
   b How is IVF done?
3. a What are the advantages of IVF described in the article?
   b Write down some arguments against using IVF in this way.
4. What is *your* opinion about the article?
5. Write down a list of things you would need to find out about to help you to decide whether you would be for or against the new law.

B1.2 Genes and DNA

What do genes do?

We all started off from a sperm cell and an egg cell, but we all look different to one another. We may have different coloured eyes or hair, different shaped faces, or different skin colours. These things are our **characteristics**. Many of our characteristics are caused by **genes**, which control how our bodies grow. We all have slightly different genes.

Most of our characteristics depend on combinations of several genes working together, and some characteristics are affected by **environmental factors** as well. For example, your height depends on the effect of several genes, and may also depend on whether or not you got enough food when you were growing.

Most of the **cells** in your body have a **nucleus**, and the nucleus contains **chromosomes**. Chromosomes are made of long molecules of a chemical called **DNA**. Genes are sections of chromosomes.

A

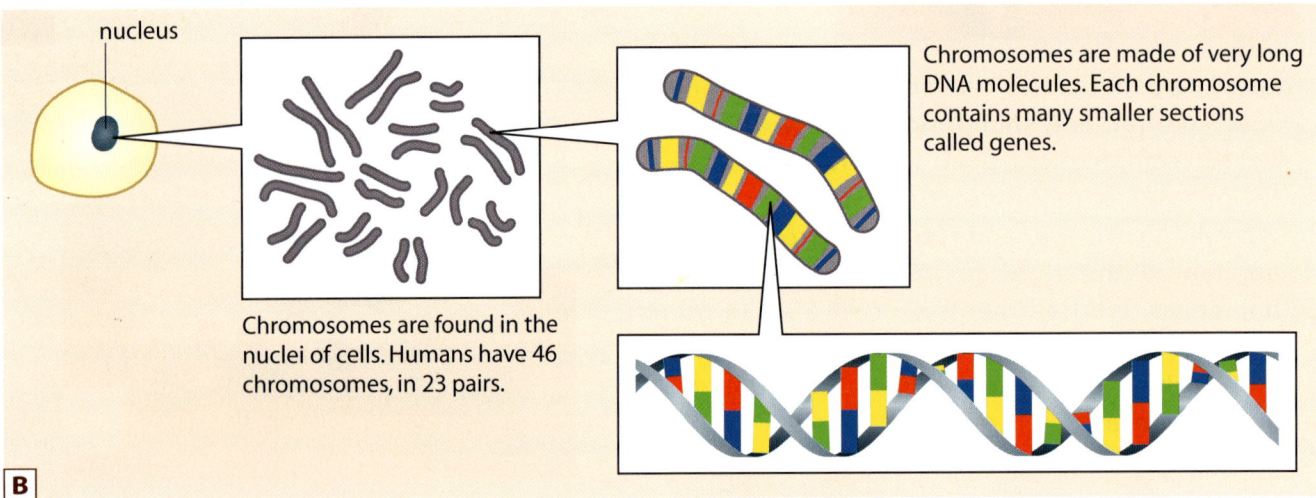

Chromosomes are found in the nuclei of cells. Humans have 46 chromosomes, in 23 pairs.

Chromosomes are made of very long DNA molecules. Each chromosome contains many smaller sections called genes.

B

? 1 a Where are chromosomes found?
  b What are they made from?
  c How many are there in human body cells?
2 What do genes do?

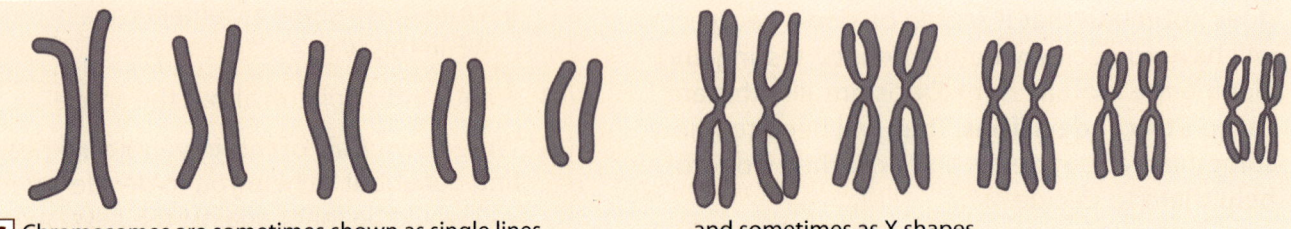

C Chromosomes are sometimes shown as single lines... and sometimes as X shapes.

You can think of genes as chapters in a book. Each chapter (gene) contains an instruction that controls one of our characteristics. The chapters (genes) are collected together into books (chromosomes), so each chromosome carries the instructions for lots of characteristics.

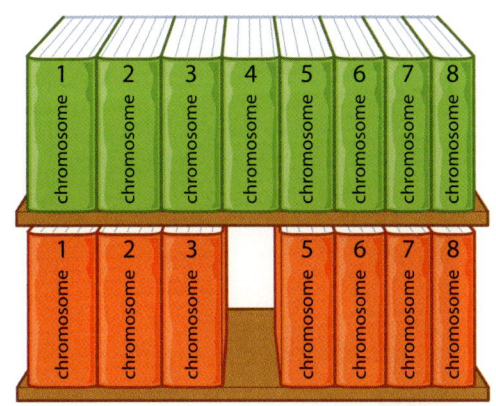

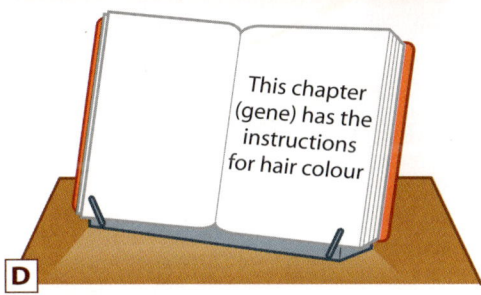

D This chapter (gene) has the instructions for hair colour

E Sometimes criminals leave hairs, blood or bits of skin at the scene of a crime. Forensic scientists can analyse the DNA and see if it matches DNA samples taken from criminals.

Genes and proteins

Genes carry the instructions for making **proteins**. Proteins are important chemicals because they make up parts of your body such as muscles, skin and hair. These are called **structural proteins**.

There are other important proteins called **enzymes**. Enzymes control the chemical reactions that happen in your body. Nearly everything that happens in your body depends on enzymes. For example, enzymes:
- help to break down food in your digestive system
- help to build new cells
- keep your nerves and brain working.

?
3 What are structural proteins?
4 **a** What are enzymes?
   b Why are enzymes important?
5 Write these things in order of size, and explain your answer:
   DNA molecule, nucleus, chromosome, gene
6 Look at photograph E. Why do you think the scene of crime officers are wearing overalls and gloves?

Summary

The _____ of your cells contain _____, and each chromosome has many _____ on it. Chromosomes are made of _____. Genes are the _____ for making _____. _____ are proteins that _____ nearly everything that happens in your body. Most of your _____ are controlled by more than one gene.

characteristics   chromosomes
control   DNA   enzymes   genes
instructions   nuclei   proteins

11

B1.3 One parent or two?

What are sexual and asexual reproduction?

All living things can **reproduce**. In most animals this happens by **sexual reproduction**, when male and female sex cells **fuse** (combine) to form a **fertilised** egg. The offspring **inherit** half of their genes from their mother, and half from their father. This is why the offspring look similar to their parents, but are not identical to them.

A These puppies have inherited characteristics from both their parents.

1 What does sexual reproduction mean?

2 Why are the offspring of sexual reproduction:
 a similar to their parents
 b not identical to their parents?

Some animals can also reproduce **asexually**. This means that one animal can produce offspring without needing a mate of the opposite sex.

The offspring produced by asexual reproduction only have one parent, so they get all their genes from this parent. All the offspring have the same genes as each other and their parent. The offspring are said to be **clones**.

3 a What is asexual reproduction?
 b Describe one way that animals can reproduce asexually.

4 What is a clone?

Bacteria and plants

Bacteria mostly reproduce asexually. If you have food poisoning, all the bacteria in you that are making you ill are likely to be clones, because they have been produced by asexual reproduction.

B Female aphids can give birth to live young which have developed without fertilisation by a male aphid.

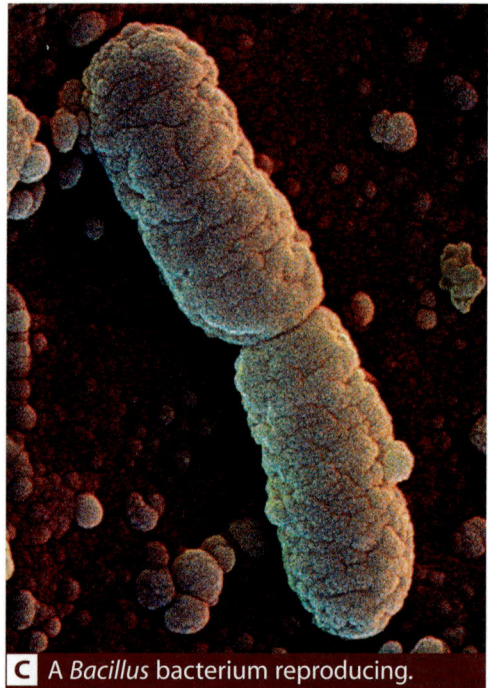

C A *Bacillus* bacterium reproducing. The 'parent' cell is splitting into two genetically identical cells (magnification x20 000).

Sexual reproduction in plants happens when an egg cell is fertilised by pollen from another plant, and grows into a seed. The plant that grows from the seed will have genes from both the parent plants.

Many plants can reproduce asexually as well. We can make this happen artificially by growing new plants from **cuttings** (parts cut off a plant). The cuttings will grow roots and develop into new plants.

A Are leaves the only parts of plants that can be used for cloning?
- How would you find out?
- What apparatus would you need?

D New plants will grow from a leaf cut from a plant.

E Strawberry plants put out runners, which produce roots and eventually grow into new plants.

F *Bryophyllum* plants grow tiny plantlets on the edges of their leaves, which can grow into new plants.

? 5 Write down three ways in which clones of plants can be produced.

Clones of an organism all have the same genes, but they may not always look the same. Environmental factors such as the amount of food, or diseases, can affect how an organism grows.

? 6 One pea plant is bigger than another. Write down as many explanations for this statement as you can.

7 Hydra are animals that live in water. Find out how they reproduce asexually.

Summary

Sexual _____ needs _____ parents, and the offspring _____ genes from each parent. _____ reproduction only needs one _____, and the offspring are all _____ (they all have identical _____). Plants, _____ and some animals can reproduce asexually. Differences between clones can be caused by _____ factors.

asexual   bacteria   clones
environmental   genes   inherit
parent   reproduction   two

13

B1.4 Specialised cells

Why are there so many different kinds of cell?

A These skaters need to use their sight and hearing to dance to the music. They need to use their bones, muscles and nerves to move their bodies, and their brains to remember the moves.

Our bodies have over 200 different kinds of cell, and each kind has a particular **function** (job). For example:
- some cells detect light and sound
- some help our bodies to move
- some carry oxygen around our bodies
- some help us to reproduce.

The different kinds of cell are **specialised**, which means they have features that help them to do their job. Egg cells and sperm cells are called **gametes** (sex cells). They are specialised to help us to reproduce.

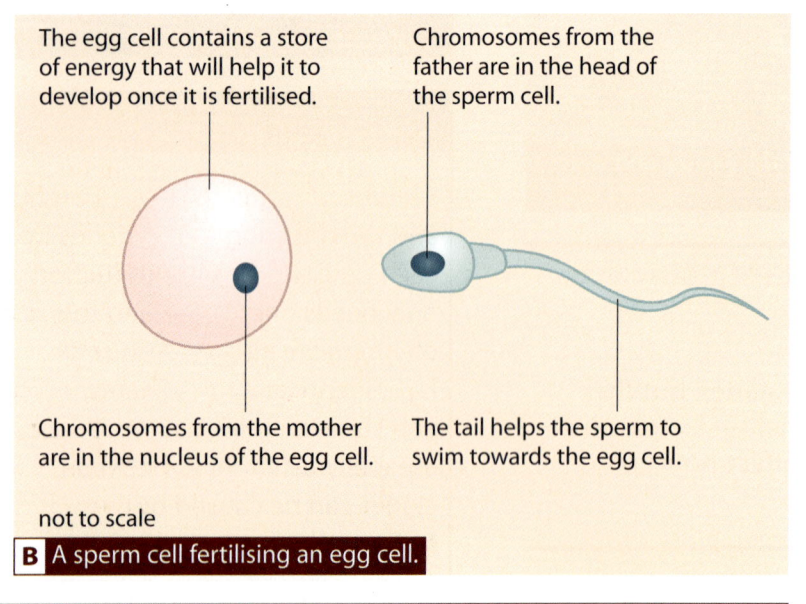

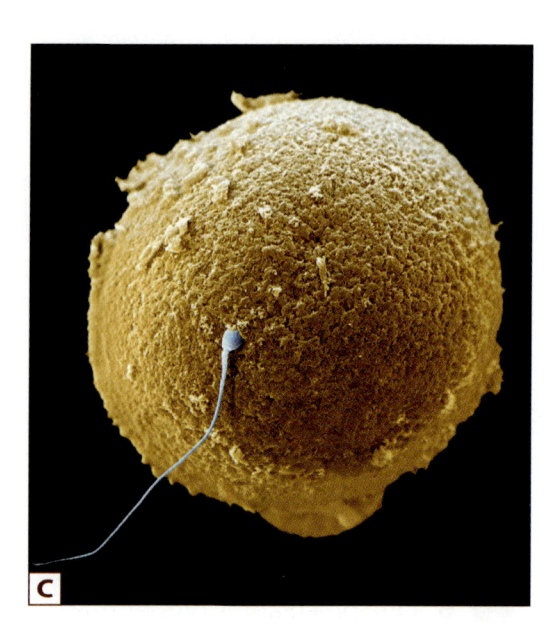

The egg cell contains a store of energy that will help it to develop once it is fertilised.

Chromosomes from the father are in the head of the sperm cell.

Chromosomes from the mother are in the nucleus of the egg cell.

The tail helps the sperm to swim towards the egg cell.

not to scale

B A sperm cell fertilising an egg cell.

C

?
1. Describe two ways in which sperm cells are specialised.
2. Describe two ways in which egg cells are specialised.

Normal body cells have 23 *pairs* of chromosomes. Gametes only have half of the chromosomes of a normal cell, so that when they fuse, the fertilised egg cell has the correct number of chromosomes.

> **?**
> 3 How many chromosomes are there in:
>   a a normal body cell
>   b a sperm cell
>   c an egg cell?
>
> 4 What happens during fertilisation?

the sperm cell contains 1 set of chromosomes (23)

the egg cell contains 1 set of chromosomes (23)

the gametes fuse in fertilisation

the fertilised egg cell contains the normal number of chromosomes (2 sets, 23 pairs)

D

After an egg cell is fertilised, it divides to make copies of itself. About four days after fertilisation it is a ball of cells called an **embryo**. The cells continue to divide, but they soon begin to specialise. All the cells still have the same genetic instructions, but different cells follow different parts of the instructions. Some cells develop into muscle cells, some develop into nerve cells and others specialise in different ways.

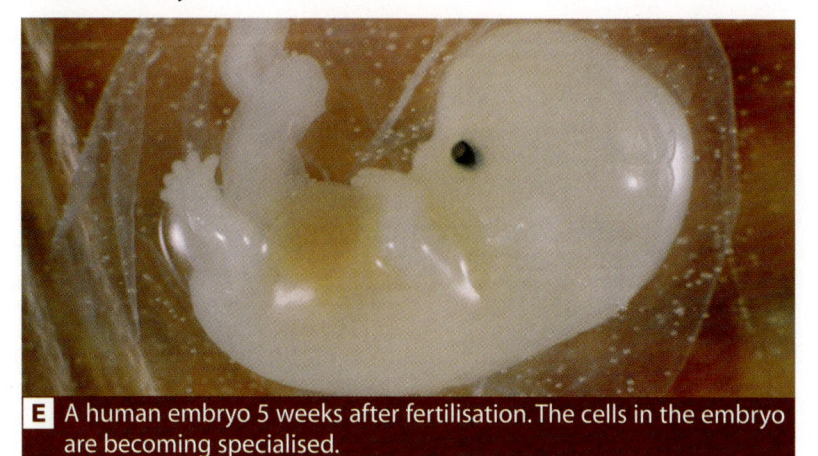

E A human embryo 5 weeks after fertilisation. The cells in the embryo are becoming specialised.

Some of the cells in your body are still dividing, so that you can grow and replace damaged cells. When a body cell divides, it produces a cell just like itself. Once human cells have become specialised, they cannot change into different types of cell.

> **?**
> 5 Why will your cells need to divide even after you have stopped growing?
>
> 6 Which is the odd one out: nerve cell, egg cell, muscle cell? Explain your answers.
>
> 7 Write down at least one way in which each of these cells is specialised:
>   a pollen grain
>   b root hair cell
>   c red blood cell

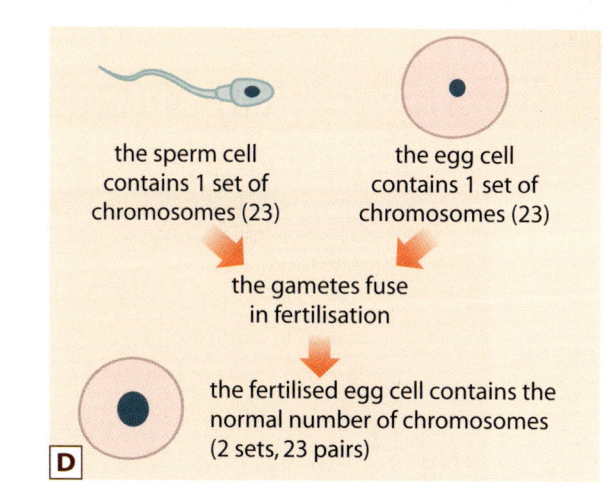

Summary

_____ contain half the normal number of _____. Everyone has lots of different types of _____, which all develop from a single _____ egg cell. This cell divides and the new cells become _____. Specialised cells have _____ to help them to carry out their _____.

cells	chromosomes	features
fertilised	function	gametes
	specialised	

15

B1.5 Sex chromosomes

How do genes produce boys and girls?

A A peahen (female) and a peacock (male).

When animals reproduce, the offspring develop into either males or females. The male and female of a species can look very different.

The **gender** of a human depends on the **sex chromosomes**. There are two types of sex chromosomes, called X and Y. Women have two X chromosomes, and men have one X and one Y. We say that women are XX and men are XY.

?
1. What are the two kinds of sex chromosome called?
2. Which sex chromosomes do men have?

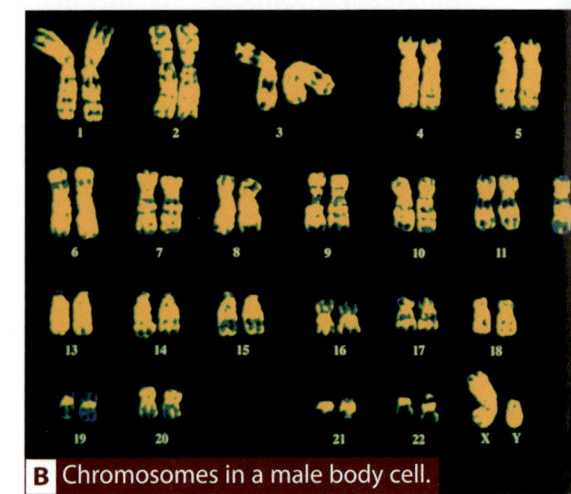

B Chromosomes in a male body cell.

This fertilised egg cell will grow into a girl.

C

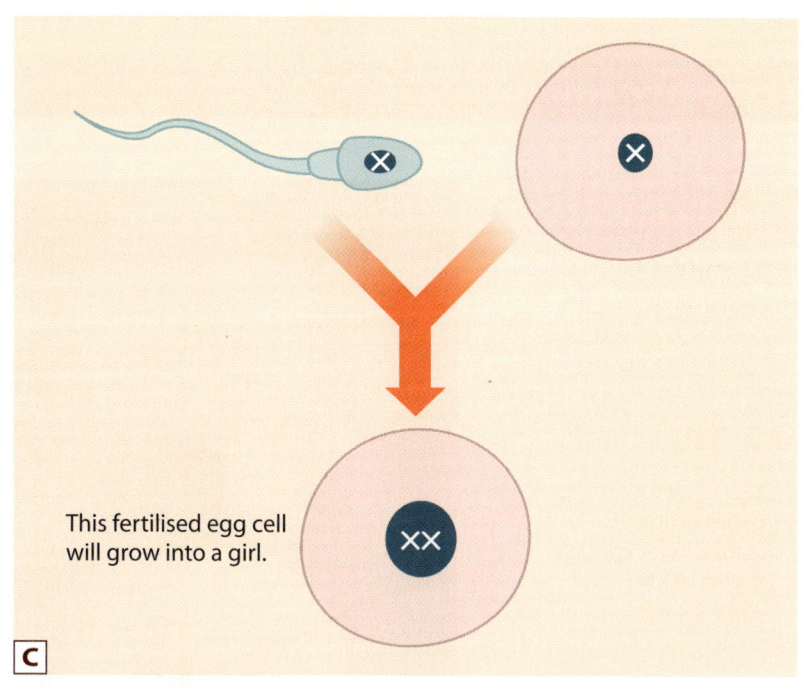

Sperm cells form in pairs, and each sperm cell gets one of each pair of chromosomes. This means that one sperm cell from each pair gets an X sex chromosome, and one gets a Y. When egg cells are formed, they all have one X sex chromosome. The gender of a baby depends on which kind of sperm cell fertilises the egg cell.

A When a couple have a baby by IVF, the doctors could test the embryos to find out if they are girls or boys. Parents could choose whether to have a boy or a girl.
- Should parents be allowed to choose the gender of their children?
- Why might parents want to choose?
- What advantages could there be to choosing the gender?
- What disadvantages could there be?

?
4 Are your sex chromosomes XX or XY?
5 Look at diagram C. Draw a similar diagram to show how the gametes could produce a boy.
6 Why do egg cells never contain a Y chromosome?
7 Which is the odd one out: egg cell, sperm cell, body cell? Explain your answers.
8 'Half of all babies born are girls.'
   a Explain why you would expect this statement to be true.
   b How could you find out if *exactly* half the babies born are girls?

?
3 a How many chromosomes are there in a normal human body cell? Choose your answer from these numbers: 23   46
  b Why must egg and sperm cells have half this number of chromosomes?

Summary

Gametes (_____ cells and _____ cells) only contain _____ of the number of _____ found in body cells. The _____ of a baby is controlled by the _____ chromosomes. _____ cells always have an X, but _____ cells can have an X or a Y. An _____ combination will grow into a girl, and an _____ combination will grow into a boy.

| chromosomes | egg | gender | half |
| sex | sperm | XX | XY |

17

B1.6 Alleles

What are dominant and recessive alleles?

The characteristics of an organism depend on its genes. For instance, some pea plants have red flowers and some have white ones, so there must be two different versions of the gene for flower colour. The different versions of a gene are called **alleles**.

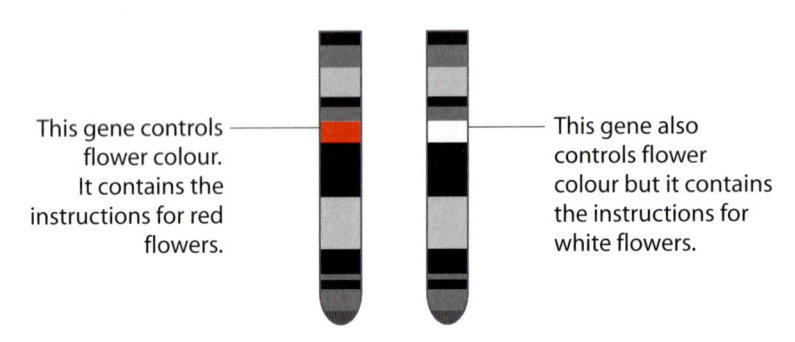

A A pair of chromosomes from a pea plant, showing different alleles for flower colour. The alleles are in the same place on each chromosome.

(Labels on diagram: This gene controls flower colour. It contains the instructions for red flowers. — This gene also controls flower colour but it contains the instructions for white flowers.)

B Pea flowers.

1 What is an allele?

The chromosomes in diagram B have one allele for red flowers and one for white flowers. The different instructions do not mix to produce pink flowers. The allele for red flowers is **dominant** (it does not allow the other allele to work), and so the pea plant has red flowers. The allele for white flowers is called a **recessive** allele. We use letters to represent the different alleles. The dominant allele always has a capital letter.

The characteristics of a recessive allele can only be seen if the organism has two copies of it. Pea plants will only have white flowers if both alleles of the gene are for white flowers.

If you breed two pea plants together, the flower colours of the offspring depend on which alleles the parent plants have. Diagram C shows what happens when you cross a plant that has two alleles for red flowers with a plant that has two alleles for white flowers.

2 The allele for red flowers is written as **R**, and the allele for white flowers as **r**. How does this tell you which allele is dominant?

3 What colour flowers would each of these pea plants have?
  a RR
  b Rr
  c rr

4 Why do pea plant gametes only have one allele for flower colour?

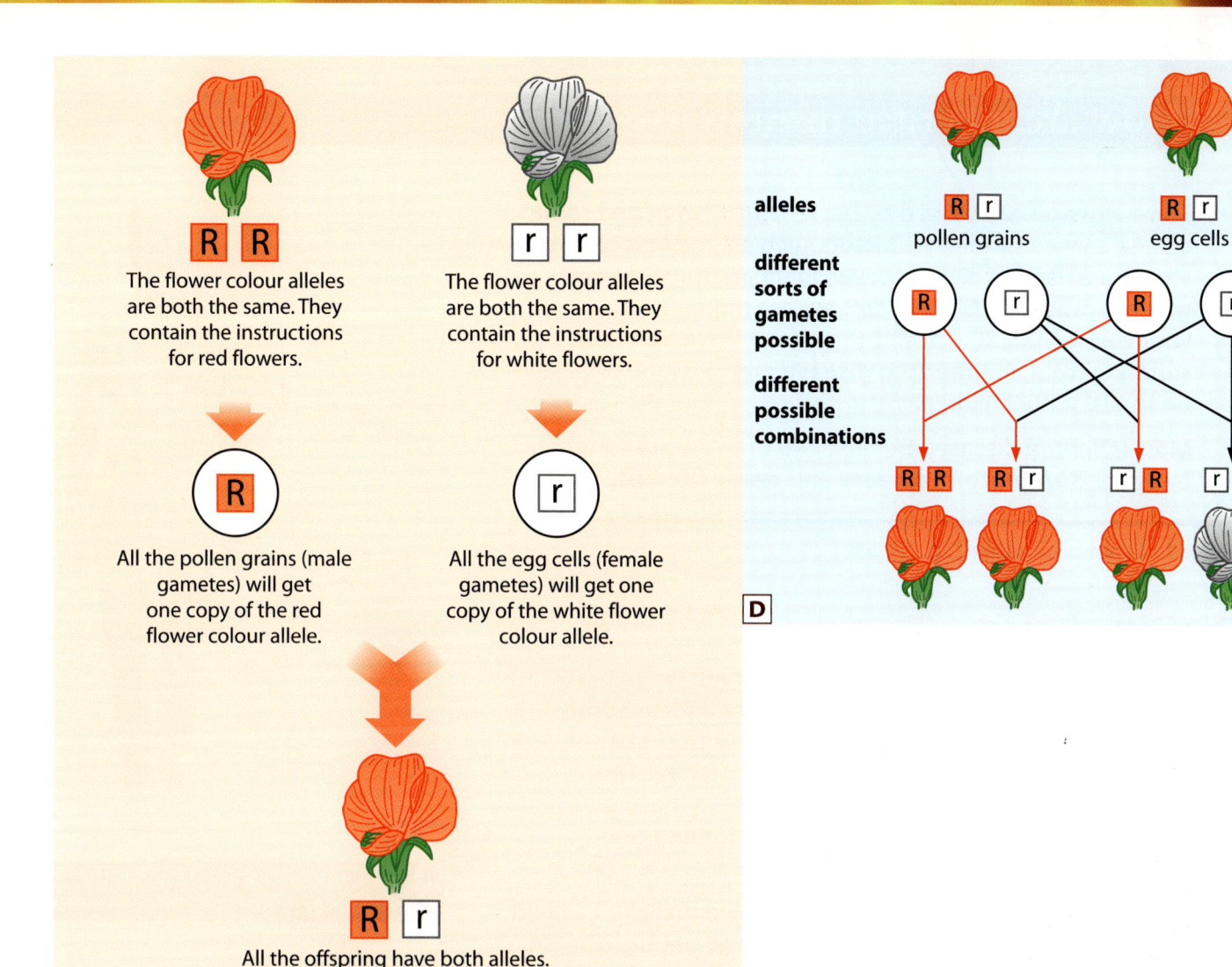

The flower colour alleles are both the same. They contain the instructions for red flowers.

The flower colour alleles are both the same. They contain the instructions for white flowers.

All the pollen grains (male gametes) will get one copy of the red flower colour allele.

All the egg cells (female gametes) will get one copy of the white flower colour allele.

All the offspring have both alleles. However, all the flowers are red. This is because red is the dominant allele.

C

alleles — pollen grains — egg cells
different sorts of gametes possible
different possible combinations

D

Some plants with red flowers have one allele for white flowers and one for red flowers. You cannot see the effects of the allele for white flowers because it is recessive. When the gametes from these plants fuse to make a new organism, some of the offspring will end up with two alleles for white flowers, and so their flowers will be white.

The offspring from the pea plants shown in diagram D are not all the same, because they inherited different combinations of alleles from the parent plants.

?
5   A pea plant has red flowers. Write down all the possible combinations of alleles for flower colour in its *parent* plants.

6   One of the first people to suggest the idea of genes was Gregor Mendel. Find out about Mendel and his work, and write a paragraph to present your findings.

Summary

Organisms have _____ copies of most of their _____. Different types of the same gene are called _____. A _____ allele only works if there are two copies of it. A _____ allele works even if there is only _____ copy of it. Offspring from the _____ parents can look _____ because they inherit different _____ of alleles.

alleles	combinations	different
dominant	genes	one	recessive
same	two

19

B1.7 Inherited diseases

How are inherited diseases passed on?

Some diseases are caused by bacteria or viruses, and some can be caused by lifestyle factors such as smoking or not eating a balanced diet. However, there are some diseases that are caused by genes. You only get these diseases if your cells contain the alleles that cause them. Someone suffering from an **inherited disease** may pass the disease on to his or her children.

Most inherited diseases are rare. Two of the more common ones are **Huntington's disease** and **cystic fibrosis**.

1 What is an inherited disease?

Huntington's disease

Huntington's disease slowly destroys nerves. People with the allele for Huntington's disease are not affected until they are about 40 years old. They first start to shake and jerk uncontrollably, and their brains are also affected. They usually die within 10 years of showing the symptoms. There is no cure for Huntington's disease, and nothing that doctors can yet do to slow it down.

Huntington's disease is caused by a dominant allele. If a child inherits one copy of the allele he or she will get the disease.

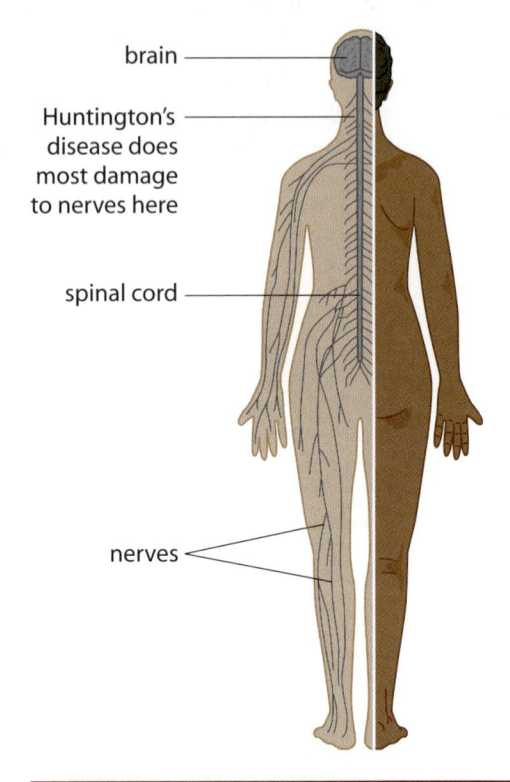

A Huntington's disease damages the nervous system.

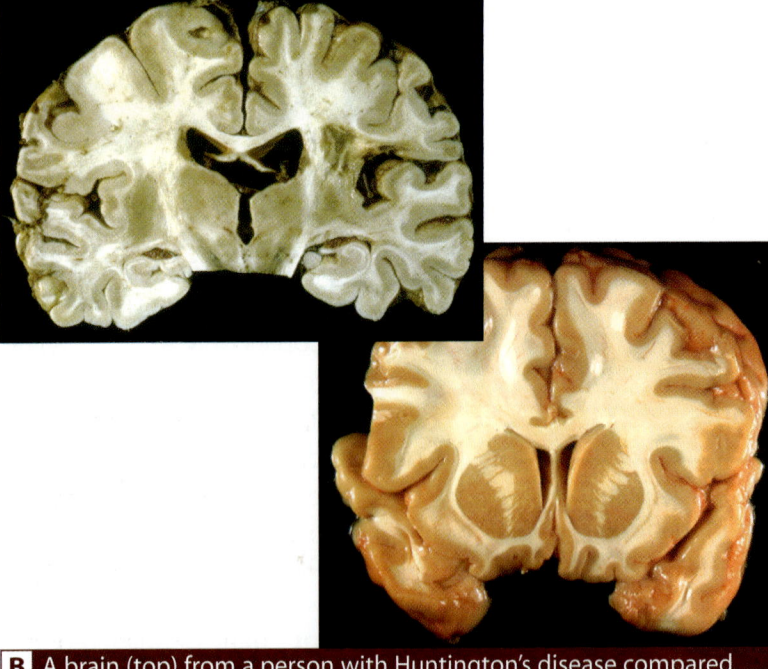

B A brain (top) from a person with Huntington's disease compared with a normal brain (bottom).

2 What are the symptoms of Huntington's disease?

3 How many alleles for Huntington's disease does a sufferer have? Explain your answer.

Cystic fibrosis

Cystic fibrosis is an inherited disease where cells that produce mucus make it thick and sticky instead of runny. Mucus sticks in the lungs, and can also block some tubes in the digestive system so that sufferers cannot digest their food properly. People with cystic fibrosis often suffer from lung infections, and may only live to about 30 years of age. There is no cure for cystic fibrosis yet.

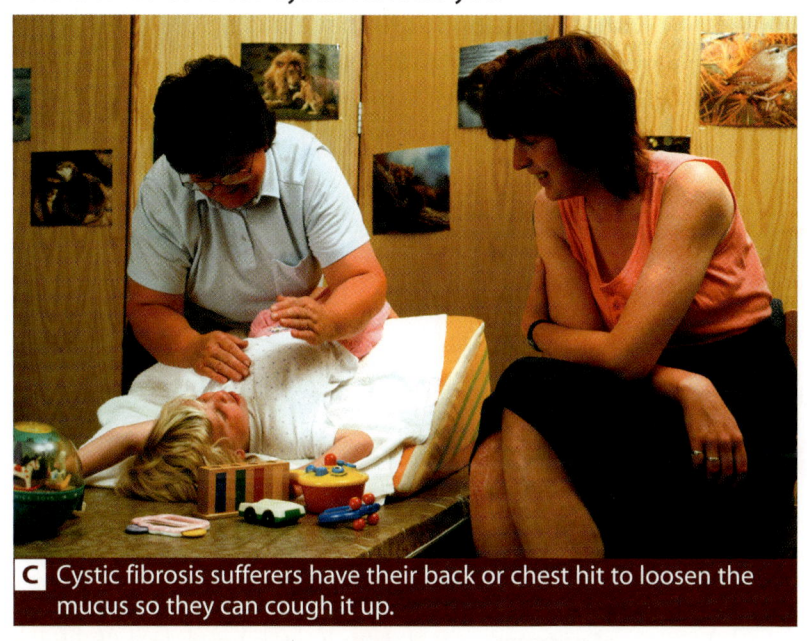

C Cystic fibrosis sufferers have their back or chest hit to loosen the mucus so they can cough it up.

? 4 Why do cystic fibrosis sufferers have difficulty:
  a digesting their food
  b breathing?

Cystic fibrosis is caused by a recessive allele, so a person will only get the disease if they have two copies of the allele. A person with only one copy of the allele will not get the disease and is said to be a **carrier**. If both parents are carriers some of their children may get two copies of the allele and so will suffer from the disease.

? 5 Look at Diagram D.
  a Why don't James and Helen have cystic fibrosis?
  b Which child has cystic fibrosis?
  c Which child is a carrier of the disease?

6 a Nadia has the allele for Huntingdon's disease. What percentage of her children would you expect to get the disease?
  b Sanjay and Nita are both carriers of the cystic fibrosis allele. What percentage of their children would you expect to get the disease?

parents' alleles

James: F f
Helen: F f

children's alleles

Mark: F f
Chloe: f f
Lee: F F

D A family with cystic fibrosis alleles. The normal allele is shown as **F**, and the recessive allele that causes the disease is shown as **f**.

Summary

Inherited _____ are caused by alleles. Huntington's disease is caused by a dominant _____. It destroys _____. Cystic _____ is caused by a _____ allele, so a person only gets the disease if they have _____ copies of the allele. Cystic fibrosis causes some cells to produce _____ which is too sticky.

allele   diseases   fibrosis   mucus
nerves   recessive   two

21

B1.8 Healthy children?
How can we stop inherited diseases being passed on?

Cystic fibrosis is an inherited disease caused by a recessive allele. Tony and Cleo are both carriers – diagram A shows the four different ways that their alleles can combine. There is a 25% chance that each baby they have will have the disease.

Huntington's disease is caused by a dominant allele. Janet has just one allele for this disease, and she will start to show the symptoms when she is about 40. Diagram B shows that each baby that Janet and John have has a 50% chance of having Huntington's disease.

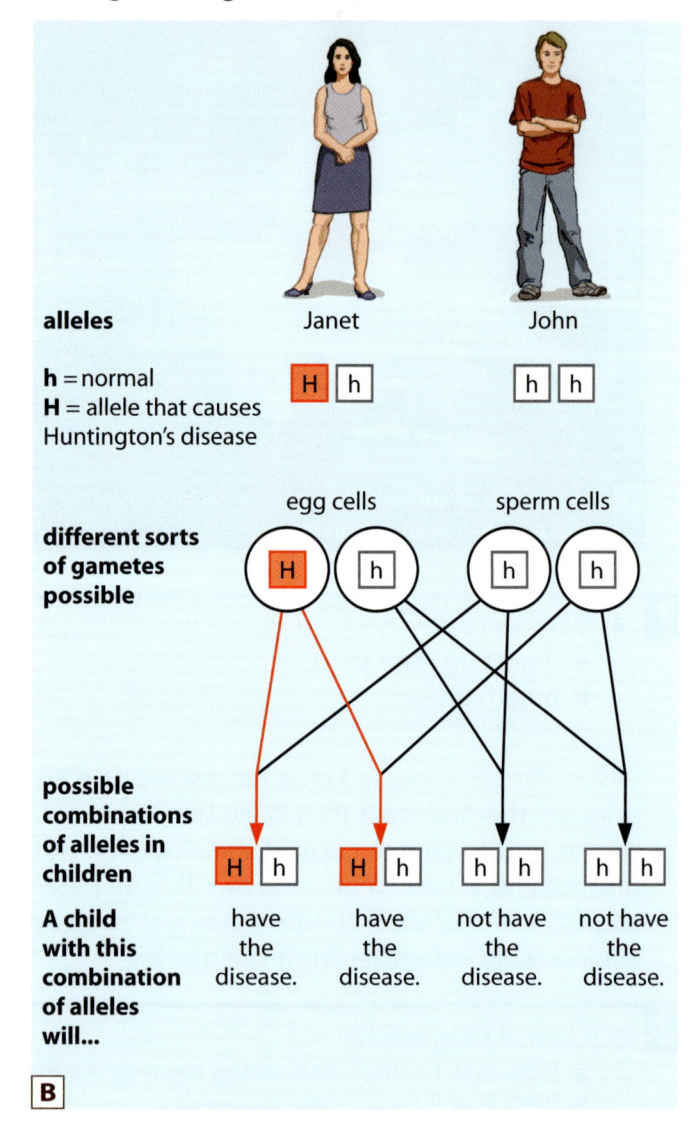

alleles — Tony — Cleo

F = normal
f = the allele that causes cystic fibrosis

Tony: F f | Cleo: F f

different sorts of gametes possible
egg cells: F, f | sperm cells: F, f

possible combinations of alleles in children
F F | F f | f F | f f

A child with this combination of alleles will…
not have the disease or be a carrier. | be a carrier but will not have the disease. | be a carrier but will not have the disease. | have the disease.

A

alleles — Janet — John

h = normal
H = allele that causes Huntington's disease

Janet: H h | John: h h

different sorts of gametes possible
egg cells: H, h | sperm cells: h, h

possible combinations of alleles in children
H h | H h | h h | h h

A child with this combination of alleles will…
have the disease. | have the disease. | not have the disease. | not have the disease.

B

?
1. What is a recessive allele?
2. What is a carrier?
3. a At what age do the symptoms of Huntington's disease start to show?
   b Between what ages do most women have children?

A Not everyone who might be carrying the Huntington's allele wants to be tested.
- Why might having the test be a good idea?
- Why might someone not want to know if they have the allele?

Scientists can test a person's genes to find out if they are carrying alleles for inherited diseases. Janet would know when she was still young that she might have the allele for Huntington's disease, because one of her parents or grandparents may have the symptoms. Janet could ask for a genetic test before she has any babies. If her result is **positive** (meaning that she does have the allele) she might choose not to have any children.

A genetic test may show that there is a risk of passing on a disease. A woman might decide to get pregnant and then have the fetus tested to see if it has the allele for the disease. A doctor carefully takes a cell from the developing fetus while it is still in the uterus and examines its alleles. If the test is positive the parents could choose to **terminate** the pregnancy (have an **abortion**).

A

C

- What would parents have to think about before asking for a fetus to be tested?

? 4 Write down one reason why a person may choose:
   a to have a test for a genetic disease
   b not to have a test
   c to have a fetus tested
   d not to have a fetus tested.

5 a Draw a diagram similar to diagram A, to show the combinations possible for a couple where only one person is a carrier of the disease.
   b What chance does each child have of being a carrier?
   c What chance does each child have of suffering from the disease?

Summary

If a person has the _____ for Huntington's disease, each of their _____ has a _____ chance of having the _____. If a couple are both _____ of cystic fibrosis, each of their _____ has a _____ chance of having the disease. Adults and _____ can be _____ to see if they have the alleles for these diseases.

| 25% 50% allele carriers children |
| disease fetuses tested |

23

B1.9 Genetic testing

What are the arguments for and against genetic testing?

Scientists can now carry out tests for many genetic diseases, but people do not always agree that these tests should be done. In many areas of science we need to consider **ethical issues** to decide whether or not something should be done.

For example, some people think that abortions should not be allowed at all, or should only be allowed if having the baby would put the mother's life in danger. Abortion is an ethical issue, and it is something we need to think about when we are discussing genetic testing.

There are lots of different views about genetic testing.

Sally and Jim: We want a family, but we want to be certain our babies will be healthy! We would rather try to adopt a baby than have a child of our own who will suffer from a nasty disease like cystic fibrosis.

Father O'Hara: Abortion is wrong, no matter what the reason! There is no point in testing fetuses. If a married couple want to be sure of healthy babies they should have themselves tested to see if they have faulty genes.

Dr Chandak: No genetic test is absolutely certain. There is still a chance that the test results may be incorrect. A 'false positive' is where the test says there is a problem when there is not. A 'false negative' is where the test says there is no problem when there is one.

Mrs Kapoor: Testing my fetus may harm it – I could have a miscarriage because of the test. And I'm not sure if I could have an abortion even if the test was positive. It would be like killing a baby!

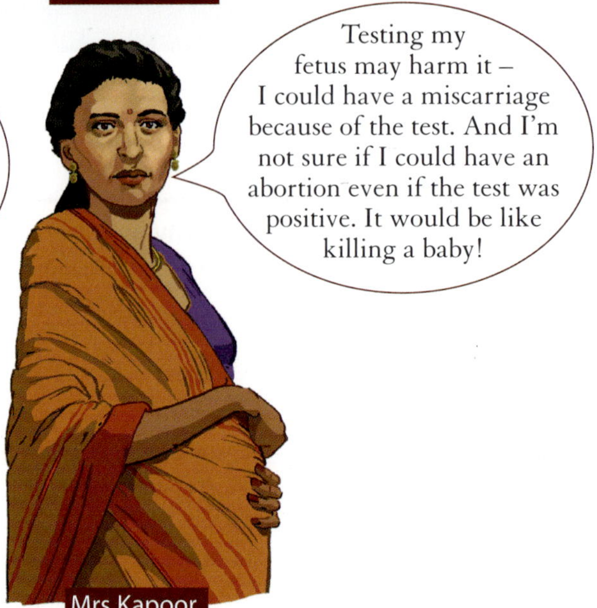

Mr Brandon: There is a test to see if I am likely to get a genetic disease. What happens if I am? I won't be able to stop myself getting it – I would just be so depressed if I knew I was going to become ill.

Carlton and Marcia: We want to have a baby using IVF treatment. The doctor says they can test the embryos before they implant them, so we can be sure that we will not pass on Marcia's cystic fibrosis gene. Choosing which embryos to implant is not like having an abortion!

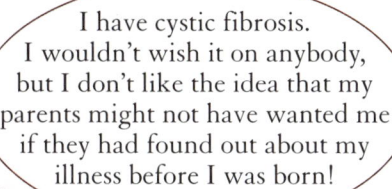

Andy: I have cystic fibrosis. I wouldn't wish it on anybody, but I don't like the idea that my parents might not have wanted me if they had found out about my illness before I was born!

Zoe: I don't think abortion is always wrong – it all depends! A fetus isn't a person until it is nearly ready to be born. Anyway, the law says that I could have an abortion any time until I am 24 weeks pregnant, and even later if there is something wrong with the fetus. They must have considered things carefully before they made that law. They know a lot more of the facts than I do.

?

1. **a** What kinds of genetic testing can be done?
   b How can genetic tests be used?
2. What are some of the ethical issues we need to think about?
3. Choose one ethical issue connected with genetic testing.
   a Write down two opposite views on this issue.
   b Suggest an argument for and against each view that you wrote down in part **a**.
4. Find out more about how abortions are carried out. Does knowing what happens in an abortion change your view about whether or not abortions should be allowed?

Summary

Scientists can test for many _____ diseases, but we need to think about _____ issues before we _____ which tests should be done, and what should be done with the _____.

decide   ethical   genetic   information

B1.10 Modifying genes

How can genetic modification be used to treat diseases?

Scientists have developed ways to **modify** (change) genes in animals. They are trying to find ways to modify genes in humans to cure some genetic diseases.

Modifying body cells

If scientists know which gene causes an inherited disease, they can try to cure the disease by putting modified genes into cells. Before **gene therapy** can be used, scientists have to work out:

- which gene is causing the problem and how to modify it
- how to get the modified gene into cells without harming the patient.

The modified genes are only put into the cells that need them. This means that a person who has had gene therapy could still pass the disease on to their children, because their egg or sperm cells will still have the allele that does not work properly.

A These GloFish went on sale in 2003 as pets. They have been genetically modified to glow red.

B Ashanthi DeSilva had gene therapy in 1990, when she was four years old. She was treated for a genetic disease that stopped her immune system working properly.

C Jesse Gelsinger died after gene therapy for a liver problem.

?
1. What is gene therapy?
2. Name two diseases that scientists may try to cure using gene therapy.
3. Write down two problems that scientists have to solve before gene therapy can work.

Modifying embryos

If an allele in an embryo is modified, all the new cells formed as the embryo grows will have the modified allele. The individual that grows from the egg could pass on the modified allele to their offspring. This technique has only been used on animals so far, but in the future it could be used on human embryos.

D Eduardo Kac asked scientists to create Alba as a work of 'transgenic art'. She glows green when blue light shines on her.

? 4 How could a modified embryo pass on the new allele to its offspring?

Designer babies

Most people would agree that modifying an embryo to replace the allele that causes inherited diseases would be a good idea if it could be done safely. However, it may also be possible to modify genes in embryos to make sure the children grow up to be tall, to have blond hair, or to be good at sport. This use of gene modification is sometimes called making 'designer babies'.

? 5 a What is a 'designer baby'?
   b Why are there no designer babies at present?

6 Think of a plus, a minus and an interesting point about this statement: A baby's genes have been modified to make it good at maths.

7 Look at photograph A and D. Do you think these animals should have been created? Explain the reasons for your answer.

A Should scientists be allowed to change the genes in embryos?
• What are the arguments for allowing this?
• What reasons might people have for opposing it?

Summary

Scientists can insert _____ genes into body cells to cure _____ diseases. This is called _____ therapy. Genes in _____ can also be modified. Genes in modified _____ could be passed on to future _____. This technique could be used in the future to create _____ babies.

designer embryos gene genetic
    modified offspring

B1.11 Cloning and stem cells

How can stem cells help to cure diseases?

Some animals can reproduce asexually by producing clones of themselves. The offspring are clones because they contain exactly the same genetic information as the parent animal. The offspring may not be exactly the same as each other, as environmental factors will also affect the way they develop.

In animals that reproduce sexually, the cells of an embryo can sometimes separate to form two separate organisms, called **identical twins**. Identical twins have exactly the same set of genes as each other, because they both started out as part of the same embryo.

> **1** What is a clone?
>
> **2** Explain these statements:
>   **a** Identical twins have the same alleles as each other.
>   **b** Identical twins do not have identical alleles to their parents.

A These identical twins have the same set of genes.

When an egg cell is fertilised it begins to divide, making copies of itself. These early cells are unspecialised, and can develop into any type of cell. These unspecialised cells are called **embryonic stem cells**. Diagram B shows how these cells can be cloned.

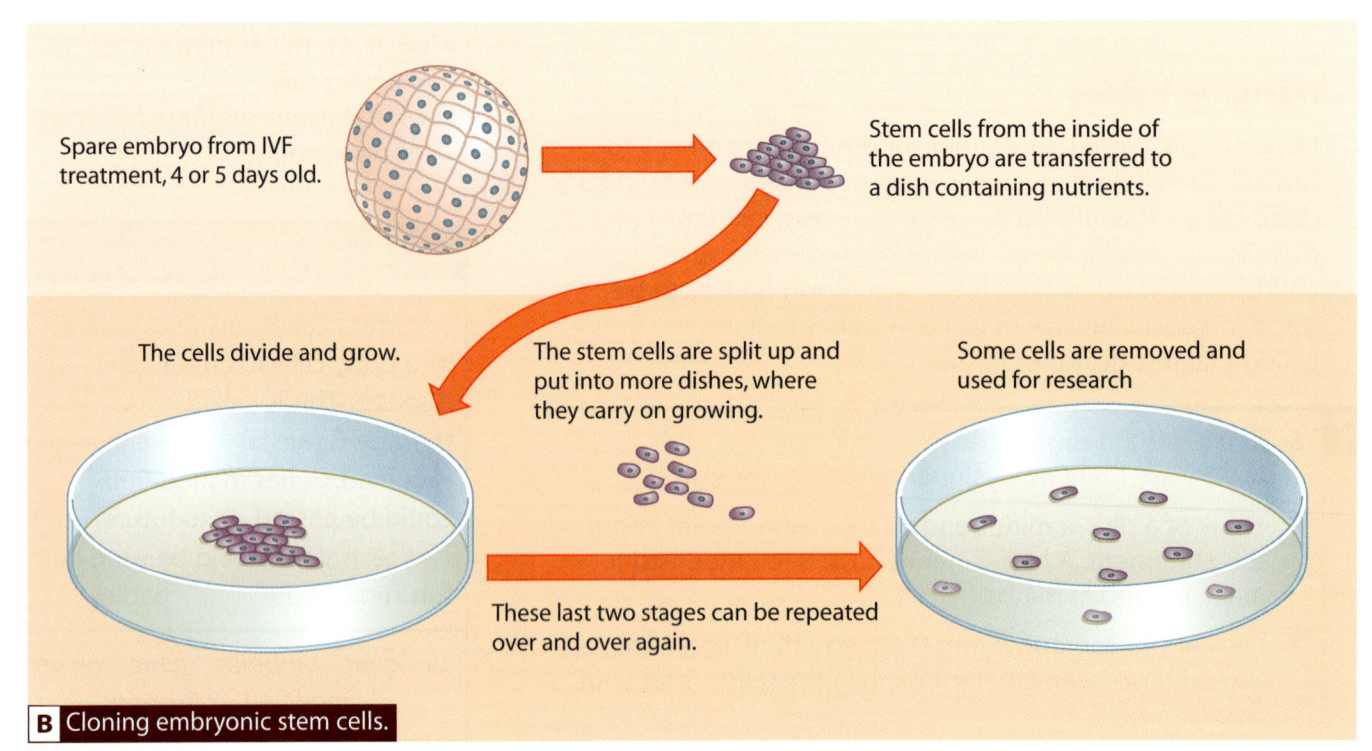

Spare embryo from IVF treatment, 4 or 5 days old.

Stem cells from the inside of the embryo are transferred to a dish containing nutrients.

The cells divide and grow.

The stem cells are split up and put into more dishes, where they carry on growing.

Some cells are removed and used for research

These last two stages can be repeated over and over again.

B Cloning embryonic stem cells.

? 3 Explain how an embryo which contains only a few cells can be used to produce hundreds of stem cells.

Scientists can use embryonic stem cells to find out about how humans and other animals develop. However, many scientists are interested in stem cells because they can be used to treat illnesses.

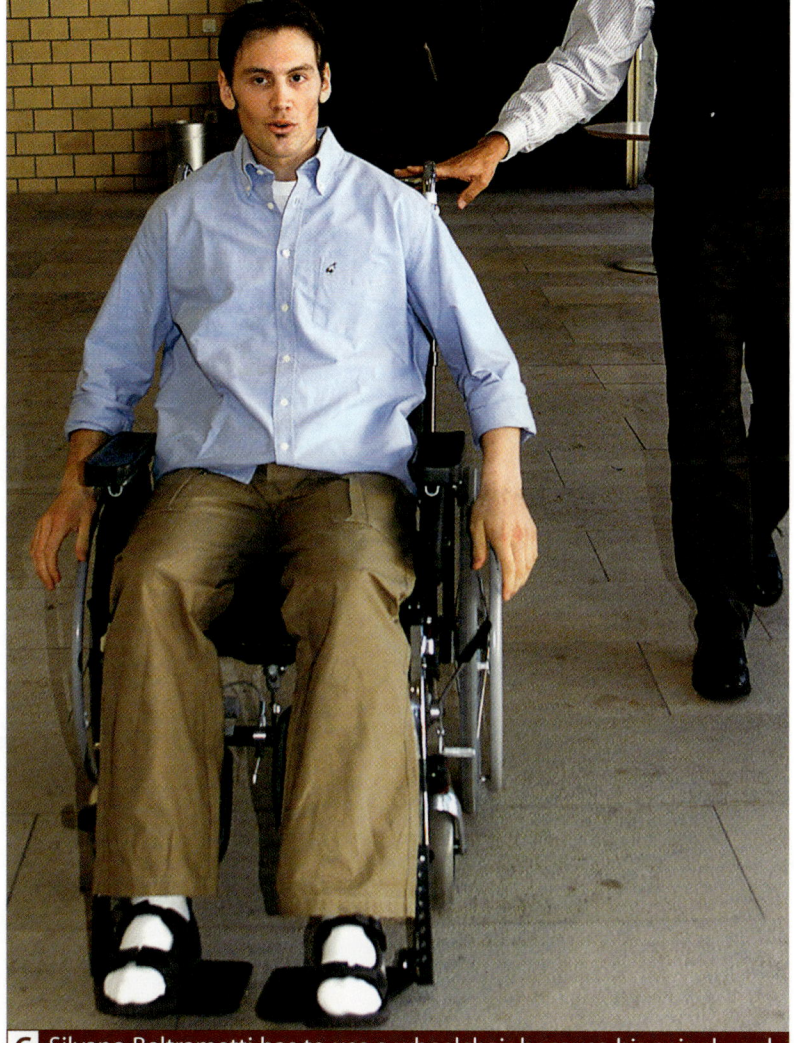

C Silvano Beltrametti has to use a wheelchair because his spinal cord was damaged in an accident. One day, it may be possible to inject stem cells into his spine where they will grow and repair the nerves.

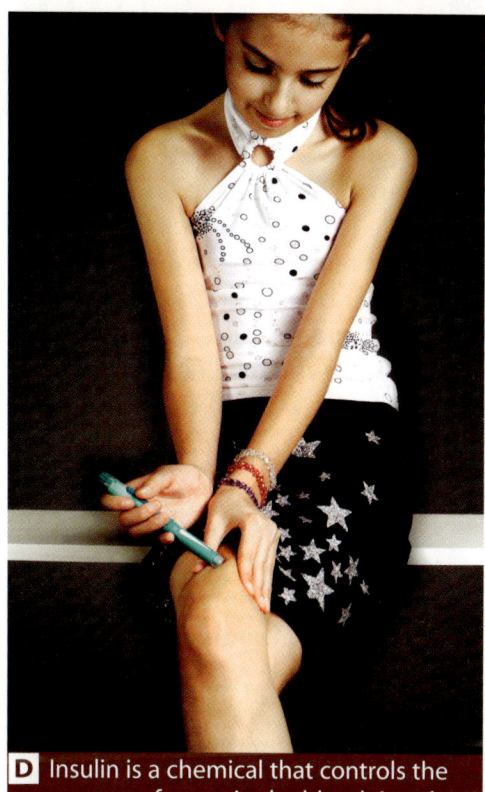

D Insulin is a chemical that controls the amount of sugar in the blood. Amy has to have regular injections of insulin because her pancreas does not produce enough. One day, it may be possible to inject stem cells into her pancreas which will grow into new insulin-producing cells.

? 4 Describe two different possible uses for embryonic stem cells.

5 Complete this sentence in as many different ways as you can. A cell is not specialised when…

6 Some diseases can be cured by transplanting organs from donors. Suggest some advantages and disadvantages of organ transplants compared to using stem cells.

Summary

Clones of _____ can occur when an embryo splits up naturally. Embryonic _____ cells are _____ cells that can grow into any type of cell. These cells can be grown from _____ left over from _____ treatments. Embryonic stem cells may be useful in the future for treating _____.

animals   embryos   illnesses   IVF
stem   unspecialised

29

B1.12 Using embryos

Should human embryos be used for treating illnesses?

When a couple have IVF treatment, the doctors usually create lots of embryos and only implant one or two. The rest are frozen. Some may be used later if the couple want another baby, or if the first embryos do not implant and grow properly. However, there are often several embryos left over, which will eventually be destroyed unless the couple allow them to be used for research.

Some arguments for or against obtaining stem cells from embryos are based on these ideas:
- Some actions are wrong, and should not be taken.
- You need to look at the benefits of an action – if the benefits are more important than the possible harm, then go ahead and do it.

We have five embryos that the clinic are keeping frozen for us. Even if we don't need them, it doesn't seem right to use them for experiments. They could have been human beings!

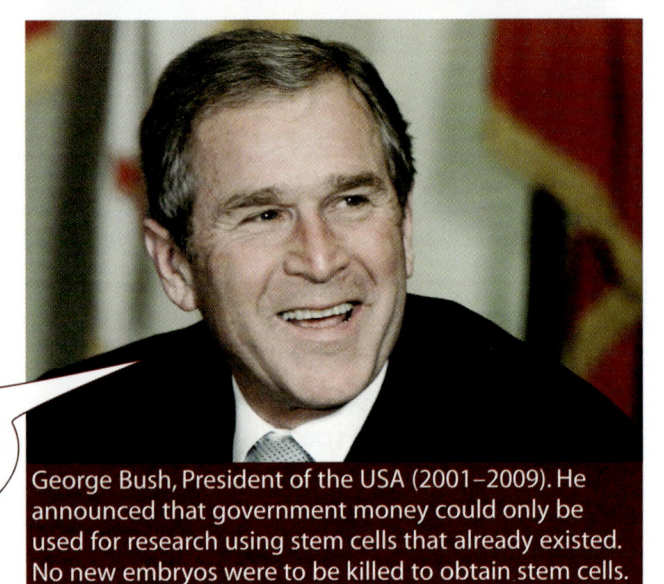

I feel too old to go through another pregnancy. I'm never going to use those frozen embryos. If they can be used to develop treatments for other people, that's great!

Gina and Atsu used IVF to have their babies.

Felicity's son was born using IVF.

Human life is a sacred gift from our Creator. We will not encourage destruction of human embryos that have at least the potential for life.

George Bush, President of the USA (2001–2009). He announced that government money could only be used for research using stem cells that already existed. No new embryos were to be killed to obtain stem cells.

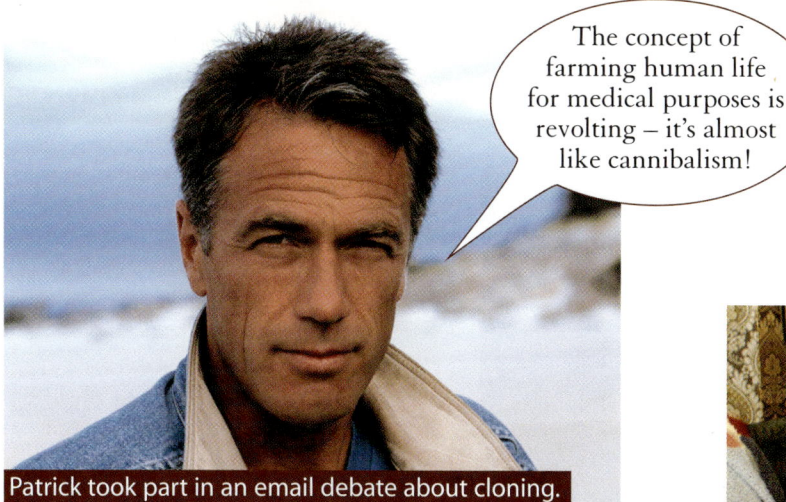

Patrick took part in an email debate about cloning.

The concept of farming human life for medical purposes is revolting – it's almost like cannibalism!

Using stem cells from embryos neither creates nor destroys life – a ball of cells is not a human being. What it does do is to give hope to millions of living human beings suffering from conditions like juvenile diabetes and Alzheimer's.

Michelle's mother has Alzheimer's disease.

Bella

Embryos created for IVF will be destroyed anyway if they are not used. Many fertilised human eggs never implant anyway. However, I don't think it is right to create new embryos on purpose for research – that's not the same thing at all!

? When you are answering these questions, you can use your own ideas as well as some of the ideas on this page.

1 Write down some of the ethical issues involved when we are discussing the use of embryonic stem cells. You might need to look back at page 24 to remind yourself about ethical issues.

2 Write down some opinions about the use of embryonic stem cells that are based on these ideas:
 a Using embryonic stem cells is wrong.
 b The benefits of using embryonic stem cells are greater than the harm it may do.

3 What is your opinion about the use of embryonic stem cells? Give reasons for your answer.

4 Embryonic stem cells may one day be used to treat diseases such as Parkinson's or Alzheimer's. Find out more about one of these diseases.

Summary

Embryos are often left over after _____ treatments. Some people think is it is acceptable to use these _____ for research into new _____ for diseases. Other people think that these _____ are potential _____ beings and should not be used in this way.

embryos   human   IVF   treatments

31

B1.13 Gene clinic

What do you know about your genes and how they affect you?

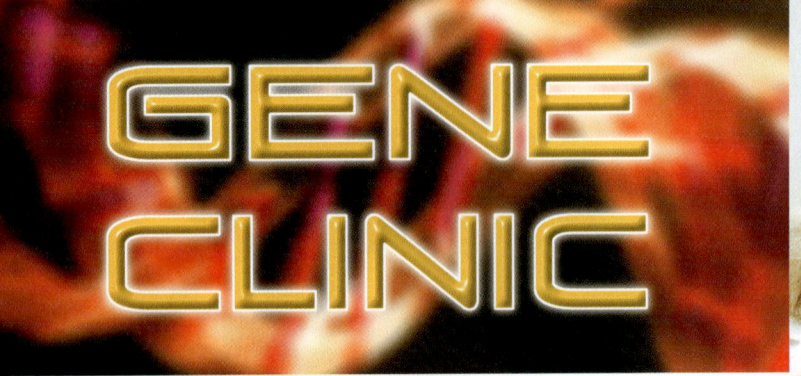

GENE CLINIC

Are you planning a family? Don't want a 'surprise package'?

Come and talk to us first – we can make sure your baby is healthy and happy, and just the way you want it!

We offer:
- genetic screening of you and your embryos
- selection of suitable embryos
- genetic modification to correct defects in health or appearance.

The services advertised by the Gene Clinic are not available yet, but they may be in the future.

The advert refers to a 'surprise package' because parents can never know exactly what their baby will be like.

1 Genes control a person's characteristics. They are found on chromosomes.
   a Where are chromosomes found in cells?
   b What chemical are chromosomes made from?

2. Genes carry the instructions for making proteins.
   a Name two different things that are made from structural proteins.
   b Enzymes are proteins. What do enzymes do?

3. Genes are passed on in gametes (egg cells and sperm cells).
   a How many chromosomes are there in gametes compared to normal body cells?
   b Why does a child inherit characteristics from both parents?
   c What are the sex chromosomes called?
   d Which combination of sex chromosomes produces a boy?

The advert offers genetic screening, which means that genes can be tested to make sure there are no alleles that cause inherited diseases.

4. Cells in your body are specialised. Name one way in which these cells are specialised.
   a egg cells
   b sperm cells

5. a Why do identical twins have the same genes as each other?
   b Identical twins may not look exactly the same. Why is this?

6. Huntington's disease is caused by a dominant allele.
   a What is an allele?
   b What does dominant mean?
   c What are the symptoms of Huntington's disease?
   d Jeff has the Huntington's allele. What are the chances of one of his children having the disease?

7. Adults could have their genes tested before starting a family.
   a Give one reason why they might want to do this.
   b Give one reason why they may not want to do this.

8. Cystic fibrosis is caused by a recessive allele.
   a What are the symptoms of cystic fibrosis?
   Sally and Asif both have a recessive and a dominant allele. We can write this as **Ff**.
   b Copy and complete this table to show the possible combinations of alleles their children could have.

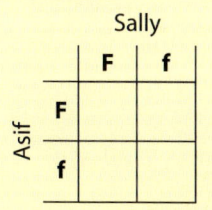

	Sally F	Sally f
Asif F		
Asif f		

   The chances of Sally and Asif having a baby with cystic fibrosis (**ff**) are 1 in 4.
   c What are the chances of them having a baby with the **Ff** combination?
   d What is a 'carrier' of cystic fibrosis?
   e Which combination of alleles does a carrier have?

9. If a couple are having a baby, the fetus could be tested to find out if it has two copies of the allele that causes cystic fibrosis.
   a Give one reason why parents may choose to have a fetus tested.
   b Give one reason why they may not wish to have the test.

There are often embryos left over after IVF treatments. Embryonic stem cells could be used in the future to treat illnesses.

10. a How are embryonic stem cells different to normal body cells?
    b Why could this be useful in treating diseases?

11. Some people think that scientists should not be researching ways of using embryonic stem cells.
    a Suggest two reasons why some people think that using embryonic stem cells is wrong.
    b Suggest two reasons why some people think this research *should* be carried out.

C1.1 Air quality

Why should we be concerned about the air?

A

B

C

Some of the ways that we affect air quality.

? 1 What do we do to change the air?

2 How could changes to the air affect us?

Take a deep breath and fill your lungs with air. You and nearly every other organism on Earth need air. Plants use carbon dioxide in the air to make food in **photosynthesis**. **Respiration**, another chemical reaction, is the reaction of oxygen with sugar in living cells. It is very similar to combustion. Animals breathe to provide every cell with a supply of oxygen.

Combustion is the scientific word for burning. It is a fast chemical reaction. Oxygen in the air reacts with a burning substance and new substances are formed which may mix with the air. We burn fuels to provide us with energy for transport and power.

Changes to the air may affect every living thing so we should be concerned about air quality. The quality of the air is affected by the chemicals that we put into the air.

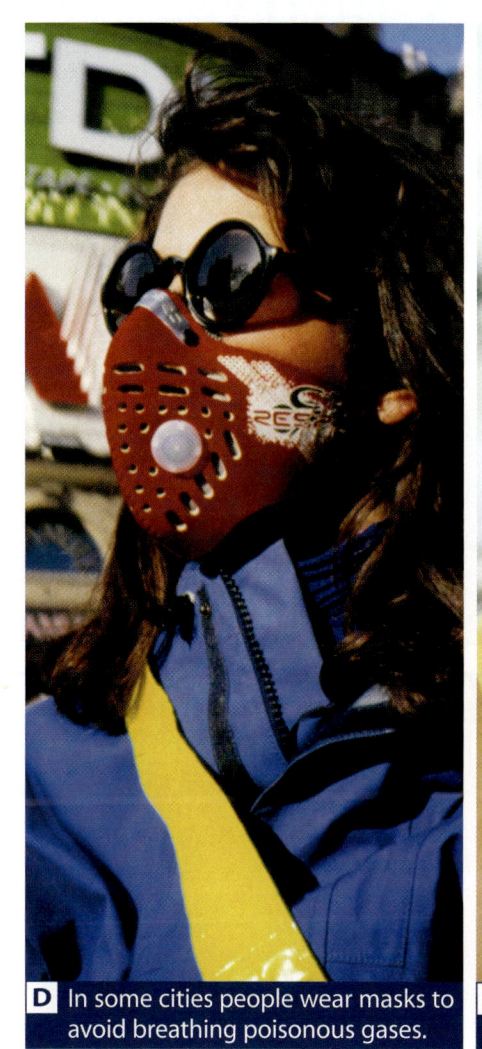

D In some cities people wear masks to avoid breathing poisonous gases.

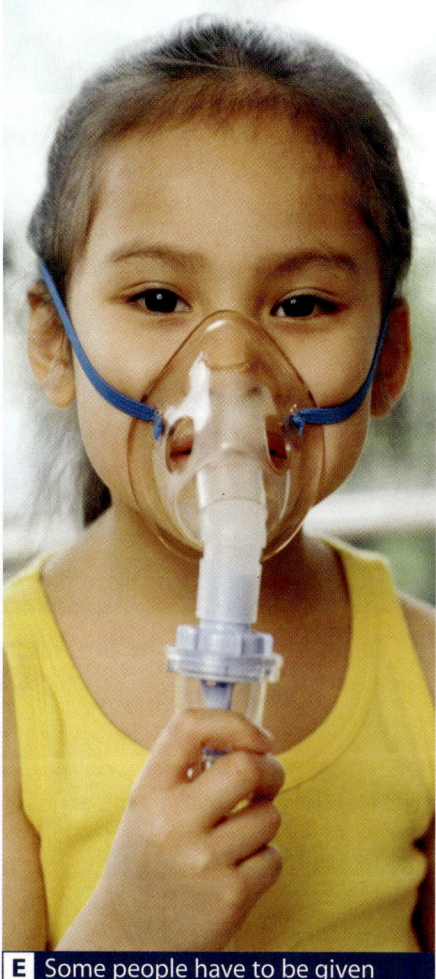

E Some people have to be given extra oxygen to help them breathe.

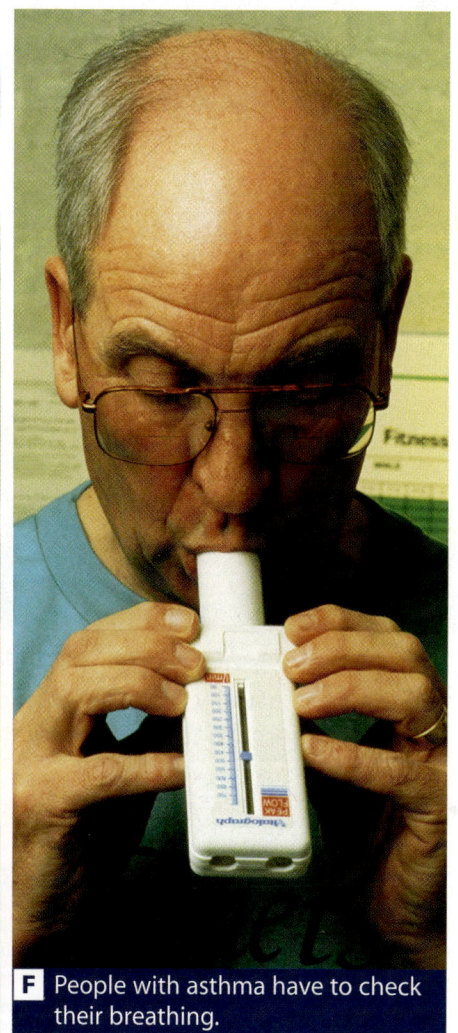

F People with asthma have to check their breathing.

A How much air goes in and out of your lungs every day?

Pollutants

A **pollutant** is a substance that is somewhere where it should not be as a result of human activity and is harmful to humans or the environment. Pollutants in the air may be gases, liquids or solids. Combustion is the main source of pollutants in the air. Later in this module we will look at where air pollutants come from. We will also examine the harmful effects that pollutants may have and the choices we have in dealing with them.

Air quality is a phrase that is used to describe how free the air is from pollutants. If the air quality is good then this means there are little or no pollutants and there is no difficulty breathing. If there are pollutants in the air, the air quality is said to be poor and people may be harmed by breathing it.

3 The gases given off by car exhausts are a major source of air pollution. There may be ways to reduce the amount of exhaust gases but they will probably make cars and fuel more expensive.
  a What can we do to reduce the air pollution caused by cars?
  b What other information do you need to give a better answer to part **a**?

4 Think of a plus, minus and interesting point about this statement: The air should be pure oxygen.

5 What happens to the air quality if a lot of people are in a closed room for a long time? Explain your answer.

35

C1.2 Looking at data on air quality

How do I make sense of data about air pollution?

A

Air quality is often poor in Mexico City but in the UK the air quality is usually good. We can check air quality in newspapers, on teletext or on the internet.

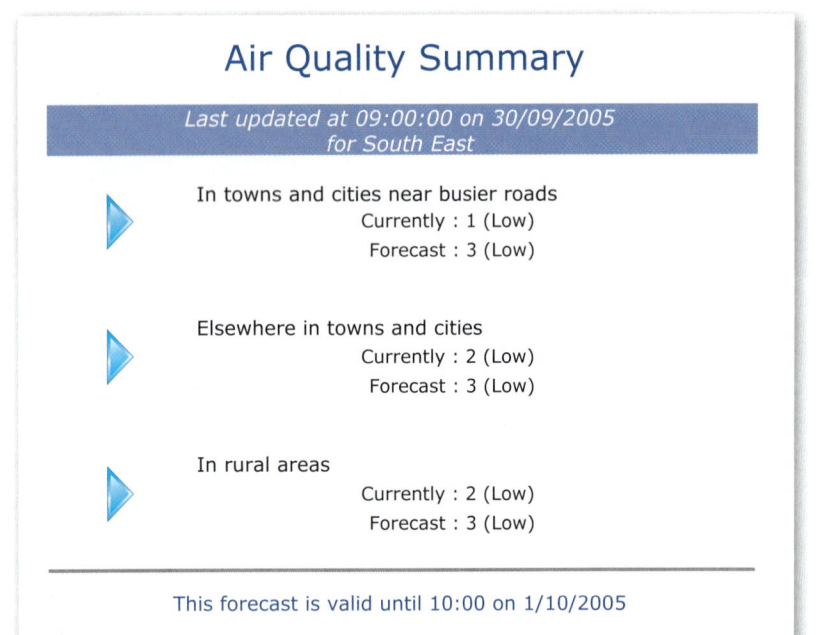

? 1 Which people need to check air quality forecasts?

Air Quality Summary

Last updated at 09:00:00 on 30/09/2005 for South East

▷ In towns and cities near busier roads
Currently : 1 (Low)
Forecast : 3 (Low)

▷ Elsewhere in towns and cities
Currently : 2 (Low)
Forecast : 3 (Low)

▷ In rural areas
Currently : 2 (Low)
Forecast : 3 (Low)

This forecast is valid until 10:00 on 1/10/2005

B Air quality forecast from an internet site.

Measuring air quality

There are **sensors** all around the UK which record the amount of different pollutants in the air. The data is sent to a computer which works out the mean amount of each pollutant every hour. The **pollution index** is a number based on the mean amounts of each pollutant. Weather forecasters decide the effect of the weather and produce an air quality forecast. Often just one word is used.

? 2 Why are some monitoring stations placed near roads?

Index number	Band description	Possible effects of the air on people
1–3	low	Even people sensitive to pollutants do not notice anything.
4–6	medium	Sensitive people may notice the pollutants but no action is necessary.
7–9	high	Pollutants could cause breathing problems in some people and they should stay indoors.
10	very high	People who suffer from asthma or other breathing-related diseases would be very uncomfortable.

C Pollution index.

? **3** Someone with asthma is having some problems breathing. In which band is the air quality likely to be?

"Air Quality – Good"

"Air Pollution Forecast – Low"

"Air Pollution Forecast – Band 3"

D Air quality can be described in different ways.

Trusting data

When you see a number on an instrument it is easy to believe that it is true, but all readings have **errors**. Usually the last figure in a reading is uncertain. There may be other reasons for a reading being incorrect – the sensor may be damaged, or in a place where the air pollution is unusual, or the computer may be faulty.

Readings are repeated a number of times. Any measurement that seems to be much bigger or smaller than the rest is called an **outlier**. The outliers are not used when a **mean** (average) of the readings is worked out. The largest and smallest of the remaining data form the **range** within which the true value should lie. The mean is the **best estimate** of the true value.

? **4** An air quality sensor is giving a 'high' reading while others in the region are giving 'low' data. Write down all the possible reasons for this.

5 The data from an air pollution sensor gives these readings:
5.22   5.17   5.20   5.42   5.19
   a Which of the readings is an outlier? Explain your answer.
   b Why do the remaining readings vary?
   c What range does the true value lie within?
   d What is the best estimate of the true value?

6 The air quality forecast for your area says that tomorrow the pollution will be high. What does this mean and what will you do about it?

Summary

Air pollution _____ collect data about _____ in the air. Data from many sensors are combined to give an air pollution word or _____. These are published to describe the air _____. There is always some _____ in the sensor readings. Scientists take many _____ to make the mean as accurate as possible.

error	measurements	number
pollutants	quality	sensors

37

C1.3 Air – a mixture

What chemicals make up the air?

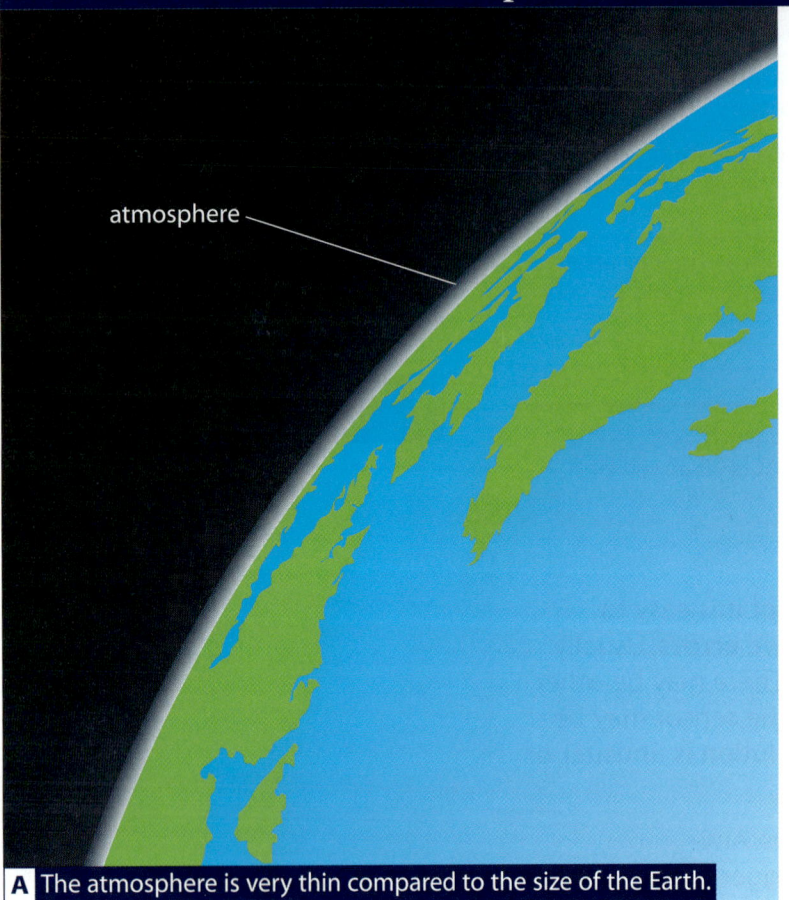

A The atmosphere is very thin compared to the size of the Earth.

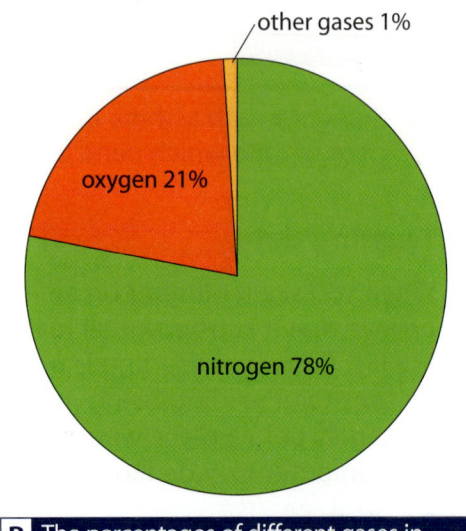

B The percentages of different gases in the air.
- other gases 1%
- oxygen 21%
- nitrogen 78%

The surface of the Earth is covered with a layer of **air** called the **atmosphere**. Without this layer life would not be possible on Earth.

Air is a mixture of many different gases, and usually there is some water vapour in the air. The amount of water vapour varies from place to place so when we talk about the amounts of different gases, we talk about the amounts in *dry* air.

?
1. What is air made of?
2. Where would you expect there to be little water vapour in the air?

Life support

Most of the air is made up of two gases, nitrogen and oxygen. It is the oxygen that supports life. The nitrogen is unreactive and does not do a lot. Winds mix up the air over the whole of the Earth so the amount of each gas only varies a little from place to place.

A How can you find the percentage of oxygen in the air? You can use this apparatus to remove the oxygen from a volume of air.

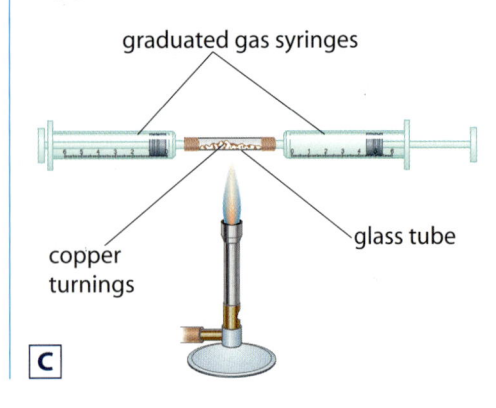

C graduated gas syringes, copper turnings, glass tube

D Forest fires would be more common if there was just a little more oxygen in the air.

> **3** Which part of the air do we need to breathe?
>
> **4** How does the amount of oxygen affect forest fires?

Trace gases

The unreactive gas, argon, makes up just less than 1% of the air. Carbon dioxide is an important part of the air but makes up only 0.04% of it. All the other gases make up just a tiny portion of the air; we say there is just a **trace** amount of each gas.

Volcanoes produce trace gases and so do other natural processes. For example, carbon dioxide is produced when dead plants or animals decay. Trace gases are also produced by industry, agriculture, transport and other human activities.

Natural processes and human activity also put dust and soot into the air. These are not gases but are tiny particles of solid materials. Soot is formed when fuels burn and dust is blown from deserts and quarries. Dead skin cells that drop off us all the time form dust too.

Some trace gases
carbon monoxide
methane
sulfur dioxide
nitrogen oxides

E

> **5** What processes produce soot?
>
> **6** Why do homes become dusty?
>
> **7** Which is the odd one out: oxygen, carbon dioxide, argon? Explain your answers.
>
> **8** Why are some trace gases considered to be pollutants?

Summary

The Earth's _____ is made up of many different _____. 78% of the air is _____ and 21% is _____. About 1% of the air is _____ and only 0.04% is _____. Other gases are present in very small amounts so we call these _____ gases. They include _____ and _____.

argon   atmosphere
carbon dioxide   carbon monoxide
gases   nitrogen   oxygen
sulfur dioxide   trace

39

C1.4 Checking the pollutants

How do we decide which substances are pollutants?

A Scientists collecting samples on a volcano need to wear face masks.

If you are unlucky enough to be near a volcano when it erupts you will soon notice the sulfur dioxide it gives off. It burns your throat and makes you cough. Breathe too much of it and you will die. Luckily, eruptions are quite rare and the amount of sulfur dioxide in the air is usually low.

Human activities produce sulfur dioxide too, such as burning coal. Sulfur dioxide is therefore a pollutant.

Hazards and risks

To decide if a substance in the air is a pollutant we need to know if it is produced by human activity and harmful. Scientists carry out tests on many substances to find out what the substance can do to the environment or to people and how much is needed for its effects to be fatal. This information is called the **hazard** of a substance. **Hazcards** show the hazards of many substances, and containers of harmful substances are marked by a hazard symbol.

97. SULFUR DIOXIDE

TOXIC

CORROSIVE

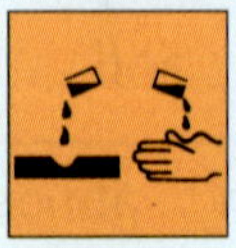

Toxic by inhalation. May cause burns. Irritating to the eyes and respiratory system. It is a choking gas with serious effects on the lungs and eyes, resulting in possible bronchitis and conjunctivitis. **Pupils with known breathing difficulties must not inhale the gas; it may trigger an asthmatic attack.**

B Part of a Hazcard for sulfur dioxide.

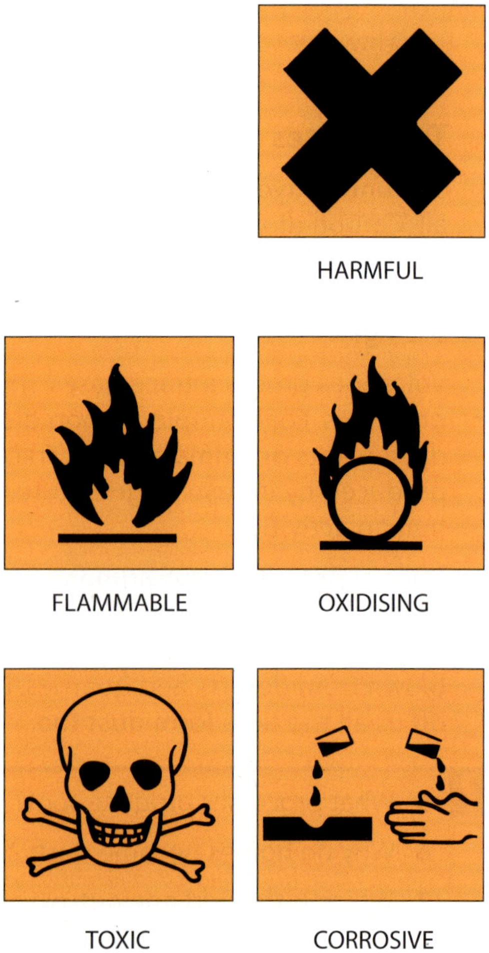

HARMFUL

FLAMMABLE

OXIDISING

TOXIC

CORROSIVE

C Hazard symbols.

? 1 What is a pollutant?
   2 a Which hazard symbol should be used for sulfur dioxide?
     b Name a natural source of sulfur dioxide.
     c Name a source of sulfur dioxide from human activities.

A substance that is harmful when there is a lot of it about may not be dangerous in small quantities. For example, pure oxygen gas could make a fire burn dangerously fast, but we need oxygen to breathe. To decide how big a **risk** an air pollutant is, you need to know:
• how hazardous the substance is
• how much of it there is in the air.

? 3 Why is there a greater risk from sulfur dioxide pollution in volcanic areas?

Many of the trace gases in the air are harmful – they are a hazard. Usually there is so little of them that the risk to health or the environment is low, but this isn't always the case. If the amounts in the air increase, the risk to the environment or to health could become high.

Pollutant	Hazard	Effect on health
sulfur dioxide	toxic	Irritates the eyes and breathing system.
nitrogen oxides	very toxic	Irritates the eyes and breathing system.
carbon monoxide	toxic	Stops the blood taking up oxygen. Prolonged exposure is fatal.
hydrogen sulfide	very toxic	Harms the nervous system. A small amount can be fatal.

D

? 4 a Which gas has the greater hazard, carbon monoxide or hydrogen sulfide?
     b If there were equal amounts of these two gases in a room, which would cause the bigger risk?
   5 Think of a plus, a minus and an interesting point about this statement: All gases in the air should be unreactive.
   6 What information do you need to decide on the risk from breathing air in a particular place?

Summary

The _____ of a substance is the harm it does to the _____ and health. A hazard _____ shows what kind of danger there is from the substance. The _____ is how large the danger is. Gases released into the air by _____ activity that are _____ are called _____.

environment   hazard   hazardous
human   pollutants   risk   symbol

41

C1.5 Making new compounds
How are pollutant molecules formed from other substances?

The air is made up of **elements** such as oxygen and nitrogen and **compounds** like carbon dioxide. Elements are substances that cannot be broken down into anything simpler. Elements are made up of tiny particles called atoms. Compounds are formed when two or more elements join together.

1 a Name two elements in the air.
b Name one compound in the air.

Molecules are groups of atoms that are joined together. Oxygen molecules are two oxygen atoms joined together. We can write this in a chemical **formula** as O_2. If the atoms are from different elements the molecule is a compound such as carbon monoxide. Molecules can have two or more atoms. The formula for carbon dioxide, CO_2, shows that there are two atoms of oxygen joined to one atom of carbon.

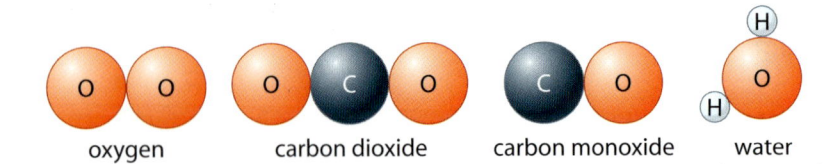

A John Dalton described how atoms of elements behave 200 years ago.

oxygen | carbon dioxide | carbon monoxide | water

B Molecules of some common gases.

There are many of ways of joining different atoms together, resulting in a very large number of compounds.

2 Nitrogen molecules consist of two atoms joined together.
   a What is the formula of a nitrogen molecule?
   b Draw a picture to show a nitrogen molecule

3 In a water molecule, two atoms of hydrogen are joined to one atom of oxygen. What is the formula for a water molecule?

Reactions

Many of the substances in the air are formed by **chemical reactions** in which atoms are rearranged into different molecules. When carbon reacts with oxygen the **reactants** are carbon atoms and oxygen molecules. The **products** of the reaction are carbon dioxide molecules. This means that the oxygen molecules have broken up and the oxygen atoms have joined to the carbon atoms. There is the same number of atoms of each element before and after the reaction.

The products of a reaction have different properties to the reactants but the atoms themselves do not change.

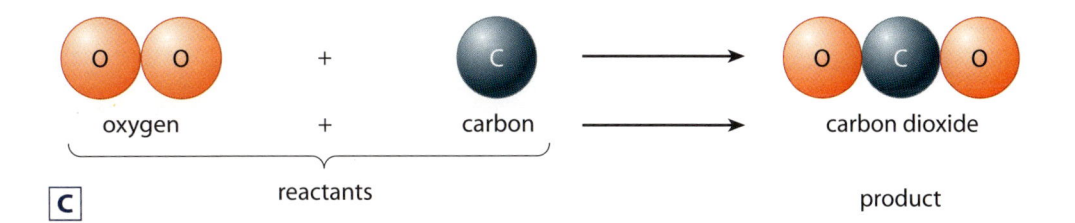

oxygen + carbon → carbon dioxide

reactants   product

C

? 4 Which statement is correct? Explain you answer
  A Carbon dioxide contains oxygen atoms.
  B Carbon dioxide contains oxygen molecules.

5 Give one difference in properties that carbon dioxide has to:
  a carbon
  b oxygen.

6 Why are the properties of carbon, oxygen and carbon dioxide all different?

7 What is the formula for nitrogen monoxide?

8 Which is the odd one out: element, atom, molecule? Explain your answers.

9 a What is formed when sulfur reacts with oxygen?
  b Which molecules have broken up in the reaction?
  c Which atoms have joined together in the reaction?
  d What is the formula for the product of the reaction?

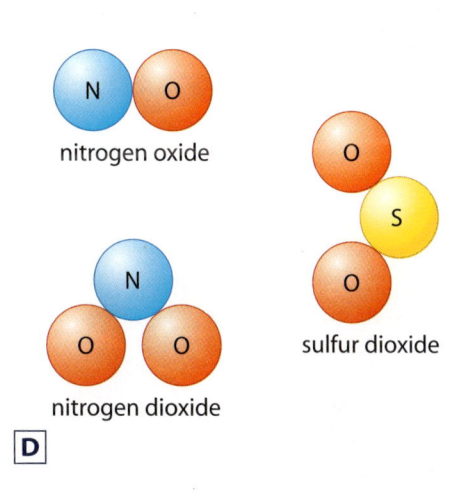

nitrogen oxide

nitrogen dioxide

sulfur dioxide

D

E Sulfur burns in oxygen to form sulfur dioxide.

Summary

The _____ of a molecule shows how many _____ of each _____ are joined together. Carbon dioxide is a _____ that contains _____ oxygen atoms and one _____ atom in each _____. In a chemical _____ the _____ of the atoms in molecules changes but the _____ of atoms of each element stays the same.

arrangement   atoms   carbon
compound   element   formula
molecule   number   reaction   two

43

C1.6 Burning fuels
What human activities release carbon dioxide and water into the air?

A This power station burns coal to generate electricity.

B We burn natural gas in our homes for cooking and to heat water.

C Ships burn fuel oil.

A **fuel** is any substance that gives out heat when it is burned. We burn **fossil fuels** to give us energy which is used in industry, transport and in our homes. Fossil fuels are substances that were formed millions of years ago from the remains of plants and animals. They contain carbon and hydrogen. The fossil fuels are coal, oil and natural gas. From oil, we get petrol and diesel fuel for vehicles and other liquid fuels for ships and aircraft.

? 1 Why is petrol a more convenient fuel for cars than coal?

Coal is mainly carbon. When it is burned it forms carbon dioxide (see diagram C on page 43).

carbon + oxygen → carbon dioxide

? 2 How many molecules of oxygen are used up for every atom of carbon burnt in coal?

A How could you show that carbon dioxide and water are formed when a fuel is burned?
- How could you collect the gases given off when a fuel burns?
- What reactions of carbon dioxide and water could be used as a test?

Petrol, diesel and natural gas are made up of compounds of carbon and hydrogen called **hydrocarbons**. When hydrocarbons are burned the atoms of carbon and hydrogen join with atoms of oxygen and form molecules of carbon dioxide and water.

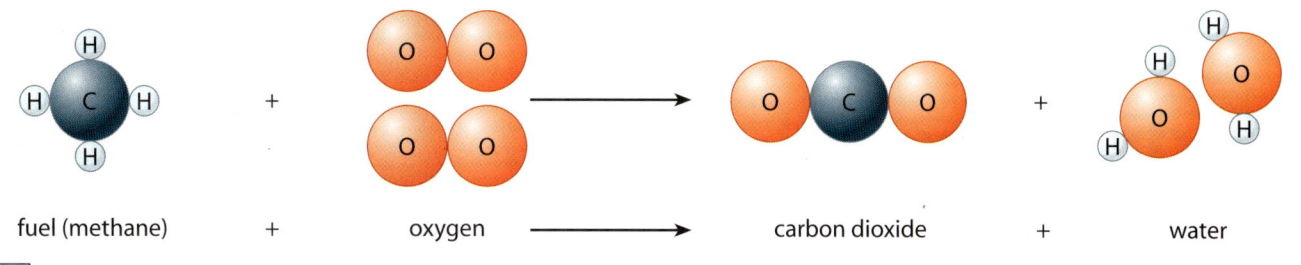

fuel (methane) + oxygen → carbon dioxide + water

D

Whenever we burn a fuel, oxygen is taken from the air and replaced with carbon dioxide and water. We burn very large amounts of fuels each year. This means that the amount of carbon dioxide in the air has increased because of human activity. Carbon dioxide does not harm health but it does affect the environment. It can therefore indirectly affect humans, so it is classed as a pollutant.

3 How many molecules of carbon dioxide are formed when one molecule of methane is burned?

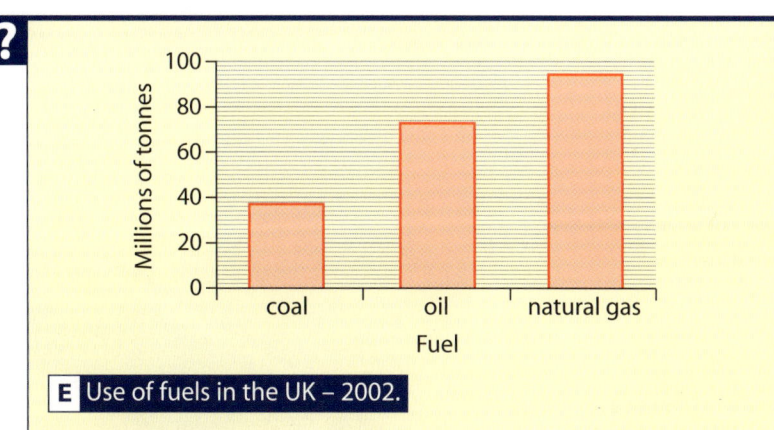

E Use of fuels in the UK – 2002.

4 Look at chart E.
   a Which fuel was used most in 2002?
   b What was the total amount of fuels used in the UK in 2002?

5 Why is carbon dioxide a pollutant?

6 Think of a plus, a minus and an interesting point about this statement: Developing countries are burning more fossil fuels.

7 When the same amounts of coal and natural gas are burned, the coal gives off more carbon dioxide than the natural gas. Why do you think the amount of natural gas used in the UK has increased recently while the amount of coal used has decreased? Give as many reasons as you can.

Summary

We burn _____ to obtain _____. Oil and natural gas are _____ and contain _____ and _____ but _____ is mainly carbon. When fossil fuels _____ they react with _____ in the air to form carbon _____ and _____. Increasing the amount of carbon dioxide in the _____ is damaging to the _____.

air   burn   carbon
dioxide   coal   energy
environment   fuels   hydrocarbons
hydrogen   oxygen   water

45

C1.7 Making pollutants

What is the source of pollutants in the air?

Burning fuels do not just form carbon dioxide and water; other substances are formed as well.

Elderly couple killed by faulty gas fire

A Carbon monoxide produced by faulty fires can kill.

Carbon monoxide

Burning a fossil fuel uses a lot of oxygen. Often there is not enough oxygen in the air to burn the fuel completely and carbon monoxide is formed instead of carbon dioxide. Each carbon atom joins with just one oxygen atom.

fuel + oxygen → carbon monoxide + water

Carbon monoxide is a poisonous gas. Carbon monoxide sensors can tell if the amount of the gas is reaching dangerous levels.

> **?** 1 Draw a diagram of a carbon monoxide molecule.

Soot

Soot is tiny particles of carbon, often called **particulate carbon**. Soot is formed when the supply of air to a fire is not enough to burn all the fuel. Coal fires, candles and diesel engines in cars all produce soot. The tiny particles are too small to be seen but they float in the air.

> **?** 2 a Is soot a solid or a gas?
>   b Why is soot sometimes called 'particulate carbon'?
> 3 a When a Bunsen burner is producing a yellow flame, is the air hole open or closed?
>   b Why is the yellow flame sooty?

B A yellow Bunsen burner flame produces a lot of soot.

A Sticky-backed plastic will trap particles of soot and dust.
- How could you use sticky-backed plastic to measure soot pollution levels?

NO$_x$

The temperature inside vehicle engines and furnaces is very high, causing some of the nitrogen in the air to react with oxygen to form nitrogen monoxide. When this escapes into the cool air it reacts with more oxygen to form nitrogen dioxide. **NO$_x$** refers to both nitrogen monoxide and nitrogen dioxide.

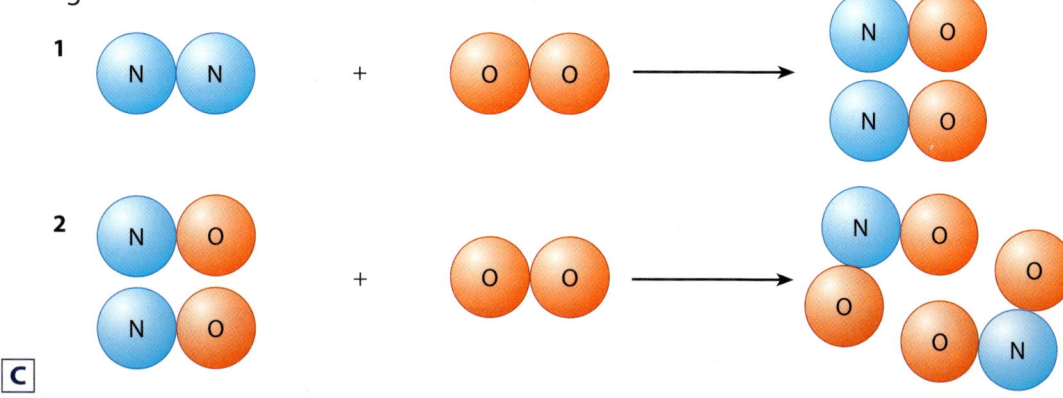

C

? 4 How are the following pollutants formed:
   a nitrogen monoxide
   b nitrogen dioxide?

5 Write down the formulae of nitrogen monoxide and nitrogen dioxide.

Dirty fuels

Fossil fuels often contain sulfur. When the fuel is burned the sulfur reacts with oxygen too, forming sulfur dioxide gas. Coal contains more sulfur than other fossil fuels.

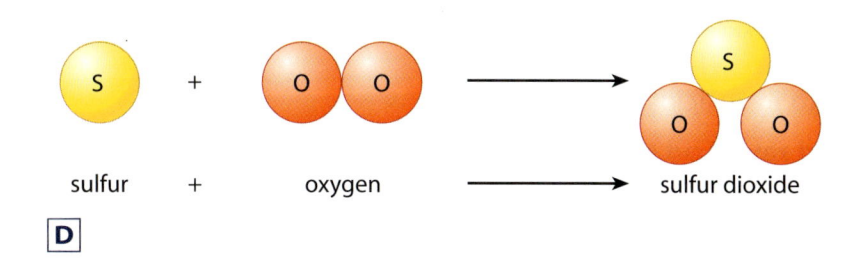

sulfur + oxygen ⟶ sulfur dioxide

D

? 6 How many atoms of oxygen are there in one molecule of sulfur dioxide?

7 Think of a plus, a minus and an interesting point about this statement: Fuels should not contain sulfur.

8 How is the formation of NO$_x$ different to the way in which other pollutants are formed by burning fuels?

E All these different gases are released into the air when fuels are burned.

Summary

When _____ fuels are burned _____ gases are formed. If there is not enough _____ then carbon _____ and _____ are formed. If the gases are hot enough _____ oxides are produced and if the fuel contains _____ then sulfur _____ is released into the air.

| dioxide | fossil | monoxide | nitrogen |
| oxygen | pollutant | soot | sulfur |

47

C1.8 Air pollutants and the environment
What happens to pollutants once they are in the air?

The burning of fossil fuels puts pollutants into the air, but they don't stay there doing nothing!

Soot

Particles of soot are washed out of the air by rain. They also settle on the leaves of plants, the outside of buildings or in the lungs of people and animals.

Up to about 50 years ago the burning of coal in cities made buildings black with soot. Most buildings have now been cleaned but soot is still a problem.

? 1 Where does soot go when it is washed out of the air by rain?

A The Houses of Parliament used to be covered with soot…

B … but after cleaning the colour of the stone can be seen again.

Acid rain

Winds can blow sulfur dioxide and nitrogen oxides long distances from where the pollution was formed. These substances react with oxygen and water to form acids.

The acids mix with rainwater to make **acid rain**. Acid rain damages plants and reacts with the stone and cement used in many buildings.

C Many trees have died as a result of acid rain.

Acid rain runs into rivers and lakes and can make the water too acidic for most animals to live in it.

? 2 How could you tell if rainfall had been acidic for a long time?

3 Pollutants produced in the UK are blown across the North Sea to Norway. What effect do you think this has on the forests of Norway?

A How would you investigate the effects of acid rain:
- on buildings made from calcium carbonate
- on machines made of steel
- on the growth of a plant such as cress?

Carbon dioxide

A lot of carbon dioxide dissolves in rainwater and the oceans. Carbon dioxide reacts with other substances dissolved in seawater and can make it more acidic.

D Shellfish make their shells from the calcium carbonate formed in seawater.

Land and water plants take in carbon dioxide and make sugars for food by the process of photosynthesis. Plankton in the oceans and forests take up a lot of the carbon dioxide that we produce. However, we are adding more carbon dioxide to the air than is removed so the amount of carbon dioxide in the air is increasing.

? 4 Calcium carbonate reacts with acids. What would happen to shellfish if the amount of carbon dioxide in seawater increased?

5 Copy and complete the table showing the processes that add and remove carbon dioxide from the air.

Add carbon dioxide	Remove carbon dioxide

6 Why is there more carbon dioxide in the air now than there was 50 years ago?

7 What effect will destruction of forests have on the amount of carbon dioxide in the air?

Summary

Soot is washed out of the air by _____ and settles on plants and _____ making them black. It also gets into people's _____. Sulfur dioxide and nitrogen _____ react with water and form _____ rain. This damages _____ and makes lakes and rivers too _____ for fish and water plants. Carbon _____ is absorbed by plants for photosynthesis and it also _____ in the oceans.

acid   acidic   buildings   dioxide
dissolves   lungs   oxides   rain   trees

49

C1.9 Air pollution and health

What effects do air pollutants have on health?

The great smog

In the past, London often had winter smogs which were thick brown fogs caused by the burning of smoky coal in open fires. Smog caused coughs. In 1952 a very bad smog lasted for days. Doctors collected data on people who died from diseases that affected breathing.

Disease	Number of deaths	
	Week before smog	Week of smog
bronchitis	74	704
influenza	47	192
tuberculosis	14	77
breathing problems	9	52
heart disease	206	525
others	595	934

A Smog deaths in 1952.

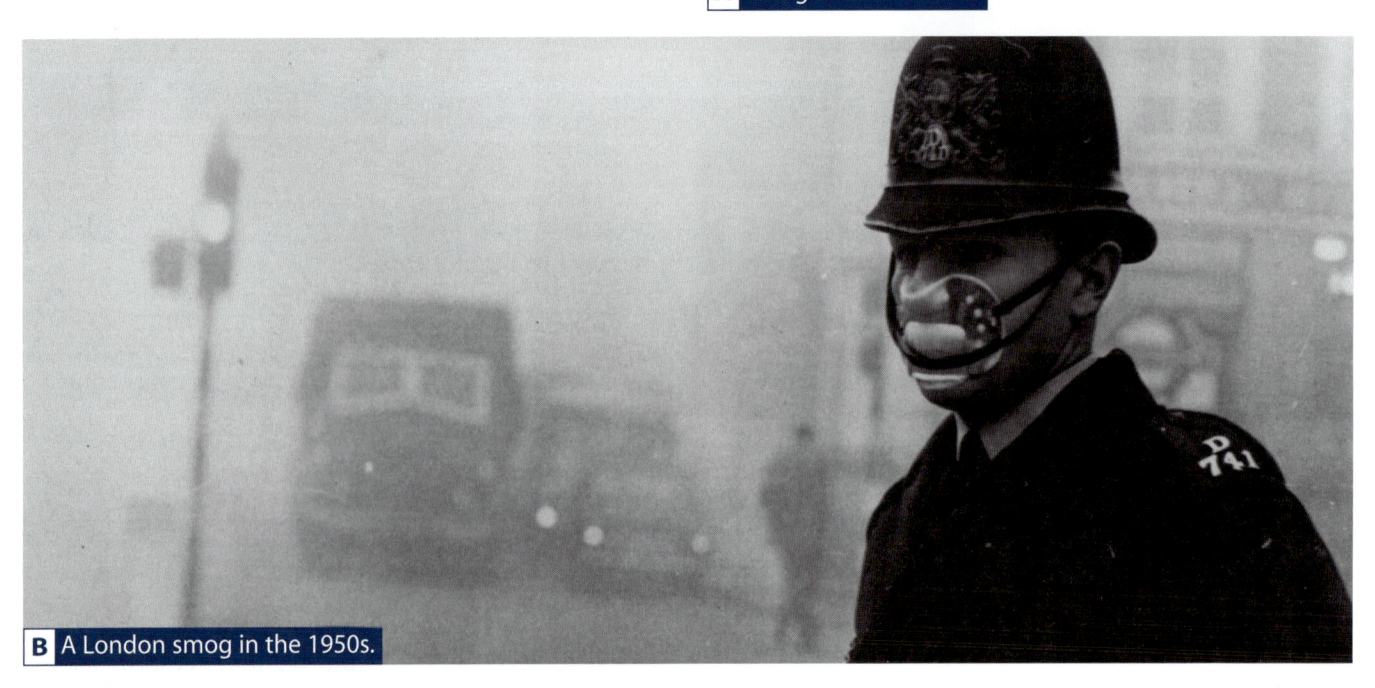

B A London smog in the 1950s.

?
1. In 1952 how many people died of tuberculosis:
   a in the week before the smog
   b in the week of the smog?
2. Which disease showed the biggest rise in the number of deaths in the week of the smog?

Scientists noticed similar effects every time there was smog. This showed that there was a **correlation** between deaths from these diseases and smog incidents. Scientists also discovered that substances in smog damage the breathing tubes. They had an acceptable **theory** for the **cause** of the deaths. After the government banned the burning of smoky coal in towns, smogs soon stopped forming.

Cause and outcome

A correlation does not always mean that one **factor** has caused an **outcome**. Let us look at the problem of asthma. Asthma causes a narrowing of the breathing tubes, making it difficult to breathe. If air quality is poor more people have asthma attacks, but scientists are not sure what causes the disease.

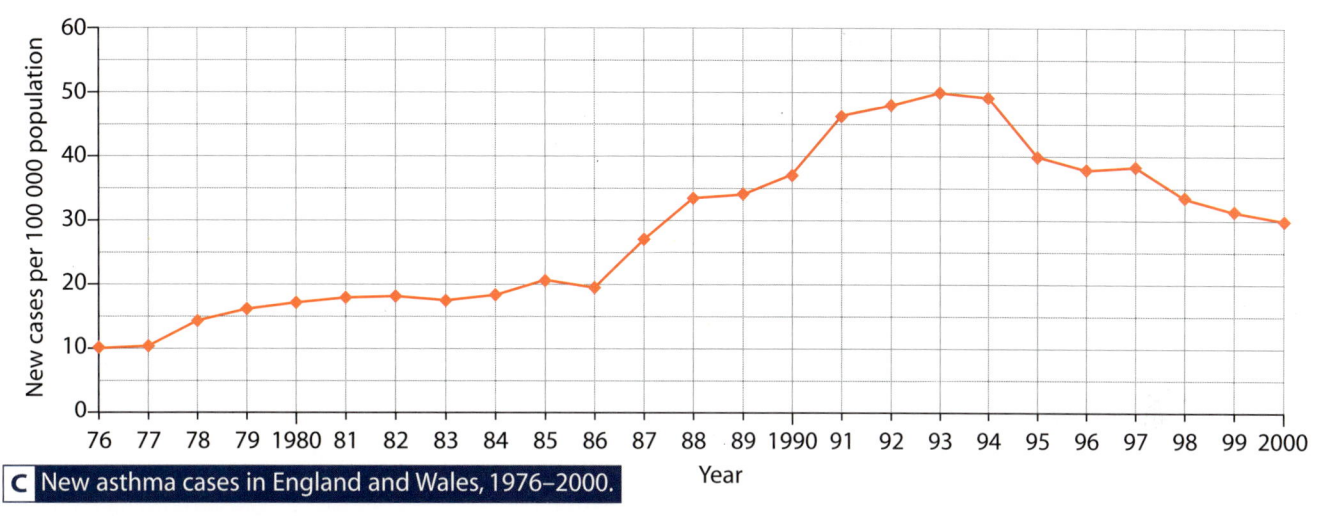

C New asthma cases in England and Wales, 1976–2000.

3 a How does the number of new cases of asthma in 1999 compare with the number in 1976?
  b Describe how the number of new cases changed between the years 1976 and 1999.
  c Between which years was the increase in new cases fastest? Explain how you obtained your answer.

Many other things were found to have increased in the same period that asthma cases had risen:
- the use of natural gas
- the number of vehicles on the roads
- the cost of chocolate bars.

Only by changing one factor and keeping the others constant can a correlation with new asthma cases be tested. Scientists still do not have a single acceptable theory for the cause of asthma.

4 Scientists could test whether sulfur dioxide caused asthma by making healthy people breathe the pollutant and counting how many became asthmatic. Why don't scientists do this experiment?

5 Which of the factors mentioned could be a cause of the rise in asthma cases? Give reasons for your answers

6 Explain this statement: A correlation between two factors does not prove that one causes the other.

Summary

Two factors show a _____ when they show a similar pattern. One factor may be the _____ that affects the other factor. In the 1950s, deaths from _____-related diseases _____ whenever there was _____. A _____ that showed that _____ in smog caused the deaths was proved. It is difficult to test one _____ that could be the cause of asthma.

breathing	cause	correlation
factor	increased	pollutants
	smog	theory

51

C1.10 Pollution and power stations
How can we cut pollution caused by power stations?

A All these machines use electricity.

Electricity is a very useful form of energy. It is generated in power stations mainly by burning fossil fuels. This produces much of the pollution in the air. To improve air quality we must find ways of reducing the amount of pollutants produced in power stations.

Here are some ideas for how we could do this.

- **Produce less electricity**

If we can find ways of using less electricity we will not need to burn as much fossil fuel in power stations. We could turn off electrical appliances, such as TVs and lights, when they are not in use. We could buy fridges and other machines that are designed to use less energy. We could insulate our homes better so that less electricity is needed for heating.

- **Stop releasing pollutants into the air**

Sulfur could be removed from fossil fuels before they are burned so that no sulfur dioxide is formed. The furnaces in power stations could be designed to burn the fuel to produce less soot, carbon monoxide and nitrogen oxides. Alternatively the pollutants could be removed from the waste gases before they are released into the air. The only way to produce less carbon dioxide and water is to burn less fuel.

- **Generating electricity in different ways**

Burning fossil fuels is not the only way of making electricity. **Nuclear power** or **hydroelectric** schemes are used in many places and these do not burn fossil fuels. **Renewable** sources of energy such as wind or **solar power** produce electricity without causing air pollution. However, all these methods require expensive new machinery.

B Solar cells turn the Sun's energy into electricity.

C Hydroelectric power stations use the energy from water stored behind dams to generate electricity.

?
1. Why will removing the pollutants from burning fossil fuels increase the cost of electricity?
2. Why will replacing power stations that burn fossil fuels make electricity more expensive?
3. Suggest three ways by which you could reduce the amount of electricity you use at home.
4. How can we reduce the amount of carbon dioxide produced?

Controlling pollution

The air quality in the UK has improved in the last 30 years, as the government has passed laws controlling the amount of sulfur in fuels, and limiting the amounts of sulfur dioxide and nitrogen oxides that power stations are allowed to produce. There are targets to continue to reduce the amounts of these pollutants produced in the future.

D Wind is a clean source of power.

?
5. Think of a plus, a minus and an interesting point about this statement: All electricity should be generated by wind power.
6. Why does the government need to pass laws controlling the amount of pollution produced by power stations?

Summary

Burning _____ fuels to produce _____ is one of the main causes of air _____. We could improve air _____ by producing _____ electricity, by removing pollutants from _____ gases or by using _____ sources of energy. The government passes laws to _____ the amount of _____ that power stations are allowed to produce.

_____ control   electricity   fossil   less
pollution   quality   renewable   waste

53

C1.11 Pollution and transport

How can pollutants in emissions from transport be reduced?

A The engines of road vehicles burn petrol or diesel fuel.

We all travel from place to place and we buy goods that have come from all parts of the world. Some ways in which pollution from transport could be reduced are described here.

- Use cleaner fuels – some sulfur has been removed from 'low sulfur fuels' so less sulfur dioxide is formed when the fuel burns.

B This car uses hydrogen as its fuel which only gives off water when it is burnt.

- Use a **catalytic converter** – this helps the nitrogen oxides and carbon monoxide formed in the engine react to make nitrogen and carbon dioxide. However, catalytic converters only work well if the engine runs for more than about 10 minutes.

?
1. Which air pollutants are reduced by using low sulfur fuel?
2. Why are catalytic converters not much use on short journeys?

- Use less fuel – small cars use less fuel than large ones. Engines could be made more efficient so they waste less energy. The faster we move the more fuel is used, so travelling more slowly would also use less fuel.
- Use **public transport** – one full bus or train replaces a lot of cars but uses less fuel.
- Increase **taxes** – the government could increase the tax on cars or fuel. The tax on each car depends on how much air pollution it produces. Big cars produce more pollutants than small cars. Parking charges could also be increased.

3 a Why is the tax on small cars less than on large cars?
b How can the government try to stop people using cars in cities?

- Make anti-pollution laws stricter – the amount of pollutants a vehicle produces is checked by the annual MOT test. Vehicles that fail have to be repaired or scrapped.
- Use electric vehicles – an electric vehicle produces no air pollution. It gets its power from batteries. The electricity could be provided by new power stations which do not cause pollution.
- Cycle or walk – on short journeys it is almost as quick as using a car, produces no pollutants and keeps you healthy.

C Cars are charged for driving on these city streets. Perhaps it would be cheaper to leave the car at home and use public transport.

D This vehicle charges its batteries by plugging into the electricity supply.

4 Why would electric cars not be an improvement if the electricity came from power stations that use fossil fuels?

5 Think of a plus, a minus and an interesting point about this statement: Cars should be banned from city centres.

6 A bus travels 2 km on a litre of fuel; cars travel about 12 km on a litre of fuel. If every car carries just the driver, how many people must take the bus in order to save fuel?

Summary

Road _____ are a major source of air _____. Reducing the use of _____ fuels could be achieved by using different fuels such as _____ or by using _____ vehicles. Increasing _____ may encourage the use of _____ and trains by making private cars more _____ to run.

buses   electric   expensive   fossil
hydrogen   pollution   taxes   vehicles

55

C1.12 Making choices about air quality

What decisions can be made to improve air quality?

A Smoke from forest fires in the Amazon shows where land is being cleared by burning.

Air quality has improved in some parts of the world. London no longer has thick brown smogs because laws have been passed to improve air quality. Globally, however, air quality is getting worse as more fossil fuels and wood are burned. Some difficult choices will have to be made.

? 1 What will happen if nothing is done to improve air quality?

International choices

Leaders of all the countries of the world meet to discuss air pollution and other problems. Suggestions are made that may help, but at the start of the 21st century no decisions have yet been reached. Some leaders are unwilling to make choices that will help air quality but make their country poorer. The problem is that most solutions mean burning less fossil fuel, making it expensive for a country to change to other methods of obtaining energy.

? 2 Why would a developing country not want to reduce the amount of fossil fuels burnt?

National decisions

In the 1980s the UK government insisted that new cars should be fitted with catalytic converters. Decisions like this cost money but general health would improve if air quality was improved. In the future, governments will have to make more choices like this. Some decisions may not be popular.

? 3 Why is increasing fuel tax unpopular, even though it may improve air quality?

B Some people do not approve of the high tax on fuel in the UK.

Your turn

Even small groups of people can make a difference. An example is the 'walking buses' that have been organised in some places, where parents supervise a group of children walking to school. By not using cars for the 'school run' they are reducing the amount of fuel burned and improving the air quality in their area.

> **?** **4** What are the advantages and disadvantages of 'walking buses'?

We can all make choices that make small improvements. We can turn off lights that are not needed, walk or cycle instead of using a car, or take a train on long journeys. Each choice we make reduces air pollution a little. There are 6 billion people on Earth. Lots of small contributions add up to big improvements in air quality.

C A 'walking bus' saves energy, keeps the air cleaner and improves health.

D In a city, a cyclist can travel just as fast as a car and produces no pollution.

> **?** **5** Describe one thing you could do to improve air quality.
> **6** Air quality is worse in some countries than others. Write down as many explanations for this statement as you can.
> **7** What can local governments do to encourage people to cycle or walk instead of driving?

Summary

If nothing is done to improve air quality it will get _____ in the future. Choices must be made by _____ and by _____. Governments can make _____ and raise _____ that force people to improve air quality. Individuals can choose to save _____ or use cars _____.

energy   governments   individuals
laws   less   taxes   worse

57

C1.13 Looking at air quality

What do you know about air quality and how it can be improved?

Josh and Emily live in a small town. The streets in the town centre are clogged with traffic and Josh and Emily think that the air quality is poor. They have decided to do a project to investigate air quality in their town and find ways of improving it.

A Josh and Emily have started their research.

1 Josh and Emily want to know what gases make up the atmosphere. They have a bar chart but it has lost its labels. Which gases are represented by the columns 1, 2 and 3? You can choose from: argon, helium, oxygen, nitrogen.

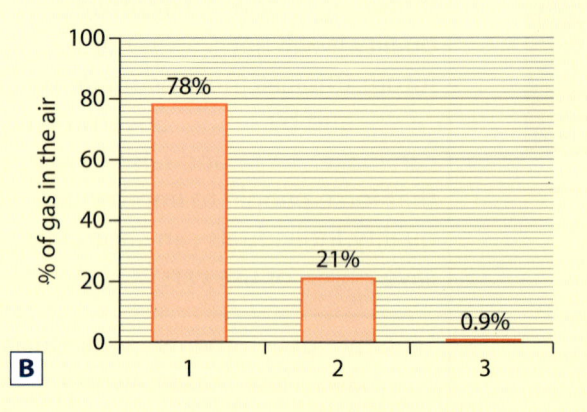

B Bar chart: % of gas in the air — Column 1: 78%, Column 2: 21%, Column 3: 0.9%

2 Emily says she knows that the fuels used in cars are compounds of carbon and hydrogen, but is not sure what happens when the fuel burns.
   a What gas in the air is used up when these fuels burn?
   b What substances are formed when these fuels are burned in car engines?

3 a Josh says that he thinks nitrogen monoxide is also formed in car engines, but where does the nitrogen come from?
   b The formula for nitrogen dioxide is NO_2. How many atoms of nitrogen and oxygen are there in one molecule of nitrogen dioxide?

4 Josh is worried that the poor air quality may be causing asthma in people. He has found some data on asthma.

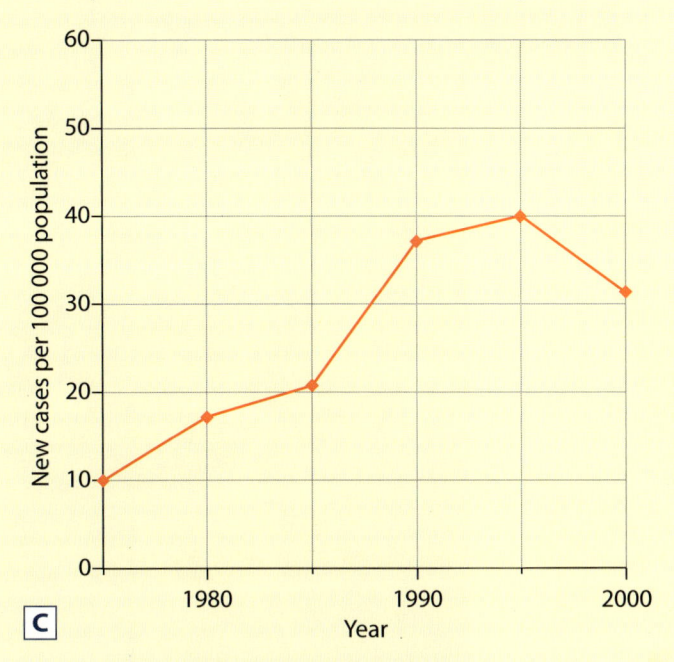

C

a How many new cases of asthma were reported for every 100 000 people in 1995?
b Josh thinks that the number of new cases of asthma is growing each year. Is this true? Explain your answer.
c What other data does Josh need to show that there is a correlation between air pollution and the number of new asthma cases?

5 Emily has found out that catalytic converters are fitted to cars. Catalytic converters convert some pollutants into less dangerous substances. Copy and complete the table to show Emily how the amount of each substance is changed by the catalytic converter. Tick one box in each row. One has been done for you.

Gas	Increases	Decreases	Stays the same
carbon monoxide		✓	
carbon dioxide			
nitrogen oxides			
argon			
nitrogen			

D How catalytic converters affect gases.

6 Emily and Josh have used sticky cards to collect soot in the centre of town and in their school playing field. Using a microscope they counted the number of soot particles collected in the millimetre squares marked on the cards.

Card	Number of particles per mm²				
school field	19	21	20	22	18
town centre	33	29	20	32	30

E Soot data.

a Which measurement taken in the town centre is probably an outlier?
b Emily and Josh calculated the mean for the other four results taken in the town centre.

$$\frac{\text{total of results}}{\text{number of results}} = \frac{124}{4} = 31$$

Why did they calculate the mean?

c Between which values does the true value for the town centre probably lie?
d Look at the results for the school field. Calculate the mean for all five results for the school field. Show your working.
e Josh wrote a conclusion: 'This investigation proves that there is more soot in the air in the town centre than in the school field'. Do you agree with Josh? Explain your answer.

7 Josh thinks that power stations also cause air pollution. There is a coal-burning power station near the town.
a Coal often contains sulfur. What pollutants are formed when coal is burned?
b Suggest ways that pollution from power stations could be reduced.

8 Emily and Josh would like to end their project with some suggestions on how to improve air quality in the centre of town. They think that one way would be to reduce the number of vehicles that use the streets in the town centre. Give Emily and Josh three ideas about how this could be done.

59

P1.1

The Earth in the Universe

Where do you live?

A

You might have written an address like this at some time, but usually we stop at the postcode. We live on a **planet** that is one of nine planets that go around our own special star – the Sun. The Sun and the planets are called the **Solar System**. Our Sun is just one of billions of stars that make up our **galaxy**, the **Milky Way**, and our galaxy is just one amongst the billions that can be seen looking deep into space using telescopes.

Here are some questions that you may have thought about:

- How old is the Earth?
- Why is it the way it is, with mountains in some places, plains in others and oceans in between?
- Is it a safe place to live?
- How long will it stay safe?
- What might threaten life on Earth?

Scientists study many things, including trying to answer questions like the ones above. We are interested in the answers, particularly if the answer is likely to affect us personally. We do not worry too much when we are told that the Sun will only burn for another 5000 million years, but when we read that a massive **meteorite** could smash into the Earth in 10 years time it seems to be a lot more important!

B

60

Bam Earthquake
Over 25 000 dead, over 100 000 homeless

Pinatubo erupts! Thousands evacuated.

C

Hollywood hype or real risk?

If you were told that a meteorite could hit the Earth, you would need to ask more questions before you started to panic. You could ask:

- How can scientists know this?
- How certain are they that a disaster will happen?
- What will it do to life on Earth?
- Can we do anything to stop it happening?
- Can we do anything to increase our chances of survival?

In this module we will look at what we know about the Earth, the forces that shaped it and its place in our Solar System. We will look at the different ideas suggested by scientists and other thinkers to explain why the Earth is the way it is, and test the different ideas and explanations to see which seems the best. Some of the things that we now accept as scientific facts were once thought not just to be wrong, but wicked or crazy!

?

1 Put the following events in order of how often you think they happen, most frequent first: meteorite impacts, earthquakes, volcanic eruptions.

2 a Which type of event do you think is most dangerous?
  b Explain your answer to part **a**.

3 a Do you think that meteorite impacts with the Earth are always dangerous?
  b What do you need to know to decide whether an impact is dangerous or not?

4 The size of earthquakes is sometimes measured using the Richter Scale, but this does not tell us how dangerous an earthquake is. What else do you need to know to judge how dangerous an earthquake is?

61

P1.2 The face of the Earth

What is the structure of the Earth, and how is the Earth changing?

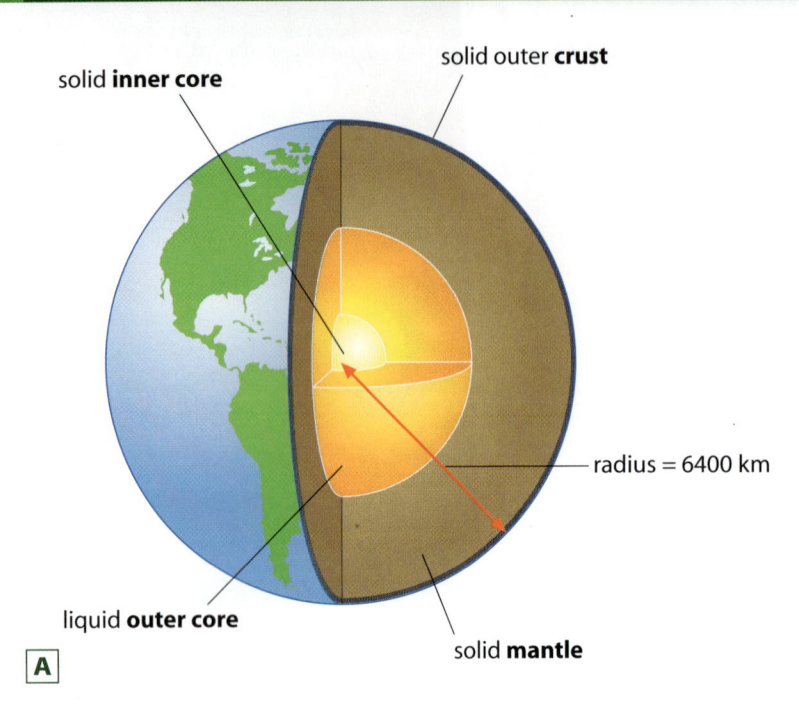

A

- solid **inner core**
- solid outer **crust**
- liquid **outer core**
- solid **mantle**
- radius = 6400 km

The Earth is shaped like a sphere that is slightly squashed at the poles. The solid surface that we live on is called the **crust**. The crust under the sea is called **oceanic crust**, and is made of denser rocks than the **continental crust**.

The photographs on these pages show some views of the Earth's crust as it is today. Rocks are being **weathered** (broken down) all the time. This can happen in different ways. Broken bits of rock can be carried away by water, ice or the wind. This is called **erosion**.

?
1. a Name the four main layers in the structure of the Earth.
   b What is the difference between the two kinds of crust?
2. a What does 'weathering' mean?
   b What does 'erosion' mean.

B The Lyngen Peninsula in Norway.

C The ice in the glacier wears rocks away and carries the broken pieces downhill.

D These pinnacles in the Arizona desert have been worn away by the wind.

E The sea is gradually eroding the white cliffs of Dover, on the south coast of England.

Weathering and erosion are usually very slow processes. The speed at which rocks are weathered depends on how hard the rocks are and what it is that is wearing them away. Hard rocks take a very long time to wear away. Soft rocks are worn away more quickly.

Even very hard rocks like granite show wear after a hundred years or so. The oldest rocks on the Earth are about 4 billion years old, so the Earth must be older than this. If all the mountains had been made at the same time as the Earth they would have been eroded by wind and water by now.

Worn bits of rocks are carried away in streams and rivers, and eventually deposited as **sediments**. Some sediments get buried and eventually become new rock. The processes of **sedimentation** and erosion can help us to understand past changes to the Earth.

? 3 What processes weather and erode rocks?

? 4 a How do you think the Earth would look now if all the mountains had been made when the Earth was formed?
b Why do you think that there are very high mountains on the Earth now?

5 Think of a plus, a minus, and an interesting point about this statement: Rocks should not wear away.

6 Find out the names of three high mountain ranges from different parts of the world.

Summary

The Earth consists of a solid _____ core, a liquid outer _____ and a solid _____ and _____. Mountains are _____ and eroded by the action of _____ and _____. These processes are very _____ but the Earth is very _____. If all the mountains had been formed when the Earth was made, even the highest would have been _____ away by now.

core   crust   inner   mantle   old
slow   water   weathered   wind   worn

63

P1.3 Continental drift

What was Wegener's theory about mountain building?

A Fossils of sea creatures are sometimes found at the top of high mountains. This is evidence that the mountains rose after the Earth was formed.

B Alfred Lothar Wegener.

In 1915 Alfred Wegener (1880–1930) published his theory of **continental drift**. Wegener thought that the continents of Africa and South America had once been joined together but had slowly drifted apart over millions of years. He gave the following evidence for his ideas:

- The shapes of the continents seem to fit together.
- Fossils of similar plants and animals are found in the two continents.
- There are similar rocks where the two continents may have been joined.

?
1. What did Wegener notice about the shapes of South America and Africa?
2. What other evidence did Wegener have to support his idea that South America and Africa were once joined together?

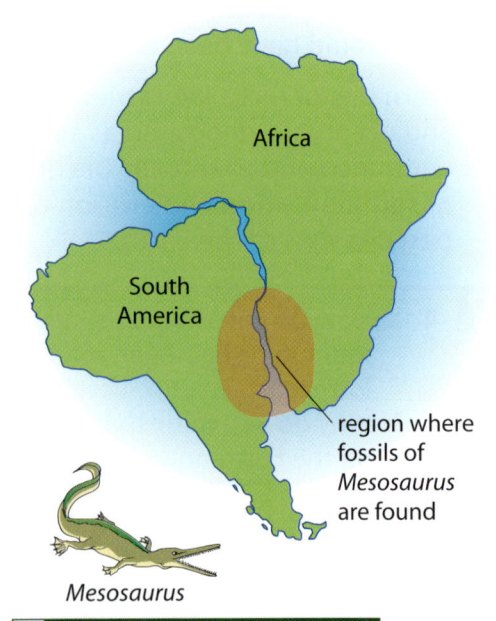

Mesosaurus

region where fossils of *Mesosaurus* are found

C Evidence for continental drift.

Wegener also suggested that all the other land masses were once joined together in a 'supercontinent' called Pangaea. This broke up over 200 million years ago and the fragments drifted apart. He was not the first person to suggest that the continents had once been joined, but he was the first to provide evidence to support his ideas.

This idea suggested that mountains could have been formed when the huge masses of land crashed into each other and parts of them were slowly pushed upwards by the tremendous force of the collision. This would explain the folds that can be seen in the rocks in some mountains.

D Pangaea.

E Folds in the French Pyrennees.

3 a What was Pangaea?
  b What happened to it?

4 How does the idea of continental drift explain how mountains are formed?

Wegener's theory of continental drift was not accepted by most other scientists in his lifetime. There were several reasons for this:
- They did not see how great masses of rock could just drift around, ploughing through other great masses of rock.
- There were other explanations suggested for the similar fossil finds in Africa and South America.
- They could not detect the movement of the continents, and thought this was a very big idea with not much evidence for it.

5 Why wasn't Wegener's theory accepted in his lifetime?

6 An older theory of mountain building said that the Earth was hot when it was formed, and gradually shrank as it cooled.
  a How would this explain the formation of mountains? (*Hint:* what might happen to the surface if the inside got smaller?)
  b Why don't scientists agree with this idea today?

Summary

Wegener thought that the continents were once _____ together. This explained why the coast of _____ seemed to fit together with _____. His evidence was the similar _____ found on both sides of the Atlantic and the matching _____ types. Mountains were formed where continents _____ and made the rocks fold. Most other _____ did not agree with Wegener's theory.

| Africa | collided | fossils | joined |
| rock | scientists | South America |

P1.4 Plate tectonics
What is the theory of plate tectonics?

More evidence

Scientists continued to study rocks and fossils all over the world, and started to make detailed surveys of the ocean floors. In 1948 an undersea survey discovered **oceanic ridges** (mountain ranges) that run down the middle of the oceans. They also discovered deep **oceanic trenches** in other parts of the oceans. **Radioactive dating** of rock samples showed that the rocks in the ocean floor were much younger than most of the rocks that formed the continents.

? 1 What new evidence was found under the sea in 1948?

A The mid-Atlantic ridge.

Plate tectonics

The theory of plate tectonics explains why these oceanic ridges and trenches occur, as well as explaining all the observations that Wegener used to back up his theory.

According to plate tectonic theory, the surface of the Earth is made up of large pieces, or **tectonic plates**, that can move around slowly. The plates consist of a part of the crust and the top part of the mantle beneath it. The mantle is solid, but heat energy from **radioactive decay** inside the Earth allows parts of it to move very slowly. Movements in the mantle move the plates on the surface of the Earth.

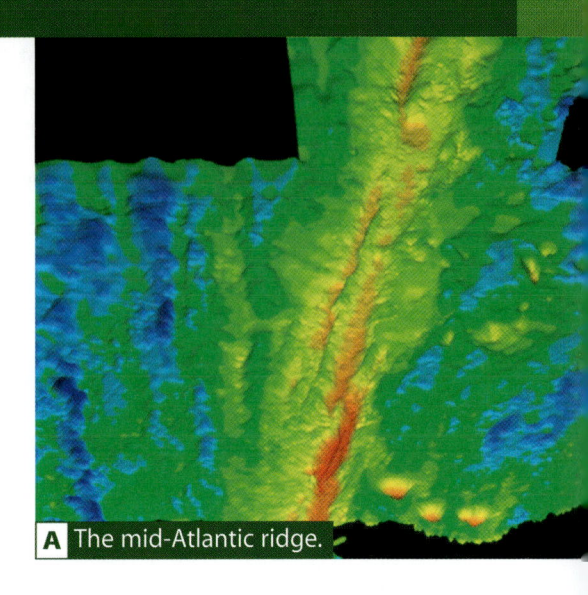

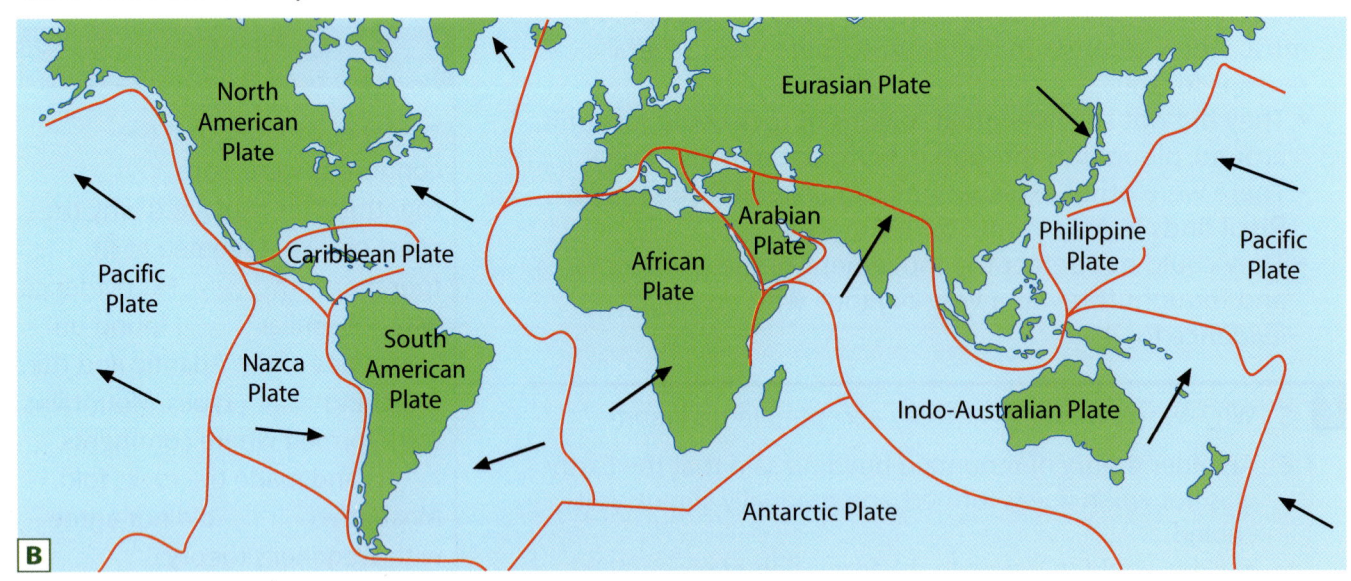

B

? 2 a What are tectonic plates?
b How can these plates move?

Oceanic ridges are formed as two plates move away from each other. As the plates move, part of the mantle beneath the crack melts and forms liquid rock called **magma**. This forces its way up to the surface where it cools and solidifies to form new rocks. This **seafloor spreading** is making the oceans wider.

? 3 What is seafloor spreading? Explain in as much detail as you can.

If the floors of the oceans are spreading, then in other parts of the world the plates must be getting smaller. Diagrams D and E show what can happen when plates move towards each other.

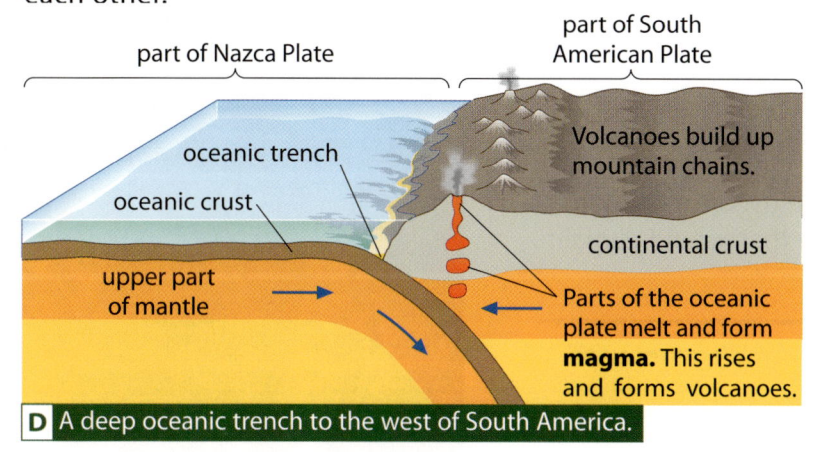

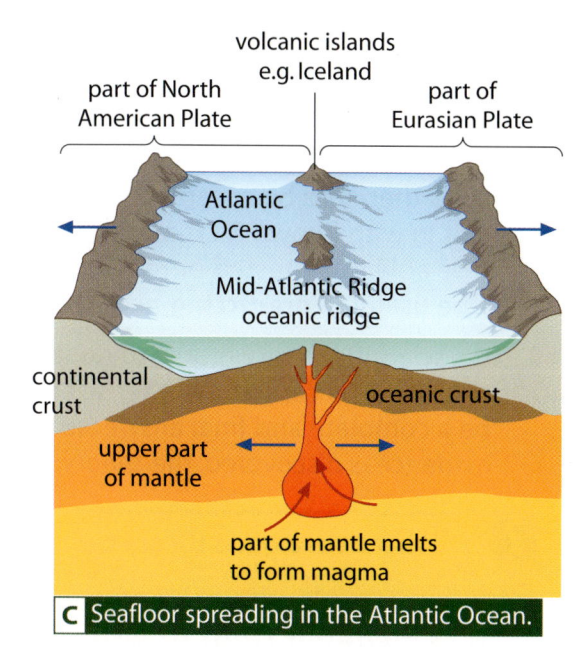

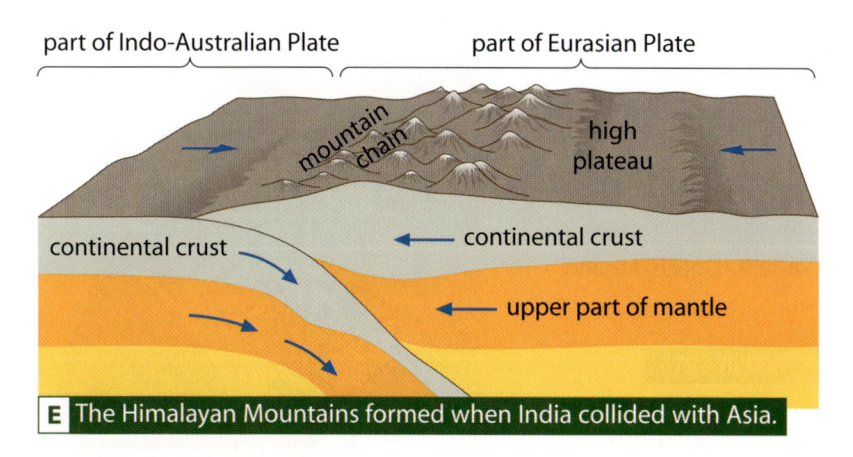

C Seafloor spreading in the Atlantic Ocean.

D A deep oceanic trench to the west of South America.

E The Himalayan Mountains formed when India collided with Asia.

? 4 Describe two different ways that mountain ranges can be built up.

5 A mountain is not the same height as it was 10 years ago. Consider all the possible reasons for this statement.

6 Describe some differences between Wegener's theory of continental drift, and the theory of plate tectonics. (*Hint*: think of which part of the Earth moves.)

Summary

The surface of the Earth is divided up into large sections called tectonic _____. These move around slowly, using energy from _____ decay. Oceanic ridges form where two _____ plates drift apart. Ocean trenches form where _____ crust is forced beneath _____ crust. Mountains form where plates move _____ each other.

continental   oceanic   plates
radioactive   tectonic   towards

67

P1.5 Weighing the evidence
Why are some theories accepted and not others?

For a theory to be accepted by other scientists it has to:
- fit in with known facts and not disagree with them
- be able to be tested or repeated by other scientists
- be useful in **predicting** new ideas or evidence.

If a scientific theory is able to do these things then it is likely to become accepted by other scientists. However, it may not be a complete and final answer to a problem. If new evidence is discovered, the theory may have to be changed.

1 What does a good theory help other scientists to do?

Was Wegener right or wrong?

Wegener based his theory on his observations and on evidence collected by other scientists. He used the evidence and his imagination to produce a theory that would explain the evidence.

2 Write down three pieces of evidence that Wegener used. You may need to look back at page 64.

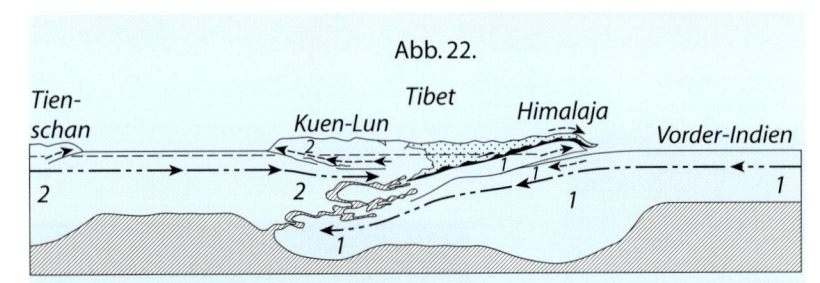

B An illustration from Wegener's book, first published in 1915.

Wegener's theory of continental drift was not accepted by most other scientists in his lifetime. They did not say that all his evidence was wrong, but they thought that there could be other explanations for it.

3 Give one scientific reason why Wegener's theory was rejected.

4 How do you think other scientists found out about Wegener's ideas?

A This fossil tree fern is about 250 million years old. It is found on several continents.

C Some scientists said that there were once 'land bridges' that allowed animals and plants to spread across different continents.

The new theory

In 1930, towards the end of Wegener's life, new evidence about the structure of the Earth was discovered. By the late 1960s Wegener's ideas had been developed into the new theory of plate tectonics that scientists still use to explain and predict many events, including volcanoes and earthquakes.

D Map of the Mid-Atlantic Ridge.

E The submersible Alvin, which is used to study oceanic ridges.

This theory is now accepted by most scientists because:
- there is a lot of evidence to **corroborate** (support) it, from lots of different scientists
- it explains *how* the plates can move.

New observations that agree with predictions increase confidence that a theory is a good explanation for what happens. If observations do not agree with predictions then either the observation is wrong or the prediction is wrong. If several new observations do not agree with predictions, then scientists may change the theory to account for the new observations.

?
5. What new evidence was discovered that led to the plate tectonic theory? You may need to look back at page 66.
6. Why was the plate tectonic theory accepted when Wegener's theory had been rejected?
7. **a** What did the 'land bridge' theory attempt to explain?
   b Suggest why this is no longer believed.

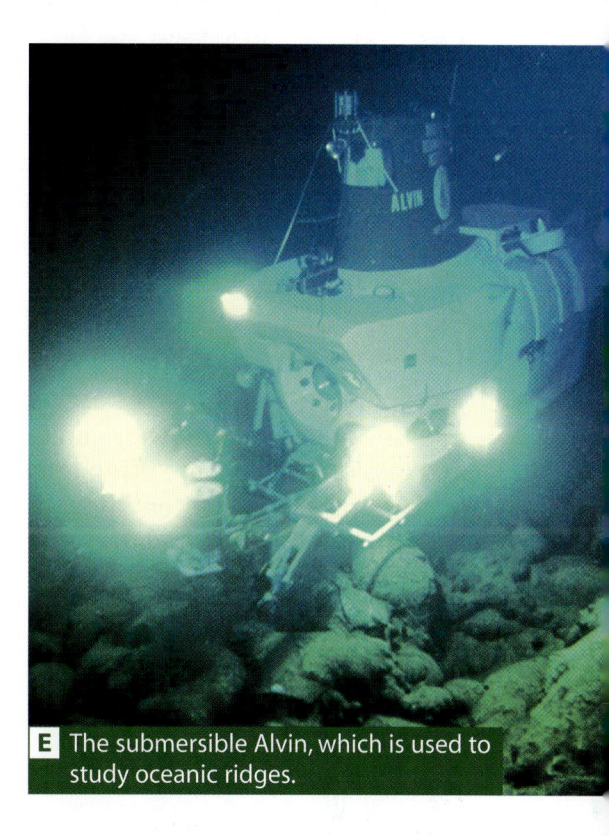

Summary

A theory must fit observed _____. Other scientists must be able to _____ it and make _____ using it. Observations that _____ with the predictions increase _____ in the theory.

agree   confidence   evidence
predictions   test

69

P1.6 Geohazards 1 – Volcanoes

How can we reduce the damage caused by volcanoes?

A Lava from the Eldfell eruption destroyed houses on the island of Heimaey.

Volcanoes and earthquakes are produced by enormous releases of energy, and they can cause massive destruction and loss of life. They are often referred to as **geohazards**. Records of these disasters show that they are most likely to happen along the boundaries of the tectonic plates.

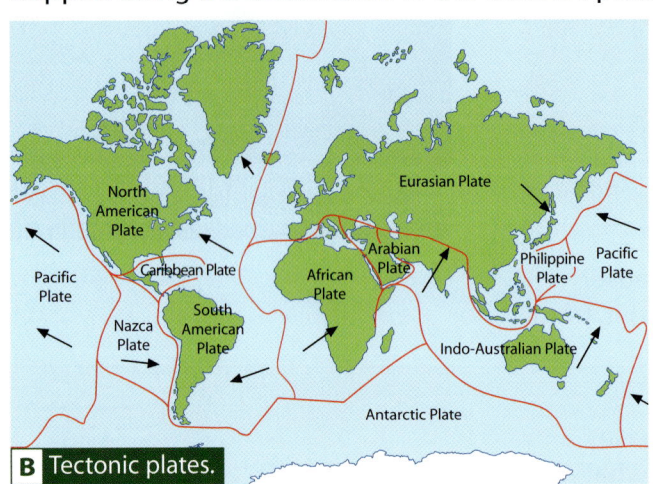

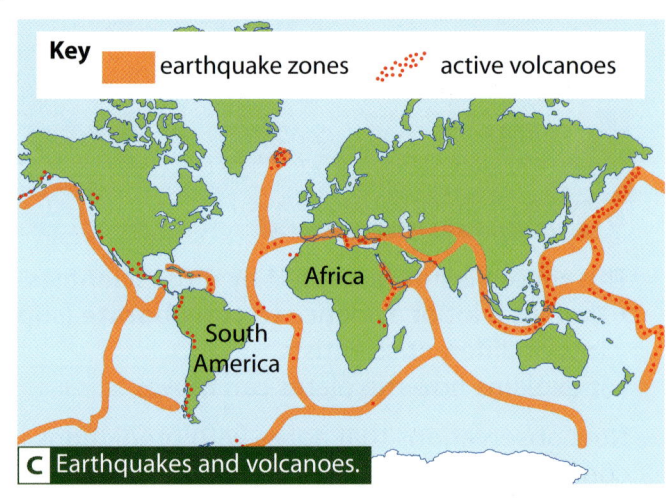

B Tectonic plates.

C Earthquakes and volcanoes.

? 1 What is a geohazard?

2 Look at maps B and C. What do you notice about the locations of earthquake zones and volcanoes?

In a volcanic eruption, magma builds up in a chamber beneath the volcano. The pressure builds up until magma is forced out through cracks or **vents** in the volcano. The molten rock is called **lava** when it is on the surface. The hot lava burns anything in its path.

? 3 What is the difference between magma and lava?

It is not just lava that can kill people. A **pyroclastic flow** is made up of a cloud of hot gases, ash, dust and rock that flows down the side of an erupting volcano very rapidly.

An eruption often covers the surrounding land with thick layers of ash. If there is also heavy rainfall, or if a lake or river bursts its banks, the water and ash can form a fast-moving mudflow. This can kill people and destroy farmland and property.

E A mudflow in Japan.

D Pyroclastic flows can move faster than cars and lorries!

4 Describe three different ways in which a volcanic eruption can damage property.

Scientists cannot stop volcanoes from erupting. However, they can help to reduce the damage by trying to predict when a volcano will erupt. **Public authorities** in areas near active volcanoes have plans to evacuate people when an eruption is predicted. Some buildings can also be protected against falls of ash.

On 15th June 1991, Mount Pinatubo in the Philippines erupted violently after lying **dormant** (not erupting) for over 500 years. Scientists had been monitoring the volcano carefully, and over 55 000 people were evacuated. The eruption killed around 400 people and left 400 000 people homeless. Damage continued after the eruption due to mudflows caused by heavy rainfall.

5 a What can scientists do to try to reduce the damage caused by volcanoes?
  b What can public authorities do?

6 Why are volcanoes likely to occur at plate boundaries? You might need to look back at page 66.

7 Which is the odd one out from this list: lava, magma, pyroclastic flow, mudflow? Explain your answers.

Summary

Earthquakes and _____ are geohazards, and they are most likely to happen at the _____ between _____ plates. Lava, pyroclastic flows and _____ from a volcano can kill people and damage _____. Scientists can try to _____ eruptions, and public authorities can _____ people from danger areas.

boundaries   evacuate   mudflows   predict   property   tectonic   volcanoes

P1.7 Geohazards 2 – Earthquakes
How can we limit the damage from earthquakes?

A Earthquake damage, San Francisco, 1989.

People who live in San Francisco know that earthquakes are inevitable (bound to happen). This is because the city is built on the boundary between two tectonic plates that are trying to slide past each other. The San Andreas Fault zone is along this plate boundary.

Friction between the massive blocks of rock stops them moving smoothly, so the plates move from time to time in rapid jerks. This sudden movement causes **earthquake waves** to spread out from the initial movement.

?
1. Name the fault zone that San Francisco is built on.
2. What is happening at the plate boundary along this fault?

B The San Andreas Fault zone.

What can we do to protect people from earthquakes?

Throughout history major earthquakes have killed many thousands of people and destroyed towns and cities. Earthquakes are more common in some places than in others.

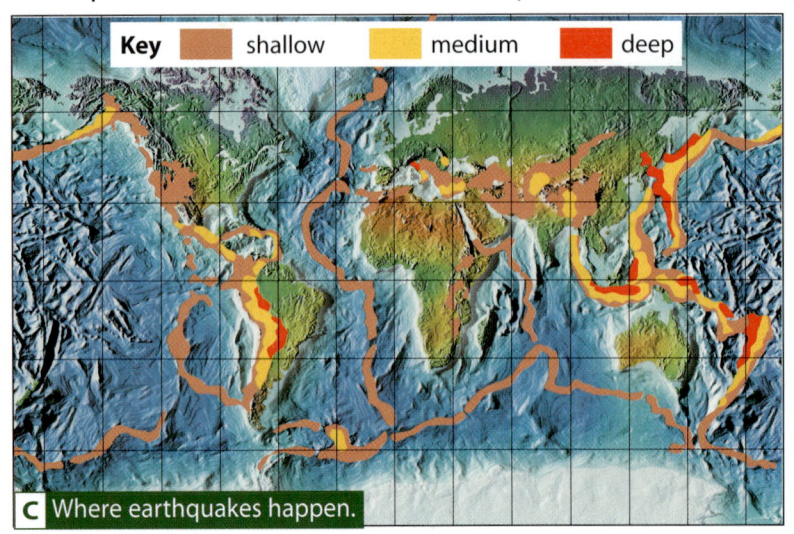

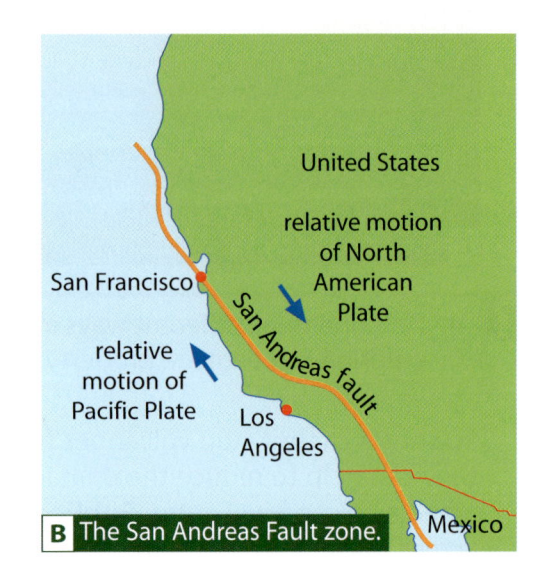

Key: shallow   medium   deep

C Where earthquakes happen.

?
3. Look at map C, and compare it with map C on page 70.
   a. What do you notice about the places where most earthquakes have happened?
   b. No major earthquakes have occurred in Central Africa or Australia. Suggest a reason for this.

Scientific knowledge can help us to reduce the number of people killed in earthquakes. One obvious precaution is not to live near plate boundaries, but this is not always possible. Some big cities grew before people were aware of the risk.

Careful design of buildings can help them to withstand earthquakes without collapsing. New buildings can be built so that they can move to absorb the energy of an earthquake. Some buildings have flexible foundations, so the building does not move as much as the ground does. They are also designed not to collapse.

D The Imperial Hotel, Tokyo, designed by architect Frank Lloyd Wright, successfully withstood the 1923 earthquake.

Predicting earthquakes can be more difficult than predicting volcanic eruptions. Scientists know *where* earthquakes are likely to happen. They can try to predict when the next earthquake will happen based on what has happened in the past, and on measurements of forces and small movements in the ground. However, there is often no warning.

4 Why shouldn't new towns be built near plate boundaries?

5 How can buildings in earthquake zones be made safer?

6 How can scientists try to predict earthquakes?

7 Look at the part of map C that shows South America. Some earthquakes start deeper within the Earth than others. Suggest a reason why the deep earthquakes are further from the coast than the shallow ones. (*Hint:* you may also need to look at diagram D on page 67).

Summary

Earthquakes are most likely to happen at the _____ between the _____ plates as they slowly move. Scientists can _____ where earthquakes are more likely to happen but cannot say exactly _____ they will occur. The _____ of buildings can help to protect people from earthquakes.

boundaries   design   predict
tectonic   when

73

P1.8 The Solar System

What is in the Solar System?

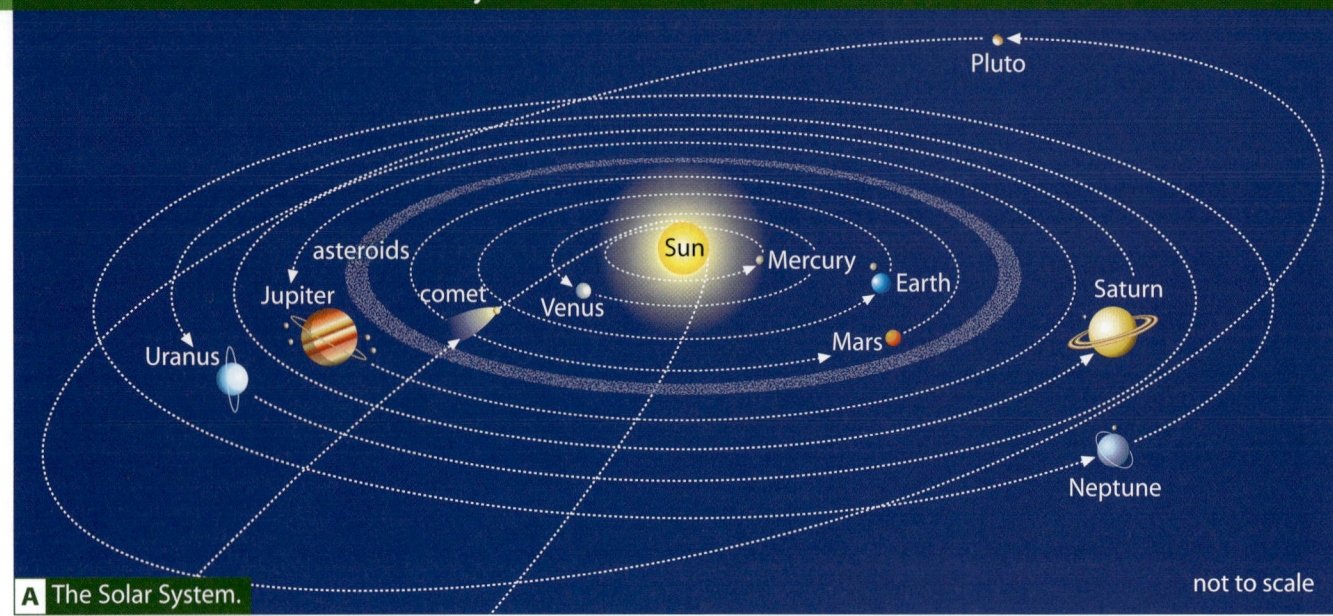

A The Solar System.

not to scale

Diagram A shows the Solar System. The Solar System consists of:
- a star (the Sun) which makes its own light and heat
- nine planets orbiting the Sun
- **moons** (natural **satellites**) orbiting some of the planets
- **asteroids**
- **comets**.

The Earth is the planet we live on. It takes one year (365 days) to orbit the Sun.

> 1 Name three different kinds of body that orbit the Sun.
> 2 Which are the nearest planets to the Earth?
> 3 Which planet is:
>   a nearest to the Sun
>   b furthest away from the Sun?

Asteroids are pieces of rock that orbit the Sun, but are too small to be planets. The smallest ones are only the size of a pebble, but the biggest (Ceres) is nearly one third of the diameter of our Moon.

> 4 Where are the orbits of most of the asteroids?

B Halley's Comet.

Comets are largely made up of ice, frozen gases and a small amount of rock. They usually have very long, elliptical orbits. When they get close to the Sun, some of the water and gases evaporate and form the 'tail'.

> 5 What is the difference between:
>   a an asteroid and a moon
>   b an asteroid and a comet?

Asteroids, shooting stars and meteorites

Some asteroids move in irregular orbits that cross the orbit of the Earth. Asteroids the size of pebbles and small rocks frequently enter the Earth's atmosphere. Friction with the air heats them to very high temperatures, and most of them burn up. The asteroids that burn up in our atmosphere are called **meteors** or 'shooting stars'. Some of the larger ones actually reach the ground; these are called **meteorites**.

Once in a while the Earth is hit by a bigger piece of rock. These **impacts** from large, fast-moving objects leave **craters** when they hit the Earth. The bigger they are and the faster they move, the more energy they have and the more damage they cause.

C A small meteorite, about the size of a bowling ball, hit a car in the USA in 1992.

D This crater in Arizona, USA, was formed by a meteorite about 50 metres across and travelling at about 60 000 km/hour.

E The Moon has no atmosphere to protect it from meteorite impacts.

A How can you investigate the factors that affect the size of a crater?

?
6 What two factors decide how much damage a meteorite hitting the Earth could do?

7 Which is the odd one out from this list: comet, asteroid, moon? Explain your answers.

8 There are many more craters visible on the Moon than on the Earth. Suggest as many reasons for this as you can.

Summary

The _____ takes one year to orbit the Sun. The Sun is also _____ by planets, asteroids and _____. Meteors are fragments of _____ which enter the Earth's atmosphere and _____ up. If they hit the ground they are called _____. The danger from a meteorite increases with its _____ and _____.

burn	comets	Earth	meteorites
orbited	rock	size	speed

P1.9 Asteroid impact!

Could life be destroyed by an asteroid?

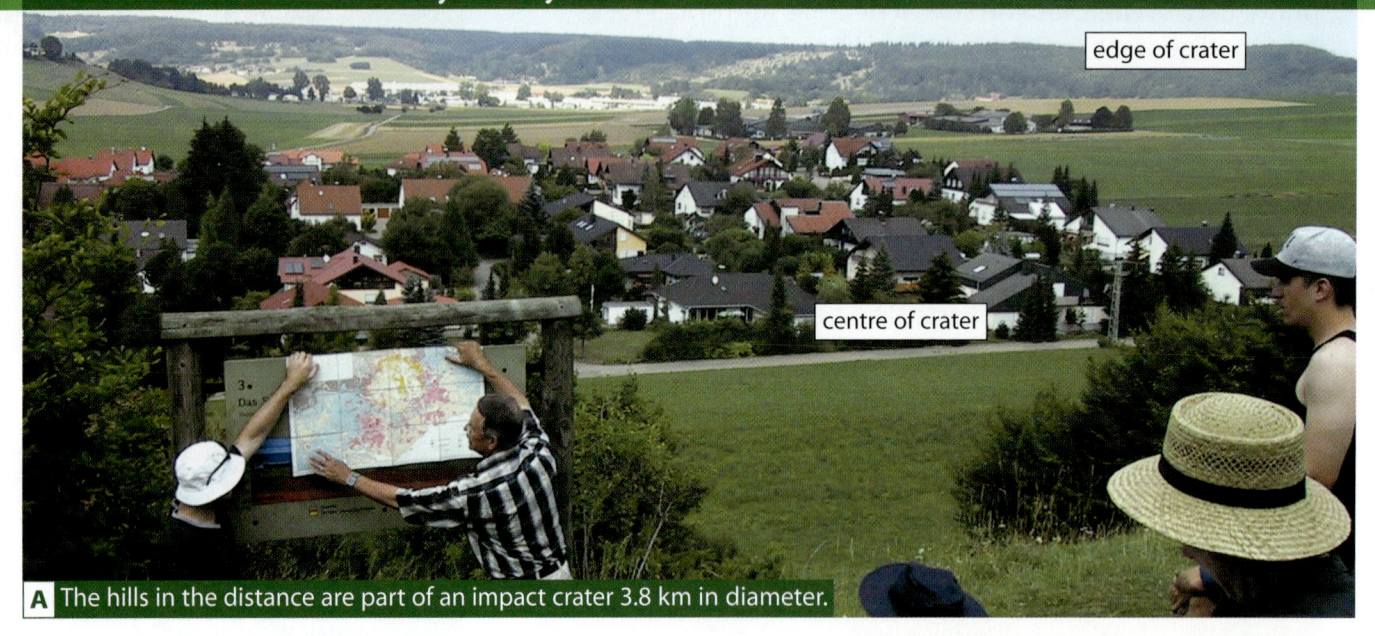

A The hills in the distance are part of an impact crater 3.8 km in diameter.

The Earth's atmosphere protects us from meteors smaller than about 50 m across, but large pieces of rock could reach the surface of the Earth before they burn up. The impact of an asteroid 2 km across could throw enough dust into the atmosphere to cool the Earth for a few years and cause great food shortages.

Scientists are trying to observe as many asteroids as they can to work out their orbits. If we have enough warning that an asteroid could hit the Earth we may be able to destroy it or change its course.

An asteroid big enough to cause a global disaster hits the Earth on average once or twice in every million years. This means you have a 1 in 20 000 chance of being killed by an asteroid impact. However this is not a very helpful statistic, because it doesn't tell you when the next big impact will happen.

?
1. What protects the Earth from most meteors?
2. **a** Why is it important to find all the asteroids in the Solar System?
   b Why is it most important to find the ones that are bigger than 50 m across?

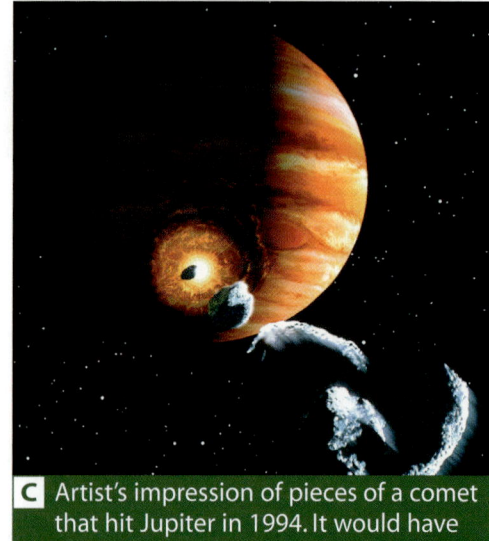

B An artist's impression of a large meteor strike.

C Artist's impression of pieces of a comet that hit Jupiter in 1994. It would have caused a major disaster if it had hit the Earth.

The extinction of the dinosaurs

There is evidence that the Earth has been hit by very large meteorites several times in its history. Scientists have found evidence of an impact about 65 million years ago. The dinosaurs and many other species became **extinct** at about the same time. Some scientists have a theory that the impact caused climate changes that killed off the dinosaurs.

Most scientists accept that there was a large impact about 65 million years ago. However, there is evidence that some species of dinosaur had died out at least 20 million years before the impact. There are also many other theories about the cause of the extinctions.

D An artist's impression of the crater formed by the impact that may have killed the dinosaurs. The actual crater is now beneath the sea and the jungle in Central America.

E Volcanic activity may have caused climate changes that killed off the dinosaurs.

3 a How could a meteorite impact have killed off the dinosaurs?
 b Why do many scientists not agree with this idea?
 c Give one other possible cause of the extinction of the dinosaurs.

4 Only about 150 meteorite impact sites have been discovered on the Earth. Why are some of them difficult to locate?

5 What problems do you think scientists will have to overcome if they need to destroy or deflect an asteroid?

Summary

Asteroids sometimes _____ the Earth. Rocks smaller than about _____ usually burn up in the _____, but larger ones could hit the ground. The _____ of a 1 km _____ could change the _____ and cause food shortages. If we can _____ an asteroid before it hits the Earth we may be able to _____ it or _____ its course.

50 m   asteroid   atmosphere   change   climate   destroy   detect   hit   impact

77

P1.10 Studying the stars

How do we find out about the stars?

A These telescopes detect radio waves produced by stars.

Geologists can study the rocks that the Earth is made from by digging up samples and testing them, but astronomers can only study the stars by detecting the radiation they produce.

> **1** Write down two different kinds of radiation produced by stars.

Large telescopes on the Earth are usually built on high mountains so they are above most of the clouds and dust in the atmosphere. They need to be away from towns and cities, because **light pollution** interferes with observations.

The stars are a long way from the Earth. Because the distances are so big, astronomers use a unit called a **light year**, which is the distance that light travels in one year. Light travels at 300 000 km/s, so a light year is about 9 500 000 000 000 km!

Proxima Centauri is 4.3 light years away, and is the nearest star to our Solar System. This means that we are seeing light that left the star 4.3 years ago. For a star 5000 light years away, we are seeing it as it was 5000 years ago.

B The Sun is the nearest star to the Earth. We can see the light radiation it gives out.

> **2 a** What is light pollution?
> **b** Why is this a problem for astronomers?
>
> **3 a** What is a light year?
> **b** Why do astronomers use light years?
>
> **4** Why can we only see Proxima Centauri as it was over 4 years ago?

Some stars seem to change position very slightly at different times of the year. This is called **parallax**, and happens because stars are at different distances from us. Astronomers can work out the distances to nearby stars by carefully measuring the angle of the star at different times of year compared with the background of more distant stars. The change in the angles is very small, so measurements have to be very accurate. This way of measuring distances only works for nearby stars.

The brightness of a star depends on how bright it really is, and on how far away it is. Astronomers know how bright some kinds of star really are, so if they make careful measurements of how bright they are when seen from Earth, they can work out how far away they are. This is how the distances to far off stars are estimated. These measurements have to be very accurate, because a small mistake could make a big difference in the distance calculated.

?
5 Describe two ways of measuring the distances to nearby stars.

6 What are the advantages and disadvantages of having a telescope in orbit around the Earth?

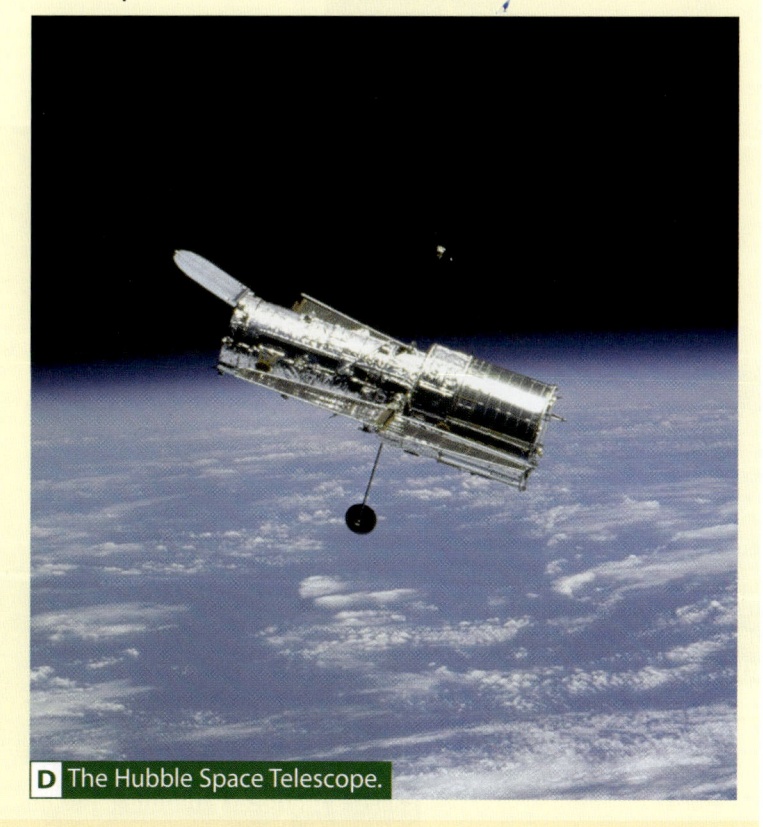

D The Hubble Space Telescope.

7 Why is the parallax method less accurate for more distant stars?

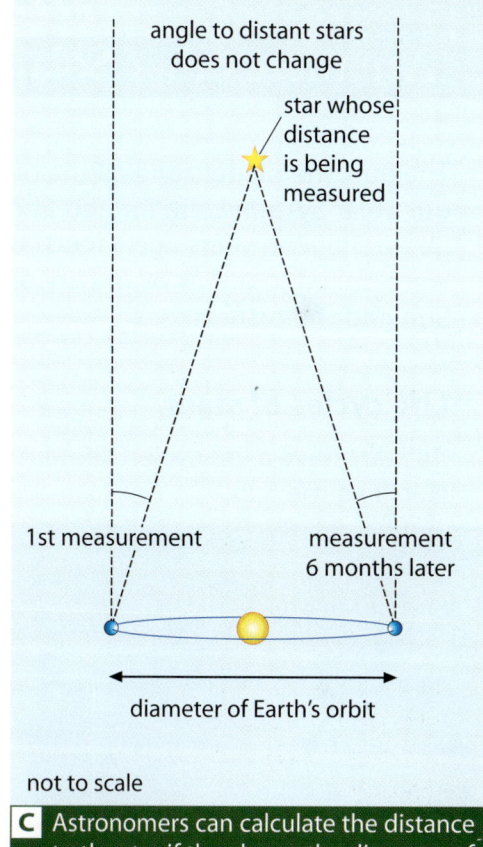

C Astronomers can calculate the distance to the star if they know the diameter of the Earth's orbit and the two angles.

Summary

Light travels at _____ km/s. Distances in space are measured in _____ years. Other stars are so far away that we see light that left them many _____ ago. The distance to stars can be calculated by measuring _____ or the relative _____.

| 300 000 | brightness | light |
| parallax | years | |

79

P1.11 The Sun and other stars

Are there other Solar Systems in the Universe?

The Sun, the planets and all the other objects that make up our Solar System were formed at roughly the same time, about 5 billion years ago. Clouds of dust and gas in space were pulled together by gravity, and eventually formed the Sun and the planets.

Life cycles of stars

All stars have a life cycle. Diagram B shows the life cycle of stars like the Sun.

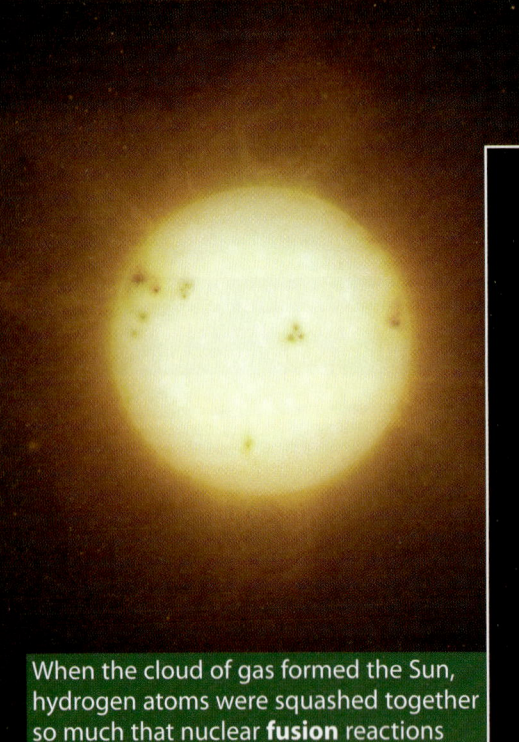

A How the Solar System might have looked when it was forming.

When the cloud of gas formed the Sun, hydrogen atoms were squashed together so much that nuclear **fusion** reactions started. The reactions produce heat.

B

Eventually the Sun will have used up all the hydrogen fuel in its centre. The inside of the Sun will collapse, and the outer layers will cool and expand to form a **red giant** about 100 times its present diameter which will destroy the Earth.

After about 1000 million years the red giant will throw off a shell of gas and dust called a **planetary nebula** (although it has nothing to do with planets!). The rest of the star will shrink to form a small, hot **white dwarf** star.

?
1. How did the Solar System form?
2. What provides the energy for the Sun?
3. What will happen to the Sun when it has used up all its hydrogen?

Stars bigger than the Sun may explode at the end of their life cycle. When this happens, nuclear reactions in the exploding star form new elements. All of the elements in the Solar System except hydrogen and helium were made in stars that existed before the Solar System was formed.

Evidence for life?

As far as we know, Earth is the only planet in the Solar System with life on it. Spacecraft have looked for signs of life on other planets, but so far there is no evidence of life now, or life that existed in the past.

C Europa is one of Jupiter's moons. Scientists think there may be liquid water below its icy surface, and it is possible that there may be life there.

Astronomers have detected planets orbiting around other stars. Even if only a small proportion of stars have planets, there are so many stars in the Universe that scientists think that it is likely that life exists somewhere besides Earth.

5 a Which is the only planet with life?
b Why do scientists think there may be life on Europa?
c Why do scientists think it is likely that life exists elsewhere in the Universe?

6 Some scientists think there may have been liquid water on Mars once. Find out what evidence there is for this.

4 Our bodies contain a lot of carbon and oxygen. Where did these elements come from?

Summary

The _____ System was formed from a cloud of _____ and gas. Nuclear _____ reactions inside the Sun provide energy. Some stars _____ at the end of their life cycle, and create new _____. Astronomers have detected _____ around other stars, and think there may be _____ somewhere else in the Universe.

| dust | elements | explode | fusion |
| life | planets | Solar | |

P1.12 The Milky Way and beyond

What is beyond the Solar System?

A This is the Eagle Nebula, one of the places where new stars are forming in our galaxy.

B The Andromeda galaxy is the nearest large galaxy to the Milky Way. It is about 100 000 light years across, and 2–3 million light years away.

Our Sun is one star of more than 200 billion stars that make up the Milky Way – our galaxy. The Milky Way is just one of billions of galaxies in the Universe. Astronomers have discovered many galaxies beyond our own using powerful telescopes. They are not all the same size or shape.

We cannot see what shape the Milky Way is, because we are inside it. However, astronomers have made careful measurements and observations of the stars in our galaxy, and think that it is a spiral galaxy, similar to the ones shown in photo C.

?
1. a What is a galaxy?
   b What is the name of the galaxy that our Sun is a part of?
2. a What shape is the Milky Way?
   b How do astronomers know this?
3. Write these things in order of size, starting with the smallest: Sun, Earth, Universe, Milky Way.

C Galaxies like the Milky Way.

The expanding Universe

In 1929 an American astronomer called Edwin Hubble made a very important discovery about our Universe. His observations of distant galaxies showed that they are moving away from us.

If the Universe is expanding now, then in the past it must have been smaller. Most scientists think that the Universe began in a '**Big Bang**' about 14 000 million years ago and has been expanding ever since.

The Universe may continue to expand in the future, or it may stop expanding and start to get smaller again. The fate of the Universe depends on how much mass there is in the galaxies, because the more mass there is, the more likely it is that gravity will stop the expansion. However, it is very difficult to find out how much there is.

D On a very clear night you may see a band of stars stretching across the sky. These stars are part of the Milky Way.

?
4 a Write these things in order of their age, starting with the oldest: galaxies, the Earth, the Universe, the Sun.
    b Explain your answer to part **a**.
5 a What did Hubble discover about other galaxies in the Universe?
    b How do scientists explain this?
6 Which is the odd one out: galaxy, nebula, star? Explain your answers.
7 Suggest why it is difficult to work out how much mass there is in the Universe.

Summary

The Solar System is part of a _____ called the _____. The Universe started in the _____ about _____ years ago, and is expanding.

14 000 million   Big Bang   galaxy
Milky Way

83

P1.13 Planet for sale!
What do you know about the Earth?

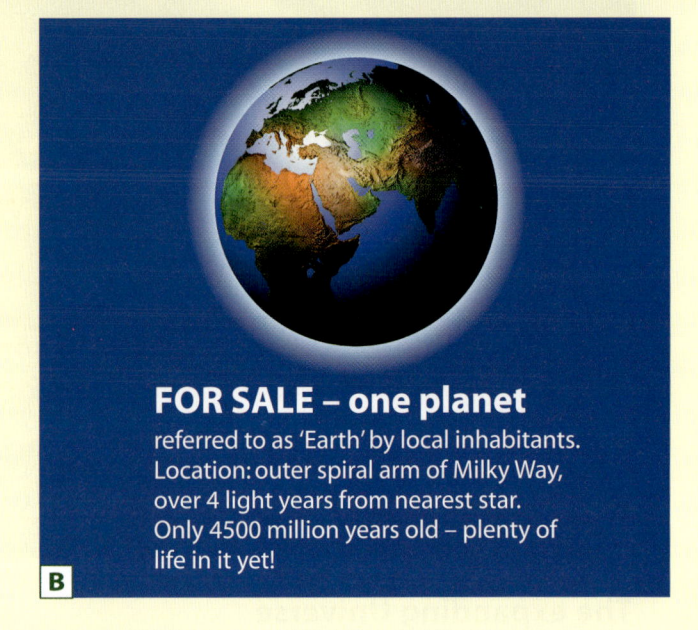

A

B

FOR SALE – one planet
referred to as 'Earth' by local inhabitants. Location: outer spiral arm of Milky Way, over 4 light years from nearest star. Only 4500 million years old – plenty of life in it yet!

Attractive scenery –
mountain ranges, oceans, rivers and plains

C

1. Explain the meanings of the following words:
   a planet
   b star
   c galaxy
   d Universe
   e Big Bang

2. a How did the Solar System form?
   b What will happen to the Sun in the future?
   c How do scientists know what will happen to the Sun?
   d Where did most of the elements that make up the Earth come from?

3. a What is a light year?
   b How can astronomers measure the distances to stars?
   c Why can't we see any stars as they are now?

4. Alfred Wegener suggested the theory of continental drift.
   a What was Wegener's theory?
   b What evidence did Wegener have for his theory?
   c What did other scientists think about Wegener's theory?

D

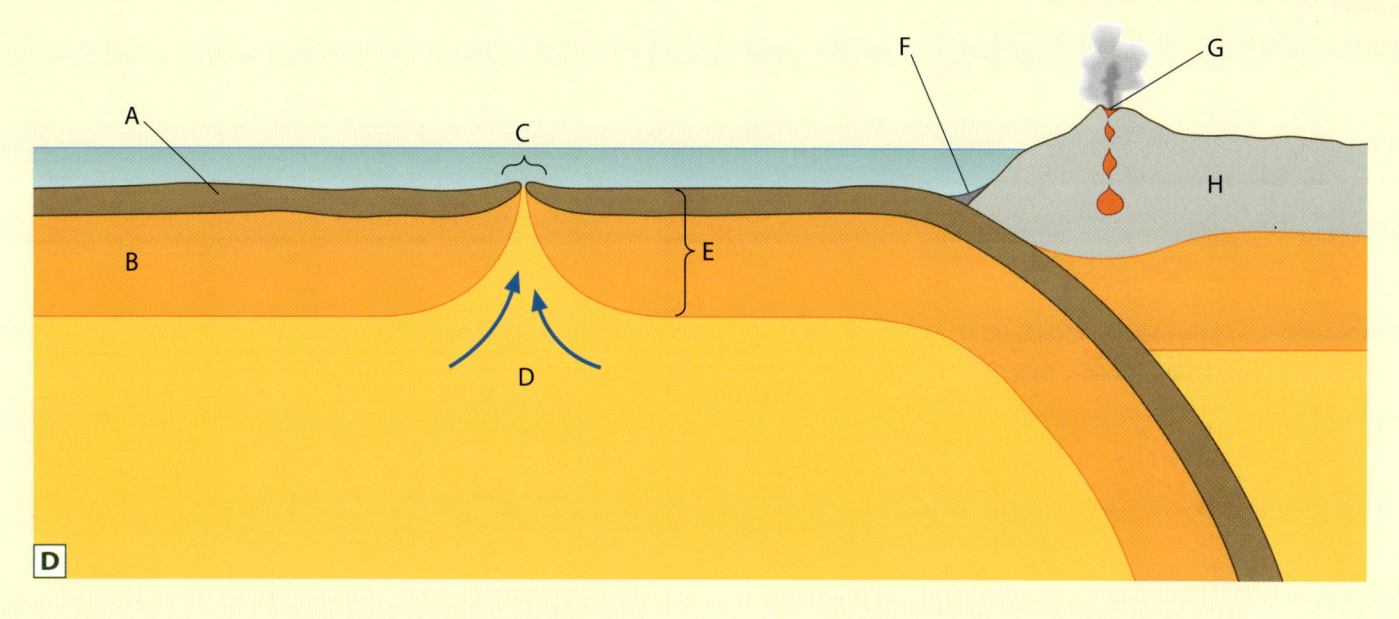

5 Name the parts labelled A to H in diagram D.

6 How does the theory of plate tectonics explain:
   a the formation of mountains
   b seafloor spreading?

7 a Where do most earthquakes occur?
   b What can public authorities do to protect people against earthquakes?

8 a Why do most volcanoes occur near the edges of the tectonic plates?
   b Describe three different dangers from volcanoes.

9 The Solar System includes asteroids and comets as well as planets and their moons.
   a What happens to very small pieces of rock if they enter the Earth's atmosphere?
   b What could happen if a large asteroid entered the Earth's atmosphere?
   c How can we try to prevent this happening? Explain in as much detail as you can.

10 Most scientists agree that a large asteroid hit the Earth about 65 million years ago, at about the same time as the dinosaurs became extinct.
   a How could the asteroid have killed off the dinosaurs?
   b Why do many scientists disagree with this idea?

Some minor geohazards, but nothing to worry about!

E

B2.1 Keeping healthy

How can we prevent diseases?

Health matters, 2 May 2015

Instead of an injection have a banana!!

Scientists have developed the world's first edible **vaccine** against a virus that causes severe diarrhoea.

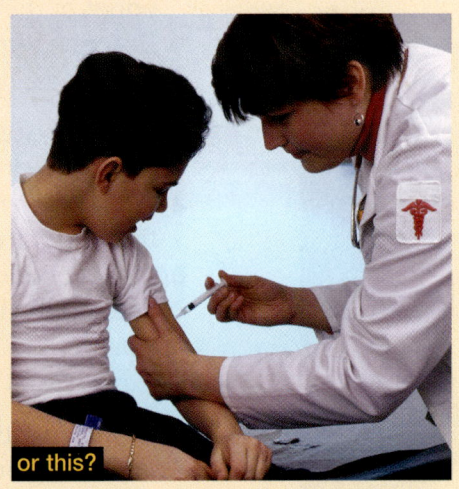

Would you prefer this ...   or this?

The vaccine has taken many years to develop and has cost a lot of money. Scientists added genes from the Norwalk virus to banana plants. The bananas were fed to laboratory mice, to find out if the vaccine protected them against the virus, and to see if there were any side-effects. The vaccine was then tested on human volunteers in clinical trials in Mexico.

The World Health Organisation says that the new vaccine will help to reduce the number of deaths of young children in the developing world. Only 80% of the world's children are vaccinated against serious diseases because it is expensive to transport and store the vaccines, and trained medical staff are needed to give the injections. Fruit containing edible vaccines could be grown locally and, without needles, the risk of infection would also be removed.

A health worker transporting vaccines.

A vaccine is a medicine containing weakened microorganisms. It is often injected into your body so that you make antibodies that kill the microorganisms. If this kind of microorganism enters your body again you will not get the disease it causes.

Children are given vaccines to protect them against many different diseases. However, not everyone agrees that children should be vaccinated. They believe that vaccines can cause harmful side-effects, and they don't want to risk their children's health. On the other hand, scientists are excited about the possibilities of developing new vaccines against the virus that causes AIDS and 'superbugs' which are difficult to control with other drugs.

Scientists are discovering more about how diseases affect our bodies. As new evidence is reported, the message on how to stay healthy can change. The way of vaccinating against diseases described in the report *could* happen in the future.

A This dangerous bacterium is a 'superbug' (magnification x25 000). Most antibiotics cannot kill it.

1 Explain how vaccines work.
2 Vaccines can be developed in different ways. Describe the stages in the development of the new vaccine mentioned in the health report.
3 What are the advantages of the edible vaccine described in the report?

However, just because we *can* vaccinate people against diseases, doesn't mean that it *should* be done. Should we encourage people to have vaccines or let them make their own decisions? To do this they need to know something about the microorganisms that cause disease, the effects of these microorganisms on their body and how vaccines work. Decisions like these are called **ethical decisions**.

B Parents need to decide whether or not to have their children vaccinated.

4 Write down some arguments against using vaccines.
5 Do you think that all children should be vaccinated against diseases?
6 What do you need to find out so that you can answer question **5** better?
7 Describe some other ways of protecting ourselves from disease.
8 Note down any words on these pages that you don't understand and try to find out their meanings.

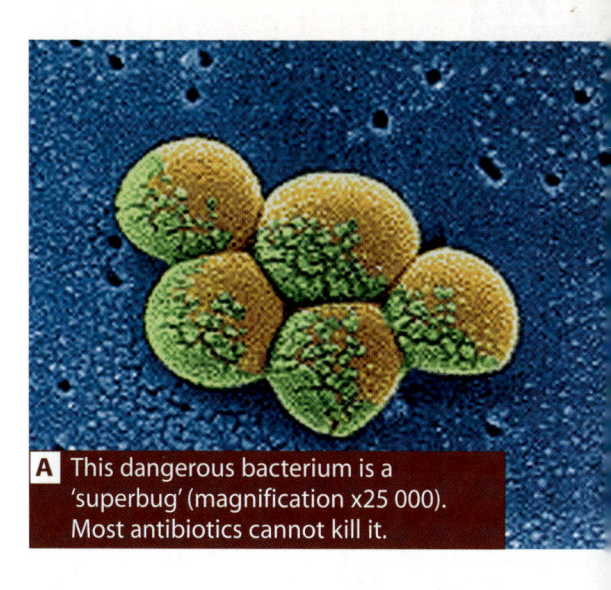

B2.2 Microorganisms and disease
What causes diseases?

A **microorganism**, or microbe for short, is any organism that you can only see clearly with a microscope. The air around you is full of microorganisms and your body is covered in them. Most microorganisms are harmless and do not affect you, but some can cause **infectious diseases**. If these harmful microorganisms get inside your body they quickly grow in number and make you feel ill. Some microorganisms can produce a 1000 million million million offspring, in just one day!

There are three main types of microorganisms.

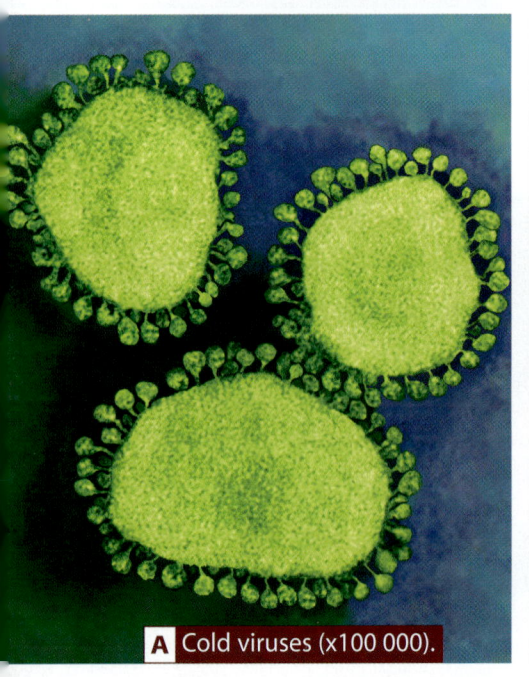

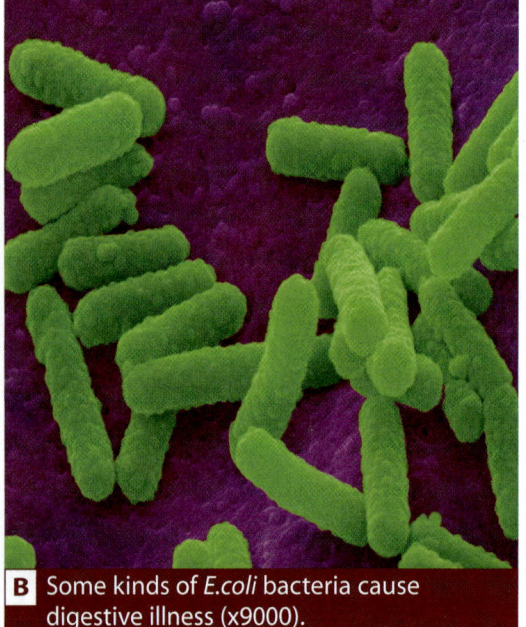

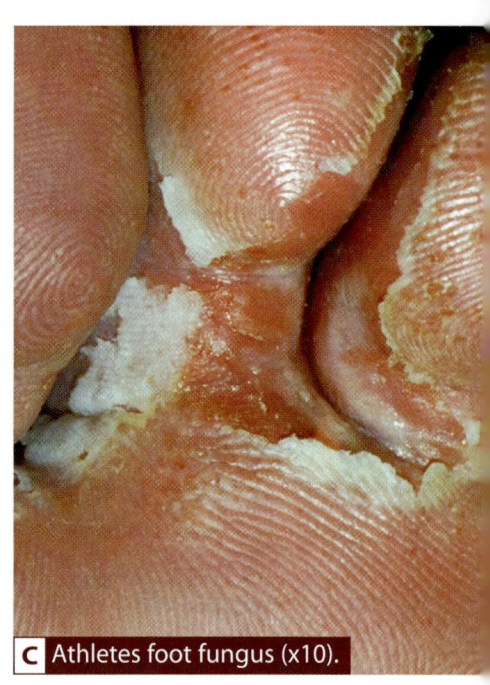

A Cold viruses (x100 000).

B Some kinds of *E.coli* bacteria cause digestive illness (x9000).

C Athletes foot fungus (x10).

Viruses can only be seen with very powerful microscopes. They cannot reproduce on their own. Viruses take over living cells and force them to make more viruses.

Bacteria are bigger than viruses. You could fit about 1000 of the bacteria in photo B on this full stop.

Fungus cells are between 10 and 100 times bigger than bacterial cells. Some fungi grow on skin and release chemicals that digest skin cells. These chemicals can make your skin red and sore.

Bacteria and fungi can reproduce on their own.

> **?**
> 1 a Write down the three types of microorganisms.
>   b Which is the smallest?
> 2 Describe two differences between a bacterium and a virus.

How do microorganisms affect you?

Harmful microorganisms cause diseases in two ways.
- They can destroy body cells. For example lung cells can be destroyed by tuberculosis bacteria.
- They can release poisonous chemicals called **toxins**. For example clostridium bacteria make a toxin that gives you one kind of food poisoning.

The effects of microorganisms on your body are called **symptoms**.

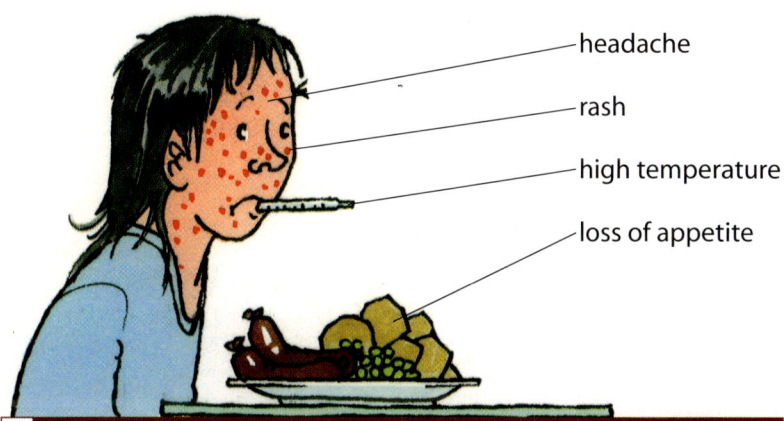

A How can you show there are bacteria on your skin?

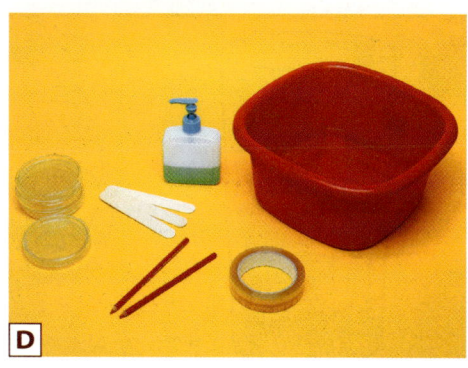

D

- headache
- rash
- high temperature
- loss of appetite

E Symptoms are caused by your body trying to fight the microorganisms causing the disease.

Disease	Microorganism causing the disease	Symptoms	How long it lasts
diphtheria	bacterium	severe fever; can also damage the heart	a few weeks, but damage to the heart can last for the rest of your life
ringworm	fungus	itchy skin rashes	a few weeks
rubella (German measles)	virus	red rash, swollen glands	2 weeks; can be fatal in babies and can harm unborn babies if the mother catches it

F Some human diseases and their symptoms.

?

3 Describe two ways that harmful microorganisms can cause disease.

4 What does the word symptom mean?

5 What are the symptoms of **a** measles and **b** mumps?

6 Which is the odd one out: bacterium, virus, fungus? Explain your answers.

7 Ben says that the definition of a microorganism is 'a small organism that causes disease'. Is he right? Explain your answer.

Summary

Microorganisms are organisms that can only be seen clearly with a _____. There are three types of microorganisms: bacteria, _____ and _____. Some microorganisms cause _____ by attacking body cells or releasing _____. The signs of disease are called _____.

diseases fungi microscope
symptoms toxins viruses

89

B2.3 Body defences

How does your body keep harmful microorganisms out?

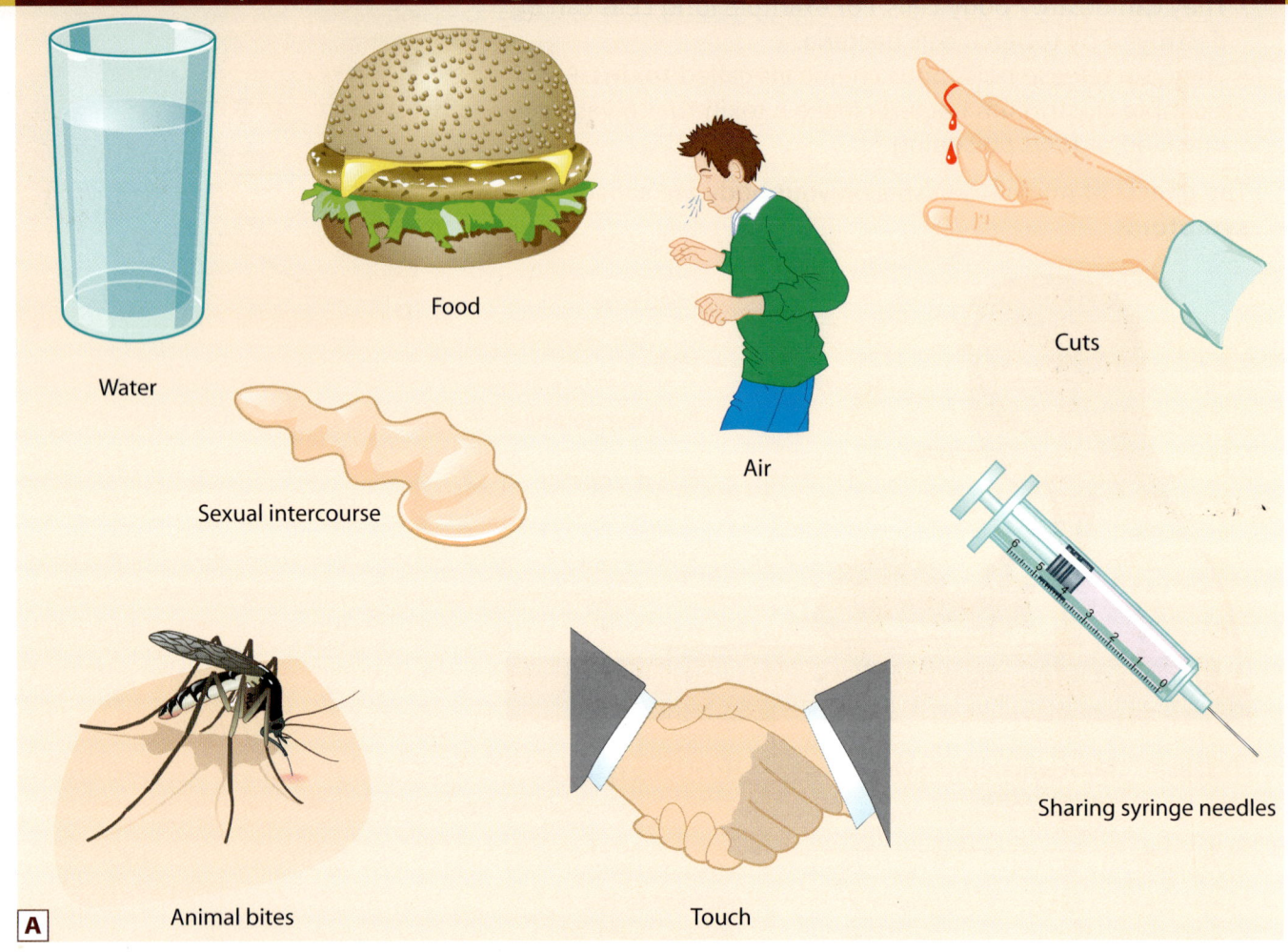

A Picture A shows how microorganisms can get into your body.

Labels: Water, Food, Air, Cuts, Sexual intercourse, Animal bites, Touch, Sharing syringe needles

? 1 Write down five ways that microorganisms can get into your body.

2 Suggest two ways of preventing a disease being spread.

What happens if microorganisms get inside you?

If harmful microorganisms get inside your body they start to reproduce quickly. They damage cells in your body or release poisonous chemicals called toxins. You don't start to feel ill until a lot of cells are damaged or a lot of toxins have built up. This means you don't start to feel ill until there are millions of the harmful microorganisms inside you.

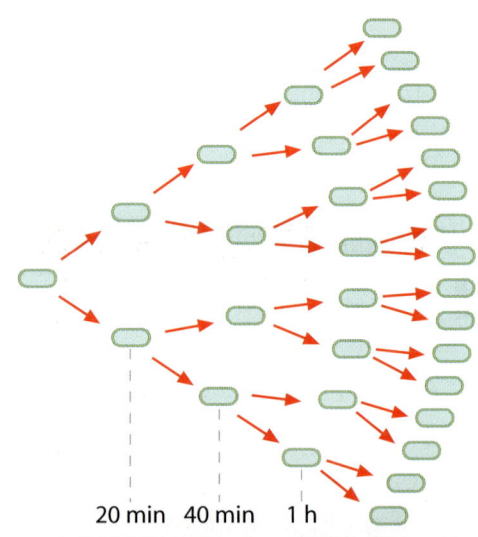

? 3 When microorganisms get inside your body why don't you feel ill straight away?

B A colony of bacteria starts with just one cell. In the right conditions the cell divides to make two cells. Two cells become four, four become eight, and so on.

20 min   40 min   1 h

Keeping microorganisms out

Your body is very good at keeping harmful microorganisms out. Picture C shows the body's defences.

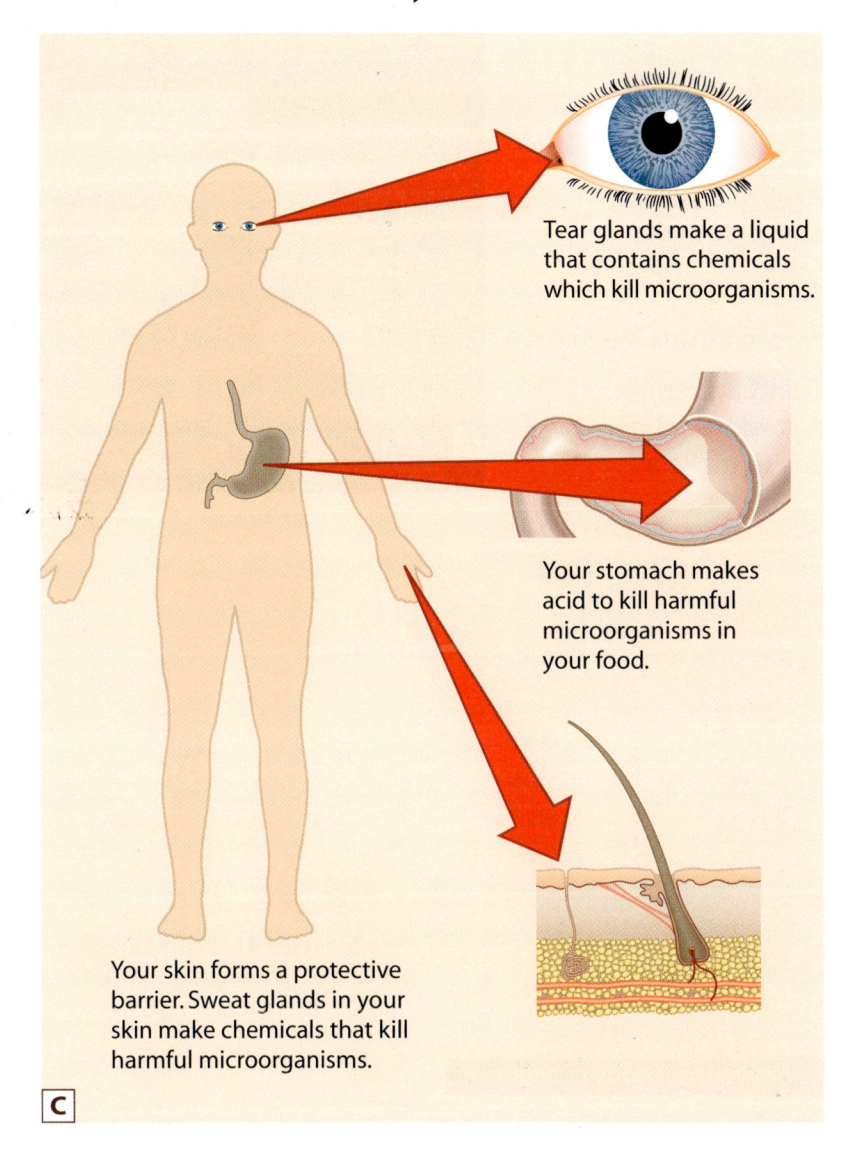

Tear glands make a liquid that contains chemicals which kill microorganisms.

Your stomach makes acid to kill harmful microorganisms in your food.

Your skin forms a protective barrier. Sweat glands in your skin make chemicals that kill harmful microorganisms.

C

? 4 How do each of these body parts protect you against infection?
  a eyes
  b skin
  c stomach

? 5 a Which of the body's defences shown in diagram C use chemicals?
  b Which of the body's defences are physical barriers?

6 Which is the odd one out: food, animal bite, dirty needle? Explain your answers.

7 Survey your class and find out who has had flu, measles, chicken pox, mumps and colds. For each disease find out:
  a how many people have had the disease once
  b how many people have had the disease more than once.

8 What do your answers to question 7 tell you about each disease?

Summary

Diseases can be passed on in many ways, such as _____, _____ or touching another person. The surface of your body is protected by _____. Your eyes are protected by _____ in your tears that kill microorganisms. Acid in your _____ kills microorganisms in food. When microorganisms get inside your body they _____ quickly. They can damage _____ or produce _____ that make you feel ill.

breathing   cells   chemicals   eating
reproduce   skin   toxins   stomach

91

B2.4 Fighting off infection
How does your body kill microorganisms?

Harmful microorganisms inside your body can be killed by white blood cells that are part of your **immune system**. These cells can:
- **engulf** or swallow up microorganisms and digest them
- make **antibodies** that attach to the microorganisms. The antibodies may kill the microorganisms or may make them clump together, which makes it easier for other white blood cells to engulf them
- destroy the toxins that the harmful microorganisms make.

Each kind of antibody can only recognise and fight one type of microorganism. When you are infected by a different microorganism your immune system needs to make a different antibody to attack it.

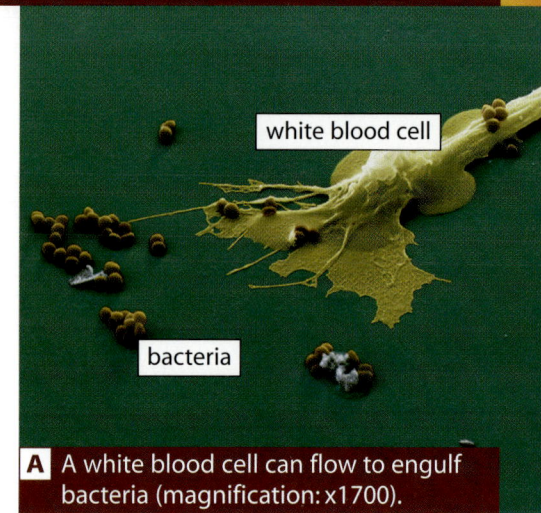

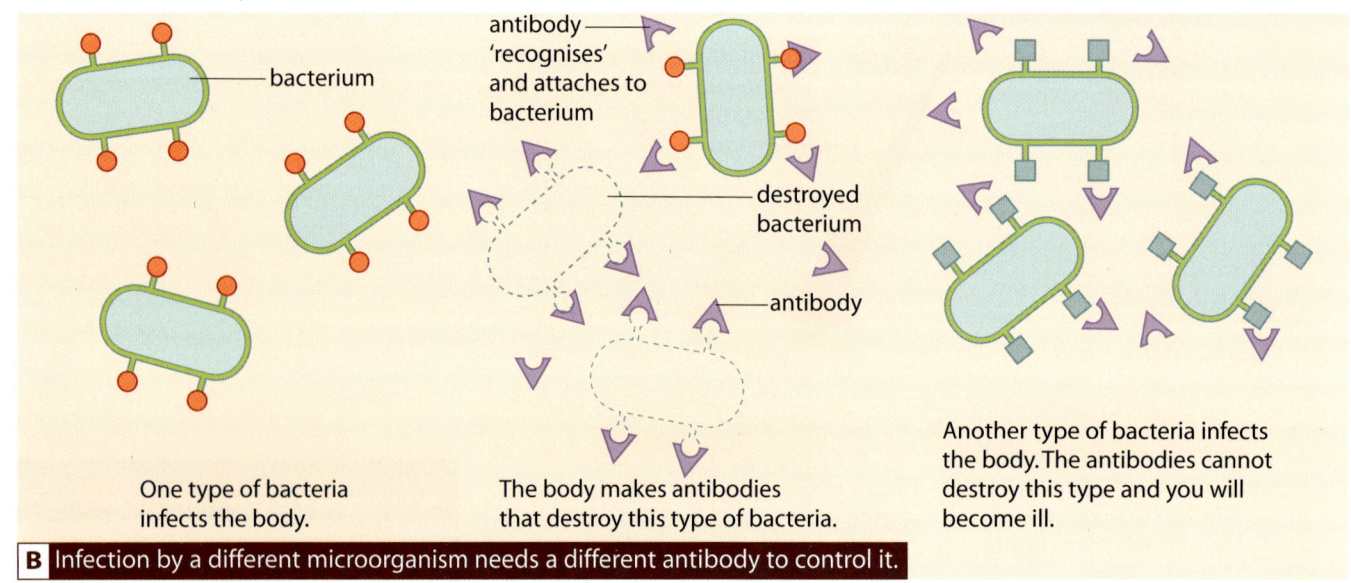

A A white blood cell can flow to engulf bacteria (magnification: ×1700).

B Infection by a different microorganism needs a different antibody to control it.

One type of bacteria infects the body.

The body makes antibodies that destroy this type of bacteria.

Another type of bacteria infects the body. The antibodies cannot destroy this type and you will become ill.

? 1 Which system in your body kills microorganisms?
2 a Describe two ways that white blood cells kill microorganisms.
  b Describe one other way in which they help to protect us.

Becoming immune

As well as making antibodies, the white blood cells also make **memory cells** that stay in your blood for years. If the same kind of microorganism gets into your body again the memory cells recognise it and make antibodies quickly so that your body fights the infection much faster. This means you won't suffer the symptoms again. You are now **immune** to that disease.

Some measles viruses get into your body.

Your white blood cells make antibodies and memory cells for the measles virus.

antibodies

The antibodies attack the measles viruses, and kill them.

If the measles virus gets into your body again your memory cells know what kind of antibody to make straight away.

white blood cell

C Becoming immune.

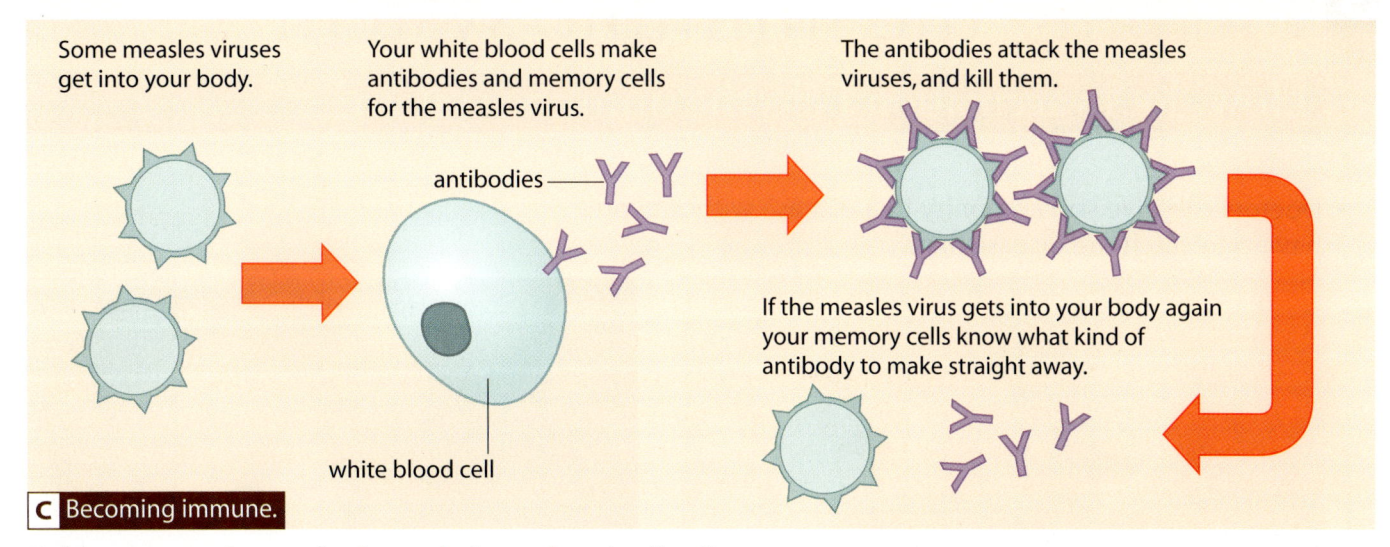

Babies can get immunity from their mother. Antibodies from the mother's blood cross the placenta before the baby is born. Babies can also get antibodies in breast milk. These can protect them from diseases like whooping cough.

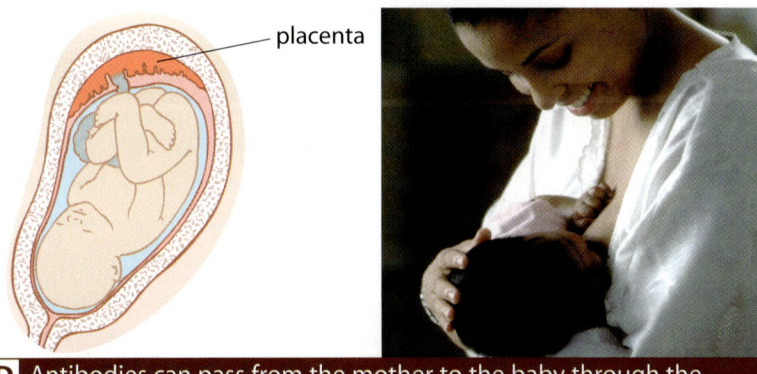

placenta

D Antibodies can pass from the mother to the baby through the placenta and in breast milk.

Antibodies can also be made outside your body, for example in other animals. These antibodies can be injected to protect you against fast-acting microorganisms such as the tetanus bacterium. Your body doesn't make memory cells in this case so you will eventually lose your immunity to that microorganism and will need another injection if you are infected again.

?
3 a What does being immune to measles mean?
   b How can you become immune to measles?
4 A measles antibody will not protect you from chicken pox. Why not?
5 Explain why memory cells are important.

?
6 Give one advantage of being given antibodies in an injection.
7 Why is it important that a young baby gets antibodies from its mother?
8 Describe three ways you can become immune to a disease.
9 The immunity a baby receives from its mother lasts about three months. Explain the benefits and disadvantages of this.

Summary

Your immune _____ attacks microorganisms that enter your body. White _____ cells can _____ microorganisms or produce _____ to them. Antibodies only _____ one type of microorganism. If the same microorganism infects you again you can make _____ very quickly. This makes you _____ to that disease.

antibodies   blood   engulf
immune   recognise   system

93

B2.5 Helping the immune system
How does vaccination help the immune system?

Doctors can give you immunity to a disease without you having to catch the disease first.

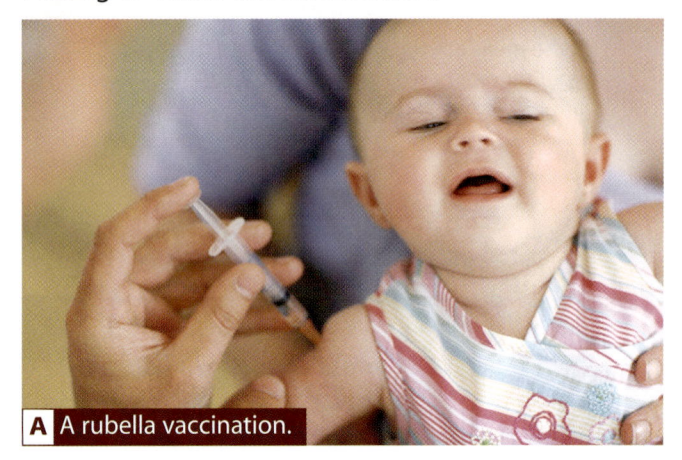

A A rubella vaccination.

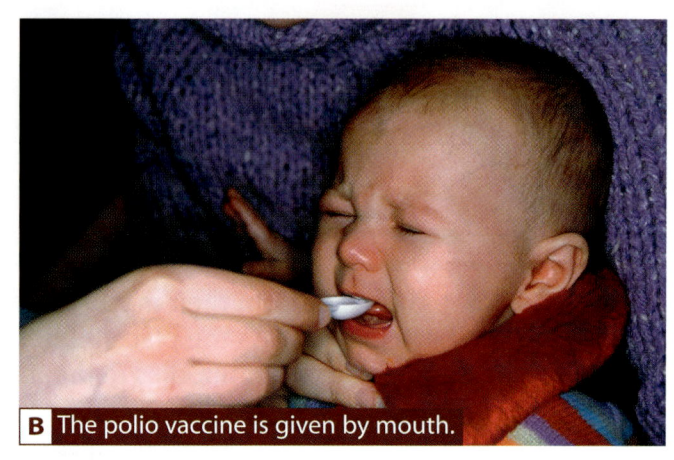

B The polio vaccine is given by mouth.

A vaccine contains a small amount of weak or dead microorganisms. It can be injected into your body or taken by mouth as a **vaccination**. The vaccine usually does not make you ill. Your immune system produces antibodies to attack the microorganisms in the vaccine. It also produces memory cells which stay in your blood. If the same kind of microorganism infects your body again you will be protected. You have been **immunised**. Vaccinations can protect you for many years, although you may need **booster** vaccinations occasionally to keep up the level of memory cells in your blood.

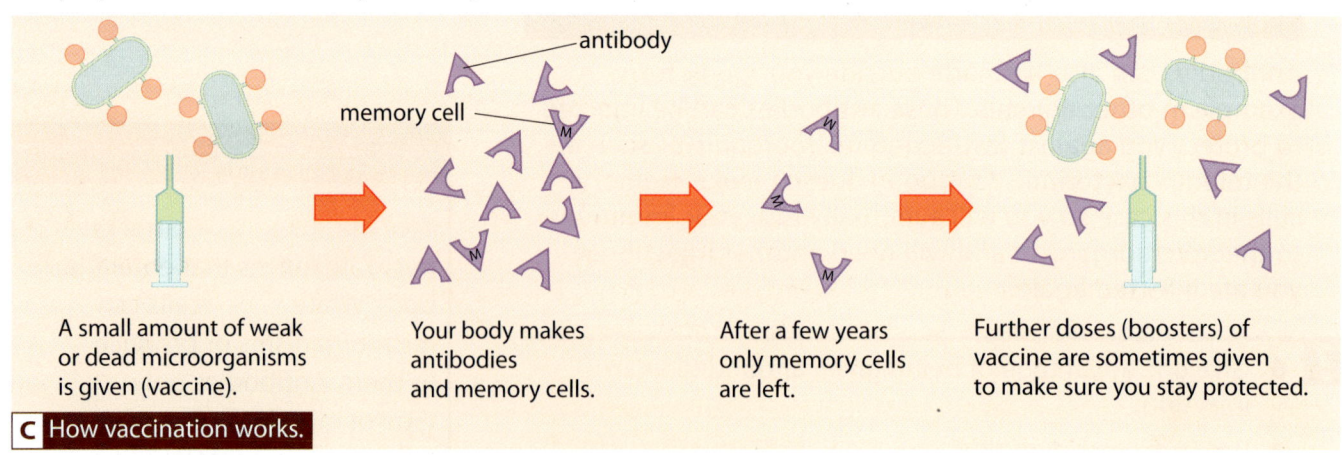

A small amount of weak or dead microorganisms is given (vaccine). → Your body makes antibodies and memory cells. → After a few years only memory cells are left. → Further doses (boosters) of vaccine are sometimes given to make sure you stay protected.

C How vaccination works.

?
1. Describe two ways you can receive a vaccine.
2. How do vaccines immunise you against a disease?
3. Why must vaccines contain weakened or dead microorganisms?
4. Why are boosters necessary?

The problem with flu

Influenza (or flu) is caused by a virus. Each year new forms or **strains** of the flu virus appear. The change in a new strain is often very small, so having influenza one year may leave you with immunity against infection in the next. But every so often a big change in the virus takes place. This causes a major outbreak of the disease because nobody has immunity. Each of these major strains needs its own vaccine, because other vaccines will not help your body to make the right antibodies.

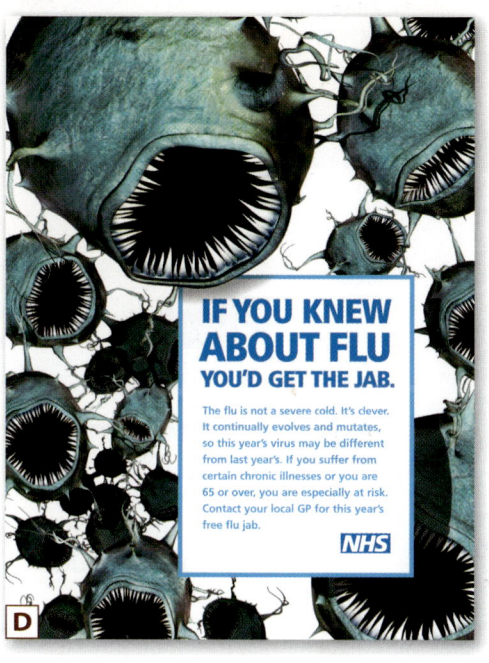

5 Why do new influenza vaccines have to be developed regularly?

D

Side-effects of vaccination

Vaccines may cause **side-effects**. These are harmful or unpleasant effects that can occur after the vaccine has been given. A vaccine will not always cause side-effects because different people react to treatments in different ways. Side-effects are usually mild, for example a slight rash, feeling 'off colour' for a few days or having a sore arm. However, side-effects can sometimes be more serious and cause the symptoms of the disease they are vaccinating against. On very rare occasions they cause permanent harm.

6 What are side-effects?

7 Explain why a vaccine can never be 'completely safe'.

8 A person does not catch whooping cough. Think of as many explanations for this statement as you can.

9 Influenza vaccines are only given widely to certain groups of the population, such as the elderly. Why do you think this is?

Summary

Doctors can give you an injection called a _____ to protect you from diseases. The _____ contains a weak or _____ form of the microorganism. Your body produces _____ and _____ cells against the disease, so you are immune. New _____ vaccines have to be made regularly, because flu viruses change. Vaccines can have _____-effects.

antibodies   dead   influenza
memory   side   vaccination   vaccine

B2.6 The good and bad side of vaccination

Why are we encouraged to have vaccinations?

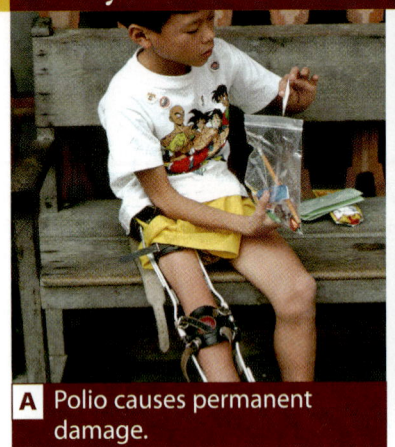

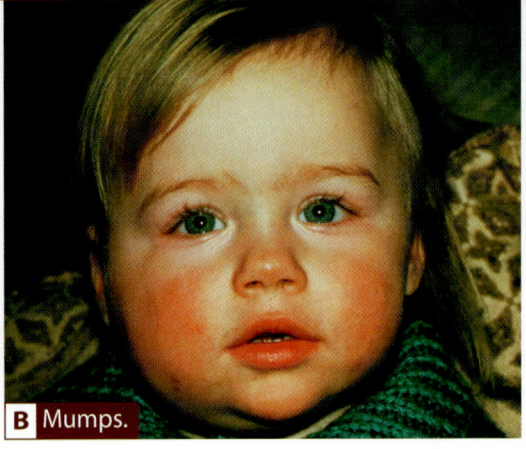

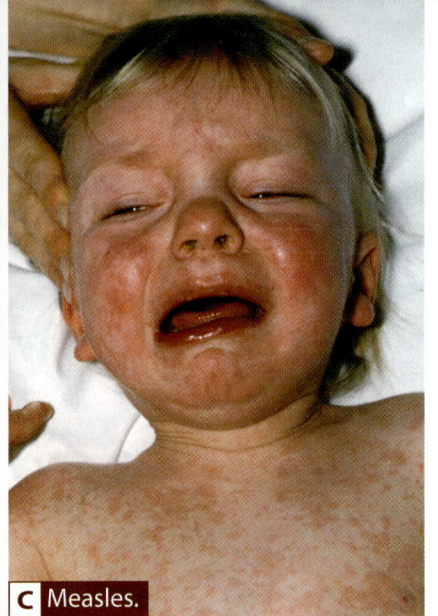

A Polio causes permanent damage.

B Mumps.

C Measles.

Many diseases such as measles, mumps, polio and whooping cough are highly infectious. They can cause death or permanent harm. Without vaccination, many hundreds of children in the UK would die each year, or would suffer complications that would affect the rest of their lives.

Whooping cough used to be a common illness in children in the UK. It causes a painful cough with characteristic 'whoops' which may last for 2–3 months. It can lead to serious lung disease and it may cause **brain damage** in young babies.

Vaccination against whooping cough started in the 1950s. Before then about 100 000 cases were reported in the UK each year. By 1973, more than 80% of the population had been vaccinated.

? 1 a What are the symptoms of whooping cough?
b What other harm can whooping cough cause?

? 2 Look at Graph D.
a Describe the shape of the graph up to 1972.
b Explain the shape of the graph up to this point.

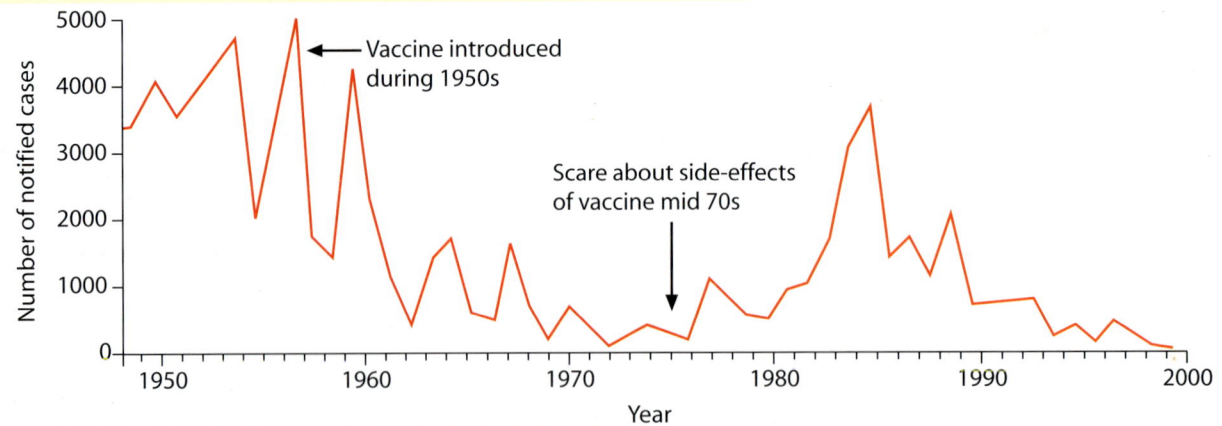

D Number of cases of whooping cough in the UK since 1948.

96

Mild side-effects of the whooping cough vaccine include fever and headache. Table E shows the severe side-effects that the vaccine may cause.

Harm caused	Caused by the whooping cough vaccine (per 100 000 vaccinations)	Caused by whooping cough (per 100 000 cases)
death	0.2	4000
permanent brain damage	0.6	2000
swelling of the brain	3.0	4000
fits	90	8000

E

3 Which side-effect of the whooping cough vaccine is the most common?

4 How does the risk from the vaccination against whooping cough compare with the risk from catching the disease?

Parents have to decide whether or not to have their child vaccinated. This means comparing the risk of catching whooping cough and being harmed with the risk of suffering damage from the vaccine.

If many people are not vaccinated, the disease can spread easily and many people may be infected. At these times, the risk of getting the disease and being permanently harmed is high.

If most people are vaccinated, then it is difficult for the disease to spread so the risk of unvaccinated people catching the disease is low. At these times people are likely to forget the dangers of the disease because they haven't seen it.

If people stop getting vaccinated because they are worried about side-effects, then there is more risk of an **epidemic**.

5 Look at graph D for the years after 1970.
 a What effect did the scare have on the number of whooping cough cases?
 b Explain why the scare had this effect.

6 Imagine you are a parent. Would you have your child vaccinated? Explain your answer using table D to help you.

Summary

Many diseases can cause _____ harm. Vaccines can protect us against these _____, but vaccines can cause _____-effects. Vaccines will only stop _____ if most people are _____. Parents must decide whether or not to have their children _____.

diseases   epidemics   permanent
    side   vaccinated

97

B2.7 Choosing to vaccinate
How do I make decisions about vaccinations?

In the UK, **mass vaccination** programmes for diseases like measles, mumps and whooping cough mean that very few people catch these diseases. Governments encourage all parents to have their children vaccinated at an early age, but it is not compulsory. Governments realise that people have:
- the right of public protection (which means that a large proportion of the population need to be vaccinated)
- the right of personal choice, because there is a slight risk from the side-effects of a vaccination.

For society as a whole, vaccination is the best choice. But for each individual it is a difficult choice for their own child. People need clear and unbiased information to help them make their decision.

Most people in this country have never seen a case of diphtheria, whooping cough or polio. They do not realise how much damage these diseases can cause. Some people even believe they do not occur any more and that there is no need to have their child vaccinated. These diseases are now rare *because* of improved vaccination.

?
1. Give one reason why a parent might not want their child to be vaccinated.
2. a. Why would governments like everyone to be vaccinated against diseases like whooping cough?
   b. Give one reason why governments do not make people have vaccinations.

Immunisation
the safest way to protect your child for life

A

There are benefits and drawbacks to being vaccinated, and there are also benefits and drawbacks if you are not vaccinated! Some of these apply to the child or their parents, and some apply to the government. For example, it costs the National Health Service money to vaccinate children, but it costs them even more to look after children if they become ill.

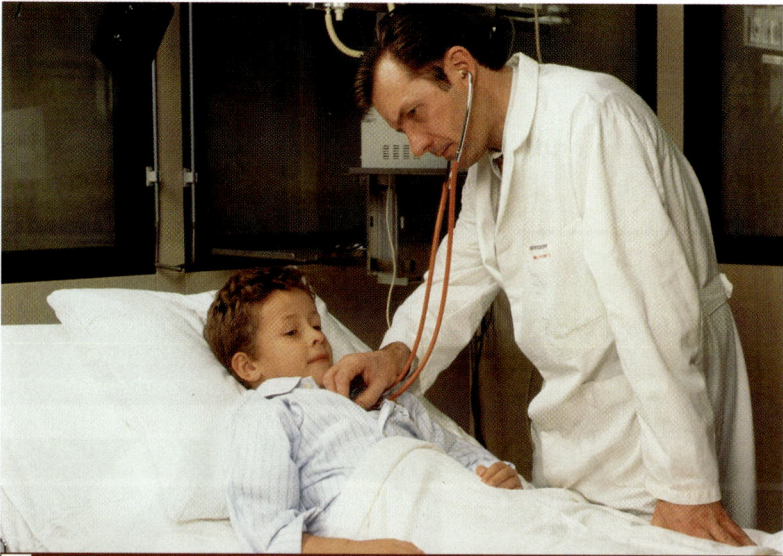

B It can cost hundreds of pounds each day to look after a child in hospital.

	Vaccinated child	Government
Benefits	Will not catch the disease and so no risk of being harmed by it.	Saves money on hospital treatment.
Drawbacks	Slight risk of side-effects for a few days after vaccination, and a very small chance of harm from the vaccine.	Costs about £4.00 for each vaccination. If vaccination causes permanent damage, it will cost a lot of money to look after the person for the rest of their life.

C Benefits and drawbacks of vaccination.

?
3 Look at Table C.
  a Why does the government want people to be vaccinated?
  b What is the benefit to a child of being vaccinated?
4 Should everyone be made to have the whooping cough vaccine? Give reasons for your answer.
5 Consider all the possible explanations for this statement: There is an epidemic of whooping cough.
6 In the UK, some vaccines are given free while some have to be paid for. How would you decide what vaccines should be given free? Explain your reasons.

Summary

Many _____ are rare today because most people are _____ against them. People need to think about the _____ and drawbacks before they _____ whether to have their child vaccinated. It is better for _____ if everyone is vaccinated, but people have the _____ to make their own decisions.

benefits   decide   diseases   right   society   vaccinated

B2.8 Antibiotics

What are antibiotics?

Some microorganisms can cause illness or even death before our immune system can destroy them. We can use **antibiotics** to kill these microorganisms. Antibiotics are chemicals that can be used to treat diseases caused by bacteria and fungi. They save millions of lives each year.

Penicillin was the world's first antibiotic and was developed during the Second World War. Nowadays there are many kinds of antibiotic that doctors can prescribe to treat diseases.

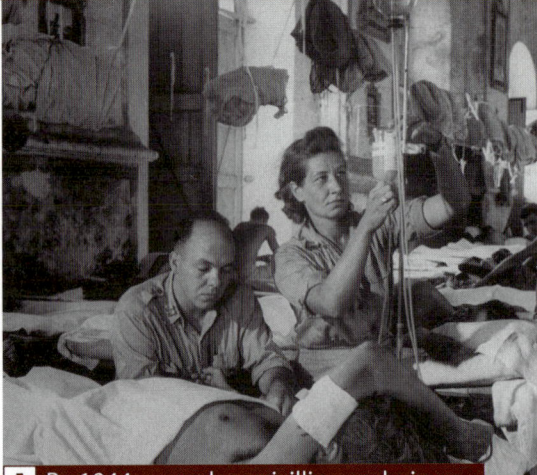

> 1 What is an antibiotic?
> 2 Why do we need antibiotics?

A By 1944 enough penicillin was being produced to treat all the British and American casualties in the war.

Antibiotics work in different ways. Some weaken the cell walls of bacteria and fungi so that they burst and die. Others stop these cells from working properly. Human cells are different so antibiotics do not usually harm them.

Antibiotics cannot be used to kill viruses because viruses are not proper cells and do not work in the same way.

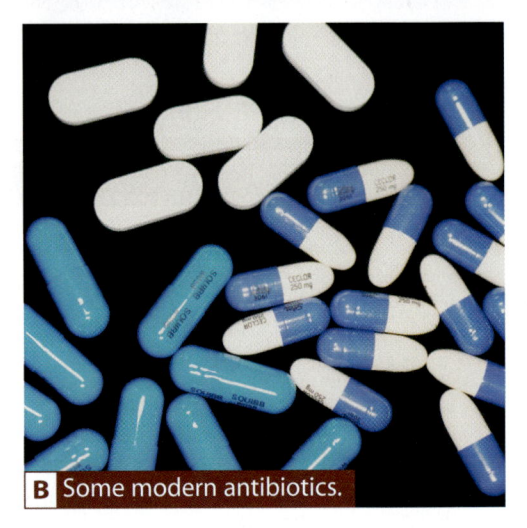

> 3 Describe two ways in which antibiotics work.
> 4 Why won't your doctor give you an antibiotic for a disease caused by a virus, such as a cold or flu?

B Some modern antibiotics.

Some bacteria and fungi become **resistant** to antibiotics. This means that antibiotics will not kill them. People who get a disease caused by these microorganisms cannot be treated with antibiotics. Antibiotic-resistant bacteria are a big problem where many antibiotics are used, such as in hospitals. Patients in hospitals are usually weakened by their illness, and catching an infection that cannot be treated may kill them.

> 5 a Why is antibiotic resistance a problem?
> b Why is the problem worse in hospitals?

Hospital 'superbug' MRSA kills!

C MRSA kills many people each year. It has become a 'superbug' because it is resistant to most antibiotics.

A How can you find out which antibiotics work the best?

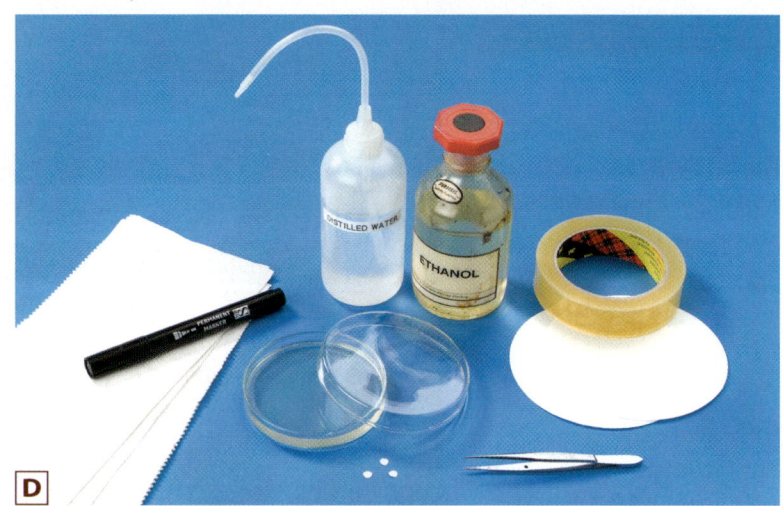

D

You can reduce the problem of antibiotic-resistant microorganisms by:
- not using antibiotics when you don't need them
- finishing a course of antibiotics when you have been given them
- thorough cleaning to stop bacteria spreading.

Scientists keep trying to make new antibiotics to treat diseases caused by resistant bacteria and fungi. However, it will also help if doctors prescribe fewer antibiotics and hospitals use better hygiene measures.

F Thorough cleaning can reduce the risk of infections spreading.

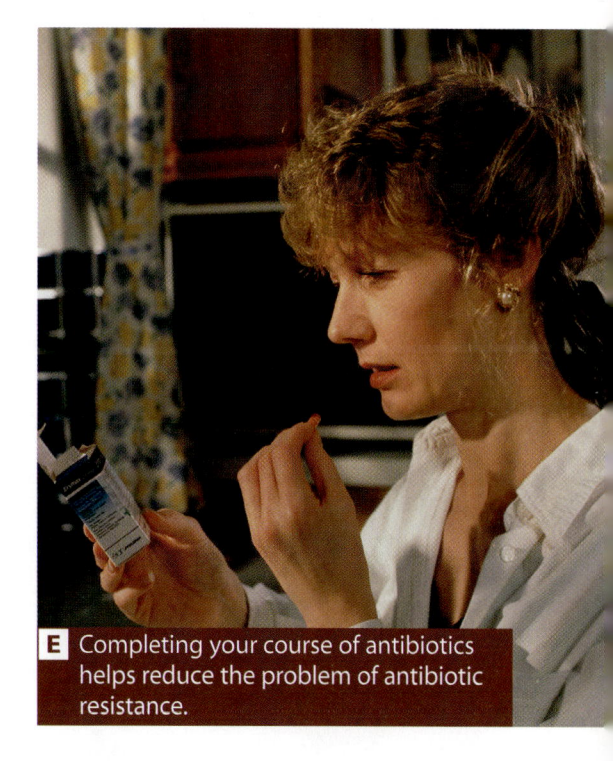

E Completing your course of antibiotics helps reduce the problem of antibiotic resistance.

?

6 Describe three ways to reduce the risk of bacteria developing antibiotic resistance.

7 James is feeling ill but his doctor will not give him antibiotics. Think of as many explanations for this as you can.

8 Suggest how hospitals can reduce the risk of spreading antibiotic-resistant bacteria.

Summary

Antibiotics are _____ used to treat infections caused by bacteria and _____. Antibiotics cannot be used to kill _____. Some bacteria develop _____ to antibiotics. To stop this happening we should only use _____ when necessary, and always take _____ of the medicine.

| all | antibiotics | chemicals | fungi |
| resistance | viruses |

101

B2.9 Testing treatments
How are new medicines tested?

Medicines are chemicals that help to make you better when you are ill, but they affect the body in different ways. Different people may have different side-effects. Medicines must be tested before they can be prescribed by doctors.

> **1** Why must new medicines be tested before they can be prescribed?

When scientists design a new medicine they start by looking at what causes the disease and how it affects the body. This gives clues about what chemicals to use to prevent or treat the disease.

New medicines are always tested first on **cultures** of human cells (a collection of cells grown in the laboratory). If these tests show that the medicine works, they are then tested on animals. If the animal tests show they are safe, they are tested on humans.

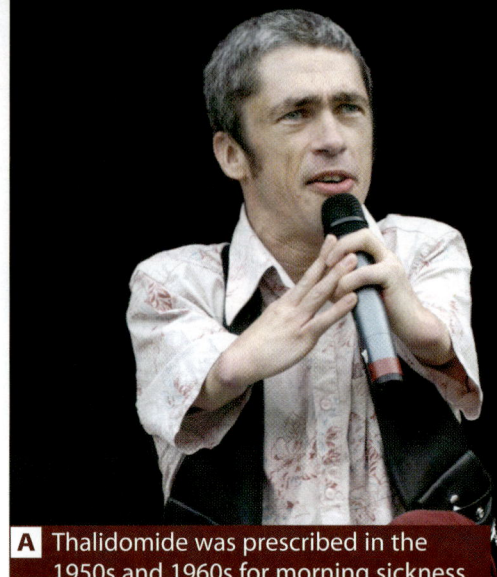

A Thalidomide was prescribed in the 1950s and 1960s for morning sickness in pregnancy. It had not been tested properly and caused malformed limbs in many babies.

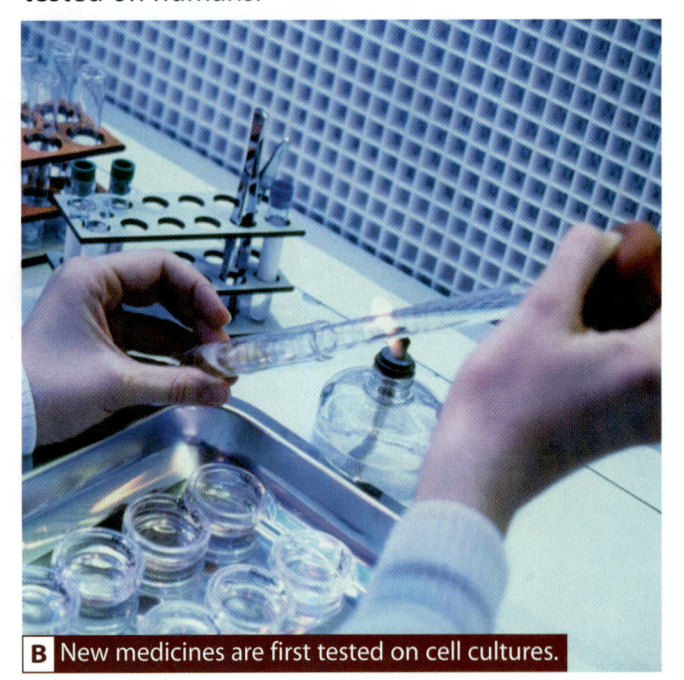

B New medicines are first tested on cell cultures.

C New medicines may be tested on animals to make sure they are safe.

> **2 a** Why are new medicines first tested on cell cultures?
> **b** Suggest one advantage of testing on cell cultures first.
>
> **3** Why are new medicines tested on animals before they are tested on humans?
>
> **4** Draw a flow chart showing the stages in the development of a new medicine.

Human trials for new medicines are first carried out on healthy volunteers to study how the medicine affects the body and to make sure that it is safe to use. Then there are **clinical trials** on patients who have the disease that the medicine treats. Trials last for 3–5 years to test thoroughly how the medicine works.

The patients are divided into two groups. One group is given the new medicine and the other group has a 'dummy pill' that doesn't contain any medicine. This is the **control** group, which shows what happens without the medicine.

Developing a new medicine is a long and slow process, and it can cost a drug company a lot of money. Before it is developed the company needs to be sure that:
- there is a need for the treatment
- it can manufacture the medicine
- enough people need the medicine so it will sell enough to get back the money it spent and make a profit.

D Drug companies advertise their medicines to try to get doctors to prescribe them.

5 Write down two reasons why medicines have to be tested before they are used.

6 a What is a clinical trial?
b What is a control group?
c Why is a control group needed?

7 Suggest reasons why developing countries cannot afford new drugs.

Summary

When a new medicine is designed, it is always tested first on cell _____. Successful medicines are then tested on _____. Clinical _____ are carried out using humans to find out how well the medicine _____ and to make sure that it is _____ to use.

animals   cultures   safe
trials   works

B2.10 The testing debate
Is it ethical to test new drugs on animals or people?

Most people agree that it is wrong to make animals suffer. Many people also agree that there are some cases in which the interests of humans are more important than the interests of animals, such as using animals to test new medicines. Many people find nothing wrong with this as long as everything is done to minimise the pain and suffering to the animal. However, other people believe that the use of animals to test medicines is wrong whatever the benefit.

Tina: We should find alternatives to animal testing. If we must use animals, they must be protected from pain and suffering.

Jeff: There are no good reasons for experimenting on animals whatever the benefits. It's cruel.

Dr McCue: If we didn't test medicines on animals we wouldn't have most of the medicines we use today. It would be very difficult to find better treatments in the future.

1. Why are medicines tested on animals?
2. Why are some people against testing medicines on animals?
3. a What do you think about animal testing?
   b Give reasons for your opinion.

Human trials

Many clinical trials take part in the developing world where poor people are willing to be paid to take part because they need the money so badly. In a trial the fee should be large enough to compensate for the inconvenience of taking part but not so large that poor people are tempted to do something they would rather not do.

Medical ethics committees decide if the possible benefits of a clinical trial are worth the possible risk to the health of the volunteers. They make sure that volunteers are carefully picked so that only suitable people take part. They should not be:
- poor people who are desperate for money
- people who have recently taken other medicines, which might affect the trial.

Sheela: I don't really want to volunteer for a clinical trial but my family needs the money.

Mr Bushe: People make their own decisions about whether to take part in clinical trials.

Dr Griffiths: If people in rich countries don't want to take part in clinical trials then it's OK for people in poor countries to do it if they want to.

Kosey: Taking part in clinical trials is an easy way to earn some money.

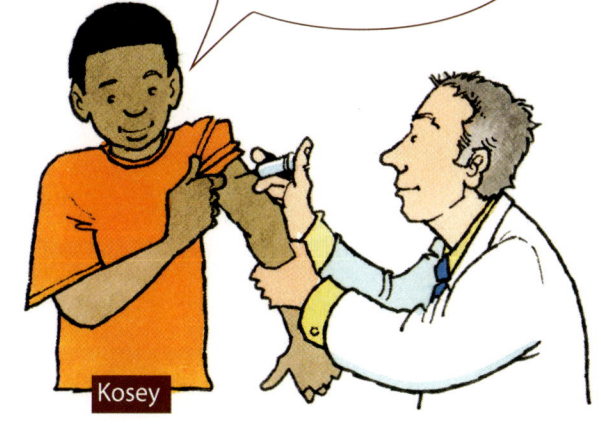

?
4. Give one reason why a poor person might agree to take part in a clinical trial.
5. Do you think it is fair to pay people in poor countries if companies cannot get volunteers elsewhere? Give reasons for your answer.
6. Most clinical trials are carried out in developing countries. Suggest reasons why this is the case.

Summary

Many people find nothing wrong with using _____ to test medicines as long as the pain and _____ are minimised. Other people believe that the use of animals to test _____ is wrong whatever the benefit. Many clinical trials take part in the _____ world where there are many poor people willing to be _____ to take part because they need the money so badly.

animals   developing   medicines
   paid   suffering

105

B2.11 Heart disease
How can we prevent heart disease?

Coronary heart disease, including heart attacks, causes more than 120 000 deaths a year in the UK. It is a major cause of death in developed countries and is becoming more common in developing countries.

> **1 a** Look at graph A. How many people die each year in the UK per 100 000 people?
> **b** What does graph A suggest about death rate in industrialised and non-industrialised countries?

Your heart pumps blood around your body through arteries, capillaries and veins. Diagram B shows how the structure of the blood vessels is related to their function. Healthy arteries have smooth walls and allow the blood to flow through easily.

Your heart muscles also need food and oxygen to keep working. The **coronary arteries** carry these to the cells in the heart muscle.

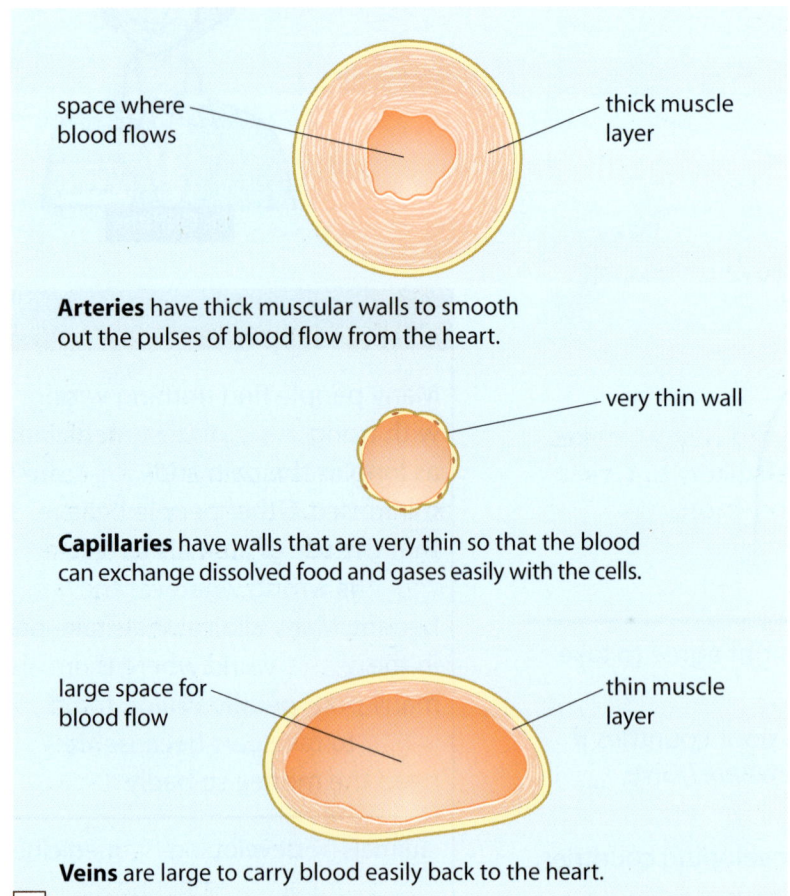

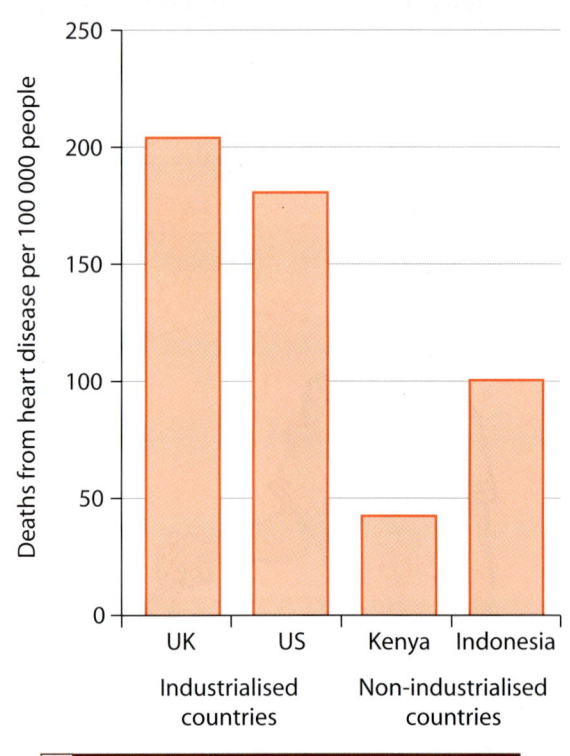

A Death rate each year from heart disease in the UK, US, Kenya and Indonesia

Arteries have thick muscular walls to smooth out the pulses of blood flow from the heart.

Capillaries have walls that are very thin so that the blood can exchange dissolved food and gases easily with the cells.

Veins are large to carry blood easily back to the heart.

B

> **2** What is transported in blood around the body?

If a coronary artery becomes partly blocked it can cause chest pains because the heart muscle is not getting enough food and oxygen. A total blockage causes a **heart attack** when the heart stops beating altogether.

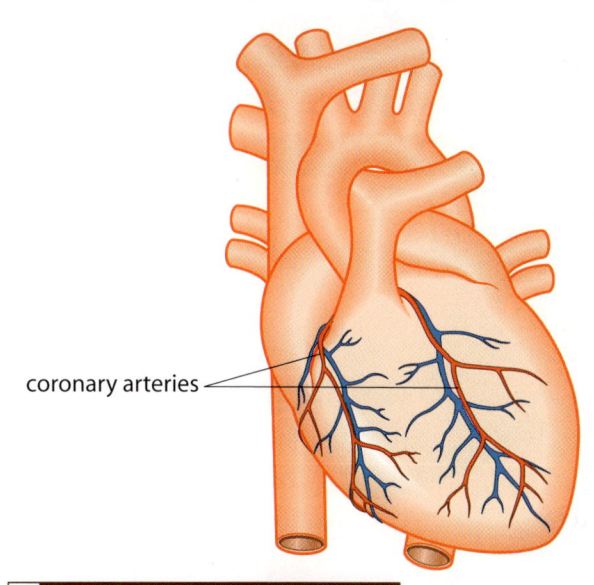

> **3** How can the build-up of a fatty plaque lead to a heart attack?
>
> **4** Why is a heart attack dangerous?

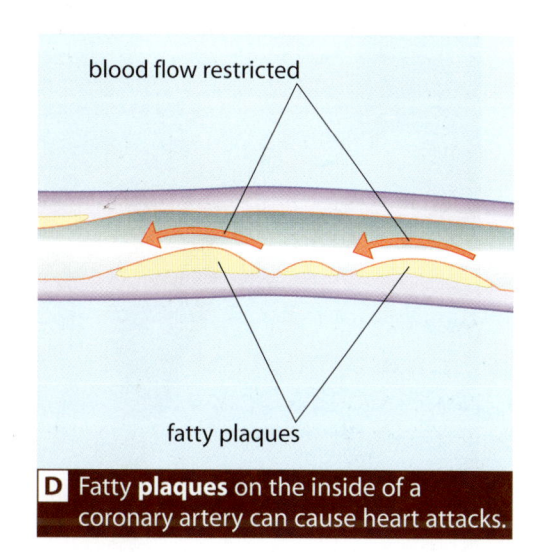

C The heart and coronary arteries.

D Fatty **plaques** on the inside of a coronary artery can cause heart attacks.

Heart disease is usually caused by **lifestyle** or genetic factors. Only very occasionally is it caused by microorganisms. The factors which most increase the risk of a heart attack are shown in table E.

Genetic factors	Lifestyle factors
• being male • inheriting genes which make you more likely to have a heart attack	• being overweight • eating a poor diet • smoking • drinking too much alcohol • being unfit • stress

E Factors linked to heart disease.

Regular exercise that makes your heart pump harder makes you fitter and reduces stress, so you are less likely to have a heart attack. It also helps your heart recover more quickly if you do have a heart attack.

> **5 a** Which of the lifestyle factors do you think would be most difficult to change?
> **b** Which do you think would be easiest to change?
> **c** Explain your answers to parts **a** and **b**.
>
> **6** Think of a plus, a minus and an interesting point about this statement: Alcohol should be banned.
>
> **7** Design a leaflet for a doctor's surgery, outlining the things that people can do to reduce the risk of a heart attack.

Summary

Heart disease is one of the major _____ of death in the UK. A heart attack happens when the heart _____ beating. This can be caused when there is a total _____ of the coronary _____. Genetic factors or _____ factors usually cause heart attacks. Eating a good _____ and taking regular _____ can reduce the risk of having a heart attack.

artery   blockage   causes   diet
exercise   lifestyle   stops

107

B2.12 Finding the cause

What causes heart attacks?

A

Scientists have tried to find out what causes heart attacks so that they can work out how to reduce the problem. There have been many **epidemiological studies** where groups of people have been studied for many factors, including lifestyle and whether or not they have had heart attacks.

Comparing people who have had heart attacks with those who haven't shows **correlations** between some factors and heart attacks. A correlation is when a change in one factor shows a similar pattern to a change in another factor.

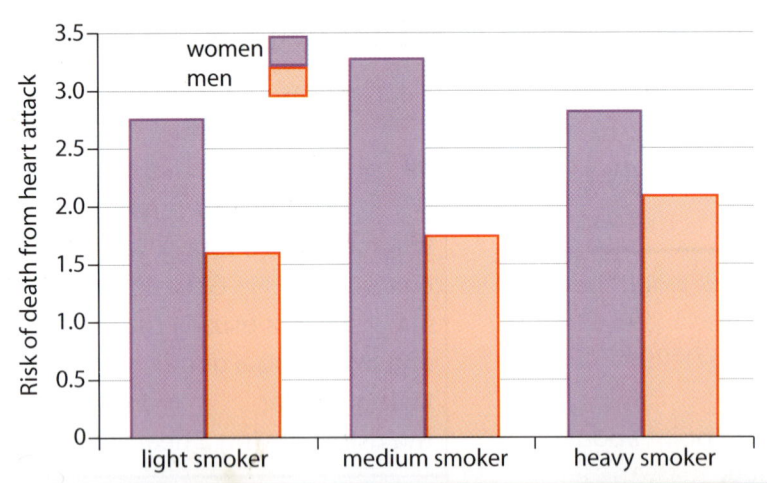

B Death rate from heart attack for smokers compared with non-smokers. A male light smoker is 1½ times as likely to have a heart attack as a man who has never smoked.

? 1 Name some of the lifestyle factors you think would have been included in studies on heart attacks.

2 When comparing groups of people, the data is first grouped by other factors such as sex. Why do you think this is so? (*Hint*: think about the other factors linked to heart attacks.)

? 3 Look at graph B.
  a Why does the graph suggest a correlation between smoking and heart disease in men?
  b What does the graph suggest about differences between men and women who smoke?

The data for graph B came from a study in Copenhagen, Denmark. The study took about 12 years and included 11 472 women and 13 191 men. This was a **reliable** study because it was made over a long time and studied many people.

Just because there is a correlation between two factors, such as smoking and heart disease, does not prove that smoking causes heart disease. To say that something is a **cause**, we need to show that there is a possible way that it may lead to the result. Studies have shown that smoking increases the amount of fatty material in the blood. This fatty material makes plaques on the inside of arteries and so can cause heart attacks.

4 Jodie's grandfather has smoked heavily since he was young, but he is now 83 and still healthy. Jodie thinks that there is no correlation between smoking and heart disease. Suggest how she is wrong.

5 Results from many other long-term studies have also shown a correlation between smoking and heart disease. Why is it important that many reliable studies are done?

Every cigarette we smoke makes fatty deposits stick in our arteries.

C

6 Draw a flow chart to show how smoking can lead to a heart attack.

Quitting smoking reduces the risk of heart attack to nearly the same as someone who has never smoked.

D Quote from World Health Organisation advice on smoking.

7 Governments in many developed countries spend lots of money on health campaigns about smoking, eating, exercise and alcohol. What effect are they trying to have?

Summary

When two factors show the same pattern we say that they are _____. For example _____ shows the same pattern of change as _____ attacks. To say that one factor _____ the other, we need to show a _____ way for it to make the other factor happen.

causes   correlated   heart
possible   smoking

B2.13 A doctor's day

How do we keep healthy?

A Doctors need to know a lot about how diseases are caused and how to cure them.

1. Name three different types of microorganism.

2. Describe three ways your body stops microorganisms getting in.

3. Explain why you should:
   a. always wash your hands before handling food
   b. put your hand in front of your nose when you sneeze
   c. clean a cut on your finger and put a plaster on it.

B Sarah is feeling unwell.

I think I might have flu.

4. Explain why you may feel ill if a microorganism infects your body.

5. a. What group of microorganisms causes influenza?
   b. Why won't Sarah's doctor give her antibiotics to get rid of the flu?

6. a. How do white blood cells help to fight disease?
   b. How do white blood cells help you to become immune to a disease?

7. a. What is an 'antibiotic resistant' bacterium?
   b. Why are resistant bacteria a problem?
   c. Describe two things we can do to try and stop bacteria becoming resistant to antibiotics.

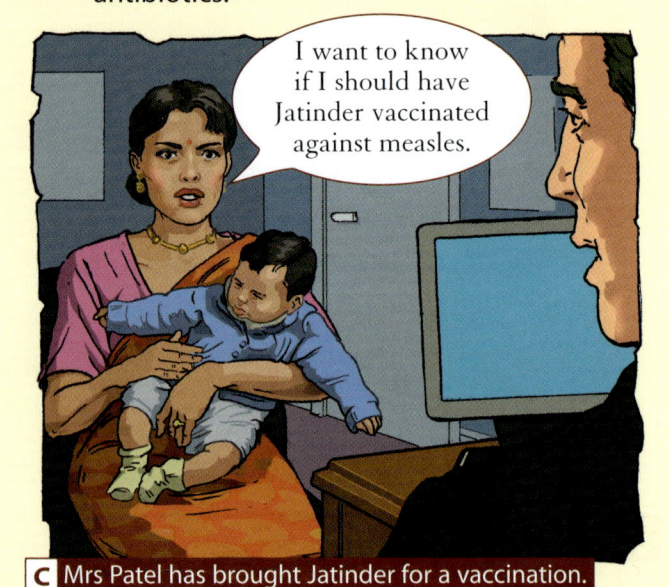

I want to know if I should have Jatinder vaccinated against measles.

C Mrs Patel has brought Jatinder for a vaccination.

8. a. What is a vaccine?
   b. How does a vaccine work?
   c. Why is it difficult to make vaccines to prevent people getting the flu?

9. a. What are the benefits to Jatinder of being vaccinated?
   b. What could be the drawbacks of being vaccinated?

10. a. Why does the government want all children to be vaccinated against measles?
    b. Why doesn't the government *make* everyone have the vaccination?

D Mrs Fraser is worried about taking a new medicine.

"How do I know these pills are safe?"

11 a Write down two reasons why new medicines need to be tested.
  b Scientists think that a chemical may be useful in treating hay fever. Draw a flow chart to describe how the chemical will be tested before it is used in human trials.

12 a Why are new medicines tested on animals before they are tested on humans?
  b Explain why some people think that we should not use animals for testing.

13 a What is a clinical trial?
  b Why are many clinical trials carried out in the developing world?
  c Suggest one reason why clinical trials should not be carried out in the developing world.

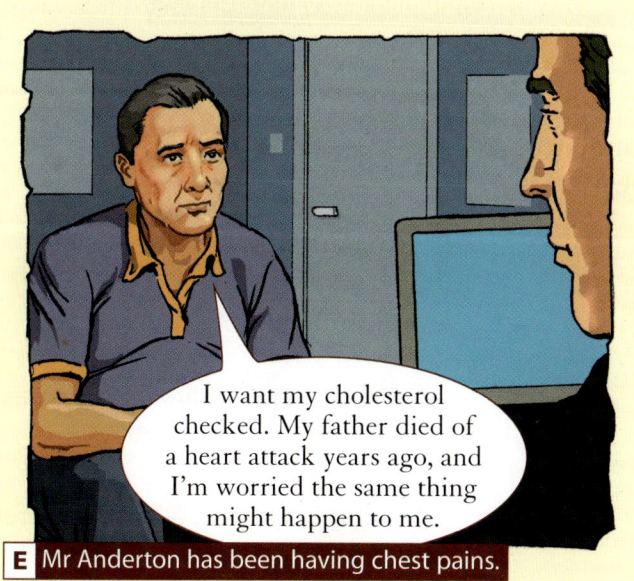

E Mr Anderton has been having chest pains.

"I want my cholesterol checked. My father died of a heart attack years ago, and I'm worried the same thing might happen to me."

14 a One artery in diagram F is narrowed where the fatty plaque has formed. Explain how the artery could become completely blocked.
  b What is a heart attack?

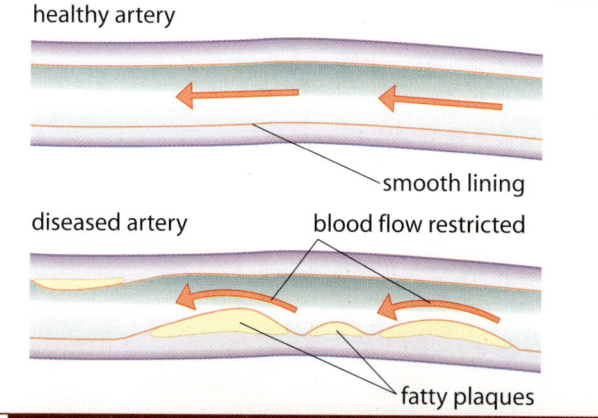

F Diagram showing lengthways section of a healthy artery and a diseased artery.

15 a List three factors that increase your chance of having a heart attack that you could do nothing about.
  b Explain how a man with a family history of heart disease can cut down his risk of having a heart attack.

16 Table G shows the results of a study on the effects of exercise on the risk of heart attacks.
  a What percentage of men between 40 and 49 who had a heart attack took regular exercise?
  b What percentage of men in the control group aged 40–49 took regular exercise?
  c Does the table show a correlation? Explain your answer.
  d What else would you need to do to show that exercise helps to reduce the risk of heart attack?

Age (years)	% of men who have had one heart attack		% of men who have not had heart attacks (control group)	
	Little or no exercise	Regular exercise	Little or no exercise	Regular exercise
40–49	91	9	64	36
50–59	87	13	70	30
60–64	85	15	75	25

G Effects of exercise on the risk of heart attacks in men.

C2.1 Material choices

What are the different materials that we use?

A Steel is used in bridges because it is strong.

B Aluminium is used in the bodies of aircraft because it is strong and light.

C Plastics have many everyday uses because they are strong, hardwearing and cheap.

D Clay can be moulded into various shapes.

We use many different materials to do things.

Many of the materials that we use are **solids** but we also make use of **liquids** and **gases**. Most useful materials are **compounds** or **mixtures**. Glass and steel are mixtures. Sometimes we use **elements**, like gold, which is used in jewellery.

Two materials may look different and be different in other ways. These differences in **properties** may make one material better for a job than another. Gold is a shiny metal that can be bent into any shape. A car could be made from gold but most cars are made of steel.

When we buy things such as clothes, cars or computers, we look at their appearance and wonder if they will do their job well. Scientists choose materials for a job by investigating the properties of the material.

> **?**
> 1 Why is steel used to make cars instead of gold?
> 2 What properties should the materials have in:
>   a a saucepan
>   b a car window
>   c a bridge?
> 3 What materials are used to make:
>   a containers for drinks
>   b clothes?
> 4 Suggest reasons why the different materials are used in question 3.

Some materials are made from rocks or substances found in the rocks. Other materials are made from plants or animals. Obtaining materials can harm plants and animals. We have to make decisions about how much damage to the environment we will allow.

E Some materials are made from rocks dug from the ground.

F Some materials are made from plants, such as cotton.

Every object we use wears out. We have to think about the effect on the environment of throwing things away.

G Many materials end up on rubbish tips.

?

5 Glass is made from rocks dug from the ground. What damage do you think this could cause to the environment?

6 Cotton is obtained from a plant grown in large fields. What damage do you think cotton farms cause to the environment?

7 What problems do you think a pile of rubbish causes to the environment?

8 Make a list of the questions you need to ask about a material to help you decide:
   a how suitable it is for a particular job
   b how harmful it is to the environment.

113

C2.2 Fit for the job

How can we pick a suitable material for a product or task?

A What properties should the rope have?

B What materials are being used here? What properties do they have?

We need to know about the properties of different materials to help us to choose the best materials for a particular job.

We use instruments such as rulers and balances to measure properties of materials.

> **1** What instrument would a kitchen inspector use to check:
>   **a** that the worktops are at the correct height
>   **b** that the fridges are keeping food cold enough
>   **c** the time taken for the oven to reach the correct temperature?
>
> **2** What instruments would you use to measure 500 g of flour and 300 cm³ water, when making dough?

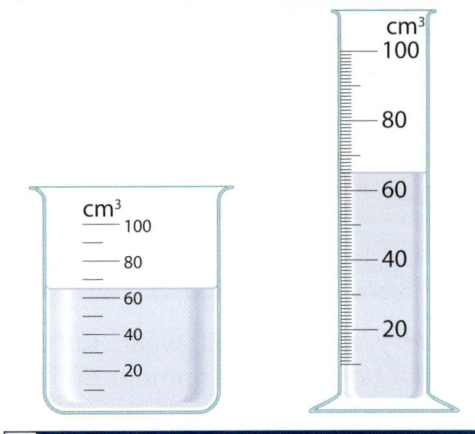

C The measuring cylinder gives the more precise reading.

We can never be sure that we have the true value of a measurement because there are always **uncertainties**. Here are a few reasons why.
- The measuring instrument may not be precise (diagram C).
- The instrument may be read incorrectly.
- The instrument may not be set correctly (diagram D).
- It may be difficult to keep the conditions constant so that an accurate reading can be taken.

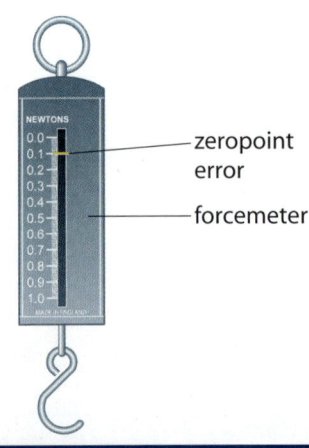

> **3** Look at diagram C.
>   **a** How much water is in the measuring cylinder?
>   **b** Do you think the beaker contains more, less or the same amount of water as the measuring cylinder? Explain why you can't be sure of your answer to part **b**.

D This forcemeter reads 0.1 N even when there is no object on it.

It helps if we repeat measurements. Readings which are very different from the others are **outliers**. The **best estimate** of the true value is found by working out the **mean** of the readings left when we leave out the outliers. The largest and smallest of the remaining data form the **range**. The true value should lie within the range.

A How can we take measurements accurately?

E

4 Emily measured the length of a bookshelf. Her measurements in centimetres (cm) were:
72 73 72 77 71
  a Which reading was probably an outlier?
  b What is the best estimate of the length of the bookshelf?
  c In what range does the true value probably lie?

5 Asha used the forcemeter shown in diagram D to measure the weight of an object. The forcemeter read 7 N.
  a What was the correct weight of the object?
  b Explain how you worked out your answer.

6 Jim heated a liquid in a beaker until it was bubbling. He put the thermometer in the liquid and waited a few moments. Then he took the thermometer out of the liquid and read it. He did the same thing five times.
  a Why would Jim's measurements be inaccurate?
  b Would Jim's best estimate be lower or higher than the true value?
  c How could Jim get a more accurate measurement?

Summary

To find the best material for a job we must _____ its _____. Each measurement has _____ but some readings will be worse than others and are called _____. The best _____ of the _____ value of the property is found by taking the _____ of the other readings.

estimate   mean   measure   outliers
   properties   true   uncertainty

115

C2.3 Comparing properties
How do the properties of different materials compare?

We can compare materials by looking at different properties.

Melting point

If a solid is heated it turns into a liquid. A pure substance does this at a temperature called the **melting point**. Mixtures are not pure. They soften and turn into a liquid over a range of temperatures.

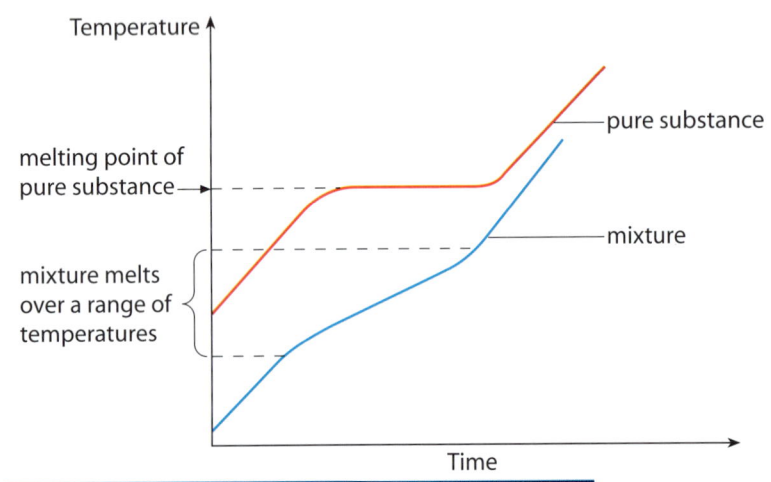

A solid ⇌ liquid (melting – gaining energy / freezing – losing energy)

B Melting curves for a pure substance and a mixture.

If a material gets hot when it is used we do not want it to melt. We need to know what the melting point of the material is so we can decide if it is suitable for the job. To measure the melting point accurately a material must be heated slowly and evenly.

C An oven dish needs to keep its shape up to about 300 °C.

D Tools used to handle molten steel must be able to withstand 1500 °C.

?
1. How could you find out if a solid material was a pure substance or mixture by heating it?

2. Look at table E.
   a. Which of these materials is suitable for making a food container for use in a microwave oven?
      (*Hint:* microwave ovens heat food to about 100 °C.)
   b. Explain your answer to part **a**.

Material	Temperature at which material starts to soften (°C)
polypropene	80
PVC	60
polythene	65
nylon	185

E

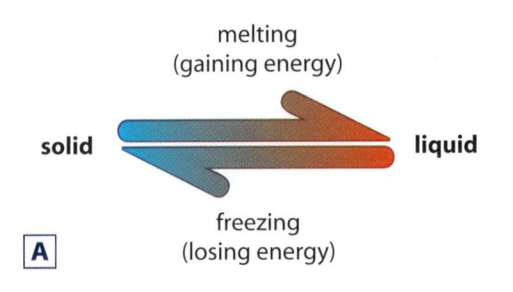

116

Density

Marathon runners often carry bottles of water with them. The bottle is made out of plastic because a glass bottle would be heavier to carry even though it might contain the same amount of water. Glass is a denser material than plastic. The density of a material is the **mass** contained in a specific **volume** of it.

E
$$\text{density} = \frac{\text{mass of material (g or kg)}}{\text{volume of material (cm}^3 \text{ or m}^3\text{)}}$$

The units for density are g/cm³ or kg/m³ depending on the units you used to measure mass and volume.

A How can you find:
- the melting point of chocolate
- the density of chocolate?

F Plastic bottles are not too heavy to carry when you are running.

G

?
3. What instruments would you need to measure the density of a lump of solid gold?

4. The mass of a piece of glass is 22 g, and its volume is 10 cm³. What is the density of the glass?

5. 1 g of polythene has a volume of 1.09 cm³. What is the density of the polythene?

6. Think of a plus, a minus and an interesting point about this statement: Different materials soften at temperatures from 60 °C to over 300 °C.

7. Glass is denser than polythene. Explain why a lorry can carry more 2 litre polythene bottles filled with mineral water than 2 litre glass bottles.

Summary

If a solid is heated it turns into a _____ when its temperature reaches its _____ point. We usually want a material to stay _____ when it is being used so we must _____ the melting _____ before choosing a material for a purpose. A material with a high _____ will have more _____ than the same _____ of a material with a _____ density. The units of density are _____.

density   kg/m³   liquid   lower
mass   measure   melting   point
solid   volume

117

C2.4 More properties

How do the properties of different materials compare?

Strength, stiffness and hardness are properties that may be important in the way we use a material.

Strength

The strength of a material is how much force is needed to break it. The material can be stretched (**tension**) or squashed (**compression**). Steel is strong when it is stretched and concrete is strong when it is squashed.

? 1 Why is concrete used for the foundations of buildings?

Stiffness

A material that bends when a force pushes on it is **flexible**. If it takes a lot of force to make the material bend it is stiff.

? 2 Why do the bumpers of a car need to be flexible?

Hardness

A hard material is difficult to scratch or cut. Diamond is a hard material. A material that scratches easily or is easy to cut is soft.

A The sails of these yachts are made of Kevlar. It is strong when it is in tension.

B When clay is being moulded it is soft.

C After it has been fired clay is hard.

Table D shows various words we use to describe the properties of materials.

Word	Means that a material…	Example
durable	…does not wear out quickly, so products made from it last a long time	stainless steel
brittle	…does not change shape when stretched or squeezed but shatters when the force is large enough	glass
malleable	…changes shape without breaking when it is squeezed or hammered	plasticine, hot steel
ductile	…can be pulled into a wire or a fibre without breaking	nylon
elastic	…returns to its original shape when a force is removed	rubber
plastic	…can be moulded into a new shape by a force	plasticine
flexible	…can be bent by a force	copper wire

D

3 What words would be used to describe the properties of:
  a a china bowl that shatters when it is dropped
  b copper used for electrical wires
  c bread dough when it is kneaded?

4 Your fingernails scratch a piece of wood but a steel nail file shapes your nails. Put the materials in order of hardness with the hardest first.

5 You are looking for a material for a mobile phone case. What properties should the material have?

6 Eddie was comparing two different types of rope for mountain climbers. He measured the force need to break each rope. He tested each rope five times.

	Force needed to break rope (N)				
rope A	2300	2400	2350	2250	2200
rope B	2800	2700	2750	2600	2650

F

  a Was a tension or compression force used to test the ropes?
  b What is the best estimate of the strength of each rope?
  c Which rope was the strongest?

A How can we test the strength, stiffness and hardness of materials?

E

Summary

A material that shatters is _____.
A material that bends is _____.
A material that is difficult to cut is _____. A material that can be pressed into shape is _____.
A strong material needs a _____ force of tension or _____ to break it

brittle   compression   flexible
hard   large   malleable

119

C2.5 Plastics, rubbers and fibres

What are the properties of plastics, rubbers and fibres?

A Polythene is a plastic used for bottles and containers.

B Tyres are made from a tough rubber.

C Polypropylene is used to make durable carpets.

Many of the materials that we use are classified as plastics, rubbers or fibres.
- **Plastics** are materials that can be moulded into different shapes by squeezing the material when it is warm. When it cools the material keeps its new shape.
- **Rubbers** are elastic materials. They can be tough like the rubber used in car tyres or soft like the rubber used in rubber gloves.
- Some materials can be drawn out into a fine thread or **fibre**. A fibre is strong and flexible. Fibres are woven for clothes and carpets and twisted to make ropes. Woven cloth is comfortable to wear because it lets the air through.

D Neoprene is a type of rubber used for wetsuits.

Some plastic materials can also be drawn into fibres. For example, polypropylene is used to make carpets.

Each material has a range of properties suitable for the job it is chosen to do.

A How can we recognise the different types of material and compare their properties?

E

?
1. Look around you and name objects made from:
   a moulded plastic
   b rubber
   c fibres.

2. Write a sentence about the properties of each type of material in question **1**, using the words from previous topics.

3. Which type of material is needed for the following uses? Explain your answers.
   a a 'bungee' rope
   b the soles of a pair of boots
   c the casing of a computer
   d a fishing net.

Materials from living things

Many of the materials we use come from plants or animals.

Plant cells make a material called **cellulose**. It forms fibres such as cotton. Paper made from wood is mainly cellulose fibres. Natural rubber is formed from the sap of certain types of tree.

We also get materials from animals. Silk is a fibre made by silk worms for their cocoons.

F Cotton can be spun into thread.

G Wool is a fibre made from protein.

H Natural rubber is formed from the sap of rubber trees. It is obtained by 'tapping' the sap.

Many natural materials have to be treated before they are usable. The sap from a rubber tree has to be heated with sulfur to make it into tough, elastic rubber.

4 Name two natural materials produced by:
   a plants   b animals.
5 What types of material are cotton and wool?
6 What properties do you think neoprene has that makes it good for wetsuits?

Summary

Examples of materials are _____ which can be moulded into various shapes, rubbers which are _____ and _____ which can be woven into cloth. Materials from _____ things include _____ and _____.

cotton   elastic   fibres   living
plastics   wool

121

C2.6 Synthetic materials
What are synthetic materials made from?

During the 20th century more and more materials were used. There were not enough **natural** materials (materials from living things) to meet the demand, and scientists discovered how to make materials from other substances. These are called **synthetic** materials. Today we use a large number of synthetic materials for many different purposes. New materials have been produced with properties that are very different from natural materials. Synthetic materials include polythene, nylon, polyester, PVC, Kevlar and Lycra.

> **1** What is the difference between natural and synthetic materials?

The starting point for many synthetic materials is a substance called a **hydrocarbon**. Hydrocarbons are compounds made up of only the elements carbon and hydrogen. Many hydrocarbons are found in **crude oil**.

Crude oil is a thick, black, tarry liquid that is found trapped in layers of rock. It is formed from the dead remains of plants and animals that lived in oceans millions of years ago. The dead matter sank to the bottom and was buried in sediments. It was crushed and heated and slowly turned into crude oil. Crude oil is a mixture of lots of different hydrocarbons. The hydrocarbons are used as fuels as well as for making useful materials.

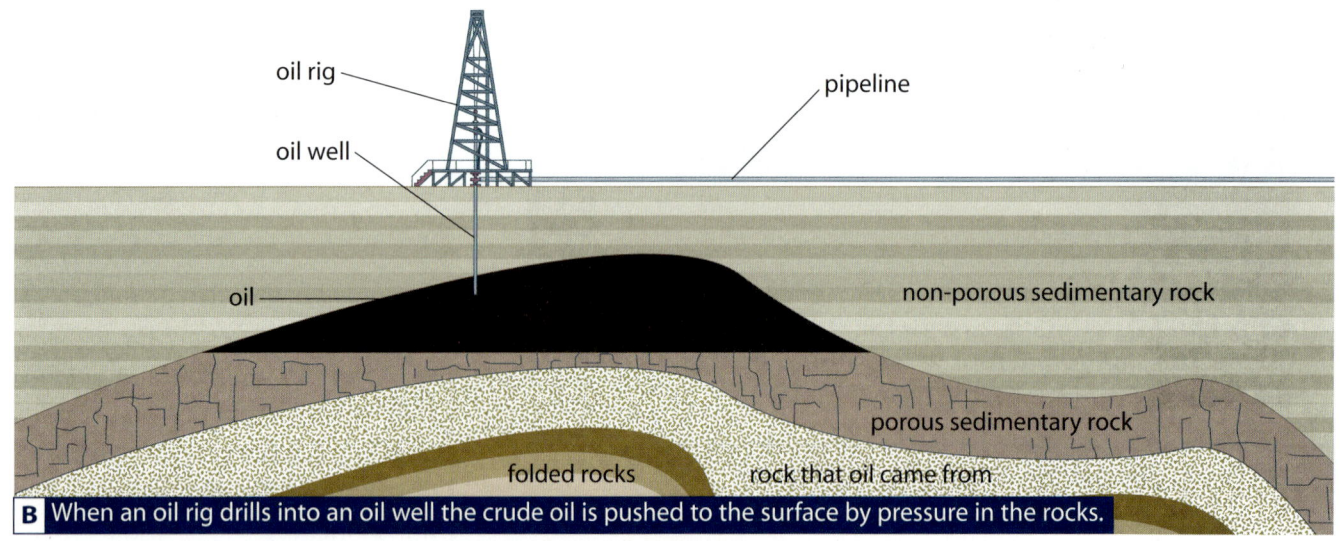

A Lycra is an elastic fibre used in clothes.

B When an oil rig drills into an oil well the crude oil is pushed to the surface by pressure in the rocks.

> **2** What is a hydrocarbon?
> **3** Where do the substances in crude oil come from?

Properties of hydrocarbons

Carbon **atoms** can join together to form a chain. Hydrogen atoms are joined to the carbon atoms, and form a hydrocarbon **molecule**. The properties of hydrocarbons depend on the number of carbon atoms in a chain.

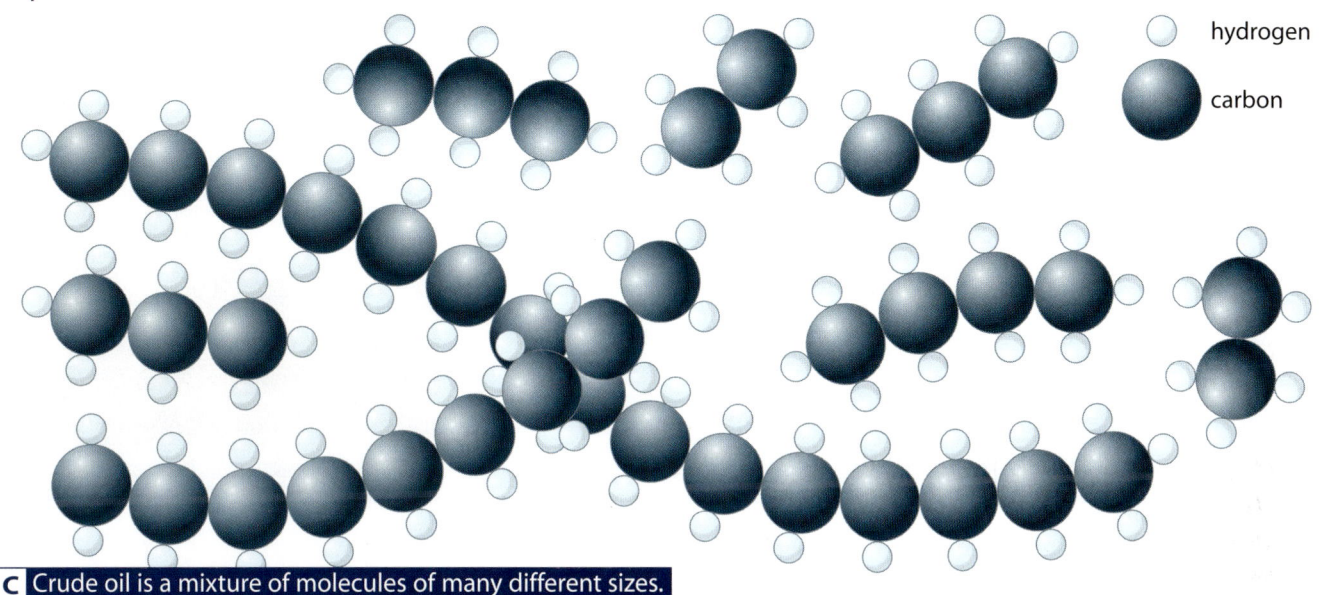

hydrogen
carbon

C Crude oil is a mixture of molecules of many different sizes.

Number of carbon atoms in molecule	Boiling point (°C)
1–4	Up to 25
5–7	40–100
8–11	100–150
11–14	150–250
15–19	220–340
20–30	over 350
Over 30	over 400

D The boiling point depends on the number of carbon atoms in a molecule.

?
4. How can we tell that crude oil is a mixture of compounds and not a single compound?
5. A hydrocarbon has six carbon atoms in its molecules. What range will its boiling point be in?
6. The boiling point of a hydrocarbon is 120 °C. How many carbon atoms could it have in its molecules?
7. The formula of a compound shows the number of atoms of each element joined together in a molecule of the compound. Look at these formulae and decide which of the compounds are hydrocarbons. Explain your answers.
   methane CH_4, ethanol C_2H_6O, ethane C_2H_4, carbon dioxide CO_2, octane C_8H_{18}

Summary

Synthetic _____ can be used in place of natural materials. Some synthetic materials are made from _____ oil, which consists of _____ molecules. Hydrocarbons have chains of _____ atoms of different lengths. The _____ of the hydrocarbon depend on the _____ of the chain.

carbon   crude   hydrocarbon
length   materials   properties

123

C2.7 Refining oil

How are different hydrocarbons obtained from crude oil?

The substances that make up crude oil have to be separated before they can be used. This is called **refining**. They are separated using **fractional distillation**.

Boiling and condensing

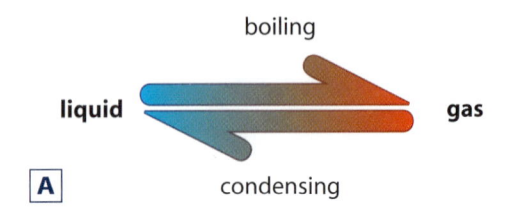

A

When a mixture of gases is cooled, each separate compound will condense when the temperature falls to its boiling point. This is how fractional distillation works.

B An oil refinery – the tall thin towers are the fractionating columns.

Fractional distillation of crude oil

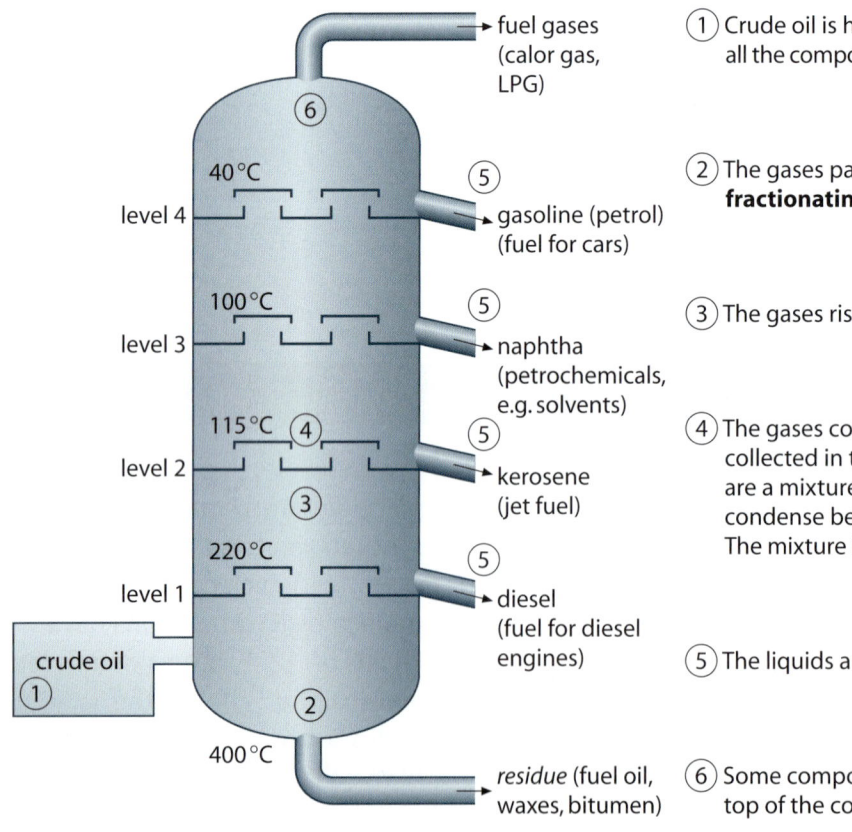

① Crude oil is heated to about 450 °C, turning all the compounds in the mixture into gases.

② The gases pass into the bottom of the **fractionating column**.

③ The gases rise and cool.

④ The gases condense into liquids and are collected in trays. The liquids in each tray are a mixture of hydrocarbons that condense between the two temperatures. The mixture in each tray is called a fraction.

⑤ The liquids are piped off from the trays.

⑥ Some compounds remain as gases at the top of the column.

Fractions from the column:
- fuel gases (calor gas, LPG) — 40 °C, level 4
- gasoline (petrol) (fuel for cars) — 100 °C, level 3
- naphtha (petrochemicals, e.g. solvents) — 115 °C, level 2
- kerosene (jet fuel) — 220 °C, level 1
- diesel (fuel for diesel engines)
- residue (fuel oil, waxes, bitumen) — 400 °C

C Crude oil is separated into fractions in a fractionating column.

1. The boiling point of water is 100 °C. At what temperature does steam turn to water?
2. Liquid A boils at 66 °C and liquid B boils at 78 °C. A mixture of the two liquids is heated to 90 °C. Which substance will turn back to a liquid first when the mixture of gases cools down?
3. In what state is crude oil put into the fractionating column?
4. Which part of the fractionating column is at the highest temperature, the top or the bottom?
5. Do large or small molecules condense first as the crude oil rises up the column? Explain your answer.

A How can we separate the substances in crude oil?

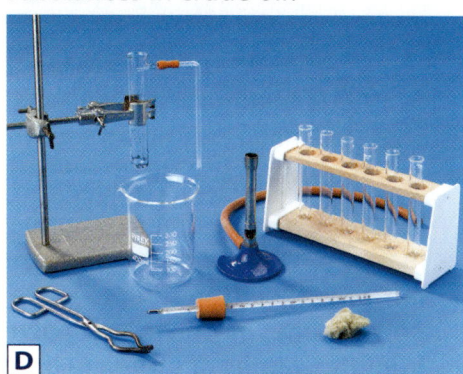

D

Using the fractions

Table E shows the uses of different **fractions** in crude oil.

Name of fraction	Number of carbon atoms in molecule	Uses
fuel gases	1–4	bottled gas for houses, caravans
gasoline (petrol)	5–7	fuel for cars
naphtha	8–11	making new substances
kerosene	11–14	aircraft fuel
diesel	15–19	fuel for cars, lorries
mineral oils	20–30	lubricating oils
fuel oil	30–40	fuel for ships, power stations
bitumen	over 40	tar for roads

E

Most of the fractions of crude oil are used as fuels. The smaller molecules in the naphtha fraction are used to make other substances. The naphtha fraction is only a small part of crude oil.

6. What are most of the fractions used for?
7. Which fraction is used to make new materials?
8. Think of a plus, a minus and an interesting point about this statement: Crude oil is too valuable to burn as a fuel.
9. Give one difference in properties between the hydrocarbons used as fuel in lorries and the hydrocarbons used to make new substances.

Summary

Crude oil is separated in a _____ column. Crude oil enters the _____ of the column as a _____. As the gas rises, different hydrocarbons _____ into liquids and are collected in _____. The compounds with the smaller molecules condense _____ up the column. Most of the fractions are used as _____. The _____ fraction is used to make new materials.

bottom   condense   fractionating
fuels   gas   higher   naphtha   trays

C2.8 Making polymers
How are polymers made?

Synthetic materials include substances called **polymers**. They are made by joining together lots of small molecules called **monomers**. The process is called **polymerisation**.

Ethene is a small molecule with just two carbon atoms. It is made from the naphtha fraction of crude oil. Ethene molecules join together to make the polymer called poly(ethene) or polythene. Each polythene chain is made from thousands of ethene monomers.

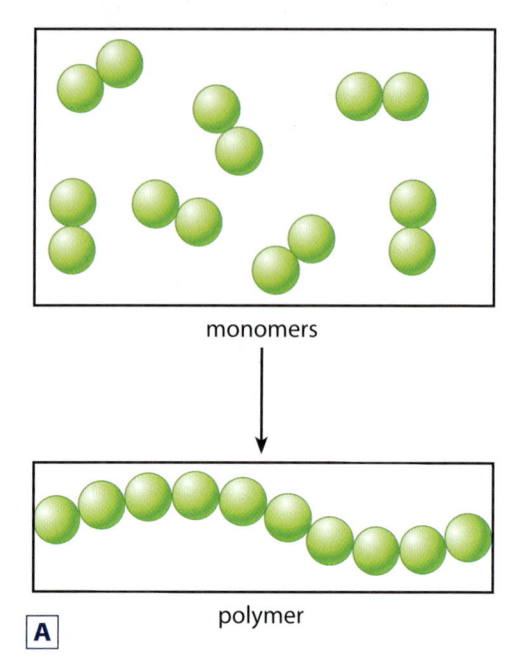

> **1** Write down the meanings of the following words:
> a monomer b polymer c polymerisation.

Different synthetic polymers are made from different monomers. Some polymers such as nylon are made from two different monomers which join up alternately. The differences in the monomers give the polymers their different properties.

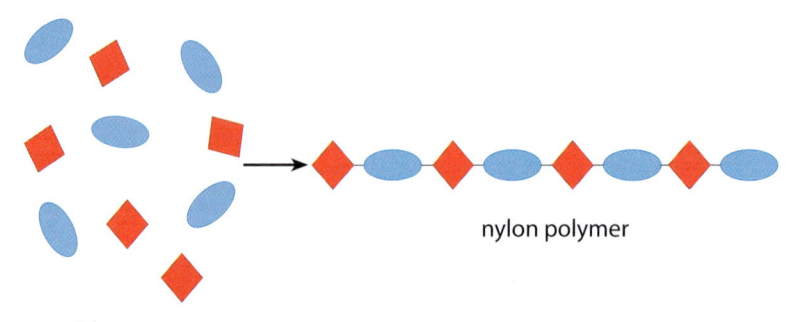

A monomers → polymer

B nylon monomers → nylon polymer

> **2** Why do you think different monomers are used to make polymers?

Polymer	Properties	Uses
poly(ethene)	flexible, cheap	bags, containers
poly(propene)	tough (doesn't break easily), can be drawn into fibres	buckets, bowls, carpets
Teflon	tough, slippery	non-stick coatings
Perspex	tough, hard, clear	unbreakable windows
polystyrene	tough, hard, can be moulded into complex shapes or 'blown' into foams	disposable cups, packaging, car dashboards
PVC	tough, hard, long-lasting	window frames, pipes
nylon	tough, can be drawn into fibres	clothes, carpets

C Polymers and their uses.

Synthetic polymers or natural materials?

Synthetic polymers have taken the place of many natural materials. Today, fishing nets are made of nylon instead of plant fibres such as hemp. PVC has taken the place of cotton for insulating electrical wires. The synthetic materials do not rot, so they last longer than natural materials.

Wine bottles are usually sealed with corks. For centuries, cork has been obtained from special trees. Sometimes the cork is attacked by microorganisms which turn the wine bad. A synthetic polymer has been made that looks and behaves just like cork. It is cheap but is not attacked by microorganisms. Many wine bottles now have a synthetic cork instead of a natural cork.

D Old and new fast food packaging materials.

E Natural or synthetic; which is best?

?

3 What advantages are there in using a synthetic polymer instead of natural cork in wine bottles?

4 Choose a suitable synthetic polymer from table C for:
   a a coating for cloth which stops dust from sticking to it
   b the casing for an MP3 player
   c unbreakable clear tumblers for a café
   d rope for a sailing boat.
   Give reasons for your choices.

5 Look at the packaging materials in photo D.
   a What are the advantages in using paper?
   b What are the advantages in using polystyrene?
   c Which material do you think should be used? Give your reasons.

6 When a polymer is made, the polymer chains end up being different lengths. How do you think this affects the properties of the polymer?

Summary

_____ is the joining together of lots of small molecules called _____ to form a polymer with a long _____ of carbon atoms. The properties of polymers differ so they can be _____ for different things. Some synthetic polymers have replaced _____ materials because they are cheaper or have better _____.

chain   monomers   natural
polymerisation   properties   used

127

C2.9 Inside polymers
Why do polymers behave as they do?

We cannot see the molecules in a polymer but scientists have **theories** that explain the properties of polymers.

There are forces between molecules that pull them together. A big force between polymer molecules means more energy is needed to pull them apart so the polymer will be tougher, stiffer and stronger.

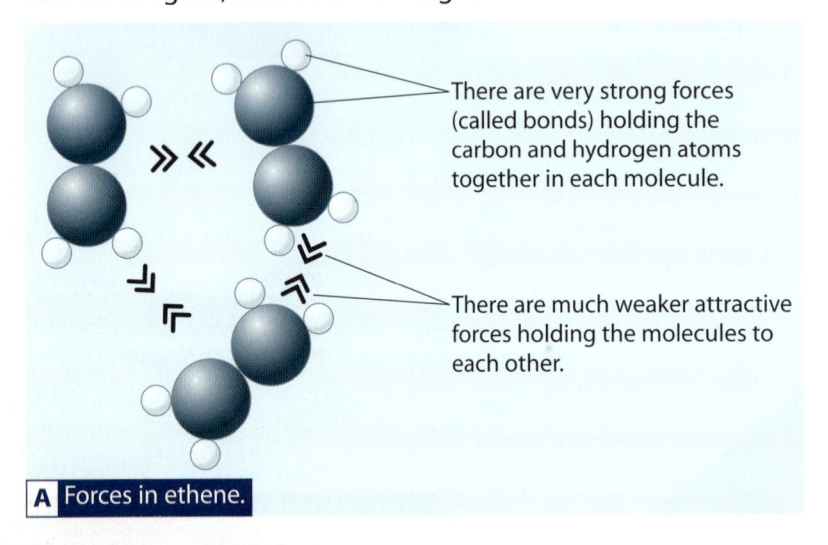

There are very strong forces (called bonds) holding the carbon and hydrogen atoms together in each molecule.

There are much weaker attractive forces holding the molecules to each other.

A Forces in ethene.

Scientists suggest that:
- the more atoms there are in a molecule, the stronger the force between the molecules
- the force is bigger when the molecules are close to each other.

Some monomers form polymers with side chains or branches. The branches stop the molecules getting close to each other. Polymers with side chains are usually more flexible and stretchy than polymers with straight molecules.

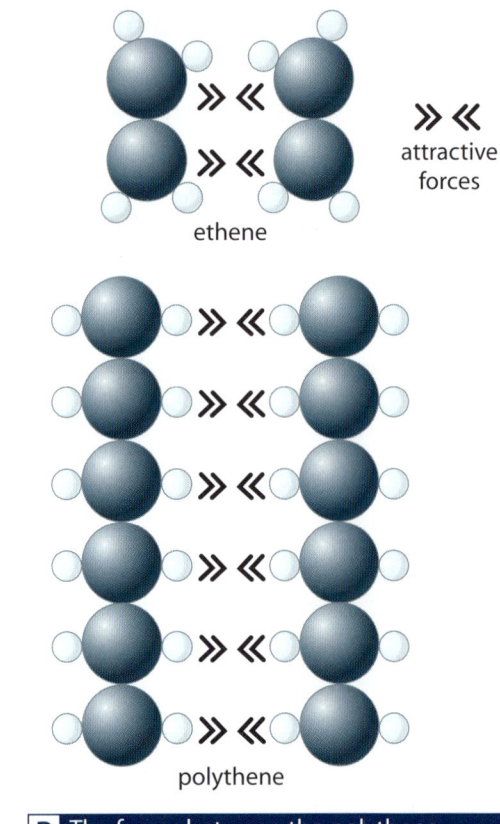

B The forces between the polythene molecules are larger than the forces between the ethene molecules.

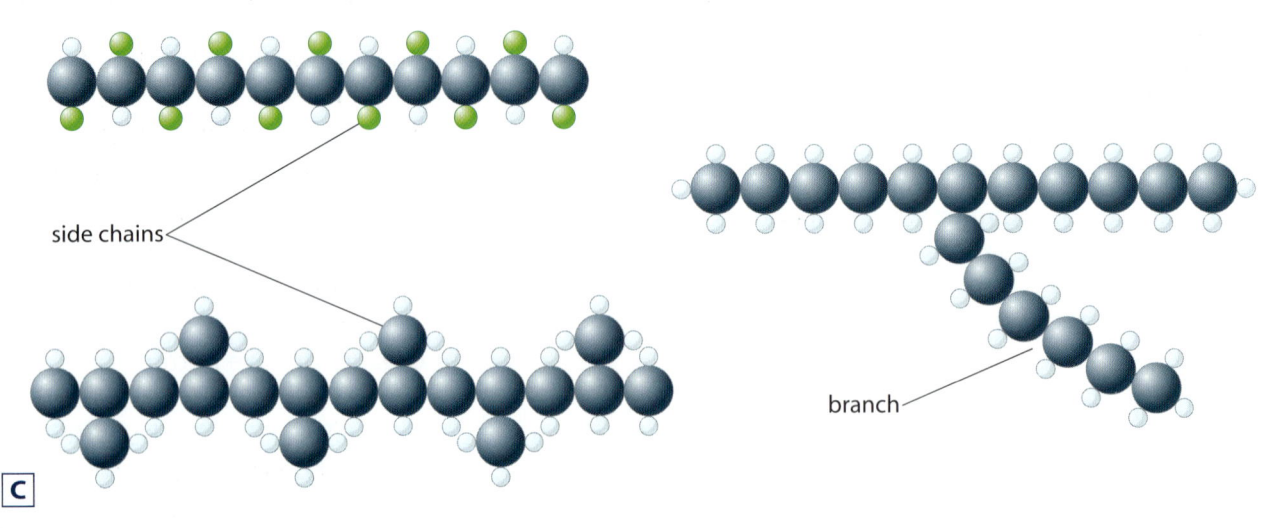

side chains

branch

C

? 1 Diagram D shows the molecules in three different polymers.
   a Why is polymer Z stronger than polymer X?
   b Which will be the strongest: polymer Y or polymer Z?
   c Explain your answer to part **b**.

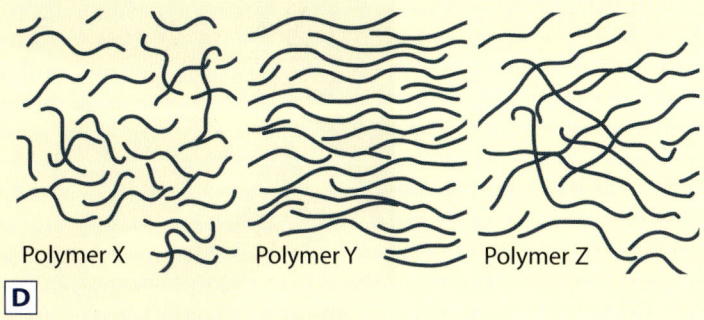

   Polymer X   Polymer Y   Polymer Z
   D

The forces between the molecules in a polymer also affect the melting point. The stronger the force, the more energy is needed to pull the molecules apart, and so the higher the melting point.

? 2 Look at diagram B. Explain why ethene is a gas at room temperature while polythene is a solid.

3 Candle wax is a hydrocarbon with more than 40 carbon atoms in each molecule. Polythene is a polymer with thousands of carbon atoms in a molecule. Why is polythene much stronger than a lump of candle wax?

4 Nylon is stronger than polythene, and softens at a higher temperature. What can you say about the forces between nylon molecules compared to the forces between polythene molecules?

Scientists think the theory about forces between molecules in polymers is successful because it predicts the properties of different kinds of polymer. They can use the theory to help them to make new polymers. The new polymers are tested to check their properties.

? 5 Look at diagram C on page 124 and table E on page 125. Why does gasoline have a lower boiling point than kerosene?

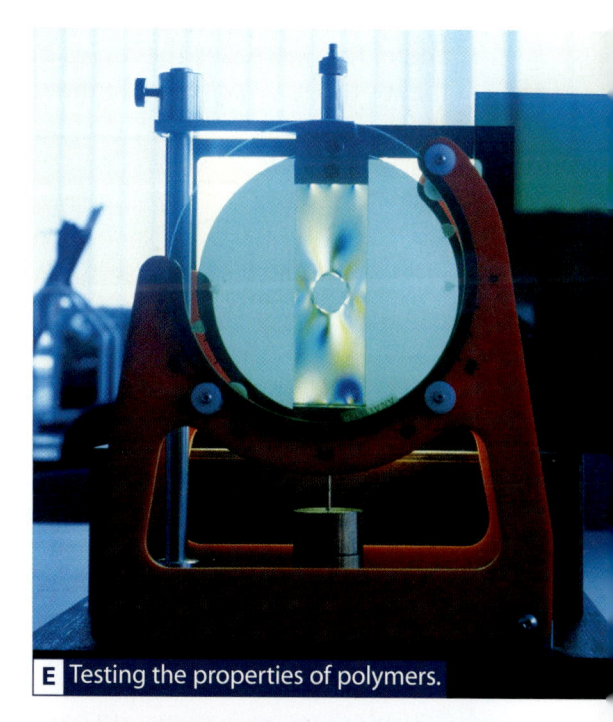

E Testing the properties of polymers.

Summary

Scientists think that there are _____ that attract molecules to each other. They think that these forces increase as the length of the molecules _____ and as they get _____ together. The strength of a _____ and its melting point depend on the forces between the _____.

| closer | forces | increases |
| molecules | polymer | |

129

C2.10 Changing polymers
How can the properties of polymers be modified?

Polymer scientists use the theory about forces between polymer molecules to predict how to change a polymer to alter its properties. They have produced many new and useful polymers. Their predictions were correct, showing that the theory is successful.

There are a number of ways that chemists can change the forces between polymer molecules.

- **Longer molecules:** Adding more and more small molecules onto the polymer increases the length of the chain. This increases the forces between the molecules and makes the melting point higher and the polymer stronger.

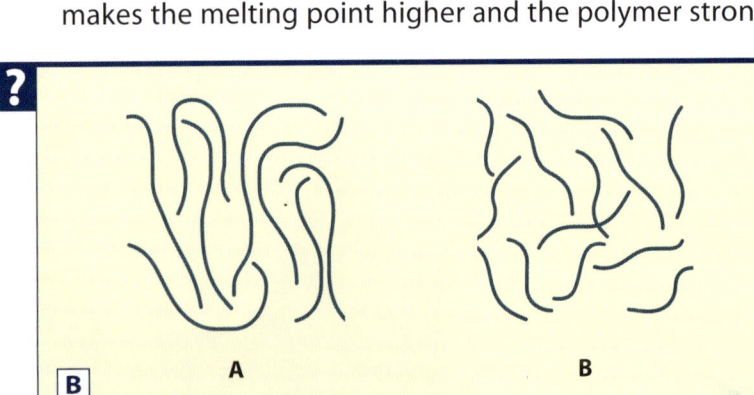

A Kevlar is a polymer used in fencing clothes. It has properties designed to protect the fencer's body.

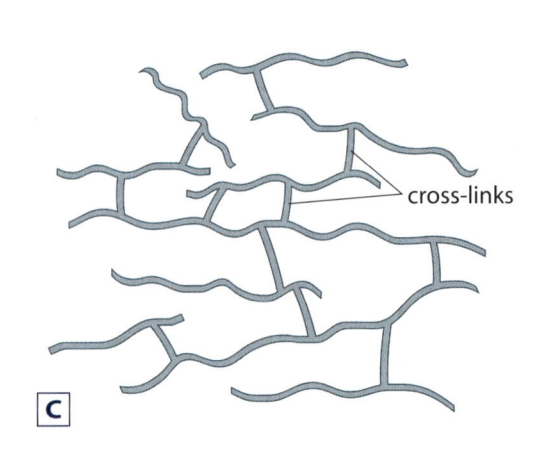

B

1. In diagram B, polymer A has molecules with about 10 000 atoms linked into a chain. Polymer B has a chain length of about 8000 atoms. Which polymer will:
   a be strongest
   b have the highest melting point?
   Explain your answers.

When polymers are made into fibres, the molecules are pulled into more regular arrangements. This increases the strength of the fibre.

2. Nylon fibres are stronger than a piece of moulded nylon. Explain why this is so.

- **Cross-linking:** Atoms in one polymer chain can be joined to atoms in another chain. The cross-links are very strong and make the polymer extremely tough and hardwearing.

3. Latex from rubber trees is a liquid. Latex is heated with sulfur to make tough solid rubber. What do you think the sulfur has done to make the rubber stronger?

C

- **Adding plasticiser:** Plasticisers are small molecules that can fit between the polymer molecules. These keep the polymer molecules apart and make the forces between the molecules weaker. A polymer with plasticiser is softer and more flexible than one without.

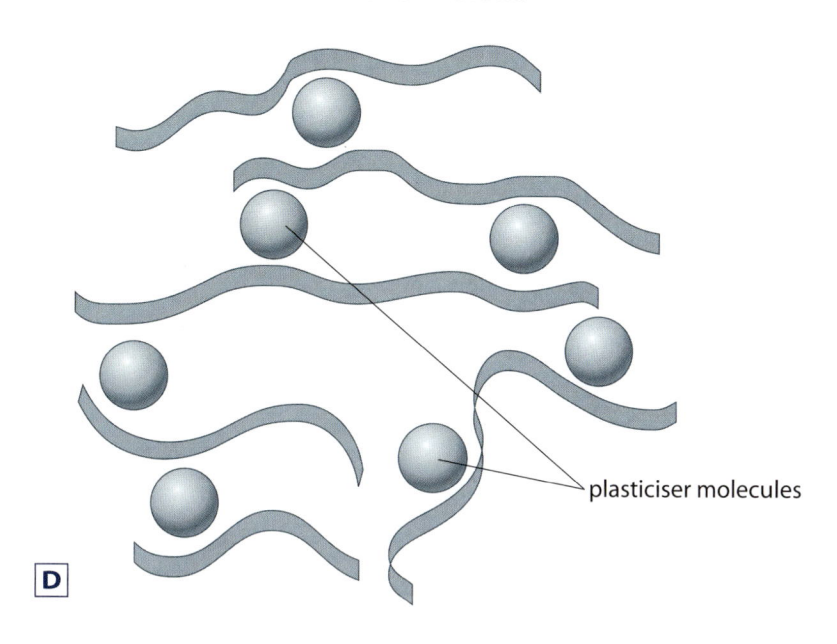

D plasticiser molecules

A How could you compare the properties of different polymers?

E

?
4 PVC used for window frames is stiff, hard and strong. PVC is also used to make waterproof coats.
   a What properties does the PVC need for a coat?
   b How can PVC be given these properties?

5 Scientists think the theory about forces between molecules in polymers is a successful theory. Give two reasons for this.

6 Which modifications would make a polymer suitable for making the body of an electric kettle? Explain your answer.

Summary

Scientists can _____ the structure of a _____ to change its properties. They can make the molecules _____ or they can join molecules together by _____. These modifications make the polymer _____. A plasticiser is a _____ molecule that separates the polymer _____ and makes the polymer _____ and more _____.

cross-links   flexible   longer
modify   molecules   polymer   small
softer   stronger

131

C2.11 Life cycle of a polymer
What is the life cycle of a polymer?

When you buy something new, you may think about the cost and you hope that the item will do the job you bought it for. You should also consider the whole **life cycle** of the product, which includes:
- the raw materials that are used to make it
- how much energy is needed
- how much waste is produced
- what happens to the packaging and the product itself when you have finished with it and want to throw it away.

Disposing of polymers

A

Even if we reuse things made of polymers they will eventually end up as waste. Natural materials will rot, but organisms cannot break down most synthetic polymers. They will last for centuries if we don't do something about them. There are three ways of disposing of waste.

- **Landfill:** Most polymer waste is simply dumped in the ground and covered with soil, but we are running out of places to do this. We could make new polymers that decompose, but this uses up resources that cannot be used again.

? 1 Disposable cups can be made from a synthetic polymer.
  a What is the raw material from which they are made?
  b What effect do you think obtaining these raw materials has on the environment?
  c The cups are transported all over the world. How could transporting the cups damage the environment?

? 2 Why can't we carry on throwing polymers into landfill sites?

- **Incineration:** Burning polymers gives out heat which could be used to generate electricity, but unless the burning is controlled carefully, poisonous gases could be given off.

B A waste incinerator.

132

- **Recycling:** Many polymers could be melted and reused, but they have to be sorted by hand before this can be done. Polymer products are stamped with a symbol which sorters can recognise, but it is still a slow job to sort them.

Local councils are responsible for collecting and disposing of waste. The government sets targets for the amount of waste to be recycled.

1 PET (polyethylene terephthalate) e.g. plastic bottles, meat packaging

2 HDPE (high density polyethylene) e.g. milk bottles, detergent bottles, oil bottles, toys, plastic bags

3 V (polyvinyl chloride) e.g. vegetable oil bottles, blister packaging

4 LDPE (low density polyethylene) e.g. plastic bags, shrink-wrap

5 PP (polypropylene) e.g. margarine containers, yoghurt containers

6 PS (polystyrene) e.g. egg cartons, fast food trays

7 OTHER (all other resins) e.g. multi-resin containers, microelectronic components

C Polymer recycling symbols.

E This post is made from recycled polymers.

? 5 a Draw up a table listing the advantages and disadvantages of each way of disposing of polymers.
  b Which method do you think should be used?
6 Synthetic polymers were invented by scientists.
  a What benefits have they provided?
  b What undesirable effects have they had?

? 3 Which method of disposing of polymers provides useful amounts of energy?
4 Polymers have to be sorted by hand. Suggest a reason why recycling companies find it difficult to make a profit recycling polymers.

D Polymers sorted for recycling.

Summary

Polymers have an effect on the _____ at every stage of their _____, including how they are disposed of. Polymer waste can be dumped in _____ sites, but these are becoming scarce. Polymers can be _____ in incinerators and the energy used to generate _____ but _____ gases may be produced. Polymers can also be _____ but sorting the many different types of polymer is _____.

burned electricity environment
expensive landfill life cycle
poisonous recycled

133

C2.12 Life Cycle Assessments

What is a Life Cycle Assessment?

A coffee machine gives you a cup of coffee in a plastic cup. You finish the drink and throw the cup away. A **Life Cycle Assessment** (LCA) of the cup would examine every stage in the manufacture and use of it and compare other materials that could be used.

?
1. How is energy used in refining crude oil?
2. Which of the following are sustainable resources? Explain your answer.
   crude oil, rubber trees, cotton plants, wool from sheep

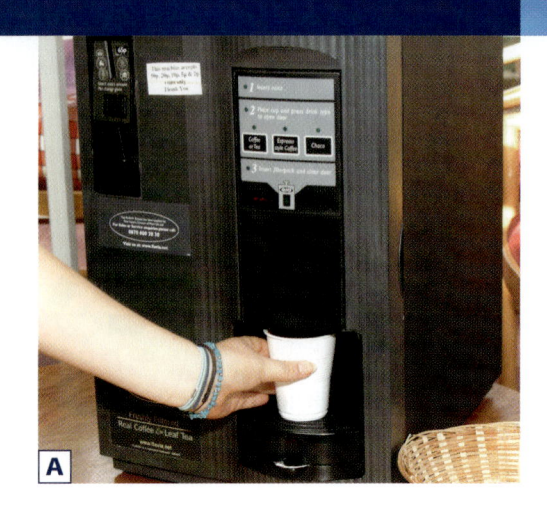

A

Using the product. Delivering the product and using it creates pollution and waste.

Disposing of the product.

Manufacturing the product. Factories replace natural habitats and produce waste.

Processing natural resources. Leaks of harmful materials can damage the environment. Transport produces air pollution and noise.

Sustainability. A sustainable resource can be replaced in a relatively short period of time and using it does not harm the environment.

Costs. The expenses of making the product and coping with the environmental problems that it causes.

Energy input. Energy is used at every stage in the life cycle of the product.

B A Life Cycle Assessment needs information about each stage in the life cycle of the product.

C

> **3** What harm could be done to the environment when crude oil is carried from an oil rig to a refinery by ship or pipeline?

Making decisions

An LCA helps us decide whether the benefits that some people get from using a material are greater or less than the costs of using it and dealing with the effects on the environment. The people who benefit may not be the same as those who are harmed by the effects.

Polymer scientists have developed many new materials with useful properties, but LCAs show that there are problems in using them. Scientists and engineers may not have solutions to these problems.

Some questions cannot be answered by scientists. An example is: 'Who should pay for disposing of waste polymers?' Questions like these must be answered by governments and citizens.

Some polymers can be used for a variety of purposes. For example, polystyrene is used for disposable cups, foam packaging, the trays in fridges and many other uses.

D What questions should we ask about these packaging materials?

> **4** Which of the following questions cannot be answered by scientists?
>   A How much energy is needed to make a polymer?
>   B How can we encourage people to recycle packaging materials?
>   C How does burning polymers change the environment?
>   Explain your answer.
>
> **5 a** Why should we recycle polymers?
>   **b** Why is large-scale recycling of polymers not economical at the present?
>
> **6** Why would it be an advantage if there was just one polymer to use?
>
> **7** Cotton and nylon are used for clothes.
>   **a** Write down the questions you need to ask to work out a LCA for cotton and nylon.
>   **b** Which material do you think causes the least harm during its life cycle? Explain your answer.

Summary

A _____ (LCA) examines the impact a product has on the _____ at every stage, from obtaining the _____ materials, manufacturing and using the product, to _____ of the waste. It also compares the _____ used at each stage in the life of the product. A _____ raw material is one where stocks can be renewed.

disposing energy environment
Life Cycle Assessment raw
sustainable

135

C2.13 A shopping trip
What's in the packaging?

Ragiv and Alex have been shopping in their local supermarket. They noticed that various materials were used as containers for the things that they bought.

Ragiv and Alex's shopping included a can of baked beans, a jar of peanut butter and a plastic bottle of toilet cleaner.

A

1 a Ragiv accidentally dropped the shopping basket. Choose a word from the following list to complete the sentences.

   tough   malleable   stiff   soft   brittle

   • The baked bean can was dented because metal is _____.
   • The jar of peanut butter broke because glass is _____.

   b Alex thought that the jar of peanut butter was heavy because it was made of glass. She decided to find out the density of the glass when all the peanut butter was removed. What quantities must Alex measure to work out the density?

Ragiv and Alex have found out that the supermarket is offering paper bags as well as polythene bags for packing goods. They wonder which is best to use. Help them by answering the following questions.

B

Ragiv wants to know which type of bag is the strongest. He tests five paper bags and five polythene bags. He hangs each bag from a hook and adds apples until the handles break. He records the number of apples in the bag when the handles break.

Bag	Number of apples in each bag				
	1	2	3	4	5
paper	17	18	17	17	16
polythene	20	16	21	19	20

C

2 Why did Ragiv test five bags of each material?

3 Ragiv noticed that the handles of the polythene bag stretched when he put the apples in it and that they stayed stretched when he took the apples out. Which word from the list below best describes this property of the material?

   plastic   elastic   strong   malleable   durable

4 Which measurement was probably an outlier? State the material and number of the bag and explain your answer.

Ragiv worked out the best estimate for the strength of the paper bag by calculating the mean. First he added up all the apples used in the paper bags.

$$\text{mean} = \frac{\text{total number of apples}}{\text{number of bags}}$$

$$= \frac{85}{5}$$

$$= 17$$

5 Calculate the best estimate for the polythene bag.

6 Which was the strongest material? Explain your answer.

Alex knows that the raw material for making the polythene is crude oil. She has some questions about how the polythene is made.

7 Crude oil is a mixture of hydrocarbon molecules. What are hydrocarbons?

8 a Table D gives some data on hydrocarbons found in crude oil. How is the boiling point linked to the size of the molecules?

Hydrocarbon	Boiling point (°C)	Number of carbon atoms in a molecule of the hydrocarbon
pentane	36	5
octane	126	8
dodecane	216	12

D

  b What state would the pentane be in at 100 °C?

9 The hydrocarbons in crude oil are separated by factional distillation. Put the letters of the sentences below in the correct order to show how crude oil is refined.
  A: When a hydrocarbon reaches its boiling point it condenses.
  B: The gases rise and cool.
  C: Crude oil is heated to form a gas.
  D: The liquids are piped away from the trays.
  E: Liquid hydrocarbons collect in trays at different heights in the column.
  F: The crude oil gas passes into the fractionating column.

10 Only a small part of the crude oil is used to make chemicals such as polymers. What are most of the hydrocarbons in crude oil used for?

Ragiv has discovered that ethene is the monomer used to make polythene.

11 What is a monomer?

12 What is the name of the process which turns ethene into a polythene?

13 The polythene used in plastic bags is very flexible but not very hardwearing. Which polymer in diagram E shows the arrangement of the polymer molecules in the plastic bags? Explain your answer.

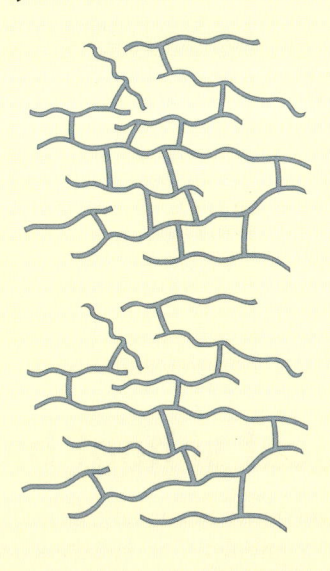

E

14 There is another type of polythene which has longer molecules than the polymer used in plastic bags. This other type of polythene is stronger. Why do longer molecules make the polythene stronger?

Alex knows that paper is made from wood from chopped down trees and polythene is made from substances found in crude oil.

15 Which of the bags is made from a sustainable resource? Explain your answer.

16 Give one way that the environment can be harmed by:
  a obtaining wood to make paper
  b collecting crude oil.

17 The carrier bags will probably end up in a landfill site. What will happen to:
  a the paper bags
  b the polythene bags?

18 Ragiv and Alex used the answers to all the questions they had asked to write out a Life Cycle Assessment (LCA) on the bags.
  a What does an LCA show?
  b What can an LCA be used for?

P2.1 Radiation and life

Is radiation useful or harmful?

This summer choose
SLOWTAN
Sun Cream

Why burn when you can tan?

Slowtan sun cream helps protect against the harmful effects of ultraviolet radiation. Using Slowtan lets you stay in the sun longer without burning.

A *Over exposure to ultraviolet radiation may cause skin cancer*

Local school bans mobile phones

Dangerfields Secondary School has banned students from carrying mobile phones. The Headteacher said, "We don't really know yet if there are risks from the microwave radiation that these phones give out. I have a duty to protect all students at the school – how could I forgive myself if in ten years time mobile phones were found to be unsafe and I had allowed innocent children to be exposed to this radiation?"

B

This week's Poll
Is Dangerfields right to ban mobile phones? Vote by telephoning the numbers below

Yes: 01234 8912
No: 01234 89

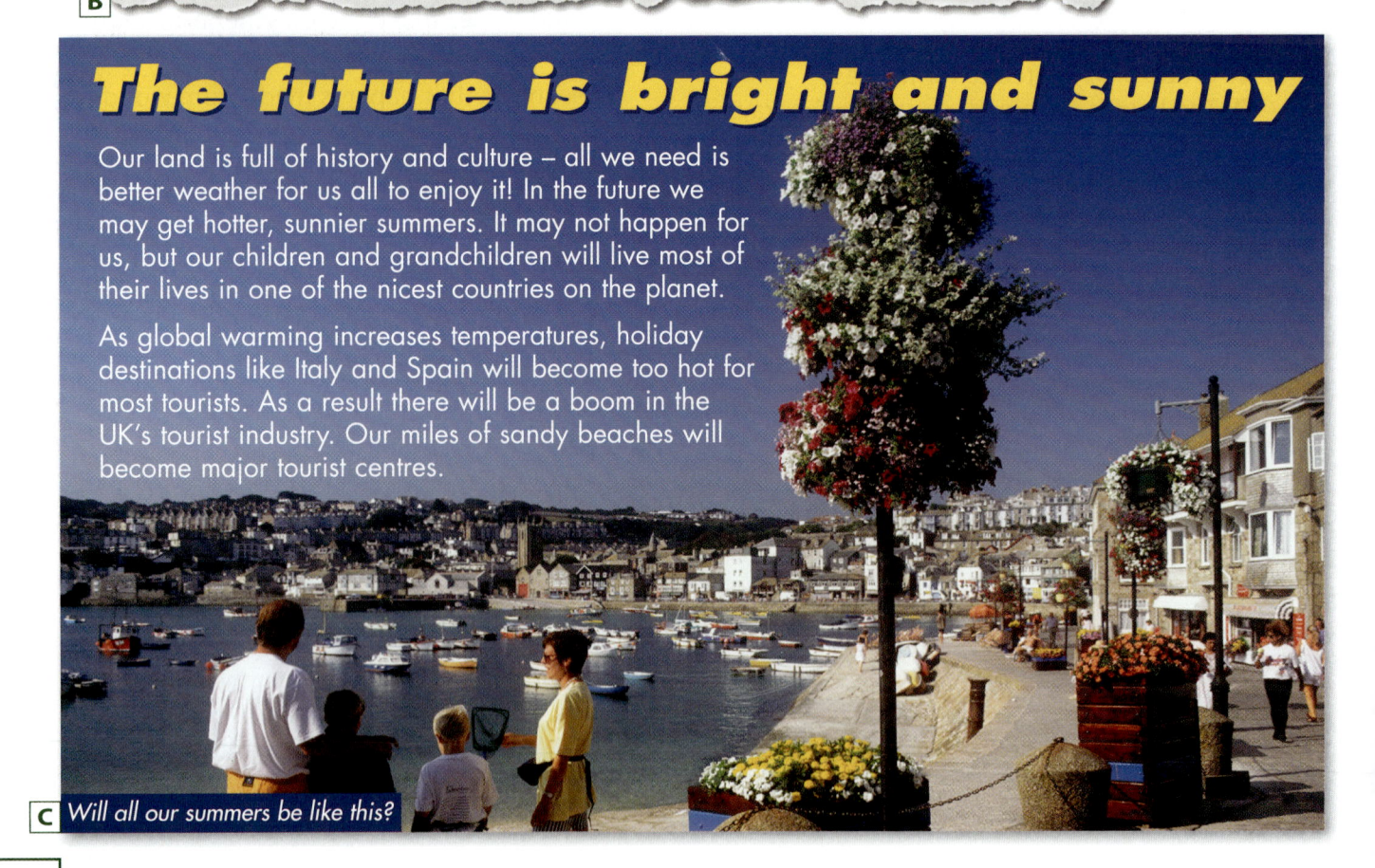

The future is bright and sunny

Our land is full of history and culture – all we need is better weather for us all to enjoy it! In the future we may get hotter, sunnier summers. It may not happen for us, but our children and grandchildren will live most of their lives in one of the nicest countries on the planet.

As global warming increases temperatures, holiday destinations like Italy and Spain will become too hot for most tourists. As a result there will be a boom in the UK's tourist industry. Our miles of sandy beaches will become major tourist centres.

C *Will all our summers be like this?*

The United Kingdom is as far north as countries like Canada and Russia but our winters are nowhere near as cold as theirs. This is partly because of the Gulf Stream, which is a current of warm water in the Atlantic Ocean. Heat energy from the Gulf Stream helps to keep the UK warm.

Global warming and the big freeze

Global warming is melting the ice caps. This could stop the Gulf Stream flowing, so the UK will not be warmed by it. Global warming could lead to a big freeze! Temperatures could regularly fall to −20 °C or even colder, and the sea around our coastline will freeze during winter.

1 a How can you protect yourself from sunburn?
       (*Hint:* there are several ways.)
    b Why do you need to do this?

2 a Do you think mobile phones should be banned in schools?
    b Give two reasons for your answer.
    c Write a list of the things you would need to find out to give a better answer to this question.

3 What causes global warming?

4 a Should we try to stop global warming getting worse?
    b How could we do this?
    c Write a list of the things you need to find out to give a better answer to this question.

5 The two magazine articles predict opposite effects from global warming. Why do you think this is?

P2.2 The electromagnetic spectrum

What types of radiation are there?

A A rainbow shows the colours of the visible spectrum – red, orange, yellow, green, blue, indigo and violet.

Visible light is **electromagnetic radiation** that we can see. Electromagnetic radiation delivers energy in 'packets' called **photons**. The photons of different colours of light deliver different amounts of energy.

Visible light is **emitted** (given out) by **sources** such as light bulbs and candle flames. The light travels from the source to our eyes. Our eyes act as **detectors**.

? 1 List the colours of the visible spectrum in order, starting with the one with the lowest energy photons.

B

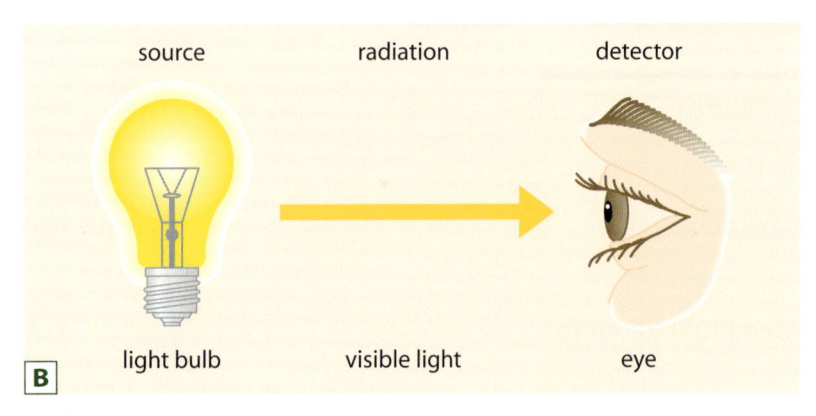

The visible spectrum is part of the **electromagnetic spectrum**. Table C shows the different kinds of radiation that make up the electromagnetic spectrum.

	Type of Radiation	Notes
lowest energy photons	**radio waves**	• emitted by radio and TV transmitters • used to send radio and TV programmes • detected by aerials and radios/TVs
	microwaves	• emitted by radio transmitters, mobile phones and microwave cookers • used to carry information and to cook food • can damage living tissue by heating the water in it • detected by aerials and radios/mobile phones
	infrared (IR)	• emitted by warm and hot objects, and by TV remote controls or car locks • detected by skin and thermometers • too much infrared can burn the skin
	visible	• emitted by hot objects • detected by eyes and photographic film
	ultraviolet (UV)	• emitted from very hot objects including the Sun • causes human skin to tan but can also cause skin cancer • detected by photographic film
	X-rays	• go through flesh but not bone • used to look at bones inside the body • can cause cancer • detected by photographic film
highest energy photons	**gamma rays**	• emitted from radioactive substances • used to sterilise medical instruments • can penetrate deep inside the body • can cause cancer

C

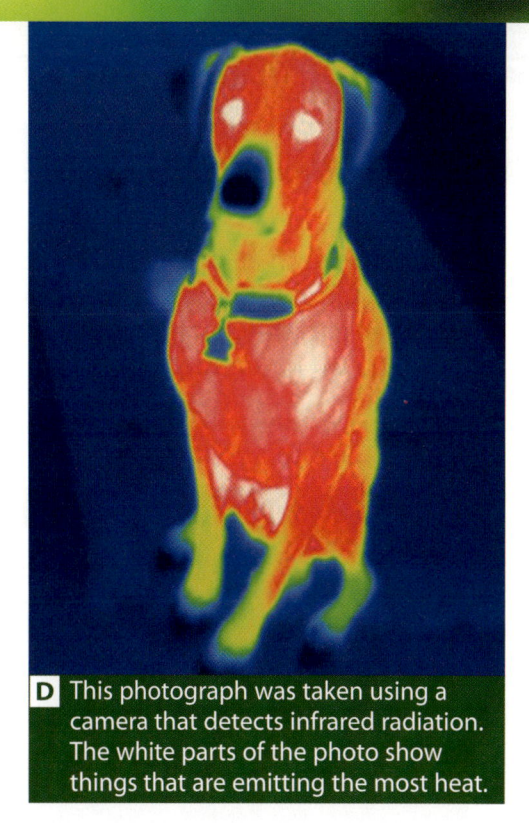

D This photograph was taken using a camera that detects infrared radiation. The white parts of the photo show things that are emitting the most heat.

?

2 List the different types of electromagnetic radiation in order, starting with the one with the highest energy photons.

3 Write down three types of radiation that can:
 a be detected by photographic film
 b cause cancer.

4 Look at diagram B. Draw similar labelled diagrams to show the following situations:
 a You can feel the warmth of the Sun.
 b A picture is sent from a mast to your TV set.

5 Which is the odd one out: microwaves, infrared, ultraviolet? Explain your answers.

6 Draw diagrams similar to diagram B to show:
 a a photo of a flower taken in ultraviolet light
 b X-rays being used to find a broken bone.

Summary

Visible _____ is part of a family of _____ radiations. Gamma rays have the _____ energy photons and radio waves have the _____ energy photons. Electromagnetic _____ is emitted by different _____, and can be detected in different ways. Eyes and _____ film can detect _____ light.

electromagnetic   highest   light
lowest   photographic   radiation
sources   visible

141

P2.3 Heating with radiation
What happens when radiation hits an object?

The particles in all objects vibrate slightly and emit infrared radiation. The hotter an object, the faster the vibration of its particles and the more infrared radiation it emits. We can feel infrared radiation, but we cannot see it.

The Sun produces most of the electromagnetic radiation we are exposed to.

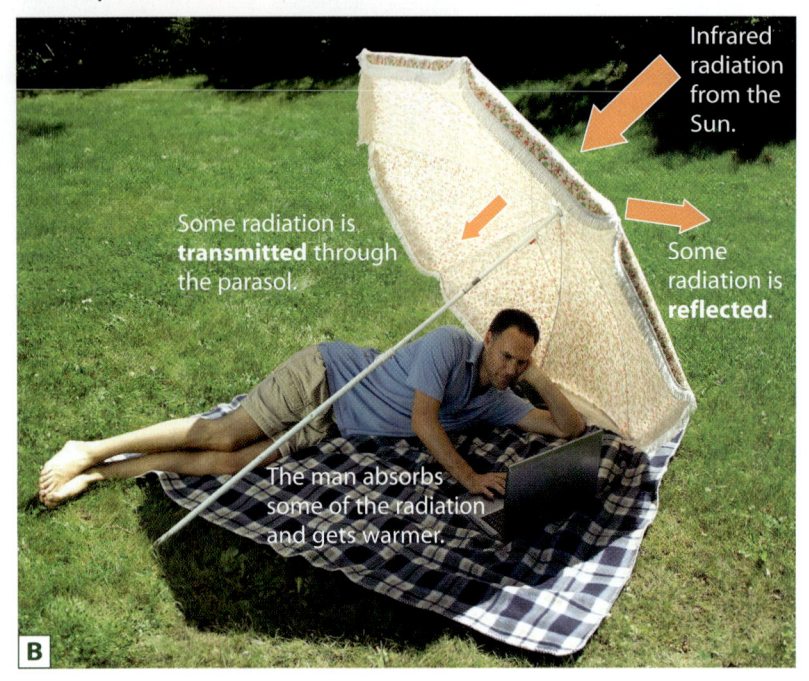

A If an object is hot enough, it also gives out visible light.

B Infrared radiation from the Sun. Some radiation is **transmitted** through the parasol. Some radiation is **reflected**. The man absorbs some of the radiation and gets warmer.

The amount of heating depends on the **intensity** of the radiation. Hot objects give off more intense radiation than cool ones.

The intensity is the amount of energy that reaches a certain area every second. The intensity depends on how many photons are absorbed each second, and how much energy each photon delivers.

A How can you find out if different colours absorb different amounts of radiation?
- What will you use as an infrared source?
- What will you use as a detector?
- How will you make your test fair?

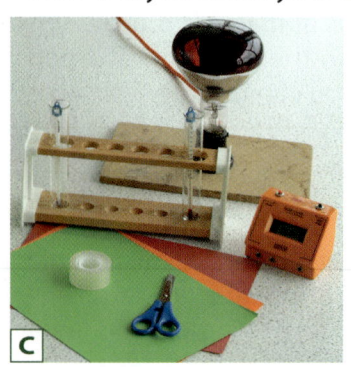

C

?
1. Look at photo B. If you covered the parasol with silver foil, how would this change:
   a the amount of radiation reflected by the parasol
   b the intensity of the radiation hitting the man
   c how warm he feels?
2. Explain your answers to question **1**, using ideas about photons and energy.
3. a Which produces the most intense infrared radiation: a candle flame or a bonfire?
   b Explain how you worked out your answer.

142

Cooking with radiation

Food can be cooked using infrared or microwave radiation. A grill emits infrared radiation, which is absorbed by the food. Microwaves can be used to cook moist food because water molecules in the food absorb the microwaves. The energy carried by the microwaves is converted to heat energy.

Microwaves can be harmful to the human body, which contains a lot of water. Microwaves are reflected by metal but they can pass through glass, so microwave ovens have a metal case and a metal screen on the door. The holes in the metal screen are too small for the microwaves to pass through. Visible light can go in and out through the holes to let you see the food inside.

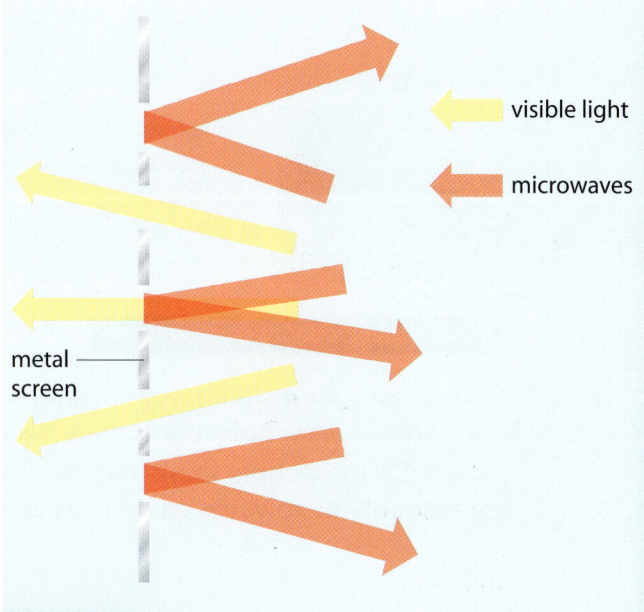

D Using infrared radiation to cook food.

E The screen on a microwave oven door protects us from harm by the microwaves.

?
4 Which kind of radiation cooks food:
   a under a grill
   b in a microwave oven?

5 Why does food cook faster under a hotter grill?

6 Explain why microwaves can be harmful to the human body.

7 Danny took the metal screen off the door of his microwave oven so he could get a better view of the food. Write a letter to him explaining why it he must put the screen back.

Summary

When infrared photons strike an object they will either be _____, absorbed or pass straight _____. Radiation _____ by objects makes them _____. Microwaves are _____ by objects containing _____, so they are useful for _____ food.

| absorbed | cooking | hotter |
| reflected | through | water |

143

P2.4 Mobile phones and microwaves

Should people use mobile phones?

Whenever a mobile phone is switched on it will be sending out and receiving microwave signals from the network. This is so the network knows where the phone is and can make it ring if the phone's number is dialled.

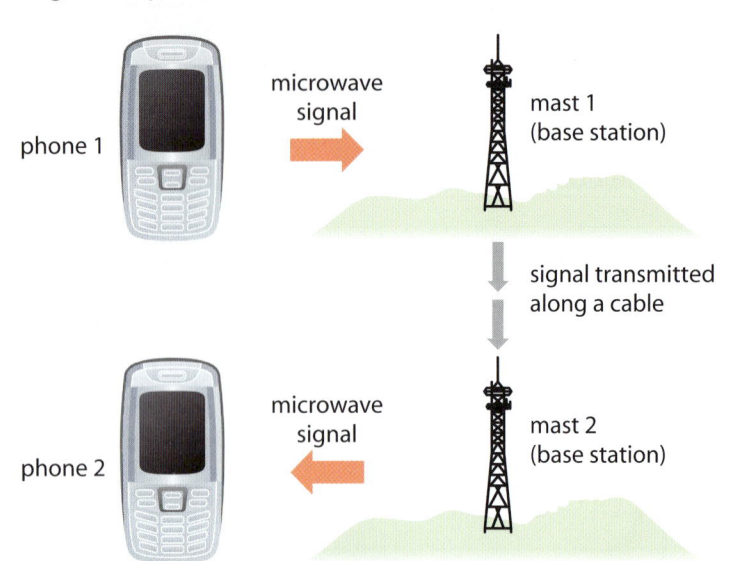

B How mobile phones communicate.

The microwaves used for mobile phones have photon energies between radio waves and the microwaves used for cooking. Some people think that there may be a health risk because the microwaves could heat up living tissue.

C Microwave radiation spreads out from the mast. The intensity of the radiation decreases the further you are from the mast.

1 Why is a signal sent and received all the time, even when you are not talking on the phone?

2 Why might you be at more risk from microwave radiation if you live close to a mast, compared to someone who lives further away?

Some scientists believe that the microwaves from mobile phone networks can damage parts of the body. Other scientists argue that the microwaves used are not powerful enough for this to happen. Some research shows that mobile phone users are twice as likely to develop cancers in areas of the brain close to the ear, but there is not enough evidence to say this is definitely linked to using mobile phones.

Children may be more at risk because their brains are still developing, and their skulls are thinner. Some people think it is 'better to be safe than sorry', and only allow children to use mobile phones in an emergency.

A Do you agree with these statements? Discuss reasons for and against each statement.

Mobile phones should be made illegal until we definitely know they are safe to use.

If you ban mobile phones you should ban cars.

D

?
3 Why might children be at more risk than adults from mobile phones?

4 Suggest one reason why scientists are not sure that mobile phones are responsible for cancers near the ears.

5 Explain why scientists may have more evidence about the dangers of using mobile phones in another 50 years time.

6 Write a letter to your local council explaining why a new mobile phone mast should not be put on top of one of your school buildings.

Summary

Mobile phones emit _____ radiation when they are _____ on. Using a _____ phone may be a health _____ but there is not enough scientific evidence to _____ this.

| microwave | mobile | prove | risk |
| switched |

145

P2.5 Ionising radiation

How does ionising radiation damage the human body?

Gamma rays, X-rays and ultraviolet light are forms of **ionising radiation**. They have enough energy to change atoms into charged particles called **ions**. Ionising radiation can damage human cells and may lead to cancer. The more ionising radiation a person is exposed to, the higher their chances of getting cancer.

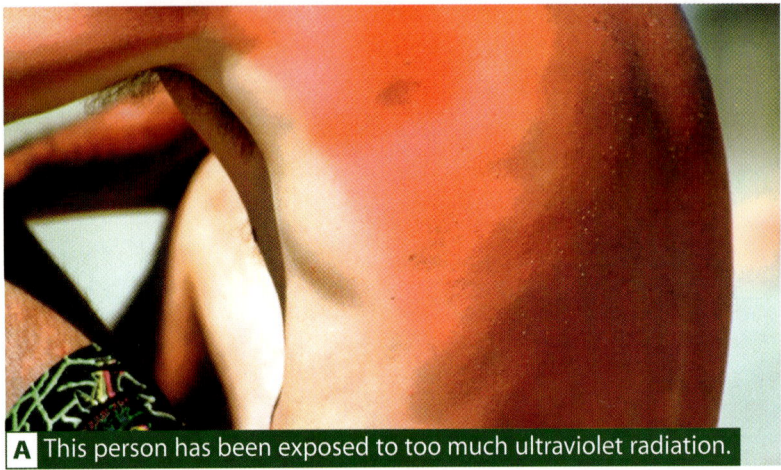

A This person has been exposed to too much ultraviolet radiation.

1 a Which forms of radiation can ionise atoms?
b What harm can ionising radiation cause to living things?

2 Which kind of ionising radiation are you exposed to most often? Explain your answer.

X-rays

X-rays are used in hospitals to scan for broken bones and look at teeth because the benefits of using X-rays for these purposes are greater than the possible risk of cancer. However, hospital workers need to reduce the risks as far as possible. They only use enough X-ray radiation to get a good picture, and only take X-ray pictures when absolutely necessary. They usually leave the room while the X-ray is being taken.

3 Which of these people should have an X-ray photograph taken? Explain your answers.
A Mrs Singh thinks her baby may have swallowed a pin.
B Danny wants to see what his bones look like.
C Sue's wrist hurts after being hit with a hockey stick.

4 Why do you think hospital workers leave the room while an X-ray is being taken?

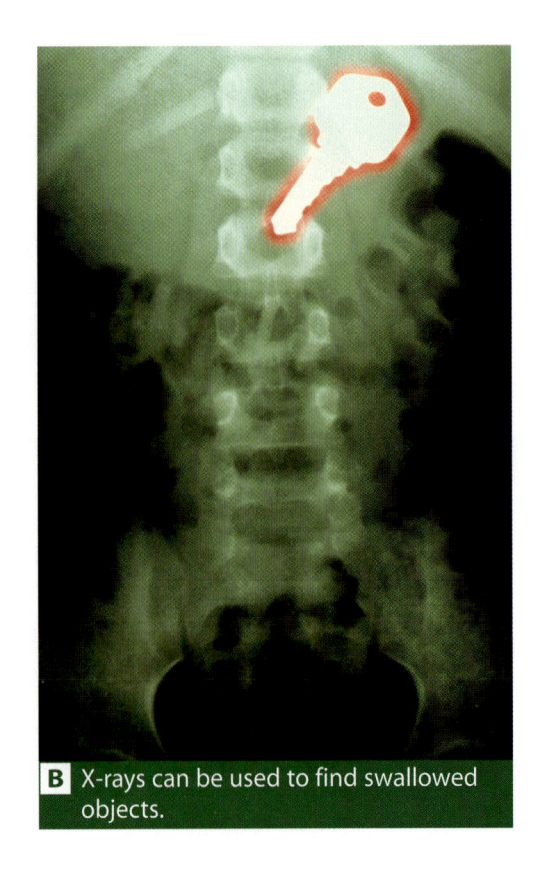

B X-rays can be used to find swallowed objects.

Ultraviolet radiation from the Sun

You cannot see or feel ultraviolet radiation, so by the time you realise you have been sunburnt, it is too late and your skin has already been damaged. If your skin is repeatedly damaged by ultraviolet radiation, you may get skin cancer.

It is quite easy to protect yourself from the harmful effects of ultraviolet radiation.

You can:
- stay in the shade, particularly in the middle of the day
- wear clothes, which will either reflect or absorb the ultraviolet radiation before it reaches your skin
- use a sunscreen, which absorbs ultraviolet radiation.

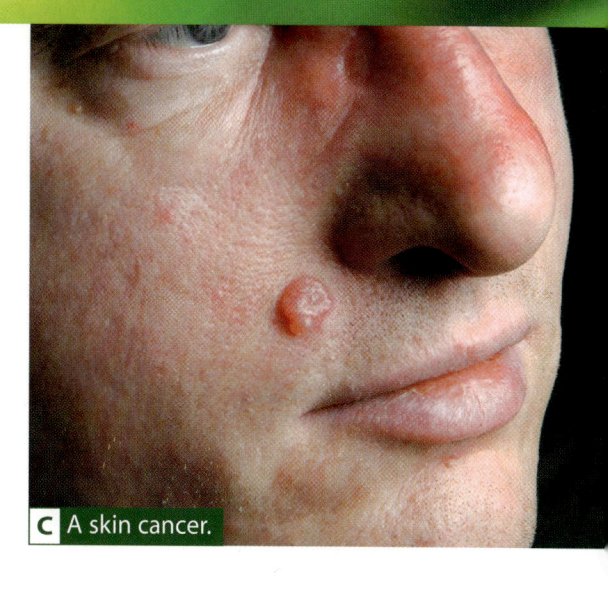

C A skin cancer.

? 5 Drawing D shows the Tanner family on their summer holiday.

D

a List the Tanner family in order of their risk of sunburn, starting with the person at most risk.
b Explain your answer to part **a**.

6 If you lived in a sunny country:
   a which area of your skin would be at most risk of skin cancer
   b what steps could you take to protect yourself?

7 Think of a plus, a minus and an interesting point about this statement: People should never sunbathe.

8 Look at drawing D. Explain why Marie could get sunburnt even though she is sitting in the shade.

Summary

There are three type of ionising radiation, _____ rays, X-rays and _____. They can damage human _____ and can lead to _____. Ultraviolet _____ comes from the Sun and can cause _____ or skin cancer. People can protect themselves by staying in the _____, wearing _____ or putting on _____.

| cancer cells clothes gamma |
| radiation shade sunburn |
| sunscreen ultraviolet |

P2.6 The ozone layer

How does the ozone layer protect us from radiation?

A Ozone at ground level contributes to pollution in cities, and can damage living tissue.

The atmosphere that surrounds the Earth is very thin compared to the size of the Earth. It contains the oxygen molecules that we need to breathe. These molecules contain two atoms of oxygen bonded together. **Ozone** is a form of oxygen with three atoms.

Most ozone is found in the **ozone layer**, between 25 and 30 kilometres above ground level. It is not a solid layer, but just a part of the atmosphere where ozone molecules are more concentrated.

? 1 Why is ozone a problem at ground level?

The atmosphere lets heat and light from the Sun pass through it. However, ozone high up in the atmosphere protects us from the harmful effects of ultraviolet radiation. This layer of ozone absorbs most of the ultraviolet radiation from the Sun so that it does not reach the Earth's surface.

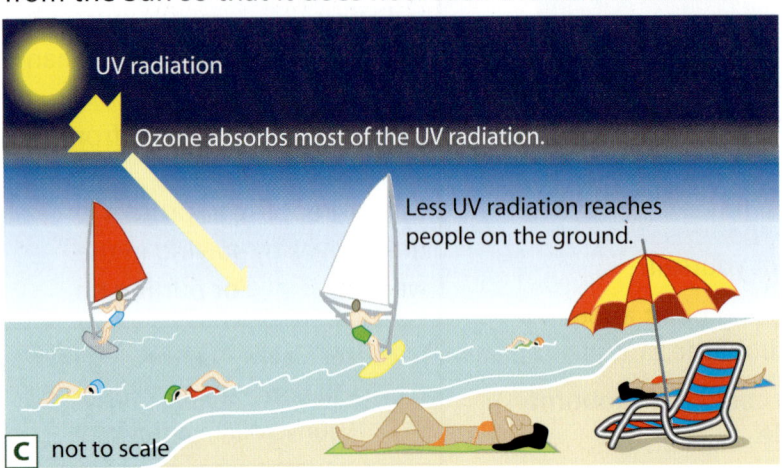

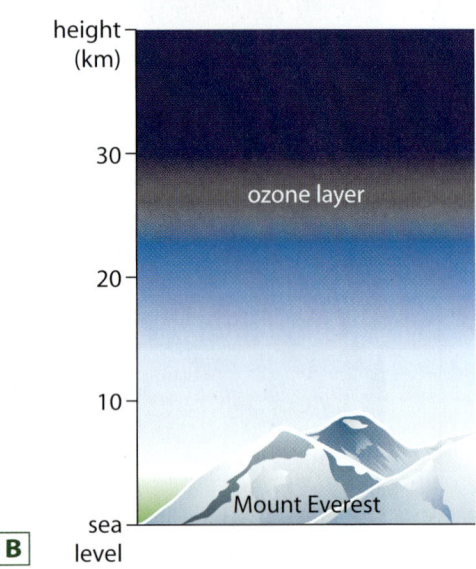

B

UV radiation
Ozone absorbs most of the UV radiation.
Less UV radiation reaches people on the ground.

C not to scale

? 2 What could happen if there was no ozone layer? Explain your answer.

148

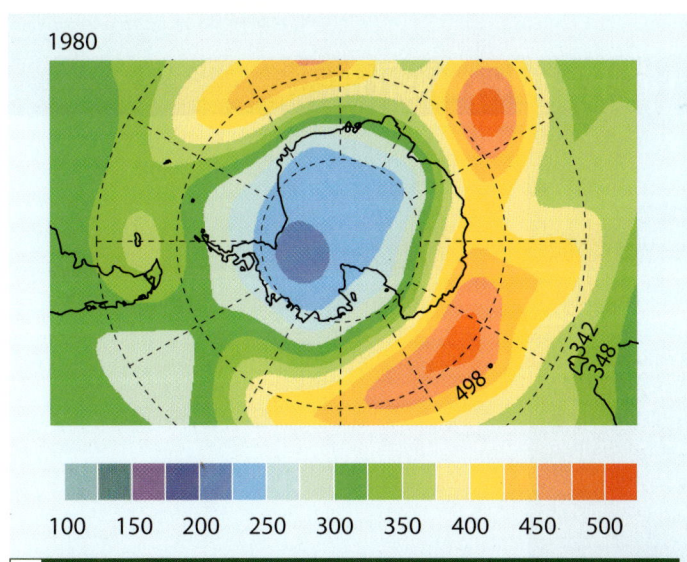

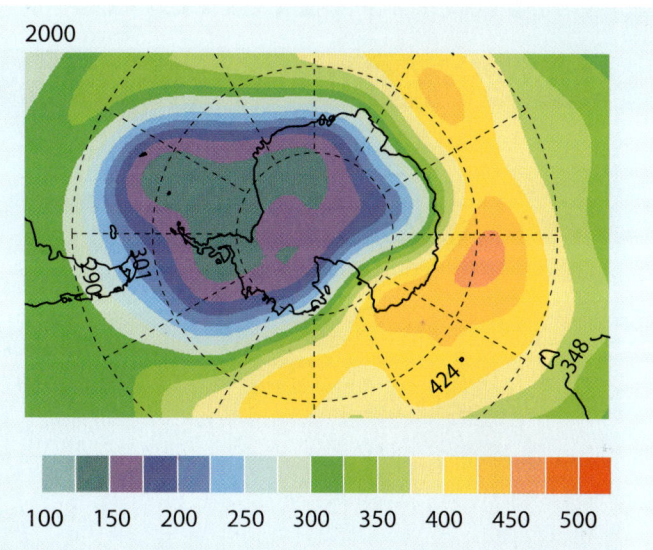

D These maps show the amount of ozone in 1980 and 2000.

The amount of ozone in the atmosphere changes with the seasons. However, in the 1970s scientists discovered that the amount of ozone over the Antarctic each spring was getting less. This decrease in the amount of ozone is sometimes called a 'hole' in the ozone layer. The amount of ozone over the rest of the world has also decreased, but not as much.

When the hole in the ozone layer was first discovered, there was a public health campaign in Australia to try to cut down the amount of ultraviolet radiation that people received. Diagram E shows a poster from this campaign.

?
3 The risk of skin cancer is higher in Australia than it is in the UK. Think of as many reasons for this as you can.

4 Explain how following the 'slip, slop, slap' advice will make you less likely to get skin cancer.

Chlorofluorocarbons (CFCs) are gases that were used in aerosol sprays, in refrigerators, and in foam packaging. Scientists think that the ozone hole is caused by these gases being released into the atmosphere. The gases react with ozone and turn it into oxygen. In 1987 there was an international agreement called the Montreal Protocol, which set out how countries around the world would cut down on the production of CFC gases. This should eventually allow the ozone layer to recover.

?
5 Why are CFC gases no longer used to make refrigerators?

6 Suggest how scientists may have found out that CFCs were responsible for the ozone 'hole'.

SLIP on a shirt
SLOP on the suncream
SLAP on a hat

E

Summary

Ozone in the _____ absorbs a lot of _____ radiation and stops it reaching the _____. Most of the _____ is found in the ozone _____, high up in the atmosphere. Gases called _____ in the atmosphere change ozone into _____, and so allow more _____ radiation through.

atmosphere CFCs Earth layer
oxygen ozone ultraviolet

P2.7 Photosynthesis

How does radiation make life on Earth possible?

A The Sun provides energy so crops can grow.

The Earth would be a very dark and cold place without the Sun. Radiation from the Sun passes through the atmosphere and provides the heat and light energy that most plants and animals need to survive.

Plants use visible light from the Sun to supply the energy for **photosynthesis**. A green pigment in the leaves called **chlorophyll** absorbs light energy from the Sun.

The plant uses the carbon dioxide, water and energy to make sugar and oxygen. The oxygen is released into the atmosphere and the sugar is used for energy or converted to starch and stored by the plant for use later.

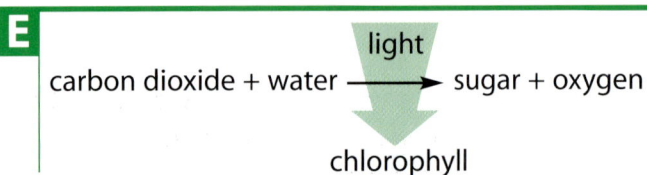

E

$$\text{carbon dioxide} + \text{water} \xrightarrow[\text{chlorophyll}]{\text{light}} \text{sugar} + \text{oxygen}$$

B

?
1. **a** Name four things that a plant needs for photosynthesis.
   b What does a plant make in photosynthesis?
2. Josie puts one plant in a sunny spot, and puts a similar plant in a dark corner.
   a Which one would produce the most oxygen?
   b Explain your answer.

Animals and plants use oxygen from the air for **respiration**. Respiration releases energy from food that is needed by the organism for growth, repair and movement.

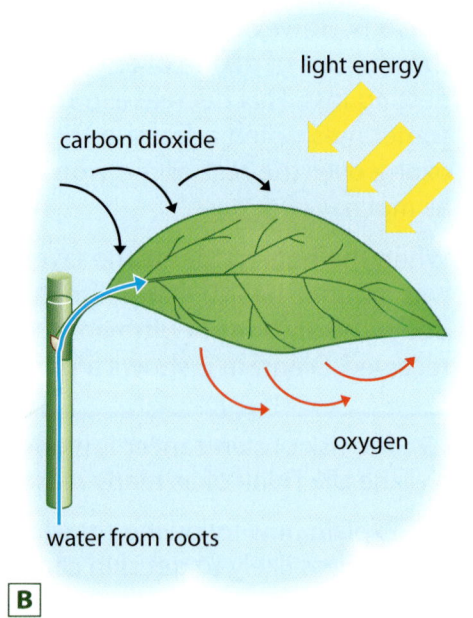

E sugar + oxygen ⟶ carbon dioxide + water (+ energy)

Respiration uses oxygen and releases carbon dioxide as a waste product. Plants recycle this carbon dioxide back into the sugars and oxygen that all organisms need for respiration.

The amounts of oxygen and carbon dioxide in the atmosphere depend on how much respiration and photosynthesis is taking place.

? 3 a How do living things add carbon dioxide to the atmosphere?
  b How is carbon dioxide removed from the atmosphere?

Plants will be very important if humans ever live in space for long periods. Diagram C shows a dome that people might live in on the Moon.

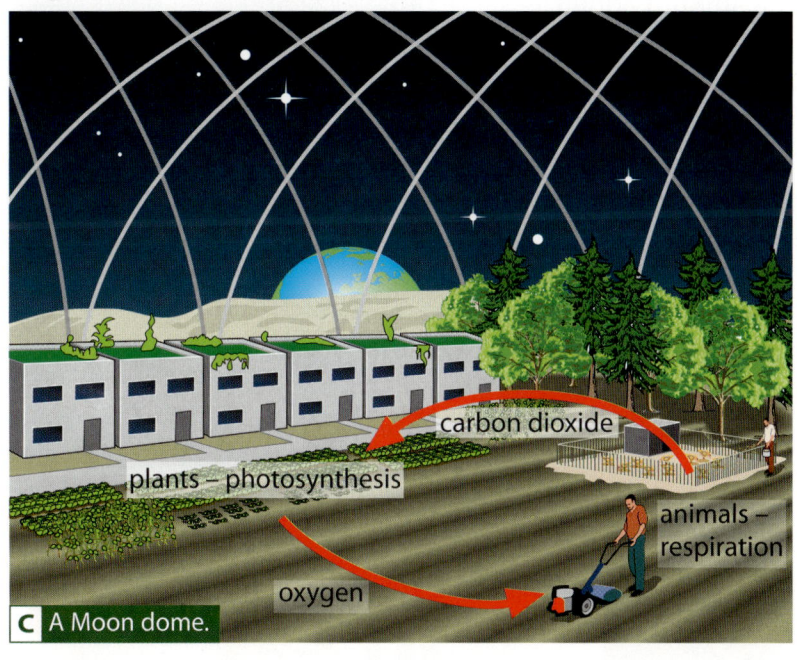

C A Moon dome.

? 4 Look at diagram C.
  a Why are plants needed in the dome?
  b Why should the dome be made of glass or clear plastic?
  c If the dome had to be made of metal, what would the people need to do to make the plants grow?

5 If the people used half the plants for food without replacing them, what would happen to:
  a the amount of oxygen in the air
  b the amount of carbon dioxide in the air?

6 Explain your answers to question **5**.

7 The amount of carbon dioxide in the air in the UK is slightly less during the summer than it is during the winter. Explain why this happens.

Summary

Plants need _____ energy from the Sun for _____. The word _____ for this process is:

carbon _____ + water ⟶ _____ + oxygen.

Animals take in _____ for _____ and produce _____ dioxide. The _____ of oxygen and carbon dioxide in the air depend on how fast _____ and _____ are happening.

amounts carbon dioxide
equation light oxygen
photosynthesis respiration sugar

P2.8 The carbon cycle

How is the amount of carbon dioxide in the atmosphere changing?

Carbon dioxide is removed from the atmosphere by photosynthesis. It is added to the atmosphere by:
- respiration of plants, animals, and **decomposers**
- burning **fuels**.

? 1 Name two ways in which carbon dioxide is put into the atmosphere.

The movement of carbon is called the **carbon cycle**.

The amount of carbon dioxide in the atmosphere remained about the same for thousands of years. The amount added to the atmosphere was balanced by the amount taken out.

A Decomposers eat dead animals and plants.

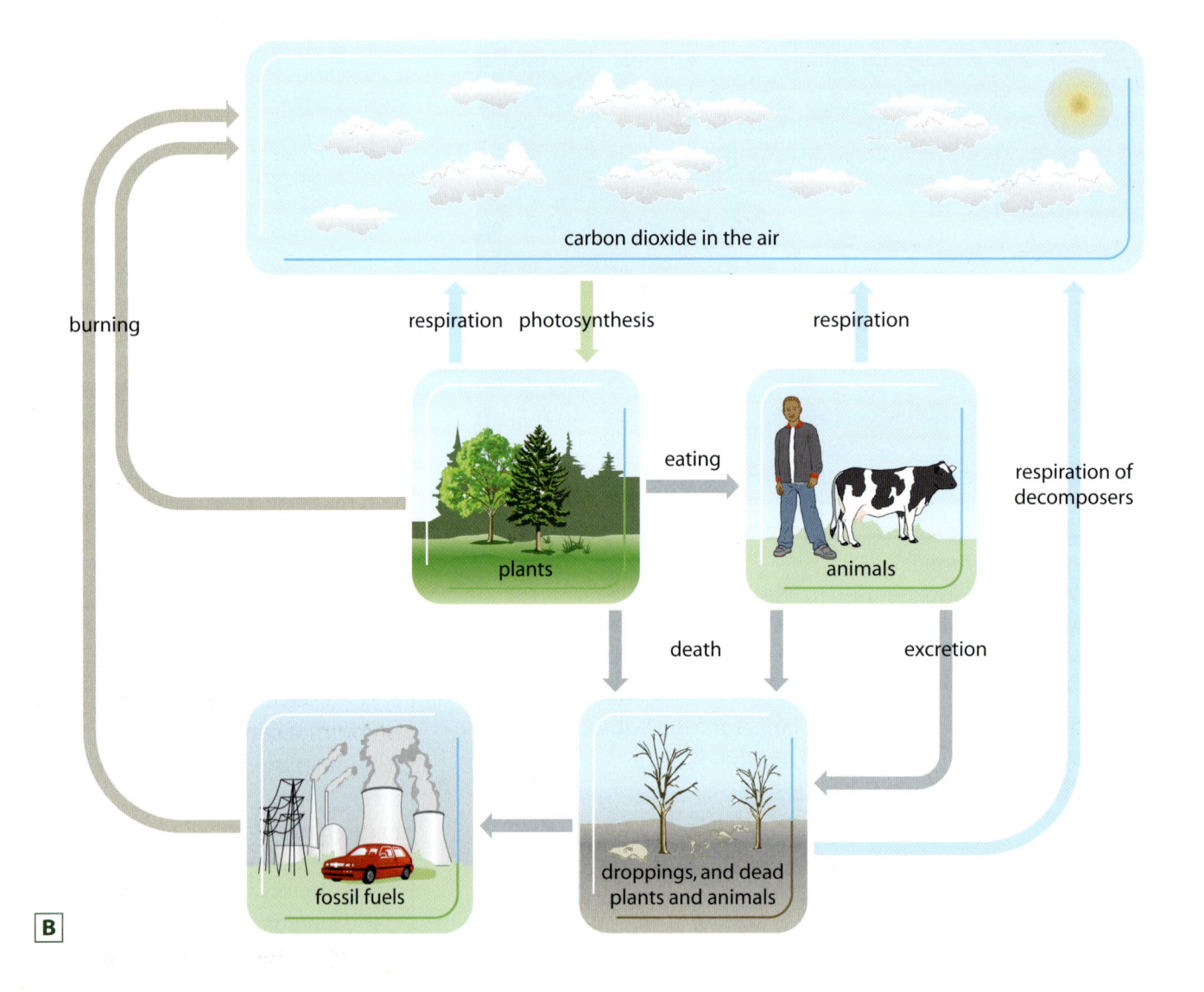

B

Graph D shows how the amount of carbon dioxide in the air has changed over the last 250 years. The increase is mostly due to humans:
- burning increasing amounts of fossil fuels to make electricity, for transport, and for heating and cooking
- burning forests to clear land.

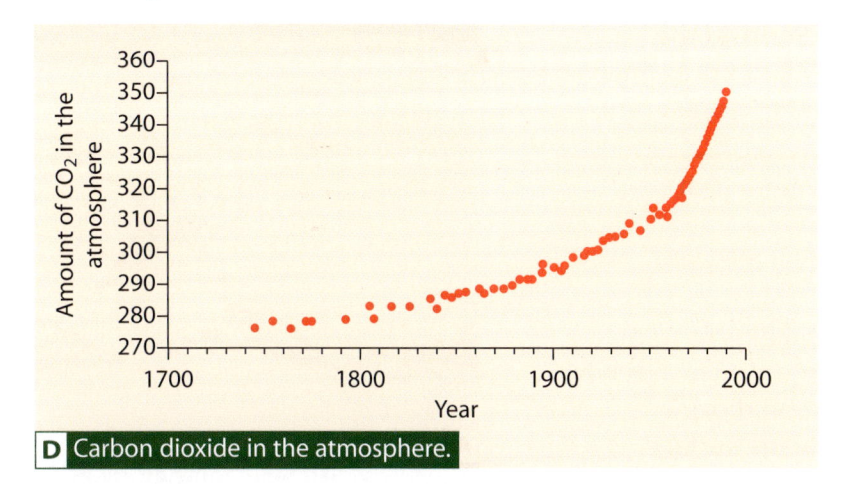

D Carbon dioxide in the atmosphere.

C The wood on this bonfire contains carbon which the tree removed from the atmosphere during photosynthesis. Burning the wood returns the carbon to the atmosphere as carbon dioxide.

Fossil fuels are made from the remains of plants and animals that lived millions of years ago. The carbon in them was originally taken out of the atmosphere over thousands and thousands of years while the plants and animals grew. When we burn fossil fuels we are putting a lot of carbon dioxide back into the atmosphere at once.

Burning forests to clear land puts carbon dioxide into the atmosphere that the trees have taken out of it. Many trees take between 50 and 100 years to grow to full size, and they took carbon dioxide out of the atmosphere while they were growing. When we burn forests, we are putting all that carbon dioxide back into the air very quickly. However, the land cleared by burning forests is often used to grow crop plants, which will remove carbon dioxide from the atmosphere again.

2 a Why did the amount of carbon dioxide in the atmosphere stay constant for thousands of years?
 b Why has the amount of carbon dioxide increased recently?

3 a Why does burning fossil fuels increase the amount of carbon dioxide in the atmosphere?
 b How does burning a large area of forest affect the amount of carbon dioxide in the atmosphere?
 c Why does burning a forest have a different effect to burning fossil fuels?

4 Which is the odd one out: coal, tree, horse? Explain your answers.

5 Look at graph D. A graph showing world population for the same years would have a very similar shape.
 a Do you think the two things are connected?
 b Explain your answer.

Summary

Plants take in carbon dioxide for _____. Carbon _____ is produced by animals, plants and _____, and when _____ are burnt. This creates a _____ called the _____ cycle. The amount of carbon dioxide in the _____ is increasing because we are _____ more _____ fuels and clearing more _____.

atmosphere burning carbon cycle
decomposers dioxide forests
fossil fuels photosynthesis

P2.9 The greenhouse effect

What is the greenhouse effect?

The Earth and its atmosphere are surrounded by empty space. The temperature of the Earth depends on the amount of radiation it receives from the Sun and the amount of radiation it emits into space. If it emits as much radiation as it receives, it stays at a constant temperature.

> **1 a** What will happen if the Earth emits more heat radiation than it receives from the Sun?
> **b** What will happen if it emits less than it receives?

Carbon dioxide in the Earth's atmosphere helps to trap heat. A greenhouse traps heat in a similar way, which is why this is called the **greenhouse effect**. Carbon dioxide is referred to as a **greenhouse gas**. The average surface temperature of the Earth is 15 °C, but if there were no carbon dioxide in the atmosphere it would be about −20 °C.

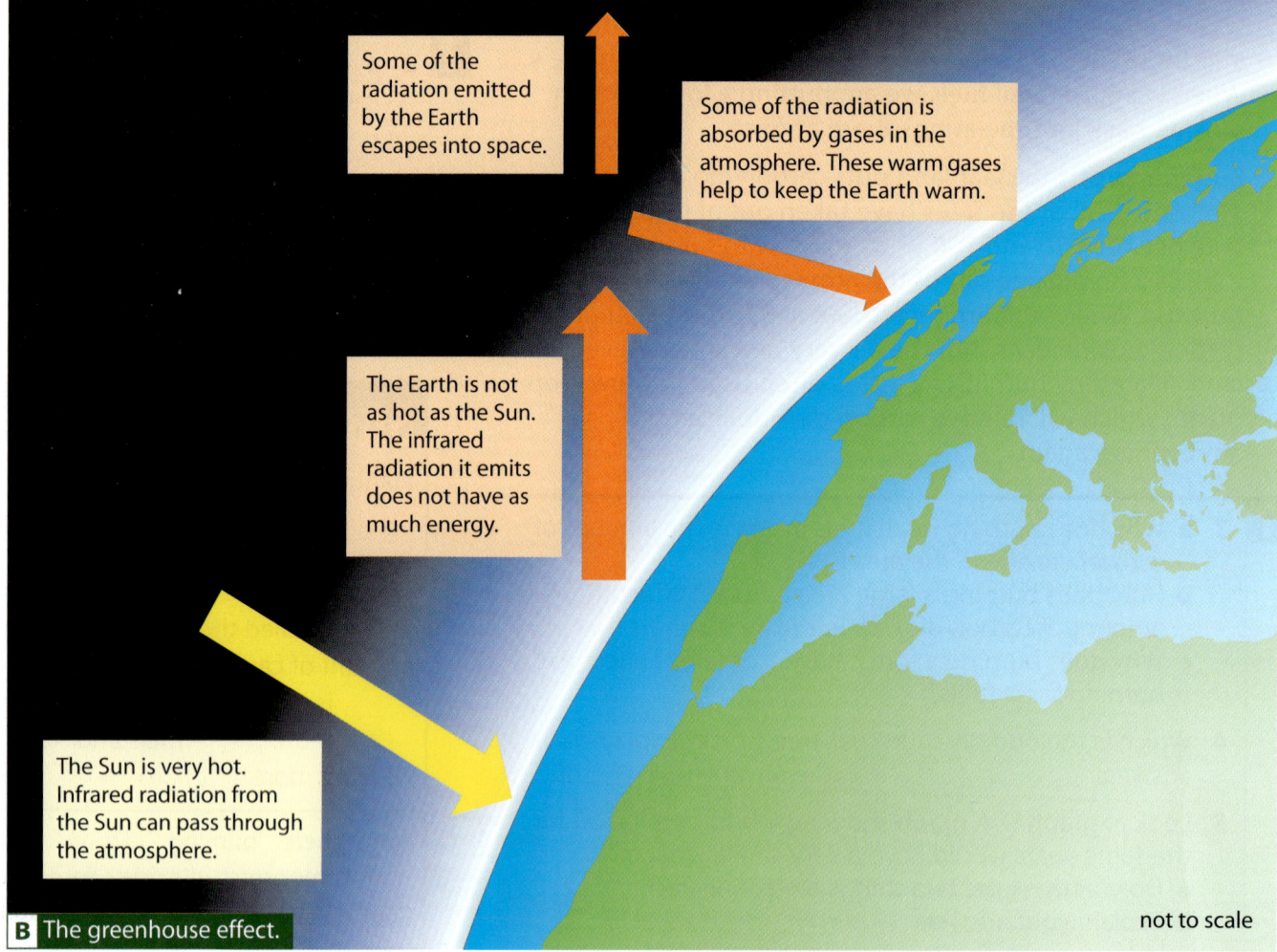

A If the Earth emitted more radiation than it received from the Sun it would cool down and become a very cold planet.

Some of the radiation emitted by the Earth escapes into space.

Some of the radiation is absorbed by gases in the atmosphere. These warm gases help to keep the Earth warm.

The Earth is not as hot as the Sun. The infrared radiation it emits does not have as much energy.

The Sun is very hot. Infrared radiation from the Sun can pass through the atmosphere.

B The greenhouse effect.

not to scale

154

? 2 a Why can radiation from the Sun get through the atmosphere?
　　b How is the radiation from the Earth different to the radiation from the Sun?

　3 a What would happen to the Earth if there were no carbon dioxide in the atmosphere?
　　b Why would this happen?

As more carbon dioxide is added to the atmosphere the Earth gets a little warmer. Diagram C shows how this happens. This rise in the Earth's temperature is called **global warming**.

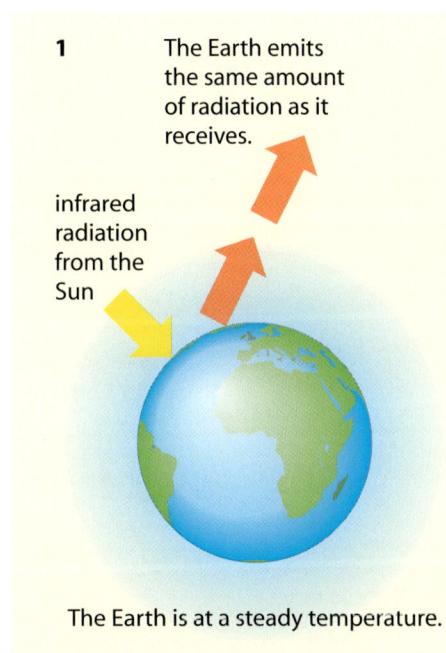

1　The Earth emits the same amount of radiation as it receives.

infrared radiation from the Sun

The Earth is at a steady temperature.

2　The Earth does not emit as much radiation as it receives.

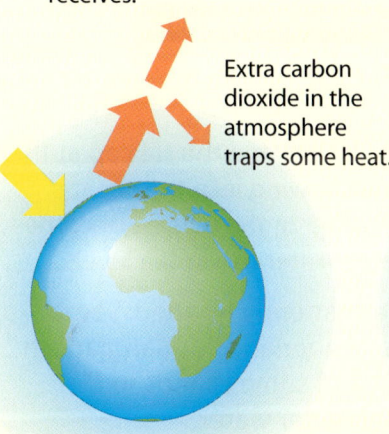

Extra carbon dioxide in the atmosphere traps some heat.

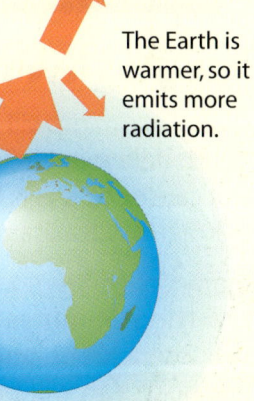

The Earth is warming up.

3　The radiation that escapes from the atmosphere is the same as the amount of radiation received from the Sun.

The Earth is warmer, so it emits more radiation.

The Earth is at a new steady temperature.

not to scale

C How global warming happens.

Scientists use computer models to try to work out what will happen if global warming continues. However, there are so many different factors to take into account that there is still a lot of disagreement about what will happen.

? 4 Look at diagram C.
　　a Why is the Earth at a steady temperature in part 1?
　　b Why is the temperature increasing in part 2?
　　c Why has the temperature stopped increasing in part 3?

　5 Which is the odd one out: oxygen, carbon dioxide, nitrogen? Explain your answers.

　6 Give two reasons why plants might grow better if there were more greenhouse gases in the atmosphere.

Summary

Some of the _____ radiation from the Sun is trapped by _____ dioxide in the Earth's _____. This is known as the _____ effect, and helps to keep the Earth _____. Extra carbon _____ in the atmosphere will make the _____ warm up even more. This is called _____ warming.

| atmosphere | carbon | dioxide | Earth |
| global | greenhouse | infrared | warm |

155

P2.10 A warmer Earth

What will happen if global warming continues?

Polar bears extinct!

Bumper crop of oranges in Greenland.

Ten more Pacific islands now completely under water.

A Some of the possible consequences of global warming.

Rising sea levels

Global warming will cause ice in glaciers and the ice cap at the South Pole to melt. The extra water flowing into the oceans will cause sea levels to rise. If the water in the oceans becomes warmer it will expand and cause a further rise in sea levels.

Many coastal regions will be permanently flooded. Some low-lying countries such as the Netherlands or Bangladesh will lose a lot of land to the sea, and some islands in the Pacific Ocean will be completely under water.

? 1 Give two reasons why global warming could cause sea levels to rise.
2 How could rising sea levels affect humans?

Climate change

Global warming will increase the amount of water that evaporates from the oceans. This evaporated water will form clouds, which could reflect more radiation back into space. Some computer models predict that this might stop the Earth warming up any further.

? 3 How might clouds stop global warming?

The extra clouds will cause more rainfall. Temperature rises could also change weather patterns, so some areas may get less rainfall than they do now and others may get more. Changing weather patterns could also cause stronger winds.

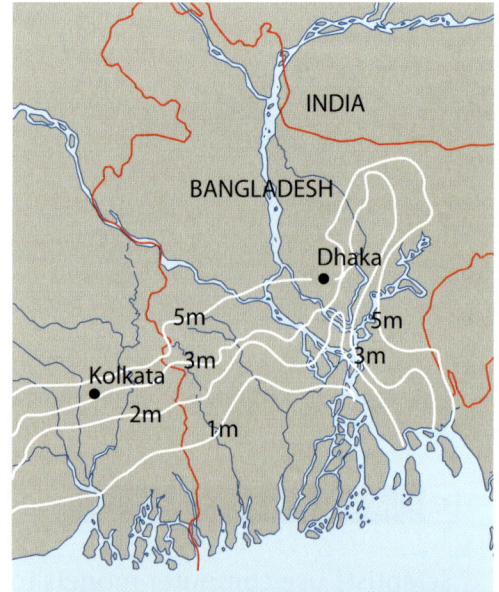

B Over half of Bangladesh will be under water if sea levels rise by 5 metres.

C Flooding like this could happen more often.

D If the Earth gets warmer, storms like this could become more common.

Effects on living organisms

Food crops are grown in the places where conditions suit them. Changes in climate could mean that we have to grow different crops. We might be able to grow new crops in some places, but in other places drier conditions may make it impossible to grow any crops at all.

E Droughts could become more common in some parts of the world.

Warmer temperatures could allow some insects to move into new areas. This may increase the spread of diseases that are carried by insects.

Some animals may be able to move to cooler regions, but many will not be able to and may become extinct. Many plants could also die out.

?
6 a Describe one possible benefit of global warming.
  b Describe three possible harmful effects of global warming on living organisms.
7 Why is global warming likely to have more serious effects on the developing world than on richer countries?

?
4 What effect would increased rain have on rivers around the world?
5 What effect would stronger winds have on:
  a houses
  b waves on the sea
  c cliffs around the coastline?

Summary

Not all scientists _____ about the effects of global _____. It may cause _____ due to increased _____ and sea _____ rises, and changes in _____ patterns. Plants and _____ will also be affected, and there may be _____ shortages in some parts of the _____.

agree   animals   floods   food   level
 rainfall   warming   weather   world

157

P2.11 The global warming debate

Are greenhouse gases responsible for global warming?

A Burning fossil fuels adds carbon dioxide to the atmosphere.

Graph B shows how the average global temperature changed between 1960 and 2000. Graph C shows how the amount of carbon dioxide in the atmosphere changed over the same period. Both temperature and carbon dioxide levels have increased, so the two factors show **correlation**. However, this does not necessarily mean that the increase in carbon dioxide has *caused* the increase in temperature. It could just be a coincidence that the two graphs have similar shapes.

> **1 a** Why do scientists say there is a correlation between carbon dioxide in the atmosphere and global warming?
> **b** Why doesn't this prove that carbon dioxide causes global warming?

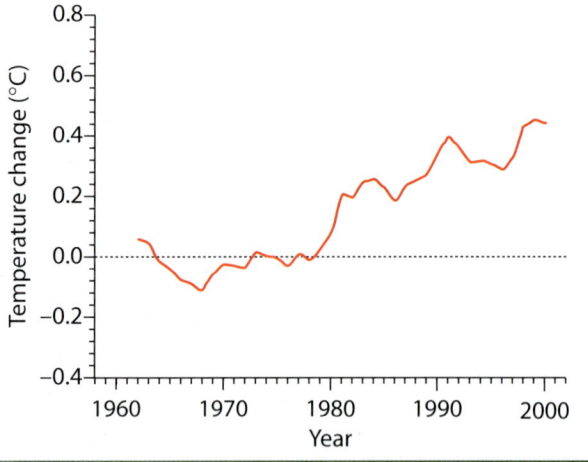

B The change in global temperature between 1960 and 2000.

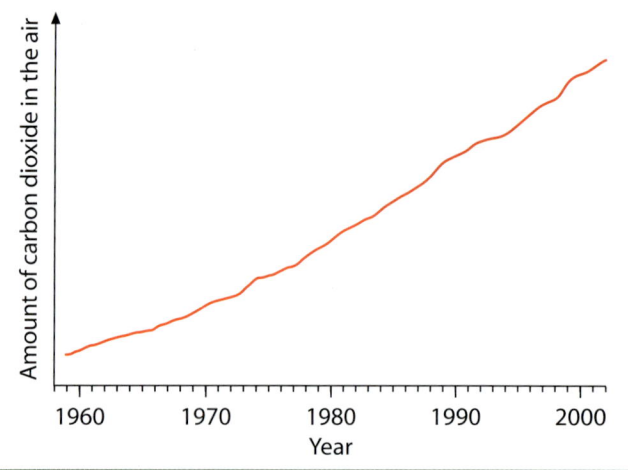

C The amount of carbon dioxide in the atmosphere between 1960 and 2000.

Scientists have estimated the temperature of the Earth all the way back to 200 000 years ago, and also the amount of carbon dioxide there was in the air. Graph D shows the results of these estimates.

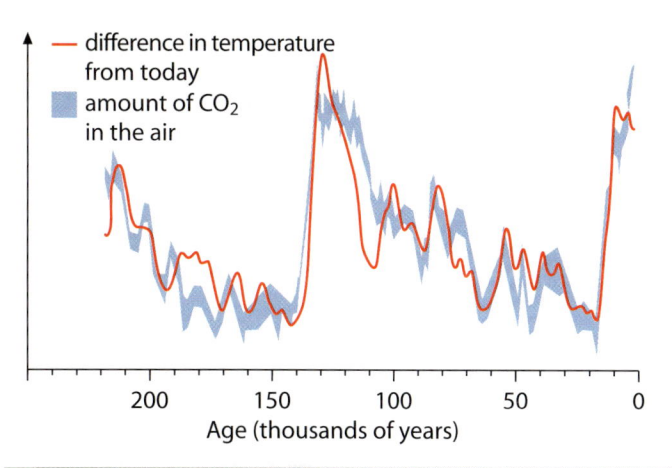

D Carbon dioxide and temperature for the last 200 000 years.

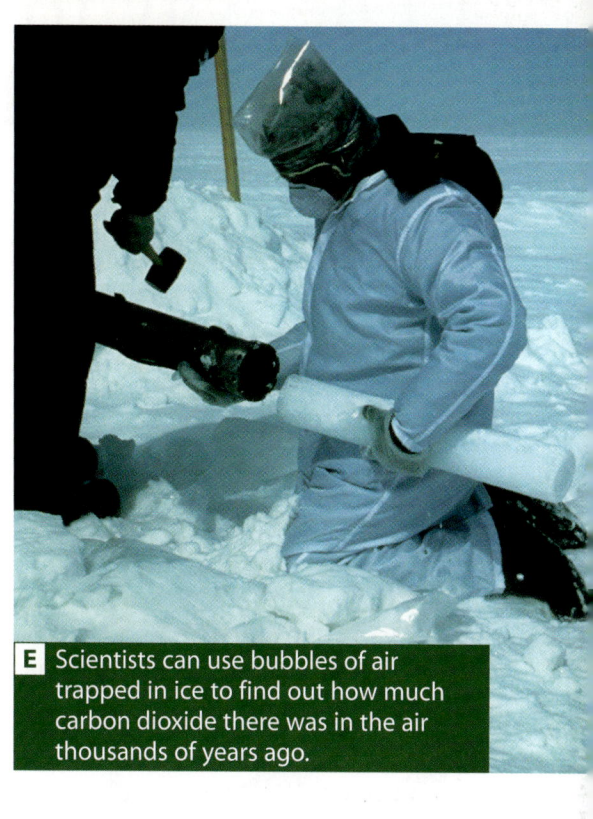

The two graphs show good correlation over thousands of years, which means that the correlation is not likely to be a coincidence. However, this still does not prove that carbon dioxide *causes* global warming. There could be some other factor that affects both temperature and carbon dioxide levels.

? 2 a Why does graph D provide better evidence that the correlation between carbon dioxide levels and temperature is probably not a coincidence?
  b Why doesn't it prove that carbon dioxide causes global warming?

Scientists have carried out laboratory experiments with different gases, and they have shown that carbon dioxide absorbs infrared radiation. They therefore have a theory which explains why carbon dioxide could cause global warming. Today, most scientists agree that the extra carbon dioxide in the atmosphere is making the Earth warm up.

If extra carbon dioxide is causing global warming, then we could try to reduce the warming effect by reducing the carbon dioxide **emissions**. We could do this by burning less fossil fuels. We could also plant more forests to use up carbon dioxide.

? 3 Give one reason why most scientists agree that carbon dioxide causes global warming.
  4 How do forests 'use up' carbon dioxide?
  5 The River Thames has not frozen for more than 50 years.
    a Explain why some people would say this is evidence for global warming.
    b Why might other people disagree with them?

E Scientists can use bubbles of air trapped in ice to find out how much carbon dioxide there was in the air thousands of years ago.

Summary

Carbon dioxide levels show _____ with _____ changes. Although this does not _____ that the carbon _____ has caused the temperature _____, most scientists accept that _____ warming is due to _____ carbon dioxide in the atmosphere. Carbon dioxide _____ could be cut by burning less _____ fuels. We could also plant more _____ to take in _____ dioxide.

carbon change correlation dioxide
emissions extra fossil global
prove temperature trees

P2.12 The way forward

What should we do about global warming?

Not everyone agrees on the risk of global warming or what should be done about it.

Mrs Sanchez: Our country is still developing. We need to clear the forests for new homes. We also need to build power stations for our new industries.

Mr Blake: We could easily cut carbon dioxide emissions by using public transport – 20 people on a bus use less fuel than 20 cars! And if we insulated our houses better we would use up less fuel for heating – we would save money as well as reducing global warming!

Mr Bushton: Not all scientists agree that burning less fossil fuels would solve the problem. It will cost us a lot of money to convert to renewable resources for generating electricity.

Mr Patel: Spend money on a wind farm or a hospital – I know which I'd choose!

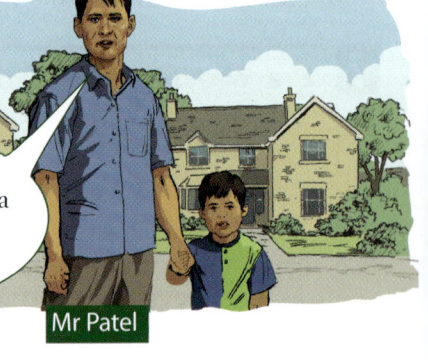

Mrs McDuff: It won't make much difference to me, but I would like my grandchildren to have a nice world to live in, without all these storms and droughts they are talking about.

Rajiv Mistry: Stopping people cutting down the rainforests will also help wildlife.

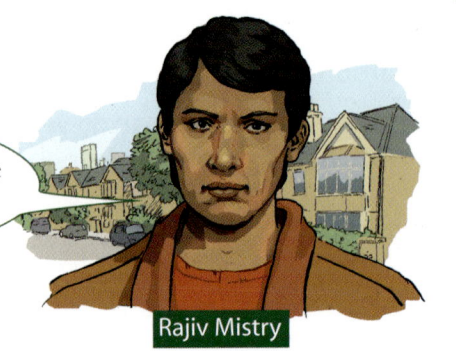

Susie Reddish: Better safe than sorry, that's what I say! Anyway – we also need oil for making plastics and there isn't an alternative to that. Oil will run out eventually, so it makes sense to cut down the amount we burn.

Ms Jeffries: I would use the bus if I could, but there is only one bus a day to my village!

Mrs Mboto: Climate change could lead to mass starvation. We cannot afford to take the risk.

Mr Penh: Each person in the USA emits over 50 times as much carbon dioxide as a person in my country. They are the ones who should change!

Miss Linton: If it gets hotter, more clouds will form. They will reflect heat from the Sun, and the Earth will cool down again. No problem!

A Discuss the different opinions on these pages.
- Who thinks we should cut emissions?
- What reasons are there for *not* reducing carbon dioxide emissions?
- What problems could there be in trying to reduce the global emissions of carbon dioxide?
- How might we solve these problems?

?
1. Write down three ways of reducing carbon dioxide emissions.
2. a Write down two reasons why people might not want to cut carbon dioxide emissions.
   b Write down two reasons for cutting carbon dioxide emissions.
3. Which people think we should be 'better safe than sorry' and reduce emissions even if the cause of global warming has not been proved.
4. a What do you think developing countries should do to reduce the risk of global warming?
   b What should developed countries be doing?
   c Do you think that developed countries should help poorer countries? Explain your answer.

Summary

Not everyone agrees on how big the _____ from _____ warming is, or how we should try to _____ it. We could try to reduce global _____ by using public _____ instead of cars, and _____ our homes.

| global | insulating | prevent | risk |
| transport | warming |

161

P2.13 Staying safe
What do you know about radiation and safety?

Stay safe!

never using microwave cookers

never using a mobile phone

staying away from mobile phone masts

Radiation is all around us – we cannot avoid it. It can damage tissues in your body, and even cause cancer.

You can stay safe by:

always covering up with clothing if you have to go outside

staying out of the Sun as much as you can

A

1 Visible light is part of the electromagnetic spectrum.
   a List the other types of radiation in the electromagnetic spectrum in order, starting with radio waves.
   b Which type of radiation has photons with the highest energies?
   c Write down one source of each type of radiation.
   d Which of these types of radiation are ionising radiations?
   e How can ionising radiations harm the body?

2 Microwaves can be used to cook food.
   a How do microwaves cook food?
   b Describe two features of microwave ovens that stop microwaves escaping from the oven.
   c Explain how these safety features work.

3 Mobile phones communicate using microwaves.
   a Why will you receive microwave radiation from a mobile phone whenever it is switched on, even if you are not phoning someone?
   b Why do people think that mobile phones might prove to be a health risk?
   c Why might the health risk be greater for children?
   d Why doesn't everyone agree on the risk from mobile phones?

Honeymoon gave me skin cancer

Mrs Sally Needham (28) recently returned from her honeymoon on the Greek island of Rhodes and doctors have told her she has skin cancer. Her husband Kevin believes the honeymoon is to blame.

"She had never been abroad before – it must have been the holiday. I'm going to sue the holiday company!"

B

4 **a** Why does Mr Needham think that the honeymoon was responsible for his wife's skin cancer?
   b How could other people travelling to the Greek island reduce the risks of getting skin cancer?
   c Which gas in the atmosphere helps to protect us from the radiation that can cause skin cancer?

Most scientists agree that the increasing quantities of carbon dioxide in the atmosphere are making the Earth warmer.

5 **a** Write down three ways in which carbon dioxide is added to the atmosphere.
   b Plants remove carbon dioxide from the atmosphere. What is the name of this process?
   c Write a word equation for this process.

SAVE THE WORLD!
PLANT A TREE!

More trees = less global warming
Help to save the planet now!

C

6 The amount of carbon dioxide in the atmosphere remained fairly constant for thousands of years.
   a Why did the amount of carbon dioxide remain constant?
   b Why has the amount of carbon dioxide in the atmosphere increased in the last 200 years?
   c How will planting trees help to stop carbon dioxide levels rising further?
   d Describe one other way of trying to stop the rise in carbon dioxide levels.

7 **a** How does carbon dioxide in the atmosphere help to keep the Earth warm?
   b Why do some scientists think that extra carbon dioxide is causing global warming? Use the word 'correlation' in your answer.
   c Describe three possible effects of global warming.
   d Why don't all scientists agree on what will happen if the Earth gets warmer?

8 There are lots of different opinions concerning what we should do about global warming, or even whether we should do anything at all. Give one reason why someone might think we should:
   a not try to do anything about it
   b cut carbon dioxide emissions to try to reduce global warming.

163

B3.1 Life on Earth

What is happening to life on Earth?

It is the year 2020 AD and the following communication has been received on Earth from the Intergalactic Federation.

From: Intergalactic Federation **Date:** 1st October 2076
Subject: Earth!! **To:** Humans of Earth!

Humans of Earth! Prepare to stand trial for the extinction of millions of species of other Earth life forms.

There has been life on your planet for over 3500 million years. During that time there have been millions of different species. Changes to conditions on Earth have caused many species to become extinct. Many others have evolved into new species, creating a great diversity of life on your planet.

A

B

C

164

About 120 000 years ago your species, *Homo sapiens*, evolved. At first you responded to your environment like other species, dying when conditions were bad for you. However, using your big brain, you developed tools that enabled you to live anywhere you wanted to. You have used the Earth's resources of space and materials for your own purposes. In the process you have crowded out other species, killed for fun and destroyed many others with the waste you produce. The rate of extinction of species on your planet is now hundreds, possibly thousands of times greater than the natural rate of extinction.

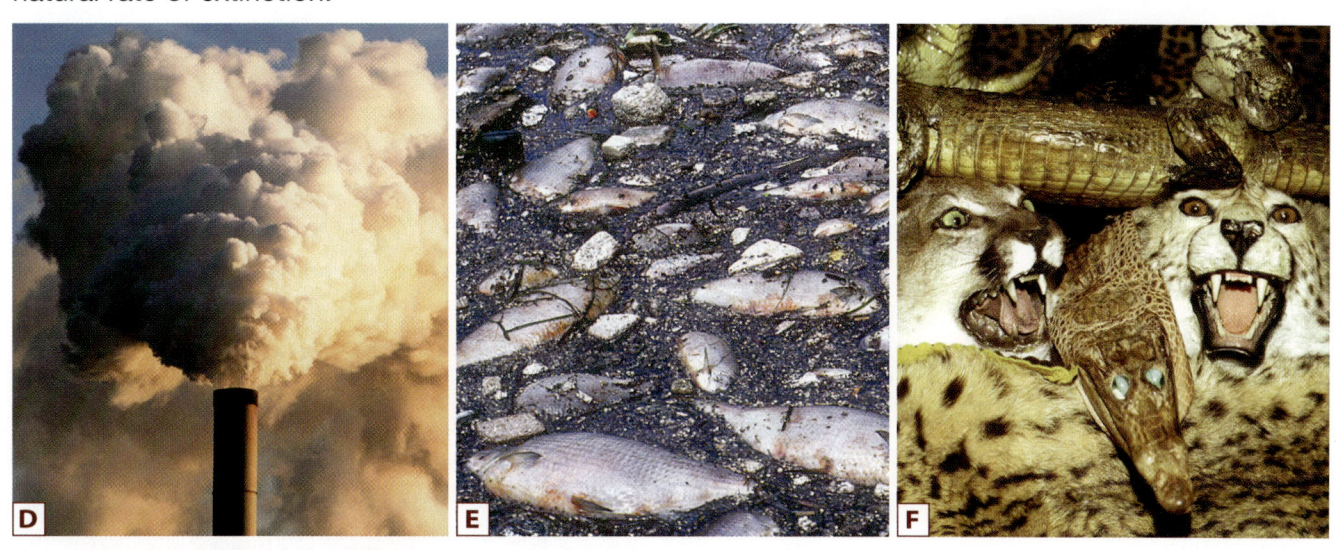

D

E

F

Now you plan to travel to other worlds and set up new colonies. You must prove to us that you can control your actions and not threaten other forms of life, otherwise we will not let you leave Earth.

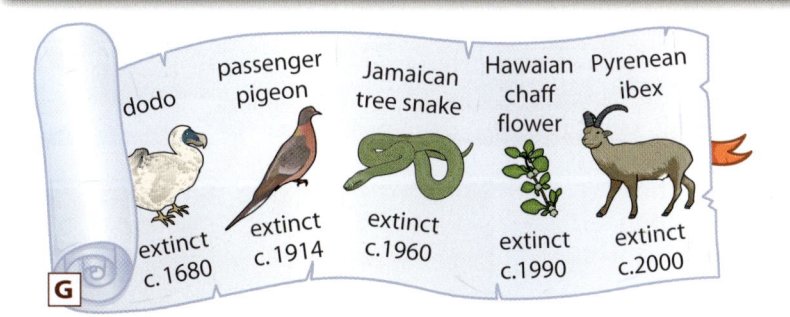

G

- dodo — extinct c. 1680
- passenger pigeon — extinct c. 1914
- Jamaican tree snake — extinct c. 1960
- Hawaiian chaff flower — extinct c. 1990
- Pyrenean ibex — extinct c. 2000

?

1. They say that life has evolved on Earth. Write a few sentences that explain what 'evolution of life' means to you.

2. People talk about the 'theory of evolution'. Theories need evidence. What evidence do you know for the theory of evolution?

3. The message tells us that millions of species have become extinct before our species evolved. This is what they mean by the 'natural rate of extinction'. Why is there a natural rate of extinction?

4. Make a list of five animals that once lived on Earth (including some that lived before humans evolved). If possible, give a reason why these animals are extinct now.

5. When humans first evolved, they were affected by the environment like other animals.
   a How are the numbers of individuals of a species affected by the environment?
   b Why are humans less affected by the environment than other species?

6. a In what ways do you think humans are increasing the rate of extinction?
   b What could we do to reduce this?

7. What do you need to find out more about to help you give better answers to these questions?

165

B3.2 Starting out

How did life on Earth start?

A These rocks in Greenland are over 3700 million years old. They contain no fossils.

The Earth formed over 4500 million years (Ma) ago. The oldest rocks on the surface of the Earth are around 4000 million years old. These contain no signs of life.

The earliest signs of life are found in rocks that are just over 3500 million years old. These rocks contain **fossils** of simple **cells** that look like **bacteria**. These cells may have arrived from other parts of our Solar System, or they might have developed here on Earth.

?
1. a For how long has there been life on Earth?
   b What is the evidence for this?
2. What evidence is there that the earliest life might have come from beyond the Earth?

The **atmosphere** of the early Earth contained no oxygen molecules. The most common gases were probably carbon dioxide, ammonia, methane and water vapour. These gases are compounds that contain the elements carbon, hydrogen, oxygen and nitrogen. These are the main elements in the compounds that make up living things.

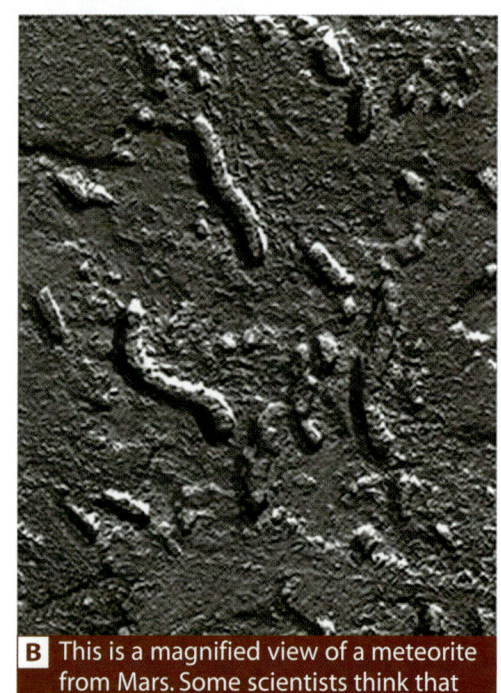

B This is a magnified view of a meteorite from Mars. Some scientists think that the marks on it are fossils of bacteria, magnification x30 000.

The early Earth was hotter than today and there were constant lightning storms. Scientists can create conditions like these using apparatus similar to diagram C. After a few days the chemicals in the flask combine to form more complex molecules, including molecules that could be used to build **DNA**. DNA carries the instructions for building new cells in organisms and for the characteristics of the organism.

DNA is an important molecule because it can copy itself exactly. This allows cells to copy themselves so that an organism can grow or reproduce.

?
3 Why is DNA important in living things?
4 Why is it important that DNA can copy itself exactly?

C — diagram showing apparatus with electrodes for spark discharge (lightning), stopcock for adding gases, atmosphere, stopcock for removing samples, condenser to circulate (reflux) atmosphere (simulating rain), water out, water in, water (ocean), heat source.

D These structures are called stromatolites. They contain bacteria. Fossils of structures like these have been found in rocks that are more than 2000 million years old.

Scientists estimate that there could be over 30 million **species** of living things on the Earth today. There are even more species that once existed but have become **extinct**. Most people believe that all these different species developed from the very simple cells that lived on Earth billions of years ago.

?
5 What evidence is there to suggest that life could have started on Earth?
6 Which is the odd one out: oxygen, water vapour, carbon dioxide? Explain your answers.
7 Draw a table to show the differences between the Earth's early atmosphere and today's atmosphere.

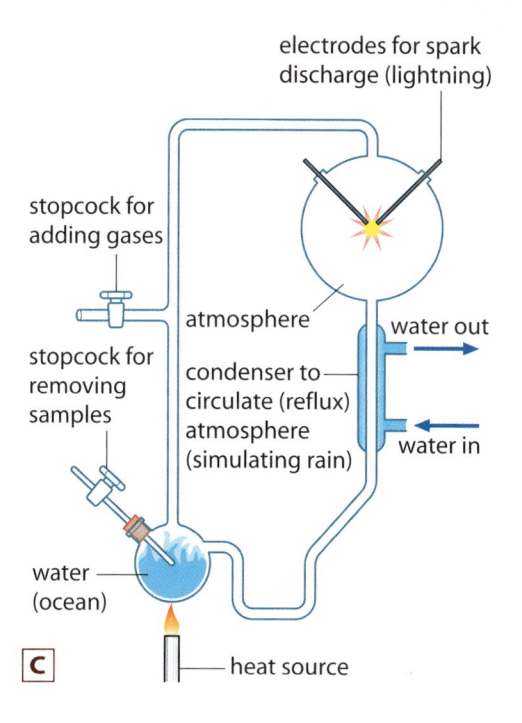

Summary

The earliest signs of _____ on Earth are fossils that look like _____, found in rocks that are over 3500 million years old. The conditions on early Earth may have created _____ that are found in living _____, including DNA. _____ is important because it can _____ itself. All the _____ on Earth have developed from these first simple living _____.

bacteria   cells   chemicals   copy
DNA   life   organisms   species

167

B3.3 Evolution of life on Earth

What is the evidence for evolution?

Fossils from rocks show us the organisms that lived on Earth in the past. We can find the age of the rocks that the fossils are found in, so we know how long ago they lived. The fossils show that the further we go back in time, the more different the organisms were to today's organisms.

Scientists can work out what the organisms looked like by studying the fossils, and see which other fossils and living species they are related to. We can link related fossil and living species in an **evolutionary tree** to show how later organisms may have **evolved** from earlier ones.

A This drawing is a reconstruction from the fossil of *Eryops* which lived 230 million years ago. It was a large predator (1.5 m long) that is most closely related to toads and frogs that are alive today.

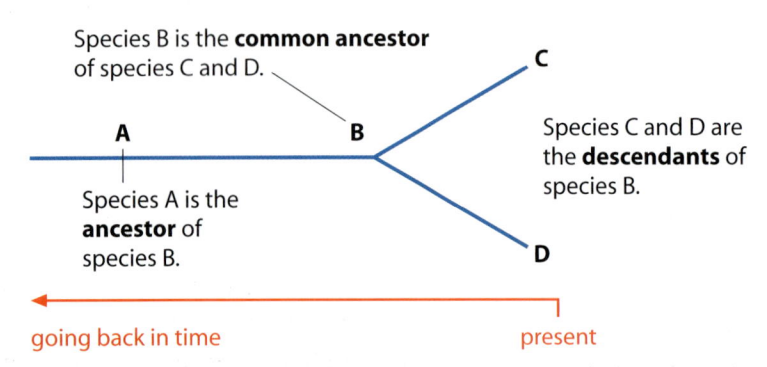

Species B is the **common ancestor** of species C and D.

Species A is the **ancestor** of species B.

Species C and D are the **descendants** of species B.

going back in time → present

C This evolutionary tree shows that fossil organism A evolved into fossil organism B which then evolved into organisms C and D.

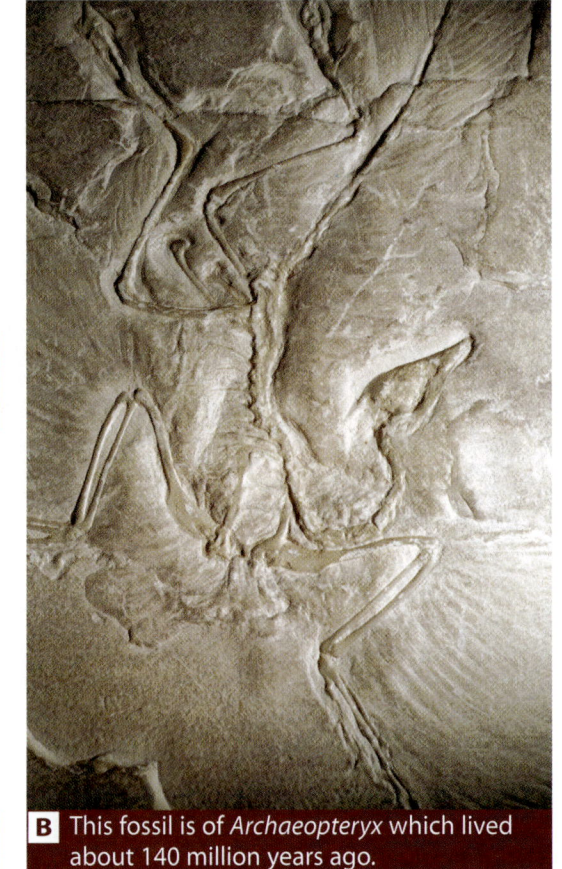

B This fossil is of *Archaeopteryx* which lived about 140 million years ago.

?
1. **a** How do scientists study organisms that lived a long time ago?
   b How do they know when these organisms lived?
2. Look at photograph B. Which living animal does the fossil of *Archaeopteryx* look most like?
3. How do you think that scientists worked out that *Eryops* (diagram A) was related to toads and frogs?

Scientists can analyse the DNA of living species. They have found that closely related species have DNA that is almost the same. We can draw a tree diagram to show how similar species are according to their DNA. These diagrams often look like the evolutionary trees made using evidence from fossils. Some DNA has been extracted from fossils, but this is very rare.

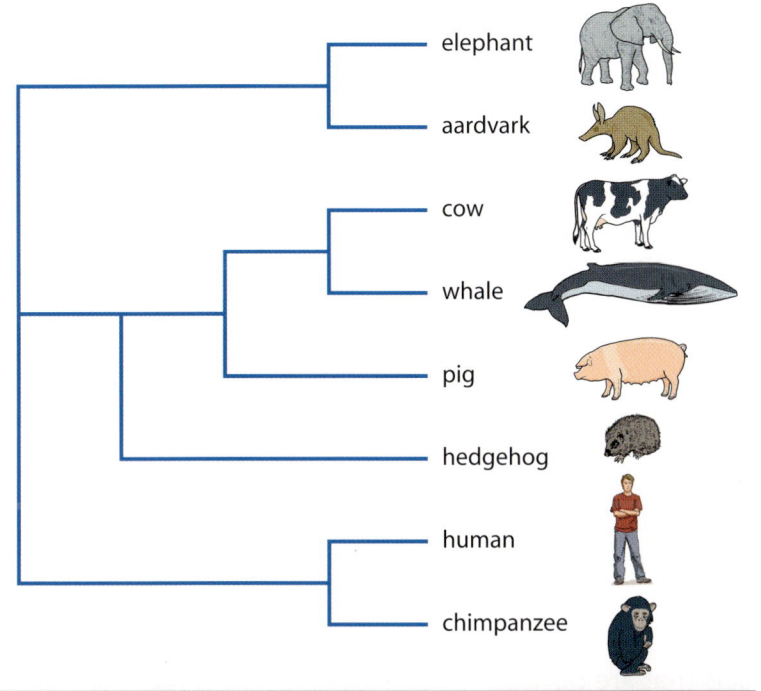

D This DNA tree diagram for mammals only shows living species. Species with similar DNA are more closely linked together on the diagram.

?
4 Look at diagram D. From DNA evidence, which animal is most closely related to humans?

5 Give one difference between an evolutionary tree diagram and a DNA tree diagram.

Most organisms do not form fossils when they die. This is because fossils only form in special situations. The dead organism must be buried by sediment soon after death, and must remain buried for thousands or millions of years. This makes it very difficult to get enough information to draw an accurate evolutionary tree.

?
6 Why must dead organisms be buried quickly if they are to turn into fossils?

7 Many fossils are found in sediments that settled in water. Explain why aquatic organisms are more likely to form fossils than land organisms.

E Scavengers will eat up everything from this kill.

Summary

Scientists can study ＿＿＿ to work out what an extinct organism looked like. They can also work out how closely ＿＿＿ different species are. We can use this information to draw ＿＿＿ to show how the species may have ＿＿＿ from one another, including humans. DNA ＿＿＿ can show how closely related ＿＿＿ organisms are.

analysis   evolutionary trees
evolved   fossils   living   related

169

B3.4 Evolution by natural selection

How does evolution happen?

We know that the species we see today evolved from different species which lived in the past. It took many years before most scientists agreed on a way that this could happen.

In 1809 a French scientist called Jean-Baptiste Lamarck suggested that a characteristic will develop (be acquired) in an organism if it is used. This **acquired characteristic** will be **inherited** by its offspring when it reproduces.

> **1** According to Lamarck:
>   **a** Which is the acquired characteristic in giraffes?
>   **b** What would need to happen so that giraffes with really long necks evolved?

In 1858 two British scientists, Charles Darwin and Alfred Russel Wallace, proposed a different idea based on these observations:
- There is **variation** between all the individuals in a species.
- Most offspring produced by an organism do not survive long enough to reproduce.

Many of the offspring die while they are still young. Darwin and Wallace concluded that only individuals that are best **adapted** to the environment survive and reproduce. They might survive because they can run away fastest from a predator or can find food most successfully. When they reproduce, their characteristics (including the ones that made them successful) are passed on to their offspring. So characteristics which increase the chance of survival are more common in the next generation. This idea became known as the theory of evolution by **natural selection**.

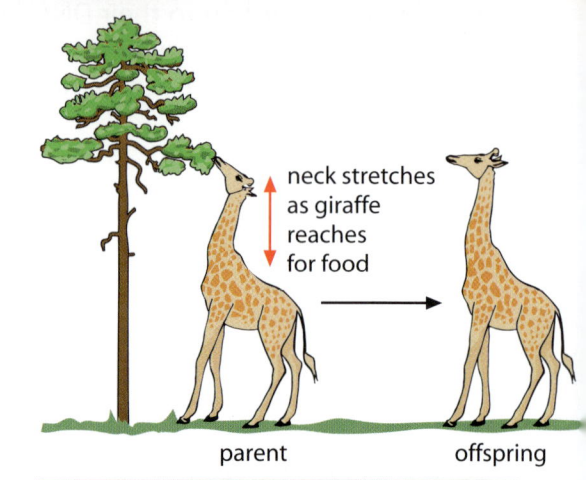

A Lamarck said that giraffes now have long necks because their ancestors stretched up to feed on tall trees.

> **2** Suggest two things that might cause the death of an individual.
> **3** Give two examples of variation between individual humans.

B How natural selection can change the next generation.

4 a Write down two things that could make an animal 'successful'.
  b Why are these successful characteristics passed on to the next generation?

At that time the only evidence that species can change over time was through **selective breeding**. This is when breeders choose individuals which show the characteristics they want and mate them. The offspring from these parents are more likely to have the characteristics that the breeder wants.

C The wolf is the ancestor of all breeds of dog.

Wolfhound

Jack Russell Terrier

D These breeds have been selectively bred for hunting.

5 Which breed of dog has been bred for:
  a hunting large animals
  b hunting animals that live in burrows?

6 Which characteristics would have been selected in dogs:
  a for breeding wolfhounds
  b for breeding Jack Russell terriers?

7 Describe one way in which natural selection differs from selective breeding.

8 Suggest as many explanations for this statement as you can: An animal has long hair.

9 Danny is thin, but he builds up his muscles by weightlifting.
  a What would Lamarck's hypothesis predict about the muscles of any children Danny has?
  b What would Darwin's theory predict?
  c Which prediction is correct?

Summary

Darwin and Wallace proposed the theory of evolution by _____ to explain how _____ change over time. This theory says that only those individuals that have _____ that are best _____ to the environment _____ and reproduce. So these characteristics become more _____ in the next generation.

adapted   characteristics   common
natural selection   species   survive

171

B3.5 Darwin's theory of evolution

When does a hypothesis become a theory?

A Two of the finches that Darwin observed.

When Darwin visited the Galapagos Islands in 1835 to collect data about plants and animals, he saw many species of finch that were not found elsewhere. Each species of finch was adapted to feed on different food. Darwin's observations helped him to develop a **hypothesis** about evolution.

Darwin used his knowledge of selective breeding to suggest how the finches evolved. He thought that a few individuals of one species of finch reached the Galapagos Islands from South America, over 500 km away. The birds competed for food. Over time, individual birds that were best adapted to feed on each kind of food survived better and produced more offspring. Eventually 13 different species of finch evolved from the original single species.

? 1 Look at diagram A.
  a Which finch has a beak that is adapted for picking insects out of cracks in tree bark?
  b Which one has a beak that is adapted for cracking large, hard seeds?
  c Explain your answers.

? 2 Use Darwin's idea to explain how a finch evolved that can pick out insects from bark.

A hypothesis is an idea that can be tested scientifically. If it explains a wide range of observations, or makes **predictions** that can be tested and are found to be correct, the hypothesis then becomes a **theory**.

? 3 What is the difference between a hypothesis and a theory?

Darwin's hypothesis caused great argument. At that time the main explanation for all the different species on Earth, and all the fossils, was that God had created them. This is not an idea that can be tested scientifically.

Many scientists soon accepted Darwin's theory because it explained many different observations, such as the older a fossil is, the more different it usually is compared to living organisms. Some scientists were unsure because they did not understand *how* characteristics were passed from one generation to the next. Now we know that genes carry information about characteristics.

B Many people made fun of Darwin's ideas.

C Peppered moths have light forms and dark forms. There are more dark forms where there are sooty trees and more light forms where the trees have light bark. This is thought to be due to natural selection by their predators.

The difficulty with testing evolution is that it takes much longer than a human lifetime for a new species to evolve. Since Darwin's time studies of animals in the wild for long periods have shown evolution happening. However, some religious people still do not believe that evolution happens.

?
4 a Why did many scientists accept Darwin's ideas?
  b Why did some scientists find it difficult to accept them?
  c Why didn't some religious people accept them?
5 Why is evolution difficult to test?
6 What do we know about genes that explains how characteristics are passed from a parent to the offspring?

Summary

Darwin's theory is _____ by most scientists to explain how _____ happens. It explains many different _____ such as the fact that _____ fossils are more different to living _____ than more recent _____.

accepted   evolution   fossils
observations   older   species

173

B3.6 Sensor and effector cells

How can organisms sense and respond to changes?

To survive, an organism needs to be able to sense changes in itself and in the environment around it. It then needs to respond to the change, or **stimulus**, in a way that improves its chances of survival. For example, if an animal feels hungry, it needs to find food; or if the temperature gets colder, it may need to find some way to keep warm.

The cells that sense changes are **sensor** (or **receptor**) cells, such as the cells in our eyes or skin. The cells that respond are called the **effector** cells. These include muscle cells. In **multicellular organisms** (organisms that have many cells), some cells are specialised to sense different stimuli and respond to them in different ways.

A A dormouse keeps warm while sleeping through the winter.

B Electric eels live in muddy water. They use pulses of electricity to navigate and to sense prey.

C Dolphins use pulses of high-pitched ultrasound to track and catch prey.

1 Copy and complete the table for human senses.

Sense	Where the sensor cells are found	What the cells respond to (stimulus)
sight		light and colour
hearing		
touch	skin	pressure, heat, cold
smell		chemicals in air
taste	tongue	
balance	ears	gravity

2 Name two senses that some animals have but humans do not have.

A How can you find out if maggots respond to light?

174

The sensor and effector cells are usually in different parts of the body. Diagram D shows how information about a stimulus produces a reaction by the effector. Sometimes the information will pass directly to the effector, but in humans and other **vertebrates** the information may also go to the **brain** as well as going to the effector.

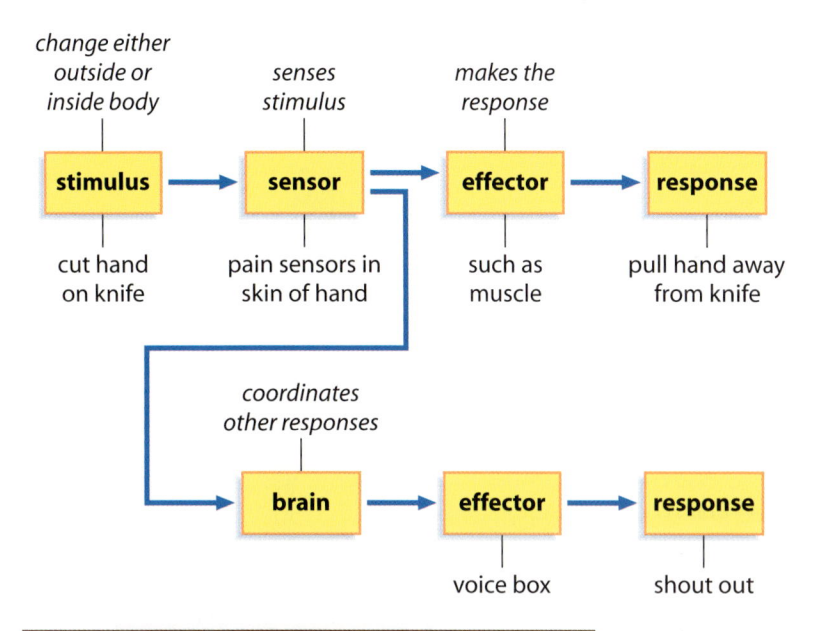

```
change either          senses           makes the
outside or            stimulus          response
inside body
    │                    │                  │
┌─────────┐        ┌─────────┐      ┌─────────┐      ┌─────────┐
│stimulus │───────▶│ sensor  │─────▶│effector │─────▶│response │
└─────────┘        └─────────┘      └─────────┘      └─────────┘
    │                    │                  │                  │
cut hand          pain sensors in        such as         pull hand away
on knife           skin of hand          muscle            from knife

                  coordinates
                  other responses
                        │
                  ┌─────────┐      ┌─────────┐      ┌─────────┐
                  │  brain  │─────▶│effector │─────▶│response │
                  └─────────┘      └─────────┘      └─────────┘
                                         │                  │
                                     voice box          shout out
```

D Information about a stimulus passes to effectors.

? 3 Describe the path that a message takes from the stimulus to the reaction, using the words in bold on diagram D.

In many reactions the information will pass to different areas of the brain, so you can compare the stimulus with memories of things like this, or with information coming from other stimuli. This means you can make choices about what to do next, so your response to the same stimulus may be different at different times. You may also respond in more than one way, so your brain **coordinates** the different responses.

E

? 4 Look at the boy in diagram E.
  a Which sensor cells have been stimulated?
  b Which effector cells might be used to respond?
  c Which part of his body is coordinating the responses?
  d Describe what choices he might make to coordinate responses and solve the problem.

5 You feel cold.
  a Describe all the different ways that you could respond to this stimulus.
  b How would these responses help ensure your survival?

Summary

Organisms sense _____ (changes in the environment) using _____ cells. Information from these cells is passed to _____ cells such as muscles by the _____. The effector cells _____ to the change so that the _____ can improve its chances of _____.

effector	nervous system	organism
respond	sensor	stimuli	survival

175

B3.7 Communication systems

What communications systems do organisms have?

Multicellular organisms have two communication systems for passing information around the body. The **nervous system** links sensors to effectors with nerves throughout the body. This system responds to changes in our surroundings.

? **1** Name the three main parts of the human nervous system.

In the nervous system, messages pass very quickly through nerves as tiny electrical signals. For example, if you tread on a pin, your brain will receive the message and send it on down to the muscles in your leg in much less than 1 second. The nervous system is the communication system that your body uses to respond very quickly to a stimulus.

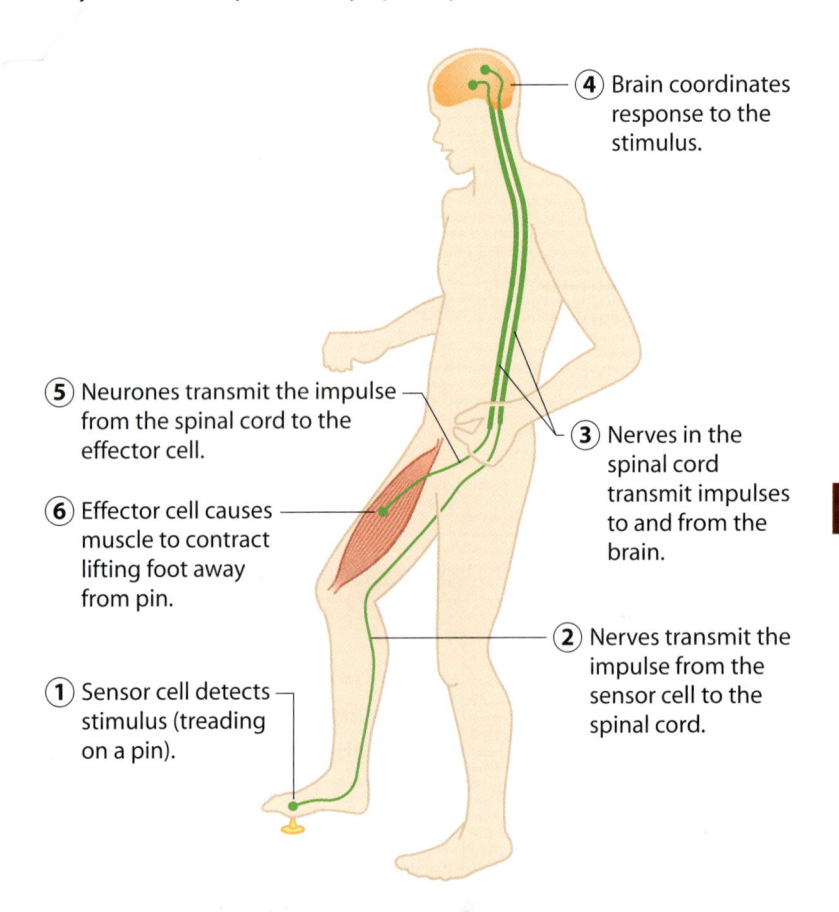

A The human nervous system.
- brain — central nervous system
- spinal cord
- major nerves

B How the message passes through the nervous system after treading on a pin.
1. Sensor cell detects stimulus (treading on a pin).
2. Nerves transmit the impulse from the sensor cell to the spinal cord.
3. Nerves in the spinal cord transmit impulses to and from the brain.
4. Brain coordinates response to the stimulus.
5. Neurones transmit the impulse from the spinal cord to the effector cell.
6. Effector cell causes muscle to contract lifting foot away from pin.

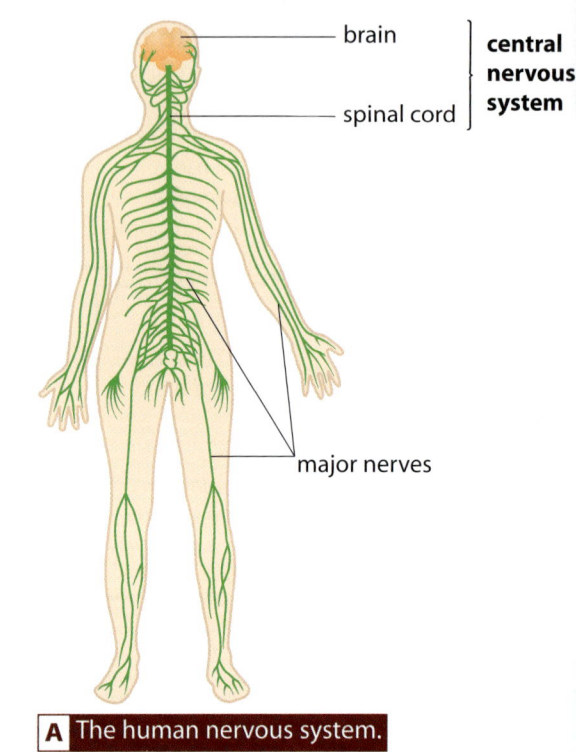

? **2** Look at diagram B. Describe how the muscles in your leg would respond to the message from your brain in this situation.

3 Think of two situations where you would need to respond quickly to a situation.
  a For each situation, explain why you would need to respond quickly.
  b Which sensors and effectors would you use to respond in each situation?
  c How do you know that you were using the nervous system to respond like this?

176

Multicellular animals also have another communication system called the **hormonal system**. This system responds to some changes in the environment, but also to changes inside the body. It uses chemicals called **hormones** to act as messengers. These are **secreted** from the sensors, which are known as **endocrine glands**, straight into the blood. The hormones travel around the body until they reach **target cells** which then respond. Your body makes many different hormones from many glands.

Hormones may stay in the blood for several hours but they are eventually removed as they are excreted in urine and are broken down by enzymes.

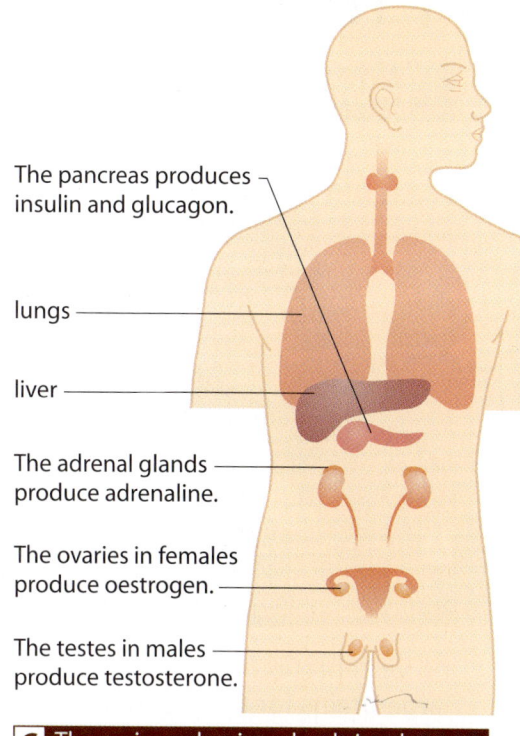

> **4** List three human endocrine glands and the hormones that they make.

Insulin is a hormone that is made in the pancreas when levels of glucose in the blood are too high. This is dangerous because it affects all body cells and can result in a **coma**. Insulin affects all cells in the body, by making them respire faster. It also causes muscle and liver cells to take glucose out of the blood until the level is back to normal.

The pancreas produces insulin and glucagon.

lungs

liver

The adrenal glands produce adrenaline.

The ovaries in females produce oestrogen.

The testes in males produce testosterone.

C The main endocrine glands in a human body.

D Eating this will put a lot of glucose into the blood. Insulin brings the level of glucose back to normal.

> **5 a** In the case of insulin, name the sensor, the stimulus, the communication system and the effectors.
> **b** What happens when insulin is secreted into the blood?
>
> **6** Why does making cells respire faster affect the level of glucose in the blood?
>
> **7** Draw up a table to list similarities and differences in the way the nervous system and hormonal system work.

Summary

Multicellular animals like you have two _____ systems in the body. The nervous system carries messages around the body in _____. The messages are small _____ signals. The _____ system uses _____ called hormones to carry the messages. _____ is a hormone that controls the level of _____ in the blood.

chemicals   communication   electrical
glucose   hormonal   insulin   nerves

177

B3.8 Human evolution

How have humans evolved?

A These macaques learned to sit in hot spring water in winter by copying other macaques.

B The lions work together to hunt and kill prey larger than themselves.

C A chimpanzee uses a 'fishing rod' to get biting ants from an anthill.

All vertebrates have a brain and mammals have relatively large brains for the size of their bodies. This allows them to develop **complex behaviour**, such as:
- learning from experience by copying others
- working and communicating in groups
- using **tools**.

These kinds of behaviour improve the chances of survival.

The first **hominid** (human-like) species evolved from an ape-like ancestor around 7 million years ago. The hominids evolved differently from those ancestors who evolved into chimpanzees because they developed larger brains. They also began to walk more on two legs than on four. Around 2 million years ago they began to use tools.

? 1 Some macaques in Japan live near hot springs. How have they learnt to keep warm when the weather is cold?

2 How is being part of a group helpful to the animals in photo B?

3 How does using tools improve the chance of survival for the animal in photo C?

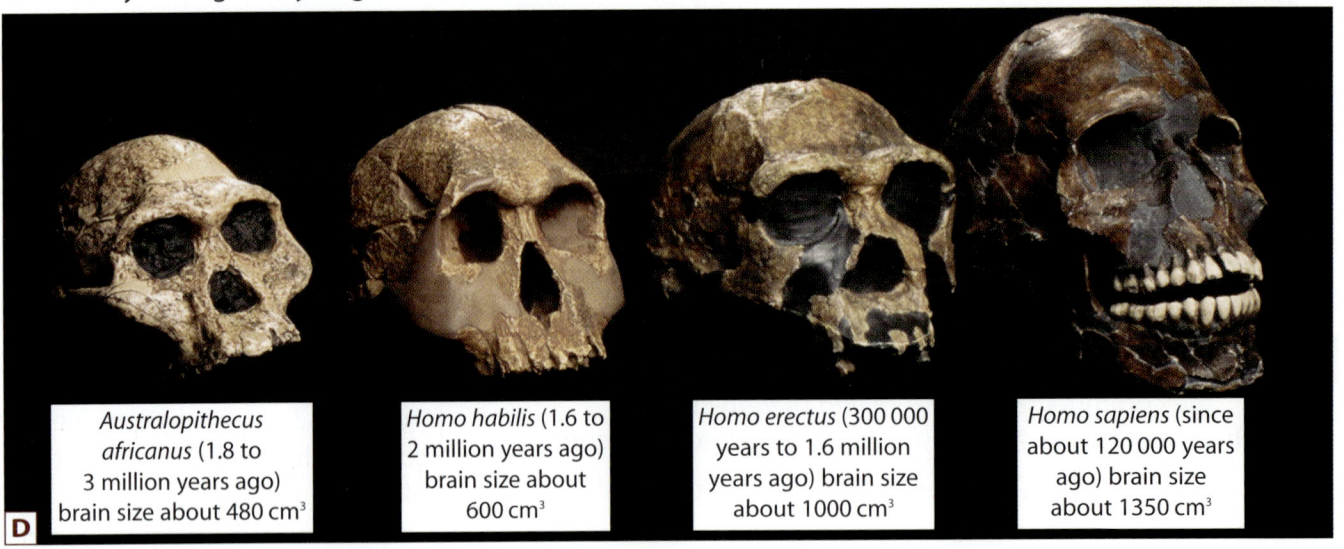

D *Australopithecus africanus* (1.8 to 3 million years ago) brain size about 480 cm^3

Homo habilis (1.6 to 2 million years ago) brain size about 600 cm^3

Homo erectus (300 000 years to 1.6 million years ago) brain size about 1000 cm^3

Homo sapiens (since about 120 000 years ago) brain size about 1350 cm^3

? 4 Describe the differences in the skulls in photo D.

5 All species of humans (*Homo*) have used tools, including hand axes and choppers. How could these have improved their chances of survival?

Many different species of hominid have evolved over the last 7 million years. More recent species have larger brains than older ones. They also show more complex behaviour, such as making more specialised tools, developing language and creating art.

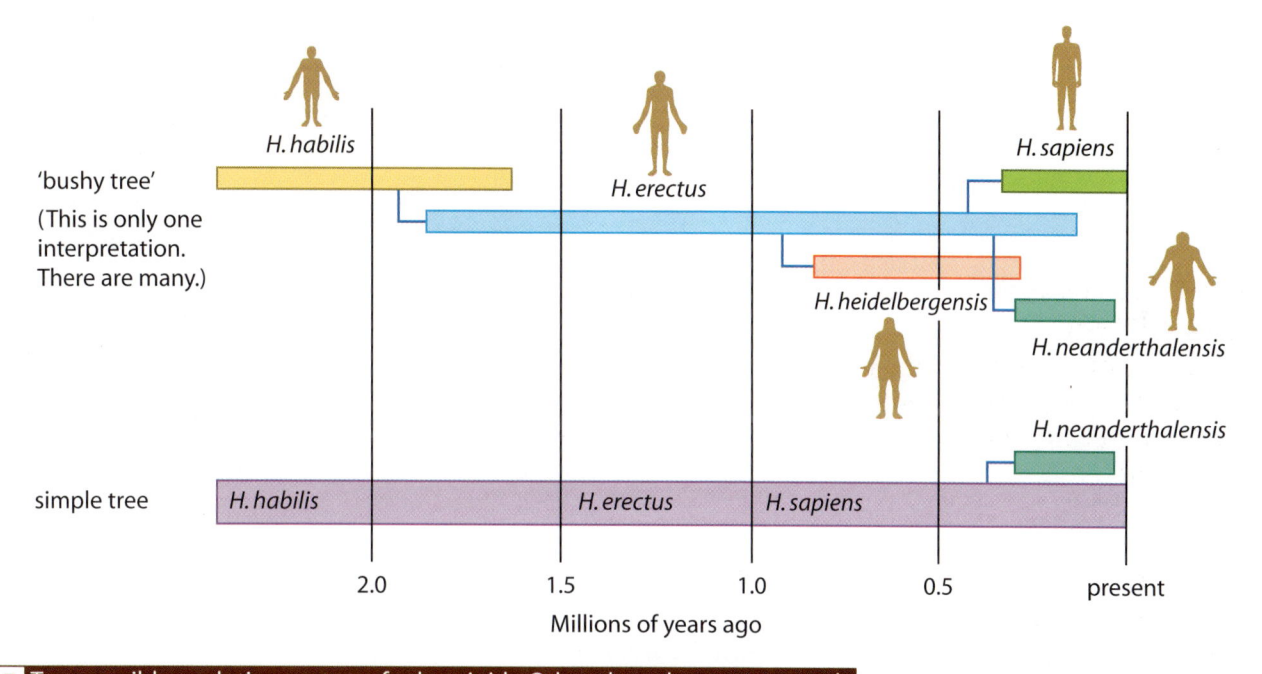

E Two possible evolutionary trees for hominids. Others have been suggested.

Diagram E shows two ways of arranging the timelines for hominid species. Some scientists arrange these time lines simply to make as few branches on the evolutionary tree as possible because they think one species evolved into another. Others arrange them to make a very bushy tree because they think that didn't happen.

6 Only one hominid species survives today.
   a Which is it?
   b What has happened to all the others?

7 A scientist who makes a simple evolutionary tree for hominids has a different explanation for what happened to *Homo erectus* than a scientist who draws a bushy tree. What are these two explanations?

Summary

Mammals have relatively large _____ for their size. This allows some of them to learn by _____, _____ in groups and use _____. The first _____ (human-like) species evolved about 7 million years ago. More recent hominid species have even _____ brains that gave them a better chance of _____. Only *Homo sapiens* still lives, all other hominid species are now _____.

brains   communicate   experience
extinct   hominid   larger   survival
tools

179

B3.9 Food webs

How are organisms linked in a food web?

A

Diagram A shows a **community** of plants and animals from the edge of a woodland. The plants in this **habitat** grow here because they are adapted to the **environmental conditions**, especially light, water and temperature. The animals are here because they feed on these plants, or on other animals that feed on the plants.

All the animals and plants in a habitat are linked in **food chains** that show how energy from food is passed from one organism to another. Food chains can be joined together into a **food web** for the habitat.

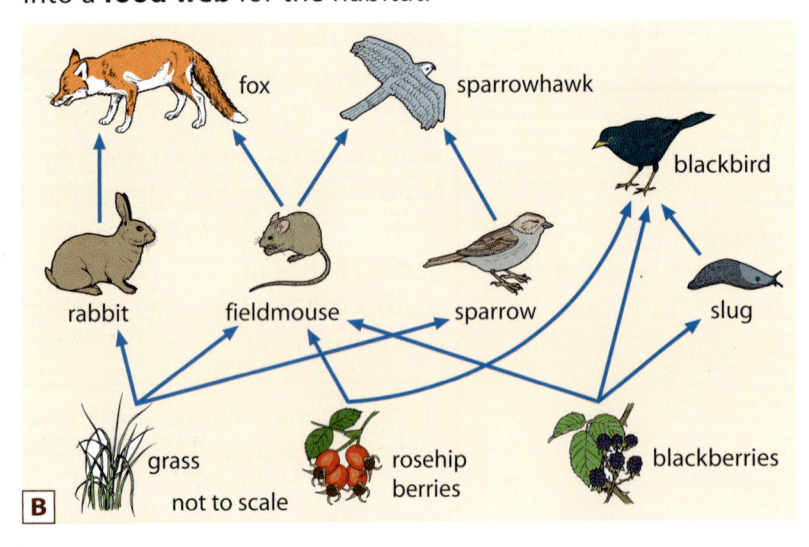

B not to scale

?
1. Name three factors in the environment that affect the growth of plants.
2. Why would a cactus not grow well in a British woodland?
3. If the conditions got drier in this habitat what could happen to the plants?
4. How would changes to the plants affect the animals in the habitat?

?
5. Look at diagram B.
   a. How many species feed on blackberries?
   b. How many different kinds of food do fieldmice eat?

180

In the food web in diagram B you can see that both blackbirds and fieldmice feed on rosehips. In a good year, when there are lots of berries, both species will have plenty to eat during the autumn and winter months. However, when there are very few berries there will be **competition** between the species. The most successful species will eat most of the berries.

? **6** Look at Diagram B.
  a If the blackbirds eat most of the berries, what can the fieldmice do?
  b If it has been a bad year for all kinds of fruit and seed, what might happen to the fieldmice?

The animals in a habitat compete with each other for resources such as food, mates or nesting sites. The plants compete with each other for light, water and space to grow.

C A fieldmouse also eats seeds.

D The trees in this woodland absorb most of the light, so that very few plants can grow on the ground beneath them.

E The koala only eats eucalyptus leaves.

A Investigate how environmental factors affect where a plant or animal species is found.

Most animals in a food web feed on several kinds of food or prey, and are called **generalist feeders**. However some, like the koala, only feed on one kind of food. These are called **specialist feeders**.

? **7** Think of a plus, a minus and an interesting point about this statement: The koala is the only animal that eats eucalyptus leaves.

8 Explain why most species of animal are more likely to be successful if they are generalist feeders.

Summary

The organisms in a _____ are linked together in a _____ that shows what eats what. When one kind of food is _____, there will be _____ between the animals that eat it. The _____ successful species might eat something else, leave the area or _____ of starvation.

community   competition   die
    food web   least   scarce

181

B3.10 Extinction

Why do species become extinct?

The fossil record contains many organisms that were once alive but are now extinct. There are many possible causes of extinction. Sometimes it happens because there is a big change in environmental conditions. For example, if it gets warmer and there is less rain, there may be long periods of drought.

A What would happen if the sea level rose?

A species may become extinct if a competitor or predator is introduced into the area where it lives. For example, around 10 000 years ago many large herd animals in northern Europe became extinct. This **correlates** with the time that populations of *Homo sapiens* were increasing and moving into these areas.

Plants and animals may also die if they become infected with a disease or a parasite (organisms that live inside other organisms). This does not usually cause the extinction of a whole species, but it might happen when a parasite or disease is introduced to an area where it did not exist before, where the plants and animals have not developed resistance.

? 1 a What will happen to most plants when there is a drought?
  b What will happen to all the small animals that used to eat those plants?
  c What might the larger animals and birds do to avoid dying?

2 Sea levels have risen and fallen many times during the history of life on Earth. Describe what effect rising sea levels in an area would have:
  a on the land animals that lived there
  b on the sea animals that lived nearby.

B This hut was made from mammoth bones by people who lived over 10 000 years ago.

? 3 a Why might *Homo sapiens* have caused the extinction of the woolly mammoth?
  b What else might have caused the extinction of the woolly mammoth?

Large changes in the environment can cause **mass extinctions**, when many species die out at the same time. The changes in conditions select for different characteristics in the new species that evolve. If conditions had changed in a different way then different new species would have evolved.

? 4 Use these table headings to make a table of all the factors you can think of that could cause a species become extinct.

Factors linked to non-living things	Factors linked to other species

5 Spring arrives 2 weeks earlier in the UK now compared with 40 years ago. Some organisms have changed to match this and others have not. Look at photo C and use the information below it to describe what may happen to the numbers of great tits.

C
- Great tits lay their eggs at the same time every year.
- 40 years ago great tit eggs hatched when most caterpillars were around.
- Today most caterpillars are around nearly two weeks earlier in the year because they feed on young oak leaves that open as soon as it starts to get warm.

Summary

The _____ record shows us that most of the _____ that once lived are now _____. Some died because of _____ in the environment, such as changes in _____. Some became extinct because of _____ with other organisms or because of _____.

changes   competition   disease
extinct   fossil   organisms
temperature

183

B3.11 Humans and extinctions

How do humans cause the extinction of other organisms?

A The numbers of giant panda are decreasing as we destroy the forests in which they live.

B The marsupial wolf of Tasmania was hunted to extinction in the early 1900s.

C Many ground-nesting birds in New Zealand are at risk of extinction from introduced predators like the rat.

D Galapagos penguins are at risk of extinction because of pollution in their habitat.

Homo sapiens is a very successful species. We eat a wide range of plant and animal foods from many food webs. We can also change our environment to make conditions suitable for us to live in. However, as we use the world to suit our needs we also affect the plants and animals around us. What we are doing threatens other species with extinction. We say they are **endangered**.

Over the past 200 years the human population has risen from less than 1 billion to over 6 billion, and it is still rising rapidly.

Group	Number of known species	Percentage of known species threatened with extinction in 2003
mammals	4 842	23%
birds	9 932	12%
fishes	28 100	3%
flowering plants	199 350	3%

E Species threatened with extinction.

1 Look at photographs A to D. Write down four ways that humans may cause the extinction of other species.

2 Which of the causes of extinction by humans is likely to be most important in the future? Explain your answer.

3 Look at table E. Why do you think that a greater proportion of mammals are threatened than other groups? (*Hint:* look back at your answer to question **1**.)

People are trying to protect and **conserve** endangered species in many different ways.

F Great crested newts are protected in the UK. You are not allowed to disturb ponds where they live.

G Elephants are killed for the ivory in their tusks. There is now a worldwide ban on trading in ivory to try to protect the African elephant.

H Crocodiles were once hunted for their skins. They are now being farmed so that wild animals are not killed.

I Scimitar-horned oryx were nearly extinct in the wild. Now individuals that have been bred in Marwell Zoo and other zoos have been released back into the wild.

?

4 Describe four ways in which endangered species are now being conserved and protected.

5 A National Park can be created to protect wildlife. Rules restrict what people can do in the National Park, such as where they can build or farm.
Describe some advantages and disadvantages of National Parks:
   a for the plants and animals that live in them
   b for the people who live in them.

Summary

Humans are causing the _____ of many other species by introducing predators, by _____, by changing their _____ to suit our needs, or through _____. We can try to _____ species from extinction by _____ the habitat where they live, by banning _____ in products from animals by _____ them so that wild animals are not killed, and by _____ them in zoos.

breeding   extinction   farming
habitats   hunting   pollution
protecting   save   trade

B3.12 Biodiversity

Why is biodiversity important?

A There are many more plant and animal species in the natural grassland than in the habitat that is being used for farming.

Biodiversity usually means the variety of living things within habitats. Some habitats, such as tropical forests and coral reefs, naturally have a higher biodiversity than others, such as moorland. When we change habitats to suit our needs, we usually reduce their biodiversity.

> **1** How do we affect the biodiversity of a habitat when we clear land to grow crops?

Habitats with high biodiversity have complex food webs. Most of the animals eat more than one kind of food.

> **2** What would happen to animals in a complex food web if one type of their food died out?

We can encourage biodiversity by leaving natural, undisturbed areas where plants and animals can live. These areas must be large enough to allow the plants and animals space to grow well and reproduce. When we use the environment in a way that does not damage the long-term survival of the organisms that live there, we are using it in a **sustainable** way.

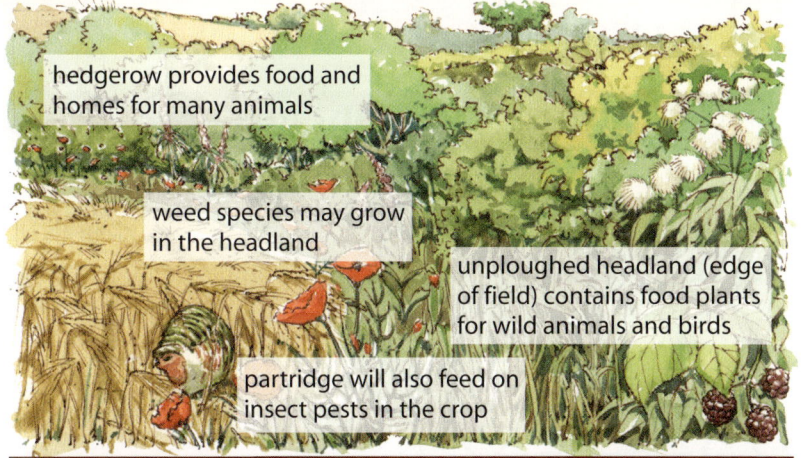

B Farmers are planting more hedgerows and leaving areas at the edges of fields unploughed to encourage wild plants and animals to return to the area.

- hedgerow provides food and homes for many animals
- weed species may grow in the headland
- unploughed headland (edge of field) contains food plants for wild animals and birds
- partridge will also feed on insect pests in the crop

3 Give one reason why planting hedgerows and leaving unploughed headlands can help wildlife.

4 a How could the farmer benefit from leaving headlands around crops?
b What disadvantage might there be to leaving headlands?

Biodiversity also refers to the amount of genetic variation in a species. In the crop field, the wheat plants are not just all the same species, they are all just one **variety** of that species, formed through selective breeding. So the genes in the wheat plants are all very similar. In the grassland, there are not only more different species of plants, there are different varieties of each species. If a disease kills one variety of grass plant in the grassland, the rest of the grass plants may not be affected.

5 What will happen in the crop field if that variety of wheat is susceptible to a disease?

C Wild potatoes contain many different genes that we might need in the future.

All the plants and animals that we use for food have varieties in the wild that contain different genes. In the future these genes could help us to improve our crops and farm animals, as they may carry characteristics for disease or pest resistance, for increased **yield**, or greater tolerance to drought.

6 The atmosphere may be getting warmer and drier in the summer in the UK. What would be the value of genes that give tolerance to drought?

7 Write a letter to a farmer explaining the benefits and possible drawbacks of sustainable farming.

Summary

A _____ that has many different _____ of plants and animals has a high _____. When we change a habitat we usually _____ the amount of biodiversity in it. If we use the habitat in a _____ way we can reduce the _____ we do to other organisms. Biodiversity also means the amount of _____ in the _____ of a species.

biodiversity   damage   genes
habitat   reduce   species
sustainable   variation

187

B3.13 Earth, life and humans

What do you know about life on Earth and humans?

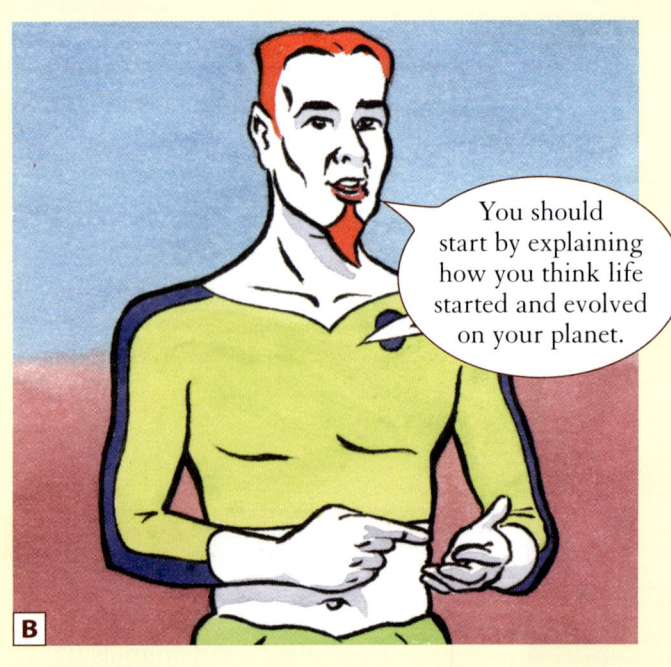

A: "This is the trial of the species called 'human' on the planet they call 'Earth'. I am here to help the humans to defend themselves."

B: "You should start by explaining how you think life started and evolved on your planet."

1. a What were conditions like on the early Earth?
   b What is the molecule called that can copy itself?
   c When did the first simple living things appear?
   d What is the evidence for this?

2. Living organisms have changed over time.
   a How do fossils show that species have changed over time?
   b How can scientists use fossils to work out how different species were related to each other?
   c Describe one difficulty in working out an accurate evolutionary tree using fossils.
   d What modern technique can be used to investigate the relationships between living organisms?

3. a How did Charles Darwin explain the evolution of different species? Describe his theory in as much detail as you can.
   b What evidence did Darwin have to support his theory?
   c Describe one other theory that has been used to explain how evolution happens.
   d Give two reasons why some people did not accept Darwin's theory when he first suggested it.

4. a What is a food web?
   b What does 'competition' mean in terms of a food web?
   c A disease that kills one type of plant can affect other plants and animals in the food web. Explain how.
   d A change in the climate can cause some species to become extinct. Explain how.

5. a How do humans detect changes in their surroundings?
   b Describe how the nervous system coordinates responses to stimuli. Use the following words in your answer: effector, sensor, brain, central nervous system.
   c Explain how the hormone insulin controls blood glucose. Name the sensor, stimulus and response in your answer.

C *Many species had become extinct on your planet before you humans evolved. Explain to us why you think this happened.*

6 Humans and some other animals can learn from their experiences, and they usually also live as part of a group.
  a Describe two ways in which living as a group can help a species to survive.
  b Describe two skills that humans need to learn to live in a group.
  c Describe four ways in which tools can help humans survive.
  d Describe briefly how hominid species have evolved since 7 million years ago.

D *Humans have caused many extinctions. How have humans done this when other species have not?*

7 Humans have caused the extinction of other species. Describe four different ways they have done this.

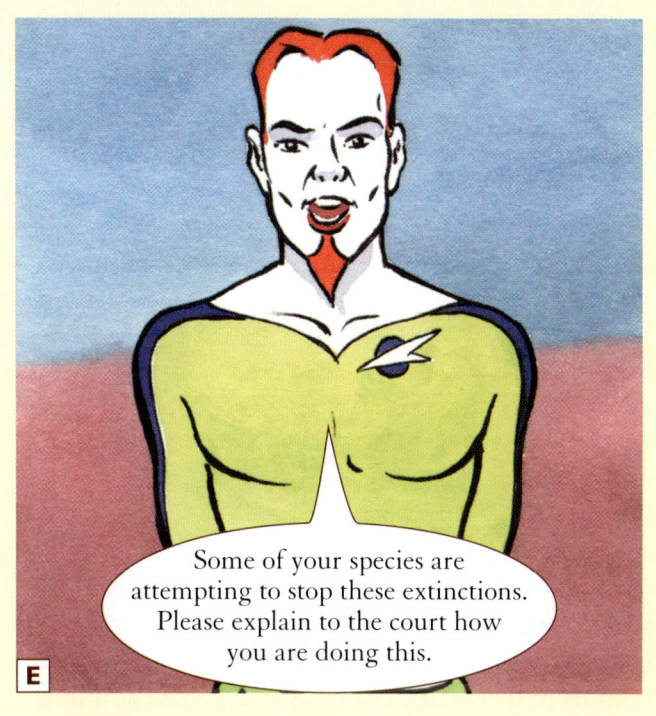

E *Some of your species are attempting to stop these extinctions. Please explain to the court how you are doing this.*

8 The time when many large Australian mammals became extinct correlates with the time that early humans were moving into this continent.
  a What does the word 'correlate' mean in the sentence above?
  b What evidence do scientists need to show that early humans caused the extinction of the large mammals?

9 a What are the two different meanings of the word 'biodiversity'?
  b How can biodiversity be increased on farmland?
  c Why is it important to keep wild varieties of crop plants and rare breeds of farm animals?

C3.1 Food matters

Why do we eat food?

THE HOURLY NEWS 16.00 August 10th 2047

FOOD BY PRESCRIPTION – IS THIS THE END OF FARMING?

Research scientists can now make all the food that we need. They start with the main elements that make up food: carbon, hydrogen, oxygen, nitrogen and sulfur. They then use these elements to make all the things needed for a healthy diet: carbohydrates, fats, proteins, fibre and vitamins. When mixed with water and small amounts of minerals, they can produce a diet that will meet anybody's requirements.

Dr Margaret Jones says 'This will have a great impact on the way that we eat. What we need to eat can be measured electronically every month, and a special mix made up specially for each person. The requirements can be recorded digitally on people's identity cards, which can then be e-mailed to the chemist who will make up the correct mixture. This should avoid the health problems connected with diet, such as obesity, diabetes and high blood pressure.

It will, however, have a major impact on farming in Britain, as there will be much less demand for home-grown food. The long-term effects on such an important industry are yet to be fully studied'.

This is not a new idea. Over 120 years ago, a chemist suggested that in the year 2000 'everyone will carry their food around with them as a little nitrogen pill, a little pat of fat, a little piece of starch and sugar, and a little jar of flavourings to suit their own taste'.

We eat food to obtain all of the chemicals that we need to stay alive. Our bodies need a variety of foods, and to be healthy we need these in the right amounts. Unfortunately many people eat too much of some foods, leading to the increasing problem of **obesity** in the UK and other developed countries. Meanwhile people in other countries, especially the developing world, eat too little, leading to **malnutrition**.

1. What would be the advantages and the disadvantages of eating your food as described above?
2. How would this change affect farmers?
3. Why do we eat food?

A A healthy meal.

B An unhealthy meal.

C These swollen bellies and stick-like arms are signs of a poor diet.

Many people are concerned about their diet, the fact that some people in the world do not have enough to eat, and also the way that food is produced. You need to know something about food and how it is grown and processed if you are going to make informed choices on these matters.

D Intensive farming.

E Free-range farming.

? 4 Think of a typical weekly food shopping trip for your family. List the main foods that you buy each week.

5 What do you think affects the choice of food that you or your parents buy? For example, price, packaging, speed of preparation, or something else?

6 Do you think about animal welfare issues when buying food?

7 a Does your family buy organic food?
  b If so, why?

C3.2 Producing food
How can we increase food production?

The population of the world has increased rapidly in the past 200 years. This means that we must now farm much more intensively so that we can get lots more food from the same area of land. At the end of 2003 the world's population was over 6.3 billion. By the year 2050, the United Nations estimates that this may have doubled.

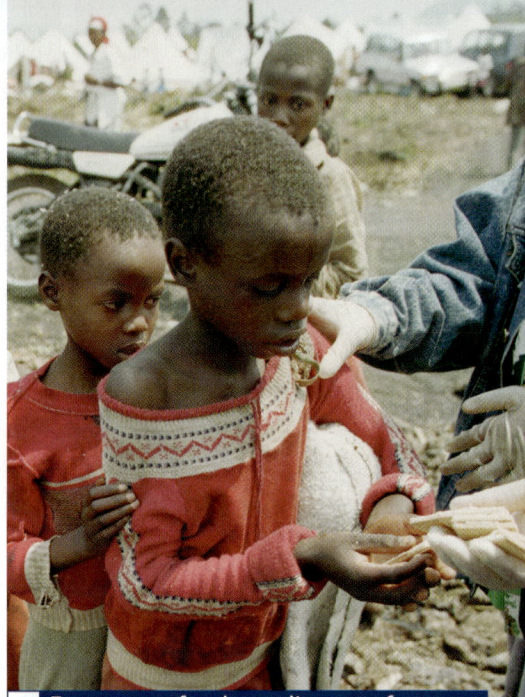

> **1** Why do we need to use intensive farming to grow food?
>
> **2** What will be the world population in 2050 according to the United Nations estimate?

Plants are similar to animals in that they need food. Plants make their own food using the process of **photosynthesis**. To do this, they need carbon, oxygen and hydrogen from carbon dioxide and water.

Plants also need other elements as nutrients to grow well. Of these, nitrogen is the most important as it is needed to make the protein molecules that are found in plant as well as animal cells. Nitrogen is essential for the development of leaves and stems and for good growth of grass and leafy vegetables. Plants absorb nitrogen from the soil in compounds called **nitrates**.

A Emergency food supplies are often needed where there have been years of drought, and in war zones where a lack of transport leads to a lack of food.

> **3** Describe three ways in which nitrates are needed for plant growth.

Growing crops absorb nutrients such as nitrates from the soil, so there will be fewer nutrients for the next crop. Some nutrients are lost to the air. Some dissolve in rain water and soak deep into the ground or are washed away into streams and rivers. They therefore need to be replaced or the land will gradually produce less and less food.

Fertilisers contain specially balanced amounts of these nutrients and can be used to replace what has been lost, so that plants grow well.

B Plants which do not get enough nitrates are stunted and have yellowish leaves.

> **4** How do we replace nutrients lost from the soil?

> **A** How can you show that plants grow better if they have added nitrates?

192

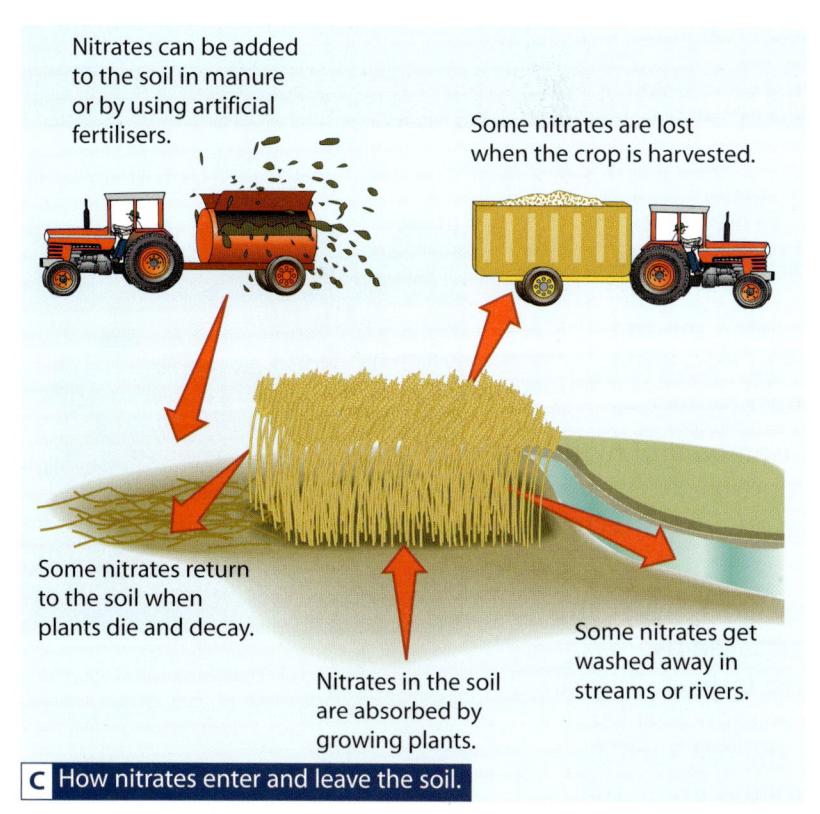

Nitrates can be added to the soil in manure or by using artificial fertilisers.

Some nitrates are lost when the crop is harvested.

Some nitrates return to the soil when plants die and decay.

Nitrates in the soil are absorbed by growing plants.

Some nitrates get washed away in streams or rivers.

C How nitrates enter and leave the soil.

Scientific knowledge about plant breeding has also helped to avoid these food shortages. For example, special breeds of cereals have been developed that provide more food from each plant. In Britain these cereals are mainly wheat and barley.

?
5 **a** Which part of the barley is used for food?
   b Suggest another advantage of having short stalks in a windy country.

6 What elements other than nitrogen are there in the fertiliser shown in picture E?

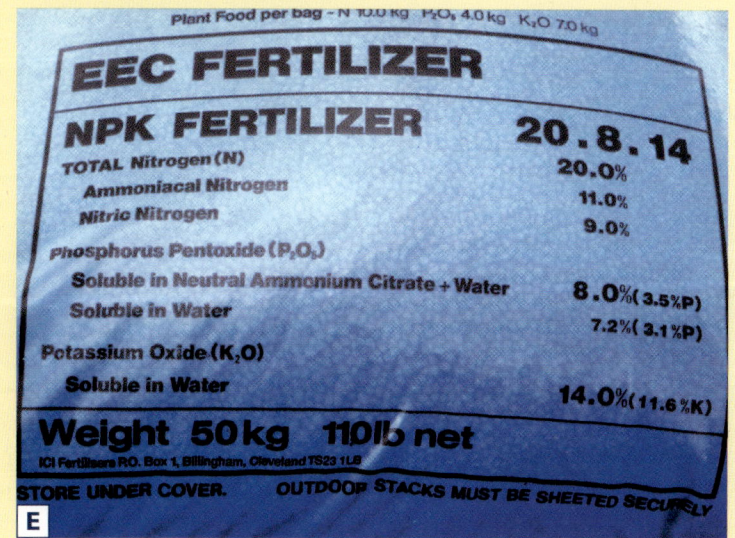

E EEC FERTILIZER
NPK FERTILIZER 20.8.14
TOTAL Nitrogen (N) 20.0%
 Ammoniacal Nitrogen 11.0%
 Nitric Nitrogen 9.0%
Phosphorus Pentoxide (P_2O_5)
 Soluble in Neutral Ammonium Citrate + Water 8.0% (3.5%P)
 Soluble in Water 7.2% (3.1%P)
Potassium Oxide (K_2O)
 Soluble in Water 14.0% (11.6%K)
Weight 50kg 110lb net

D This barley has been selectively bred so that it has short stalks. This avoids energy being wasted in growing long stalks.

Summary

We need to grow more food as the world _____ is rapidly _____. Special crops which give more _____ from each plant have been developed. We can also increase the amount grown by using _____. These contain the important nutrient _____ which is needed for healthy plant growth.

fertilisers   food   increasing
nitrate   population

193

C3.3 Intensive farming

How do intensive farmers look after their crops?

Fertilisers

Many farmers in Britain today use **synthetic fertilisers**. These allow the farmer to grow the same crop in large fields every year without using up all the nutrients in the soil. Farmers grow the crop that is most suited to the climate and soil type, or the one that will make most money.

Synthetic fertilisers increase the **yield** (the amount of food produced) of crops grown, but there are drawbacks. Growing the same crop every year can have severe effects on the structure of the soil.

Soil usually has a crumbly structure which allows water and air to penetrate easily. This structure is destroyed by fertilisers and very fine, dusty soil is formed instead. This can be blown away by the wind, causing soil erosion. Fertilisers also reduce the numbers of organisms in the soil, such as worms, which help to break down plant matter in the soil and release nutrients naturally.

A In Britain, we try to produce as much wheat as possible so we do not have to buy foreign wheat.

> **1** Why do farmers use synthetic fertilisers?
> **2** What can cause soil erosion?

Nitrates in the soil can also be washed away into lakes and rivers. Here they help the rapid growth of water plants, including algae. These block out light to plants below, which die. **Decomposers** (microbes that break down organisms) feed on the dead plants and grow rapidly, using up all the oxygen in the water. If this happens quickly, other plants and animals cannot get enough oxygen and die. This is called **eutrophication**. Nitrates may also cause water pollution.

These problems can be avoided by only using fertilisers when the plants are growing rapidly and absorb the chemicals quickly.

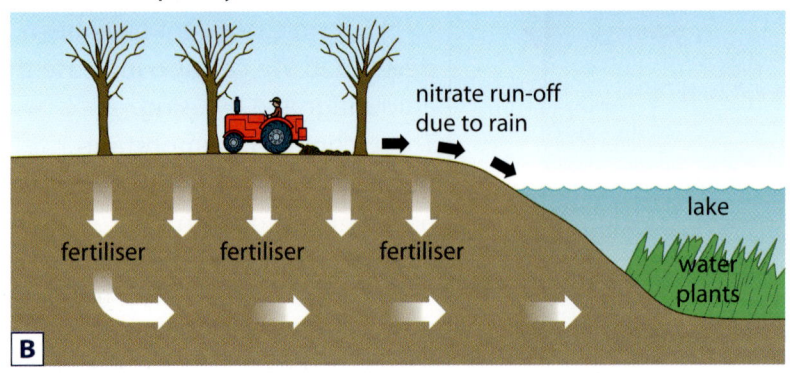

B

> **3 a** What are the advantages of using synthetic fertilisers?
> **b** What are the disadvantages of using them?

Pesticides

Growing similar crops close together causes problems if there is an infection of the crop. The pest or parasite will spread very quickly through the crops because the fields are very large. Growing the same crop year after year on the same land allows pests to attack earlier, especially if they have survived the winter in the soil or nearby wild plants.

Infections by fungi and insects such as aphids can cause severe damage to all sorts of plants. Weeds also compete with crops, taking nutrients out of the ground and reducing the yield of the crop.

An intensive farmer tries to control these pests and weeds using **pesticides**. Chemicals used against weeds are called **herbicides**, those used against insects are called **insecticides** and those used against fungi are called **fungicides**.

Herbicides may kill the crop that is being grown and they also kill wild flowers. Some farmers use selective herbicides to kill the weeds but not the crop.

Pesticides can cause problems by killing insects that might be natural predators of the insects that do damage.

C Aphids damage plants by sucking out their juices.

D Most of this field was sprayed with selective herbicide to kill the poppies without damaging the crop.

?
4 What are the differences between insecticides, herbicides and fungicides?

5 Name an insect that damages crops.

6 Describe two problems caused by growing crops close together.

7 Explain why pesticides killing other insects is a problem.

Summary

Farmers use _____ and _____ to increase the amount of crops grown. _____ kill weeds, _____ kill insects and _____ kill fungi. Intensive farming can lead to soil _____ and water _____.

erosion   fertilisers   fungicides
herbicides   insecticides   pesticides
pollution

195

C3.4 Organic farming
What is organic farming?

Organic farming is farming without the use of any synthetic fertilisers or pesticides. Instead, **natural fertilisers** are added to the soil and wildlife is used to control pests.

An organic farmer sees the farm as a whole, with the individual parts depending on one another. If animals are reared, the manure from these is spread on the ground as a natural fertiliser. This avoids the problem of loss of soil structure that happens with synthetic fertilisers, but can lead to a lack of some nutrients in the soil. In addition, manure may be more expensive to buy and difficult to apply, and pollution is still possible.

> **1** What are **a** the advantages and **b** the disadvantages of using manure?
>
> **2** Describe each year of crop rotation and explain why it is used.

Pests can be controlled naturally. If different crops are grown each year in a field, the number of pests cannot get very large as they die off in the years when the crop they feed on is not being grown. Pests can be controlled biologically by encouraging predators that feed on them.

Fallow. Only grass is grown. Cattle can feed on it and so add natural fertiliser.

Wheat. The stalks are ploughed back into the soil to replace some nutrients and to help aerate the soil.

Beans. These make their own fertiliser from the air and so make the soil more fertile.

A Crop rotation helps to keep the soil fertile.

B These pheasants feed on insect pests in the crop. Organic farmers keep more hedges to provide shelter for pheasants.

An organic farm also looks different to an intensive farm:
- The fields tend to be smaller, with boundaries such as hedges and ditches to provide homes for natural predators. Using more hedges also reduces soil erosion.
- A number of different crops are grown.

> **3** Describe two organic methods of controlling pests
>
> **4** How can you tell that a farm is organic by its appearance?

A Design a survey to find out whether people want to buy organic food, and their reasons for or against.

By 2005 there were 4010 organic farms in the UK, working about 4% of the farmland. The farms have to follow UK national standards if they want to advertise their foods as 'organic'.

More people want to buy organic food as they worry about the methods used to make food, and also the health risks of pesticide residues. However, organic food is more expensive as less is produced and amounts grown in the same area may vary.

This means that it is even more difficult for organic farmers to make a good living, especially when cheap imports from other countries are available. There is some government support to help organic farmers.

C Organic farms need a lot of labour which is more expensive.

D Organic foods are often more expensive.

?
5 Why do more people want to buy organic food?
6 Why do organic farmers make less money than intensive farmers?
7 Draw a table to show the advantages and disadvantages of organic farming and intensive farming.

Summary

Organic farmers do not use synthetic _____ or _____. Crop rotation keeps the soil _____ and prevents the build-up of _____. Animal pests can be controlled by encouraging _____. Organic farmers may make less money than _____ farmers, but are supported by the government.

fertile   fertilisers   intensive
pesticides   pests   predators

197

C3.5 Food additives
Why are food additives used?

Food additives are chemicals which are added to our food during its production. Although many people think that food additives are a 'modern invention', they have in fact been used for centuries. Saltpetre was used in the Middle Ages to preserve meat, especially important when there were no fridges or freezers. Nowadays nitrite, the active ingredient of saltpetre, is used. It prevents bacteria growing on meat that cause a rare but often deadly form of food poisoning called botulism.

A Saltpetre was dug out of the ground, purified and then used to preserve meat.

? 1 Why did people in the Middle Ages use saltpetre?

pickled chillies   pickled onions   pickled beetroot

B Vinegar has been used to preserve food for many years.

If you look at the label on any type of processed food, you are likely to find a whole list of additives. These are grouped according to what they do.

- **Colours** make processed food look more attractive, and also match our expectations of what some foods should look like. Many colours are artificial, but some are natural, such as anthocyanin (which is red) and chlorophyll (which is green)
- **Emulsifiers** and **stabilisers** keep ingredients mixed together when they would normally separate, for example oil and water in salad dressings.
- **Flavour enhancers** have little flavour of their own, but bring out the flavour in a wide range of foods. For example, monosodium glutamate is an amino acid which is used a lot in Chinese cookery.

C Strawberries and strawberry jams.

- **Preservatives** such as sorbic acid keep food safe for longer by preventing the growth of harmful microbes. Traditional methods of food preservation, such as drying, salting, pickling in vinegar and smoking are not always appropriate for all foods, although salt is often added as a flavouring.
- **Sweeteners**, such as saccharin, sweeten food without adding calories. These are used to reduce the amount of sugar in processed foods and drinks.

? 4 Look at photo D. What types of additives are in each of these foods?

5 Why do many people use sweeteners?

All additives are given **E-numbers** when they have passed a safety test and have been approved for use in the UK and the rest of Europe. European law requires that additives used in food should be clearly labelled in the list of ingredients on the label or packet, either by name or E-number.

? 6 Think of a plus, a minus and an interesting point about this statement: No additives should be used in foods.

7 Find out the names of two other types of food additive, and why they are used.

? 2 Look at photo C.
  a Which product has been artificially coloured?
  b Why do you think this was done?

3 Give two examples of foods that are pickled in vinegar.

D

Summary

Additives can be used for different reasons. _____ make food look more attractive, _____ _____ add flavour, _____ keep food for longer, _____ make the food sweet and _____ help oil and water to mix. _____ are used to tell us that additives have been approved.

colours   emulsifiers   E-numbers
flavour enhancers   preservatives
sweeteners

199

C3.6 Additives and safety
Are additives safe?

The companies that make our food often use additives to make them taste or look better, to encourage people to buy their products, or to stop the food spoiling. However, some people are concerned that there may be health risks from some additives.

'We use preservatives in all of our products to make the food keep longer. If we didn't there would be more wasted food, and we would have to charge higher prices.'

Mr Bowler – Fast Foods Ltd

'My doctor told me that I should only buy food that has reduced salt. He says that if we eat too much salt we increase the risk of high blood pressure and heart attacks.'

Mrs Evans

'I've read that the average person in Britain eats about 35 kilos of added sugar in their diet each year. They say that being overweight is unhealthy, but I feel fine'.

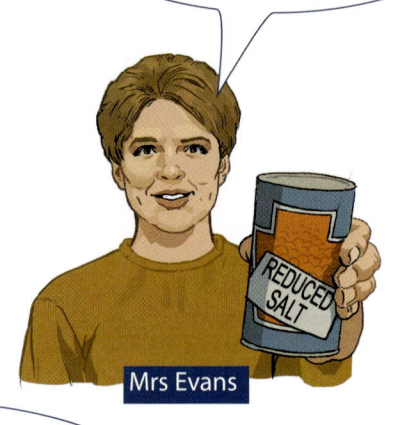

Ben

'Some winemakers added antifreeze to their wine to make it sweeter. This was only discovered when one of them claimed a tax deduction on the antifreeze! That would never be allowed now.'

Mr Green

'We do not have any freezers and it is a long walk to get any food. We try to buy food that has preservatives in it, so that it does not rot in the heat.'

Maria

A Debate the use of additives, and decide which ones should be allowed and which ones should be banned. Give reasons for all your decisions.

'My Nathan will only drink a certain kind of orange squash, and nothing else. I've been told that the colour in it may make him uncontrollable, but what else can I do? He can't go without drink.'

Mrs Taylor

Pippa

'I think that sweeteners are great. I can drink as much of this as I like without putting on any weight. I drink about eight cans a day.'

'I've read that too many colours are added to this Chicken Tikka Masala, but it doesn't seem to taste the same if the colours are left out'.

'I'm a chemist working for the **Food Standards Agency**. We check that food additives are safe, and make certain that laws on additives are kept up-to-date.'

Dr Appleton

John

?
1. List as many reasons as you can for putting additives in food.
2. Describe some reasons why additives should not be used.
3. Why do you think Ben is obese?
4. Do you think that Pippa is sensible to drink so much diet drink? Explain your answer.
5. Does the need for additives vary from country to country? Explain your answer.
6. Why do we need regulations to make our food safe?
7. Suppose that the government banned the use of preservatives. Who would suffer from this ban and who would benefit from it?

Summary

Some _____ used in this country are bad for our _____. Some additives are needed to make our food _____ to eat, while we could manage without others. Additives are controlled by the Food _____ Agency.

additives   health   safe   Standards

201

C3.7 Chemical contaminants 1

Is unprocessed food safe to eat?

A Both these mushrooms are poisonous. (Fly Agaric, Deathcap)

Not all plants are safe to eat. Many years ago, people often picked wild mushrooms in fields, but nowadays people are afraid of eating **toxic** (poisonous) mushrooms. The most deadly mushroom in this country is the Deathcap, which causes 90% of all deaths from fungus poisoning.

Some types of food are only safe to eat if they are properly cooked. For example, kidney beans must be boiled for at least 10 minutes to destroy poisonous chemicals. This is not normally a problem as most people buy canned, cooked beans.

? 1 Suggest a reason why more people die from eating Deathcap mushrooms than Fly Agaric mushrooms.

B One type of cassava must be cooked properly or it is poisonous.

C Cassava tubers.

? 2 Why is it always important to read the cooking instructions on food?

3 Why do most people use canned rather than raw kidney beans?

About 1–2% of the population are **allergic** to foods like peanuts or shellfish. If they eat even the tiniest amount of the food, their body reacts by producing special chemicals. These cause a condition called **anaphylaxis** where the mouth and tongue quickly swell, causing difficulties in breathing and even death. Many people with these allergies carry a special injection around with them, so that they can give themselves the antidote if it is needed. All foods that may cause allergic reactions must be labelled.

Some people are unable to eat certain foods because their bodies cannot deal with them. For example, some people cannot eat foods containing gluten (in wheat flour) or cow's milk. Many supermarkets now sell products for people with allergies.

> **?**
> 4 What is anaphylaxis?
> 5 Name two foods that people who cannot eat gluten should avoid.
> 6 Name three foods that people who cannot drink cow's milk should avoid.

Foods can be contaminated while they are being stored before use. For example, **aflatoxin** is a poisonous substance produced by a mould that grows on crops like peanuts and cereals. Any foods with this mould must be destroyed. About 25% of the world's food crops are affected by these moulds each year.

D People with severe food allergies always carry epipens with them.

E These foods are made especially for people who have certain allergies.

F Farmers must prevent mould growing on these peanuts.

People also worry about pesticides and herbicides that may remain in food, particularly in food from intensive farms.

> **?**
> 7 Why would farmers lose money if their crops were infected by disease?
> 8 Find out what people can use as an alternative to cow's milk.

Summary

Some plants contain _____ chemicals, and some foods are poisonous if they are not _____ properly. Some people suffer from _____ or their bodies cannot use certain foods such as _____. Harmful _____ produce chemicals called _____. Residues of _____ and _____ may remain in food that we eat.

aflatoxins   allergies   cooked
herbicides   milk   moulds
pesticides   toxic

C3.8 Chemical contaminants 2
How can harmful chemicals get into food?

Most of the food that is bought in supermarkets has some sort of packaging.

Chemicals from packaging can sometimes be absorbed by the food that it contains. For example, cling film contains chemicals that may be harmful to humans. However, these chemicals are only likely to get into foods if the cling film gets hot or if very fatty foods such as cheese or pastry are wrapped in the film.

A Do these cakes really need three layers of packaging?

B Not all food is packaged before it is sold.

? 1 a What are the advantages of packaging food?
 b What are the disadvantages?
 2 How could you stop harmful chemicals from cling film getting into food?

Packaging is meant to be used only once, and with the type of food it was designed for. A material may not be safe for other foods as the chemicals from the packaging could move into these new types of food. For example, plastic bottles in which water is sold should not be used for fruit juice. This is because the juice is acidic and chemicals in the plastic bottle may react with these acids.

C These bottles should only be used for water.

? 3 Why should you not reuse plastic bottles for other types of drink?

Another chemical used in food packaging that causes concern is called **bisphenol**. This is used to coat the insides of some food cans. When these cans are heated to kill bacteria, the bisphenol coating stops the metal of the can from contaminating the food. However, bisphenols may interfere with our sex hormones. There are now strict rules which state that these bisphenols must only be used when they do not change the quality of the food.

?
4 Why are cans of food heated?
5 What might happen to the taste of food if it was in direct contact with the metal?

Some harmful chemicals may form as the food is being cooked. Recently, scientists discovered high levels of a chemical called **acrylamide** in starchy foods that had been cooked at high temperatures. These included potato crisps, bread and crispbread. Acrylamide is known to cause cancer in animals and its presence in foods may harm people's health. Although this worried people when it was discovered, the British Food Standards Agency has advised people not to change what they eat.

D The bisphenols inside this can may be harmful.

E The way in which these foods were made may have produced a harmful chemical.

Many people can reduce the amount of harmful chemicals that they are exposed to by eating a healthy diet. This means eating more freshly prepared food rather than lots of processed food, together with plenty of fresh fruit and vegetables.

?
6 Name two other foods that contain starch, but which are not cooked at such high temperatures.

Summary

Food can be _____ when harmful chemicals form during _____. Also chemicals from _____ may move into the food. Most of these problems are _____.

avoidable   contaminated   cooking   packaging

205

C3.9 Digestion
What happens to food after we have eaten it?

Most of the food that we eat is in the form of **polymers**. These are large molecules that cannot be absorbed by the body in their natural state because the molecules are too big. **Starch** is a polymer made up of many glucose units joined together. It contains carbon, oxygen and hydrogen. **Proteins** are also polymers, made of **amino acids** that contain mainly carbon, oxygen, hydrogen and nitrogen. Both starch and proteins have to be digested – broken down into smaller molecules.

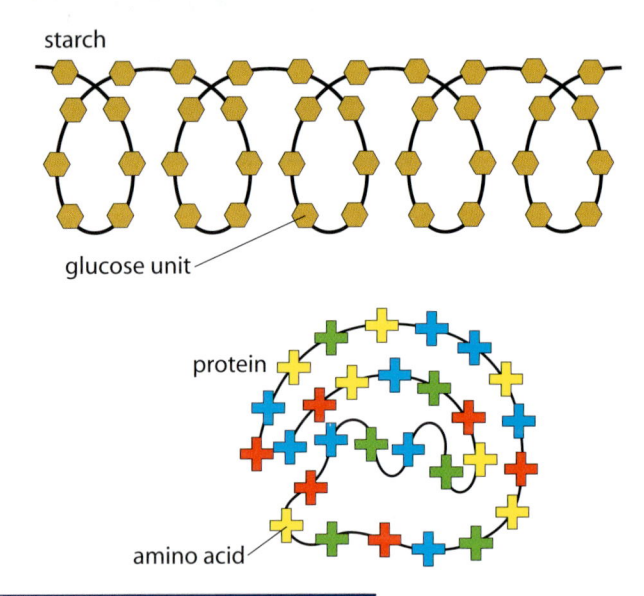

A Starch and proteins are polymers.

Cellulose is also a polymer of glucose molecules, but it is not digested by humans. It is often called **fibre**, and helps waste products move easily through our intestines. Low-fibre diets are linked to many bowel disorders, including cancer.

? 1 a How are starch and cellulose similar?
   b How are they different?

Digestion is caused by **enzymes**, which are produced and then added to food at various places in the gut. Enzymes help to break down large insoluble food molecules into smaller soluble ones that can be absorbed. Starch is broken down into **glucose**, and proteins are broken down into **amino acids**.

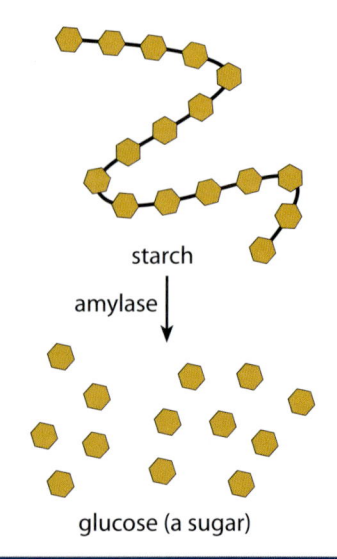

B Enzymes break down starch into glucose.

Food is chewed in the **mouth** and is mixed with saliva which contains enzymes.

gullet

tongue

Glandular tissue in the **stomach** wall makes gastric juice. This contains hydrochloric acid and other enzymes.

liver

The **pancreas** makes amylase and other enzymes, which are added to the food in your small intestine.

Undigested food passes through the **large intestine** and water is absorbed into the blood.

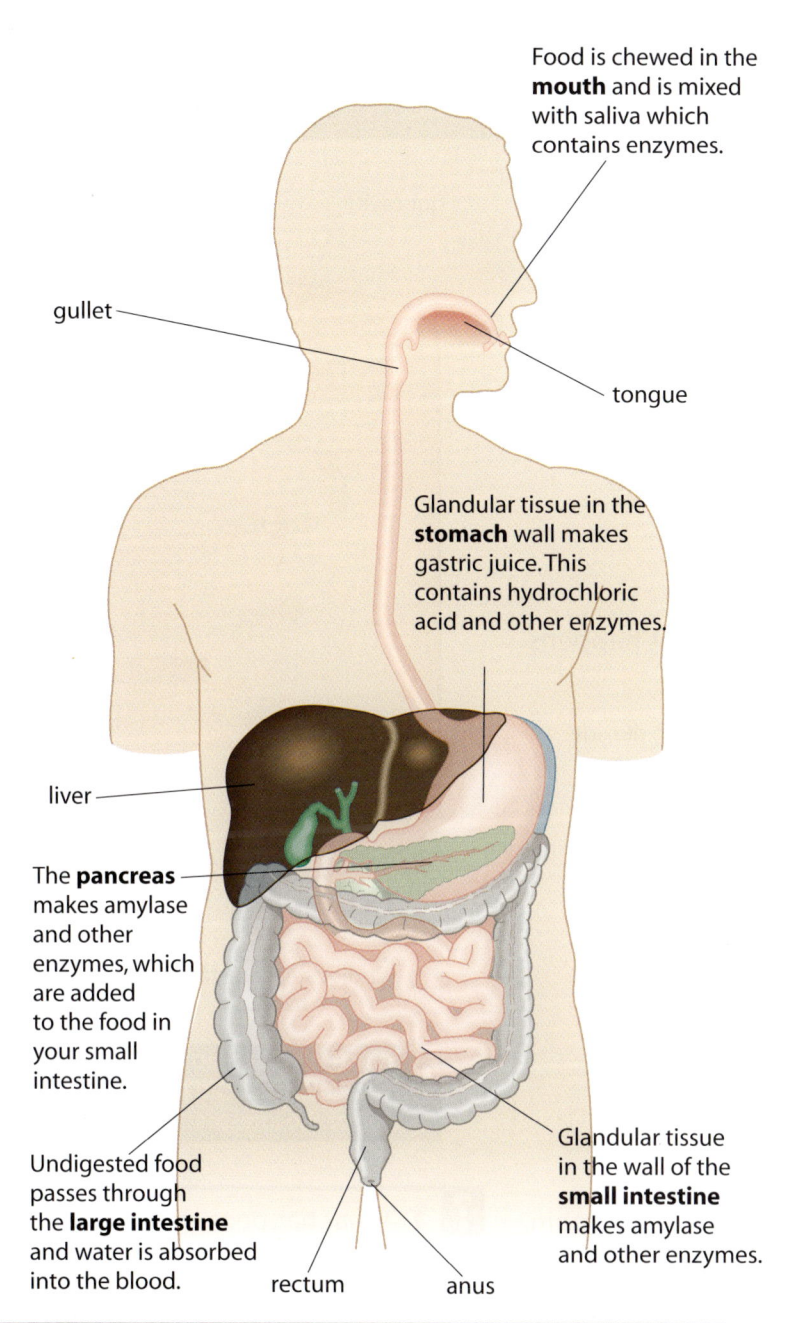

rectum

anus

Glandular tissue in the wall of the **small intestine** makes amylase and other enzymes.

C The human digestive system and the chemicals added to food.

**? **
2 List all the organs in your digestive system in the order in which food goes through them.

3 Write down two organs that produce enzymes

4 Where is starch digested?

5 Which is the odd one out: glucose, protein, starch? Explain your answers.

6 You eat a cheese sandwich and have a glass of water.
 a Which nutrients are in the meal?
 b Describe the journey of the meal through the gut.

Summary

In the _____ system, _____ are used to break down large food _____ into smaller ones which can be absorbed. Starch and proteins are both _____. Starch is converted into _____, and _____ are converted into amino acids

enzymes   glucose   molecules
digestive   polymers   proteins

207

C3.10 Using food

How do our bodies use food?

Once food has been broken down into small, water-soluble molecules, it passes through the wall of the small intestine into the bloodstream. Larger molecules cannot pass through, and are removed from the body in the faeces. The molecules absorbed into the blood are then taken to all the cells of the body which need them.

All our cells need energy. They get this energy from glucose in a process called **respiration**. This energy is used to:
- keep us warm
- allow us to move
- help us grow.

In fact, energy is used in almost every change that happens in our bodies.

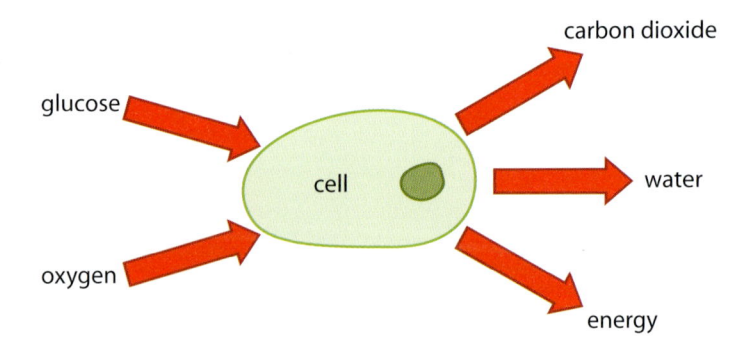

B The process of respiration happens inside cells.

Some cells also use energy to build up amino acid molecules into new large protein molecules. Muscle, tendons, skin and hair are all mainly proteins. Haemoglobin, which carries oxygen around the body in the bloodstream, is also a protein.

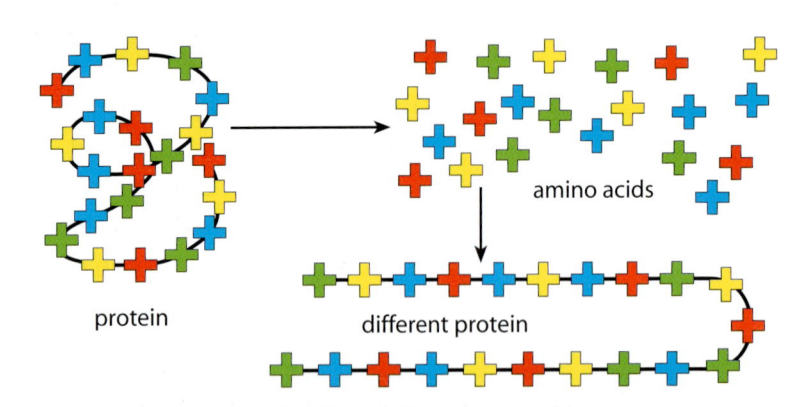

C Amino acids from one type of protein in our food can be converted into totally different new proteins.

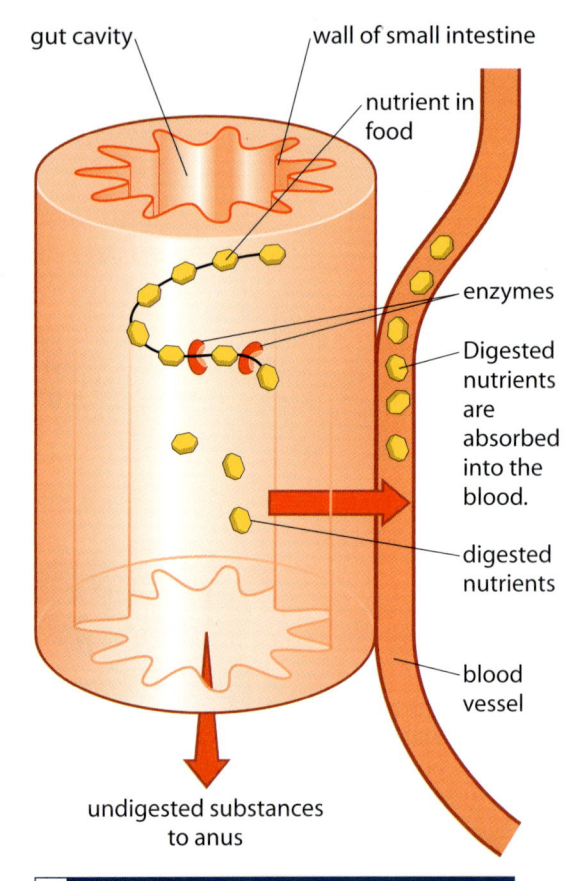

A Starch is broken up into glucose molecules that can pass through the wall of the intestine.

? 1 What happens to food when it has been broken down into smaller molecules?

2 a What is respiration?
 b Which substances are the reactants in respiration?
 c Which substances are waste products of respiration?

Any excess glucose or fats that we do not need are stored as fat under our skin. If we eat too much fat it can clog up our arteries and cause serious health problems.

> **?** 3 What happens to amino acids once they have been absorbed into the bloodstream?
> 4 Name three parts of the body which are made of proteins.
> 5 What happens if we eat too much fat?

Any amino acids that have not been turned into proteins can cause harm if they build up in cells. The blood carries the amino acids to the **liver**, where they are turned into **urea**, which is harmless. This urea is then taken to the **kidneys** and **excreted** as urine.

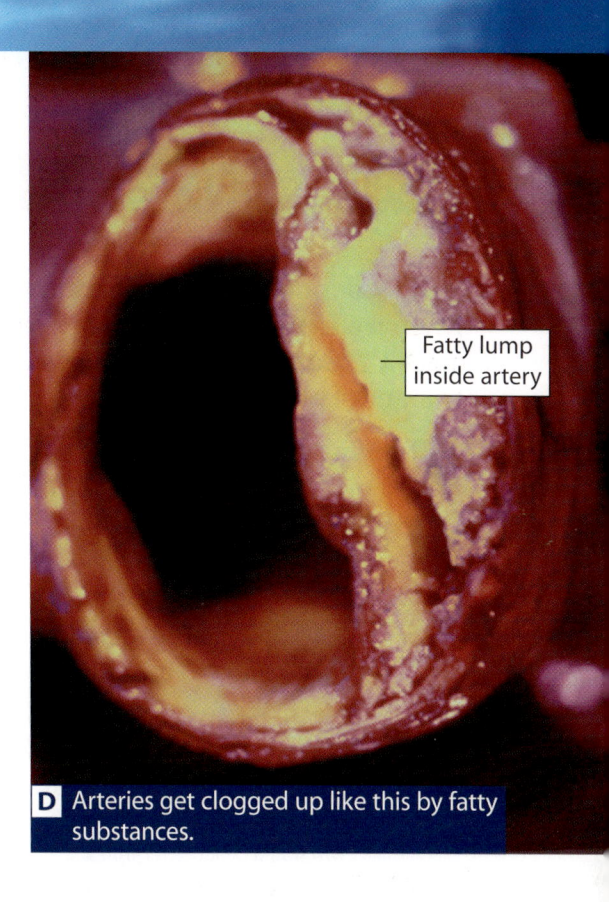

Fatty lump inside artery

D Arteries get clogged up like this by fatty substances.

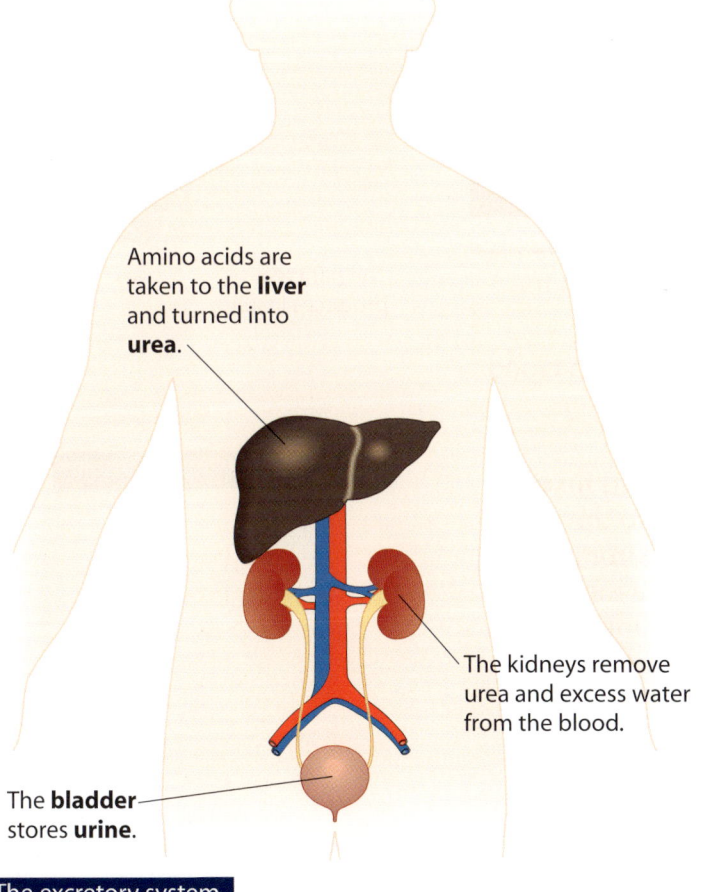

Amino acids are taken to the **liver** and turned into **urea**.

The kidneys remove urea and excess water from the blood.

The **bladder** stores **urine**.

E The excretory system.

> **?** 6 a Why do we need to excrete amino acids?
> b How does this happen?
> 7 Why might we suffer from obesity if we eat too much starch or sugar?

Summary

Our _____ need energy which they get from _____ in respiration. Amino _____ are used to make _____, such as _____, skin and hair. Any unwanted amino acids are taken to the _____, where they are turned into _____. This is then _____ via the _____. Unwanted fat can build up under the skin or in _____.

acids   arteries   cells   excreted
glucose   muscle   kidneys   liver
proteins   urea

209

C3.11 Diabetes

What is diabetes?

Many foods contain sugar, especially some processed foods. When we eat sugar it is broken down to glucose which is quickly absorbed into the bloodstream. This causes the amount of glucose in the blood to increase rapidly.

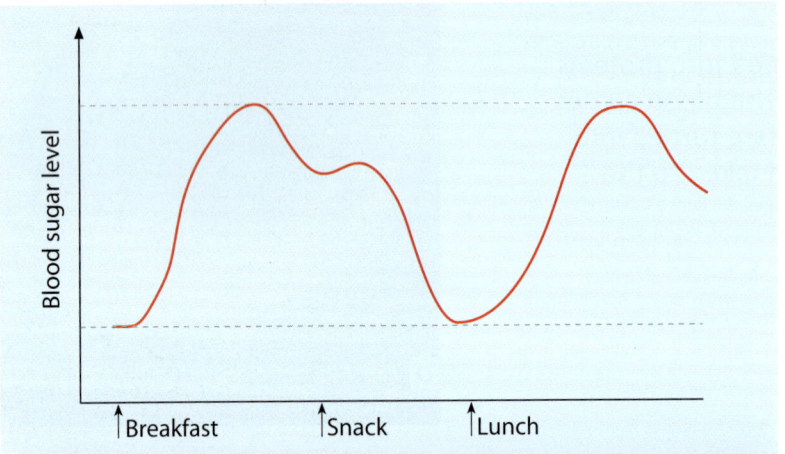

A A sugary meal gets turned into glucose, which then affects the amount of glucose in the blood.

?
1. What kind of food increases the levels of glucose in the blood?
2. Why doesn't a high protein diet have any effect on blood glucose levels?

The pancreas produces insulin.

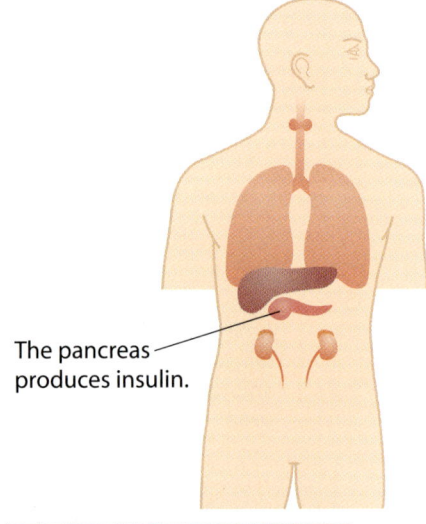

B The pancreas makes insulin.

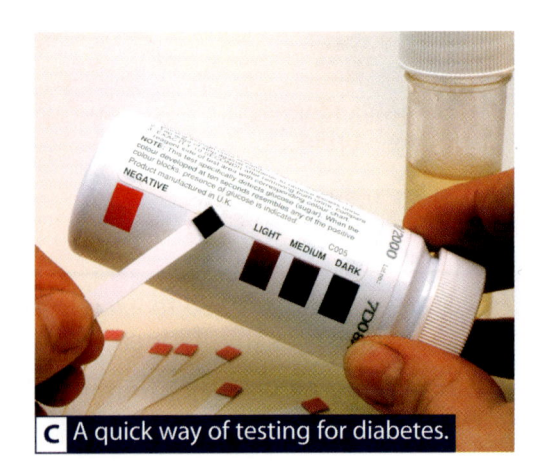

Glucose levels are controlled by a **hormone** called **insulin**, which is made in the **pancreas** and released into the bloodstream. Insulin helps cells to take glucose from the blood, which the cells use for respiration. After a meal, more insulin is made to deal with the increased amount of glucose in the blood. The glucose levels in the blood fall back to normal as the cells take it in.

People with **diabetes** (called **diabetics**) do not have enough insulin to control the amount of glucose in their blood. This means that levels of glucose in their blood can get dangerously high and lead to serious health problems.

Some of the first symptoms of diabetes are extreme tiredness, thirst and glucose in the urine. A common test for diabetes is to test urine for glucose using Clinistix.

?
3. What is insulin?
4. What are Clinistix used for?

C A quick way of testing for diabetes.

210

There are two main types of diabetes. **Type 1 diabetes** develops in young people when the pancreas stops making enough insulin. About five in every 1000 people are affected. The illness develops very quickly. It is treated by insulin injections and by eating a carefully controlled diet.

Type 2 diabetes affects at least 2% of the population. This illness develops more slowly. It happens when the body no longer responds to its own insulin or does not make enough insulin. Obesity is one of the risk factors for type 2 diabetes. It used to develop in some people after the age of 40, and is sometimes called **late-onset diabetes**. There is a lot of concern that children are now developing it because of their poor diets.

Many people with Type 2 diabetes control it by changing their diet. This means losing weight if they are overweight and eating healthy, regular meals. They need to avoid sugary foods and replace them with low-sugar or sugar-free foods. They should also exercise more.

D Although this looks painful, diabetics know that their injections are essential for their health.

E There is very little sugar in this food.

?
5 Suggest three foods that could be eaten instead of sugary things.
6 Can diabetics eat foods that contain sweeteners? Explain your answer.
7 Insulin is a protein. Why does it have to be injected rather than given as tablets?

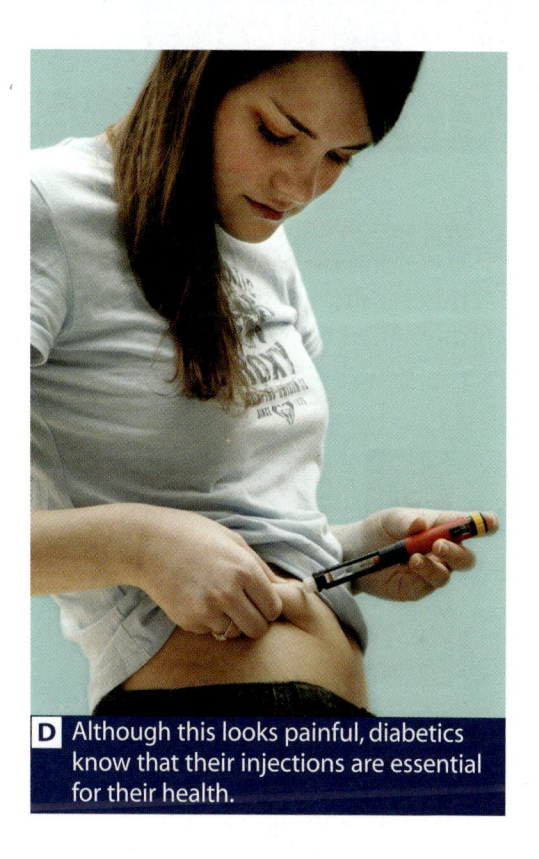

Summary

Diabetes is caused by a lack or shortage of _____. It can be treated by _____ and controlling the amount of _____ eaten. The _____ of Type 1 diabetics makes no insulin, while _____ 2 diabetics do not produce enough insulin.

injections   insulin   pancreas
sugar   Type

211

C3.12 Diet and health

Does our diet affect our health?

We are given lots of information about what we should or shouldn't be eating. 'Don't eat too much fat', 'Don't eat too much salt', 'Eat five portions of fruit and vegetables each day'. All of these are very good advice, but many people do not really understand why they are so important.

A

B Extra weight puts great strain on the heart and joints.

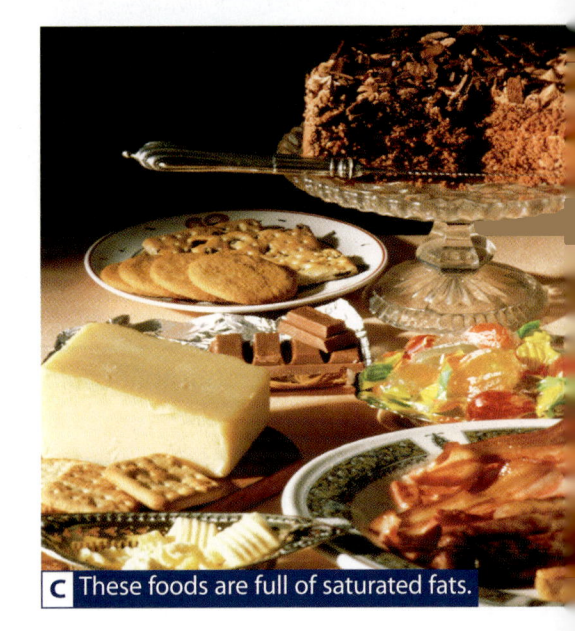

Many people today eat too much and don't exercise enough. This leads to obesity, which increases the risk of developing heart disease, high blood pressure, osteoarthritis and Type 2 diabetes. Many adults and an increasing number of children are obese.

1 What causes obesity?

Heart disease is caused when fatty substances block the arteries which supply blood to the heart muscle. The heart muscles may stop working and the person has a heart attack. Heart disease is mainly caused by eating too much saturated fat.

2 a What causes heart disease?
   b How can we try to prevent it?

C These foods are full of saturated fats.

High blood pressure can be caused by being obese and by eating too much salt. The heart has to work hard pumping blood around the body. If the pressure is not controlled, it can lead to heart disease and stroke. At the moment, 75% of the salt that we eat comes from processed foods, such as biscuits, pizza and ready meals.

D You can compare foods by checking food labels and try to reduce salt intake.

> **3 a** Why do you think salt is added to processed food?
> **b** Do you think it should be? Explain your answer.

Osteoarthritis occurs when the joints in our bodies wear away. This happens much more quickly if somebody is overweight, as the joints have to support more weight. Hip and knee joints can be replaced if the joints get very worn, although this is a serious operation.

There are other diseases linked with diet. A diet low in fibre may be linked with bowel **cancer**. This is one reason why we are advised to eat lots of fruit and vegetables each day. **Anaemia** is caused by a lack of iron and leads to tiredness. Red meat is the best source of iron, but vegetarians get enough from foods like beans, dried fruit, green vegetables and fortified breakfast cereals.

> **4** Why should we eat lots of fruit and vegetables?

Some people feel that we should not be told what to eat. However, bad diets can lead to health problems, which cost a lot of money in terms of hospital treatment and lost working days.

> **5 a** What are the risks of ignoring advice about a healthy diet?
> **b** Why do you think many people ignore this advice?
> **6** Write the script for a short radio advert to try to persuade people to eat a healthy diet.

Summary

It is important to eat a healthy _____, to prevent _____ and related diseases. Heart disease is linked with eating too much _____ and high blood pressure is linked with too much _____.

diet   fat   obesity   salt

213

C3.13 Food and its uses

How healthy is our food?

Gareth and Jack are organising the food for their Bronze Duke of Edinburgh's Award expedition. They have to plan menus for two lunches, one hot supper and a hot breakfast. This is their shopping list:

A
- brown bread for sandwiches and breakfast
- cheese – 250g.
- dried 'Super Noodles' – 6 packs for supper
- baked beans – 2 large cans
- bacon – 250 g
- sausages – 8
- crisps – 8 packs – mixed flavours
- chocolate bars – 10

B

C

1. The sausages contain preservatives. Why do you think these were added to the sausages?

2. a How is the protein in the bacon digested?
   b What happens to any spare amino acids that the body does not require?

3. Describe why eating brown bread helps the food to pass through the gut.

4. a Why was it a good idea for Jack and Gareth to include so many chocolate bars?
   b Should people normally eat so much fatty chocolate? Explain your answer.

5. Somebody suggested that the boys could pick some mushrooms to have with their sausages. Would that be a good idea? Explain your answer.

6. a What causes diabetes?
   b Would this menu be suitable for somebody with diabetes?
   c If Jack had Type 1 diabetes, what would he have to carry with him on the expedition?

214

One of the packets of crisps had the following food label.

NUTRITION INFORMATION PER PACK	
ENERGY	92 KCAL
PROTEIN	1.0 G
CARBOHYDRATE	13.7 G
FAT	3.7 G
FIBRE	1.1 G
SALT	0.8 G
ADDITIVES	

D

7 Name one kind of additive that could have been added to the crisps.

8 Why should Jack and Gareth be careful about the amount of salt that they eat?

9 What is the name of the chemical that might have formed while the crisps were cooked?

10 Gareth's father says that they shouldn't be eating food that contains additives. Describe two arguments in favour of additives, and two against.

11 Another boy in their expedition group is allergic to peanuts.
   a What will happen if he eats peanuts?
   b How could the group avoid this happening?
   c What is the name of the chemical produced when a mould grows on peanuts?

Jack was telling Gareth that his mother wanted to open a stall at the local market and was trying to decide whether or not to concentrate on selling organic produce.

E

12 What nutrients must be added to the soil to produce healthy plants?

13 What is the difference between synthetic and natural fertilisers?

14 How is organic farming different to conventional farming?

15 How would the prices for organic foods differ from those for foods grown on an intensive farm? Explain your answer.

16 The school's PE staff have organised the expedition. What are the health benefits of walking?

P3.1 Radioactive materials

What are the uses and risks of radioactive materials?

> I am an engineer in a nuclear power station. I'm amazed that people still think that nuclear power stations are dangerous. When I designed the power plant, I made sure that it could not become a nuclear bomb! Using nuclear fuel to produce electricity means that there are times when dangerous radiation is produced, but each step is closely monitored so that people inside and outside the power station are not at risk. We also produce nuclear waste, which has to be stored safely.

> My name is Kamran and I work in the medical physics department of a hospital. I use nuclear medicine to try and kill cancer cells. It is very important that the patient receives the right amount of this medicine as too much or too little could cause the patient to get very ill.

> My name is Michael. Here at Isotron we use radiation to sterilise food such as fruit, vegetables, spices and fish. Sterilised food lasts longer, but sometimes the radiation destroys some of the useful nutrients that are in the food. The food itself does not become radioactive or dangerous, so there is no need to worry about that!

My name is Jean and I work for a company called Oxford Safety. We train teachers and lab technicians so that they know how to use radioactive sources properly. I visit schools and run courses to show people how to handle, store and use radioactive materials in a safe way. If radioactive sources are not used properly, people could become very ill.

I'm called Yao-Tsan and I work for a company that makes smoke alarms. Inside the smoke alarm there is a radioactive source that sends out a stream of particles. When these particles are detected the alarm does not make a sound. However, when smoke gets into the alarm, it stops the particles from reaching the detector and the alarm sounds.

I'm not sure about these nuclear power stations. One simple mistake and we could all be killed! Just look what happened to all of those people in Russia in 1986 when the Chernobyl nuclear reactor exploded. I'm much happier getting my electricity from a coal-fired power station. I know that nuclear power stations pollute the atmosphere less, but a single accident could release enough radiation to kill a whole city!

1 What are some of the uses of nuclear radiation?

2 a Put the uses of nuclear radiation from these two pages into a league table with the best one at the top and the worst one at the bottom.
  b Explain your reasons for placing them in this order.

3 a What is your opinion about nuclear power?
  b Do you think we should use nuclear fuels to generate electricity?

4 Do you think that we should eat food that has been irradiated with nuclear radiation? Explain the reasoning behind your answer.

5 Think of a plus, a minus and an interesting point about this statement: Nobody should use radioactive substances.

P3.2 Radioactivity
What is radioactivity?

A Some foods are naturally radioactive. Different foods and drinks give out different amounts of radiation.

Radiation is all around us. It is in the air, in our food, in buildings and even inside our own bodies! This is called **background radiation**. It does not harm us. In fact scientists believe that a low level of radiation may actually be good for us.

Some foods, such as Brazil nuts, salad oil and peanuts are also naturally radioactive, because they take in radioactive material from the soil when they grow. Our homes receive radiation from a gas called **radon** that comes from rocks beneath the ground. We are constantly breathing in this radioactive gas. Some rocks, such as granite, are naturally radioactive and give out radiation.

? 1 Name three things that give out radiation.

2 What is background radiation?

? 3 a What is radon?
   b Name one place where it comes from.

4 Why is granite radioactive?

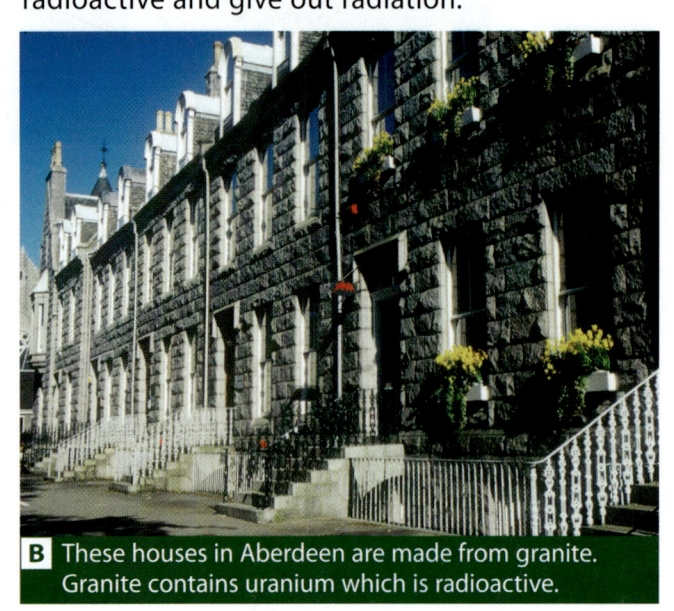

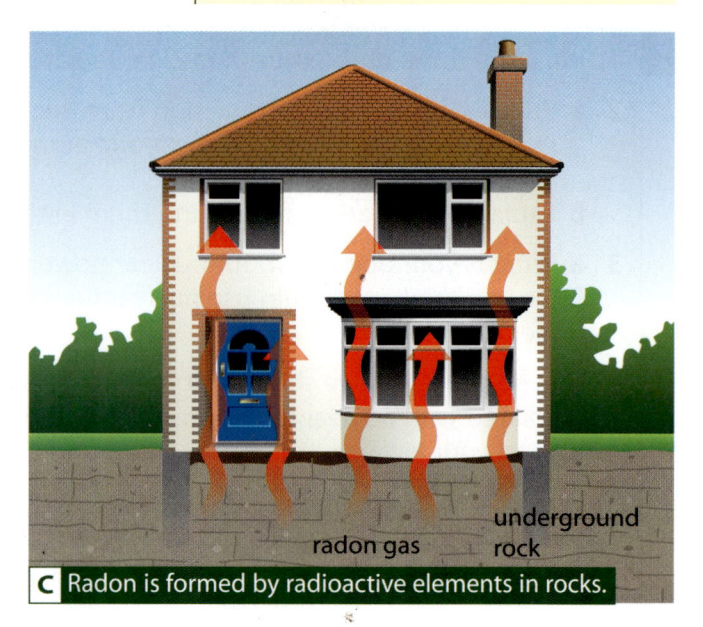

B These houses in Aberdeen are made from granite. Granite contains uranium which is radioactive.

C Radon is formed by radioactive elements in rocks.

radon gas — underground rock

Where does this radiation come from?

Everything around us is made from atoms. We cannot see atoms because they are so small. Atoms are made up of even smaller particles called **protons**, **neutrons** and **electrons**. Diagram D shows where these particles are found in an atom.

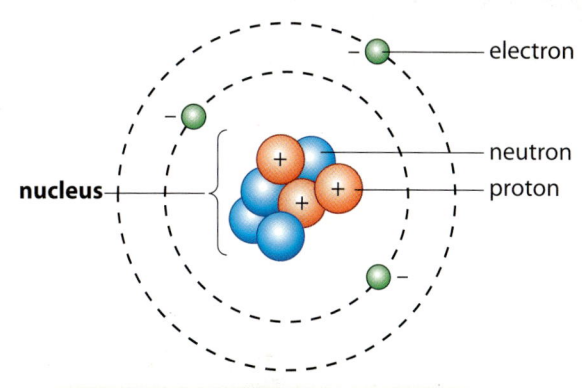

? 5 Why can't we see atoms?

There are many different types of atom. Each element has its own type of atom. The atoms of many elements are very **stable**, and they never change. For example, iron is a stable metal so its atoms do not give out radiation. However, the atoms of some elements are **unstable** and they **emit** (give out) radiation from the nucleus.

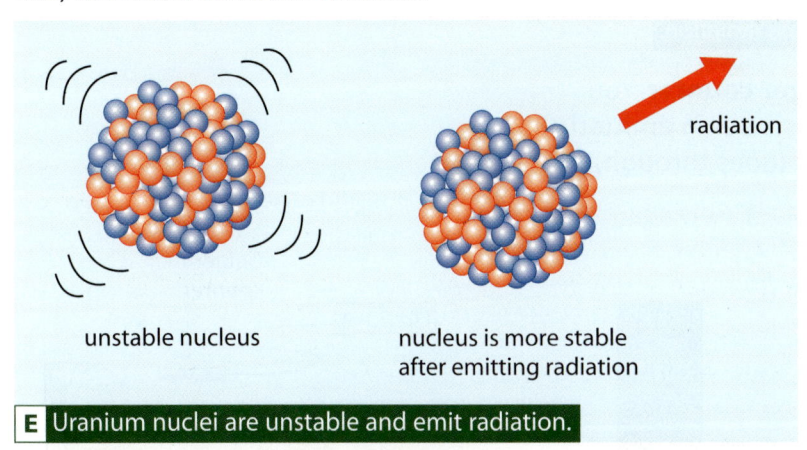

D The overall charge of an atom is **neutral** as the positive **charges** cancel out the negative charges.

unstable nucleus

nucleus is more stable after emitting radiation

radiation

E Uranium nuclei are unstable and emit radiation.

F Uranium ore.

? 6 Which part of the atom does radiation come from?

7 Think of a plus, a minus and an interesting point about this statement: All buildings should be made from granite.

8 Different parts of the country have different amounts of radon gas coming from the rocks. Find out if you live in a high or a low radon area.

Summary

There is natural _____ all around us called _____ radiation. It is found in _____ such as nuts. _____ rocks give out a radioactive gas called _____. Unstable _____ emit radiation all the time.

atoms   background   food
granite   radiation   radon

219

P3.3 Three types of radiation

What are the three types of radiation?

Unstable atoms give out radiation from their nuclei. An unstable nucleus can emit **alpha**, **beta** and **gamma** radiation. The properties of the three types of radiation are shown in table A.

Name of radiation	alpha (α)	beta (β)	gamma (γ)
Penetrates:	very short distances in air	air and paper	most things except thick lead and concrete
Absorbed by:	a few cm of air	thin metal sheet	thick lead or concrete

A The main properties of alpha, beta and gamma radiation.

Radiation can be measured using a **Geiger counter**. You can also find out which type of radiation is being emitted by seeing how the radiation **penetrates** (goes through) different materials.

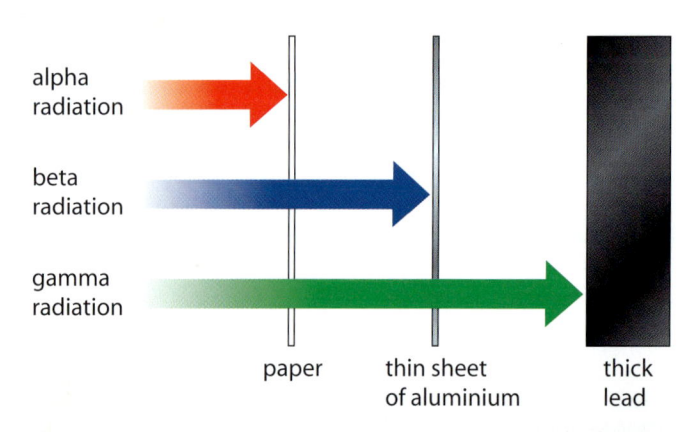

? 1 Name three types of radiation emitted from an unstable nucleus.

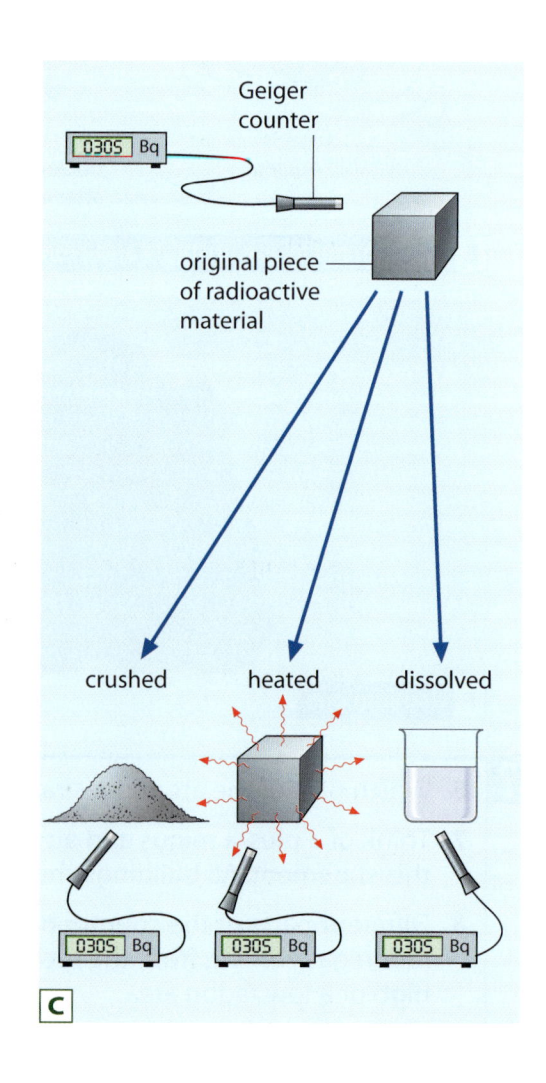

B Different types of radiation are absorbed by different amounts in different materials.

? 2 What can you use to measure radiation?
3 Which one of the three types of radiation is:
   a the hardest to stop
   b the easiest to stop?

You cannot change the amount of radiation that an unstable element emits. If a piece of radioactive material is crushed, heated or dissolved in water, it will remain radioactive and will still emit the same amount of radiation. This is because the nuclei in the atoms have not changed.

C

Even if the element is chemically reacted with another element to form a new compound, there will be no change in the radioactivity of the new compound.

? 4 Why doesn't crushing a radioactive material affect the amount of radiation that it emits?

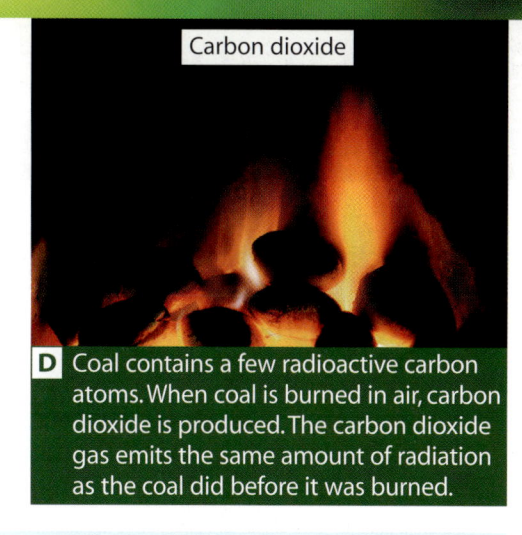

Radioactive decay

When an unstable atom emits radiation it undergoes **radioactive decay** and becomes more stable. Different elements emit different kinds of radiation.

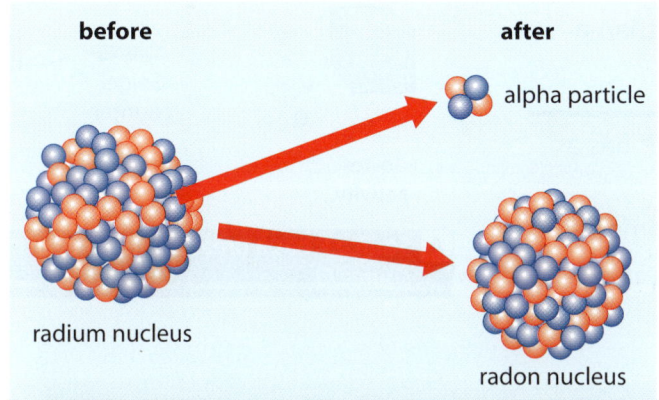

D Coal contains a few radioactive carbon atoms. When coal is burned in air, carbon dioxide is produced. The carbon dioxide gas emits the same amount of radiation as the coal did before it was burned.

E Heavier elements, like radium and uranium, become more stable by losing an alpha particle.

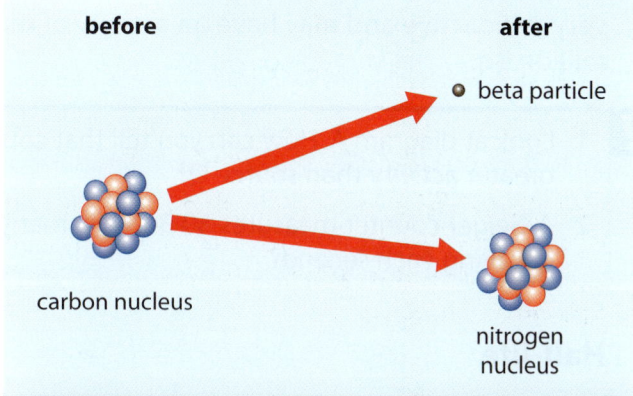

F Lighter elements, like radioactive carbon, become more stable by emitting a beta particle.

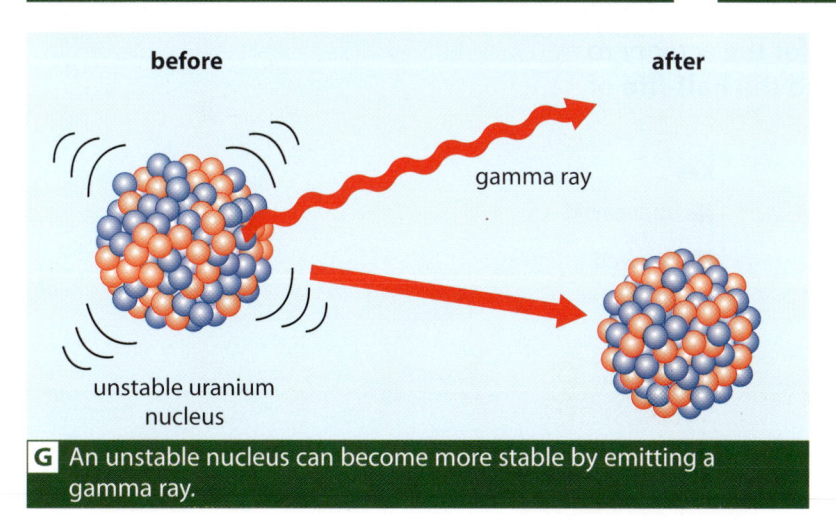

G An unstable nucleus can become more stable by emitting a gamma ray.

? 5 Plutonium is a heavy, unstable element. Which type of radiation is it most likely to emit?

6 Which is the odd one out: alpha, beta or gamma? Explain your answers.

7 Josie says that a sample of radioactive material gives off all three types of radiation. How would you test if this is true?

Summary

There are ____ types of radiation called alpha, ____ and gamma radiation. The most penetrating of these three types is ____ radiation. You cannot change the amount of radiation given off by ____, heating or dissolving the material, or by ____ it with other elements.

beta   crushing   gamma
reacting   three

221

P3.4 Activity and half-life

What happens to a radioactive material over time?

Radioactive elements constantly give out radiation. The **activity** of a **source** is the number of atoms that decay each second. The more radiation given out each second, the greater the element's activity will be.

Activity can be measured with a Geiger counter and the units of measurement are called **becquerel (Bq)**. If one atom of a radioactive source decays each second, then the source has an activity of 1 Bq. Some radioactive sources are very radioactive and may have an activity of more than a million Bq.

> 1 Look at diagram A. How can you tell that source P has a greater activity than source Q?
>
> 2 A Geiger counter measures 50 Bq. How many atoms are decaying each second?

A Source P has a greater activity than source Q.

Half-life

When radioactive materials decay, their unstable atoms change into stable atoms. As this process continues there will be fewer radioactive atoms left to decay so the activity of the source decreases. The time taken for the activity to decrease to half its original value is called the **half-life** of the material.

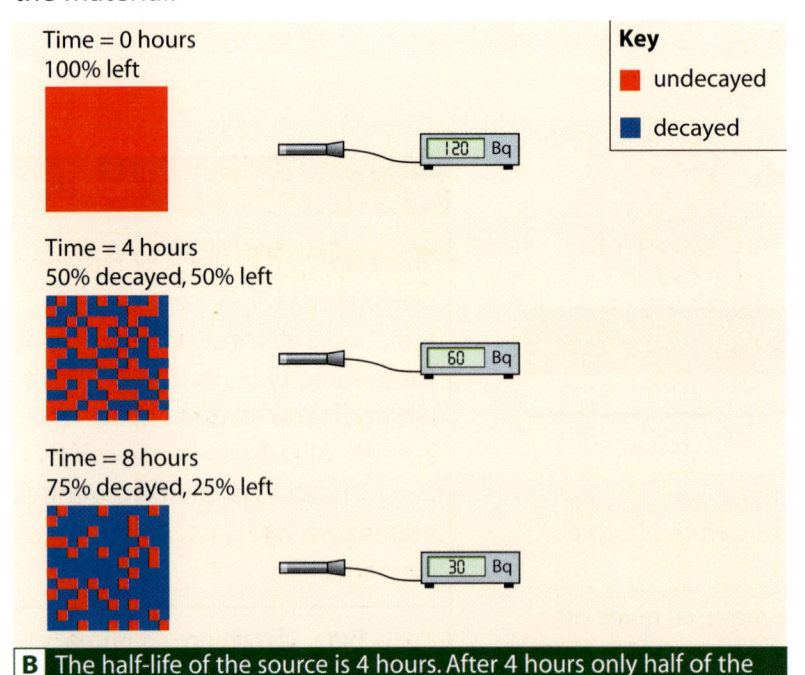

Time = 0 hours
100% left
120 Bq

Time = 4 hours
50% decayed, 50% left
60 Bq

Time = 8 hours
75% decayed, 25% left
30 Bq

Key:
- undecayed
- decayed

B The half-life of the source is 4 hours. After 4 hours only half of the radioactive atoms remain and the activity is halved.

> 3 Look at diagram B.
>   a What is the activity 8 hours after the experiment began?
>   b What will the activity be 4 hours later?

The half-life of a particular radioactive source is always the same. For example, if the half-life of a material is 8 hours, then its activity will halve every 8 hours. Graph C shows what happens.

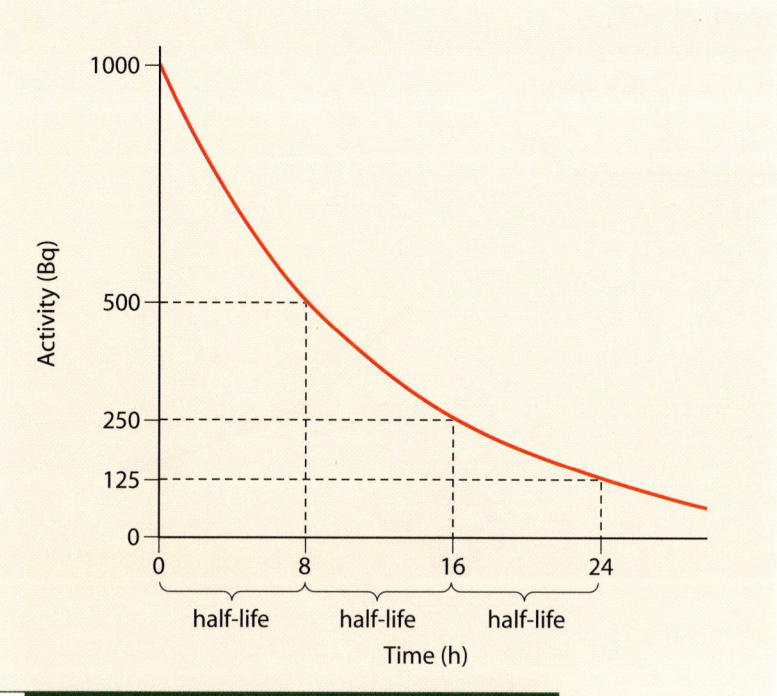

C The activity of this sample halves every 8 hours.

4 A piece of rock has a half-life of 8 hours. What fraction of the rock will remain radioactive after:
   a 8 hours
   b 16 hours
   c 1 day?

Not all radioactive materials have the same half-life. Some have fairly short half-lives and are used in hospitals to treat people with illnesses like cancer. Other materials have very long half-lives. These can be used to tell how old rocks, fossils and old relics are. Some radioactive waste from nuclear power stations also has a long half-life so it remains dangerous for thousands of years. It needs to be stored in a safe place such as a container underground, well away from people.

5 Why is it important to keep nuclear waste safe and well away from people?

6 How can the activity of a sample of rock help us work out how old it is?

7 Find out what a 'barium meal' is and what it is used for.

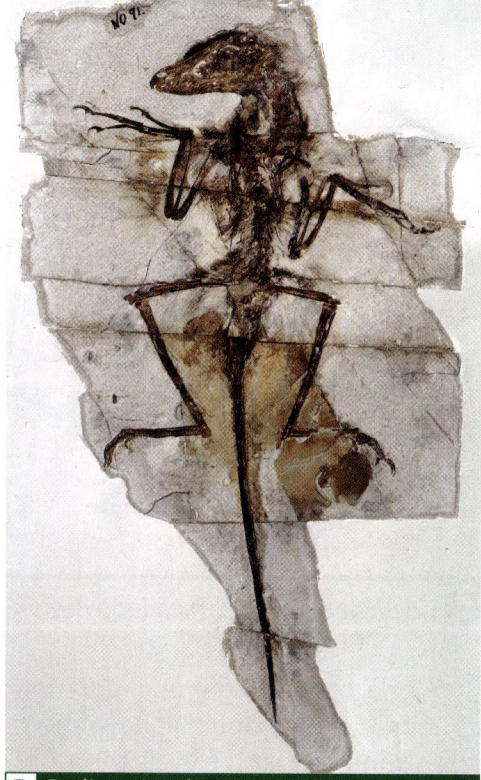

D Radioactive decay can tell us that this young *Dromaeosaurus* died about 70 million years ago.

Summary

The _____ of a source is the number of _____ that decay each second. The time taken for a source's activity to halve is called its _____. Materials with _____ half-lives remain radioactive for _____ of years.

| activity | atoms | half-life | long |
| thousands |

223

P3.5 Ionising effects of radiation

What is ionisation?

Atoms are neutral, which means they have no overall charge. When radiation hits an atom, it can make the atom become charged. This is called **ionisation** and an atom with a charge is called an **ion**.

1 What is an ion?

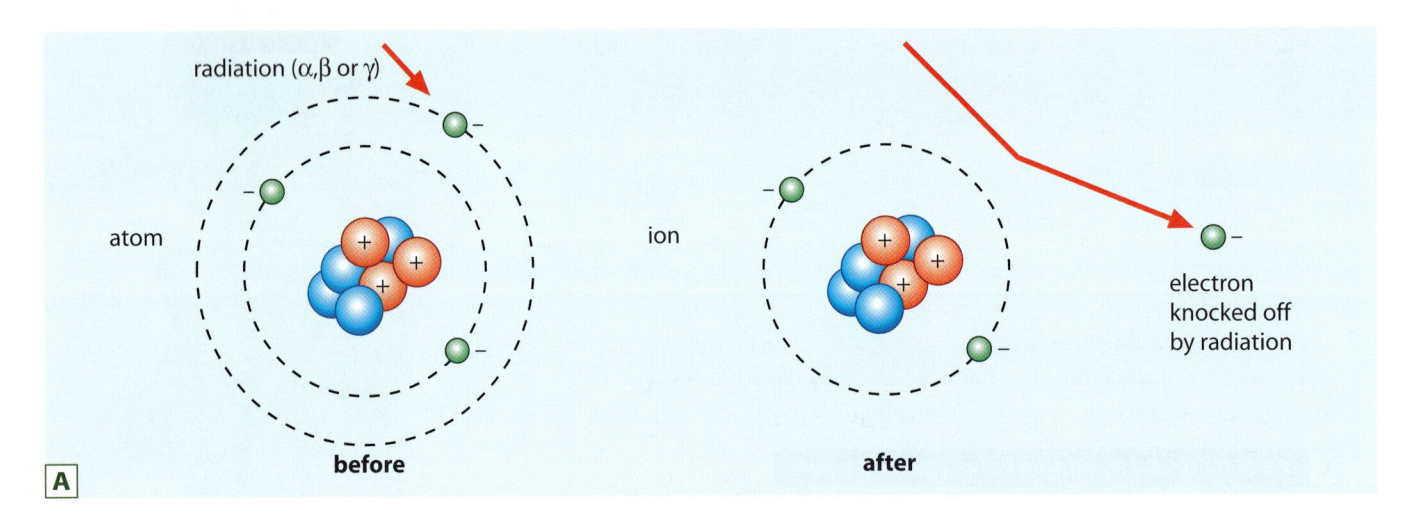

A before / after — radiation (α, β or γ) knocks an electron off an atom, turning it into an ion; electron knocked off by radiation

2 What is an atom called when it has a charge?

Alpha, beta and gamma radiation can all turn atoms into ions, but they don't all have the same effect. For every millimetre that it travels through a living cell, alpha radiation is most likely to cause damage.

B alpha — most ionising; beta; gamma — least ionising

3 Which type of radiation is most ionising?

4 a Which type of radiation is most likely to damage living cells?
b Which type is least likely to damage cells?

Uses of ionising radiation

- High-energy gamma rays can be used to kill dangerous bacteria on surgical instruments which otherwise could make patients very ill.
- Beta radiation can be used to make fruit last longer by killing bacteria and fungi on the fruit.
- Alpha radiation can kill cancer cells in the human body. Alpha particles cannot travel very far, so they are relatively harmless outside the body.

C Surgical instruments must be sterile.

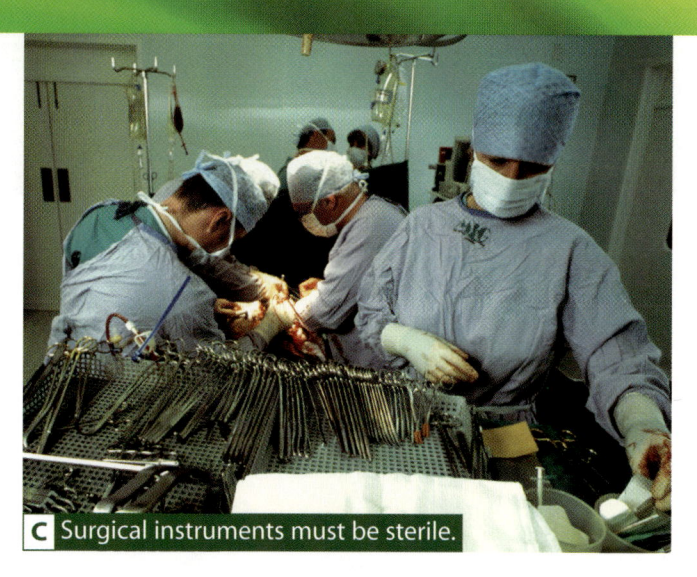

D Irradiated fruit lasts longer.

5 Describe three uses of ionising radiation.

Dangers of ionising radiation

If the cells in your body receive too much **ionising radiation**, they can be killed or they can start to divide uncontrollably and cause **cancer**. The amount of damage depends on the dose that the body receives. The **dose** is measured in **sieverts (Sv)**, and it depends on both the amount of radiation and the type. The risk of cancer increases as the dose increases.

Dose (Sv)	Effect on body
0.0025	average dose received each year by people in the UK; seen as 'safe'
3	radiation burns to skin; sterility in men and women; destroys blood cells
20	severe sickness; damage to nervous system; almost certain death in days

E Damage caused by different doses of radiation.

6 How can ionising radiation be dangerous?

7 a What unit is used to measure dose?
  b What is a 'safe' level of radiation?

8 If you receive the same amount of beta and gamma radiation, which would:
  a give you the highest dose
  b be the most dangerous?

9 Do you think the following doses of ionising radiation would be dangerous? Explain your answers.
  a 0.0001 Sv
  b 0.01 Sv
  c 50 Sv

Summary

When ionising _____ strikes an atom, the atom can turn into an _____. Ionising radiation can be used to _____ fruit and sterilise _____ instruments but it can also cause _____. The amount of damage it causes depends on the _____.

cancer   dose   ion   preserve
radiation   surgical

225

P3.6 Exposure to radiation

How are we exposed to radiation?

Natural radiation comes from rocks, the air, food and from cosmic rays from outer space. This background radiation is always present. It comes from unstable atoms when they undergo radioactive decay. The level of background radiation depends on where you are.

> **1** Look at diagram A.
> **a** Which areas in England and Wales have the most radon gas?
> **b** Are you at risk from breathing in radon? Explain your answer.

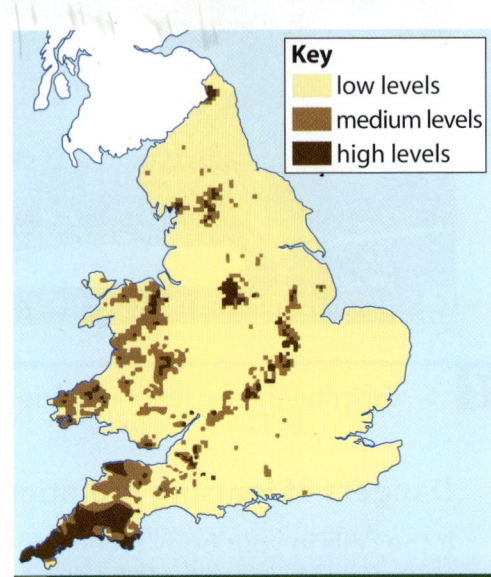

You can absorb radiation in different ways.
- **Direct irradiation** is when a body is exposed to radiation from an external source. This radiation can be absorbed by the body or it can pass straight through. The body does not become radioactive.
- **Contamination** is when radioactive materials in the form of gases, liquids or solids get into the body through the lungs, stomach or a wound.

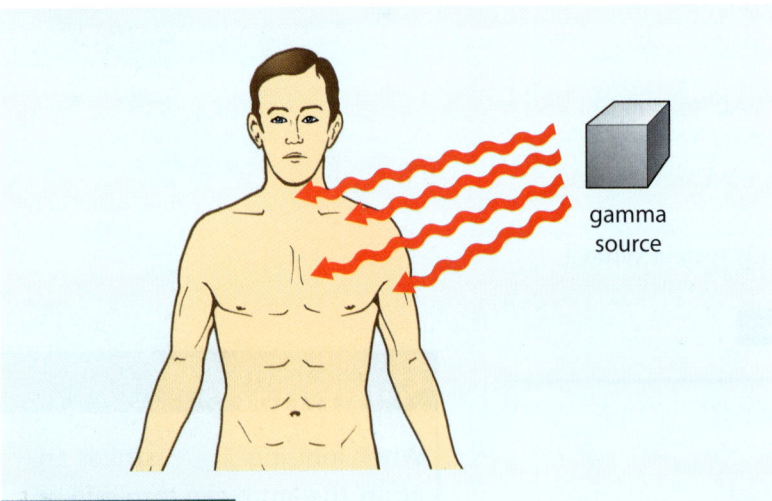

A Naturally occurring radon gas is present in different amounts throughout the country. This map shows its occurrence in England and Wales.

B Direct irradiation.

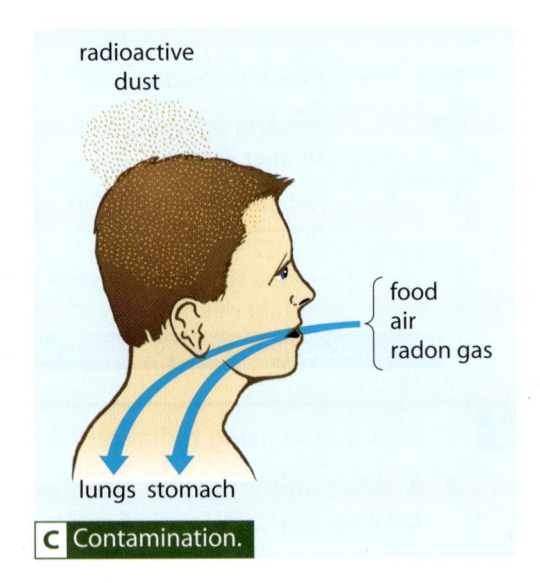

C Contamination.

Exposure to radiation

All of us are exposed to direct irradiation and we are all contaminated by the gases that we breathe in and the liquids and solids that we drink and eat. However, some people are at a higher risk of **exposure** to radiation because of the jobs that they do. Underground workers, medical physicists and workers in power stations are all at risk from **occupational radiation**.

> **2 a** What is direct irradiation?
> **b** Give an example.
> **3 a** What is contamination?
> **b** Give an example.

D A uranium miner is exposed to radiation from the radioactive rock all around him.

E This person works in a nuclear power station.

? 4 List two jobs that might have a risk of high occupational radiation.

There are strict regulations about the maximum dose that people who work with radiation can receive. Radiation levels are monitored with **film badges** which show how much beta and gamma radiation a person has been exposed to. The badges are checked regularly. Film badges are worn in hospitals and in nuclear power stations.

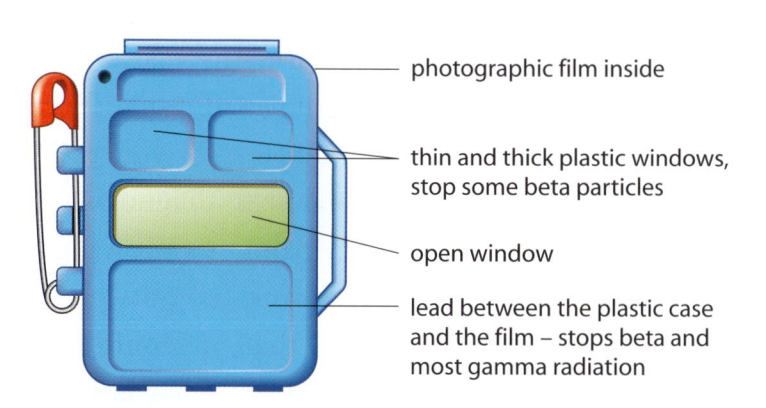

- photographic film inside
- thin and thick plastic windows, stop some beta particles
- open window
- lead between the plastic case and the film – stops beta and most gamma radiation

F A film badge.

? 5 How are workers in high-risk environments checked to make sure that they have not received too much radiation?

6 Why do certain workers need to have their film badges checked regularly?

7 a Explain how a person wearing a film badge would know if they had been exposed to too much radiation.
  b Why doesn't a film badge need to monitor alpha radiation?

Summary

_____ radiation is all around us. It comes from food, rocks and _____ rays from outer space. People are at _____ from radioactive materials by direct _____ and _____. Exposure can be checked using a _____ badge.

background   contamination
cosmic   film   irradiation   risk

P3.7 Are we safe?

Can anything be 'completely safe'?

Radiation is around us all of the time. Most of it is harmless, but we cannot say it is 'completely safe'. This is because any dose of radiation, no matter how small, may cause damage to human cells. Some of this is natural radiation and some comes from human activities.

?
1. How much radiation around us is 'natural' radiation?
2. Which two gases make up 52% of natural radiation?
3. What is the main cause of radiation from human activities?
4. a Is any level of radiation ever 'completely safe'?
   b Explain your answer to part **a**.

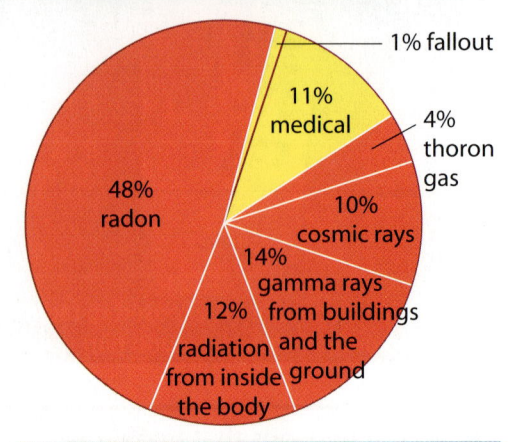

Pie chart: 48% radon, 11% medical, 1% fallout, 4% thoron gas, 10% cosmic rays, 14% gamma rays from buildings and the ground, 12% radiation from inside the body.

A 12% of the radiation around us comes from human activities.

Risks and benefits

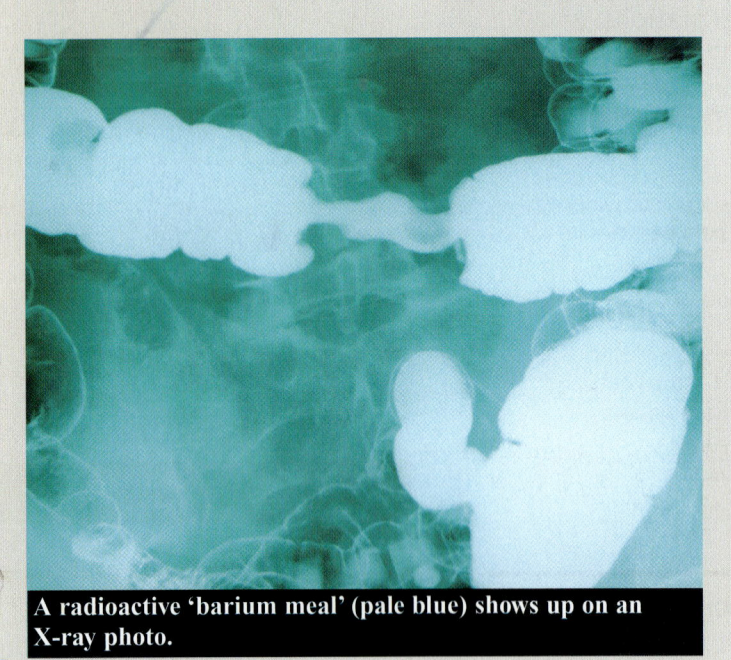

We use radiation for treating cancer and sterilising instruments, but the same types of radiation can also cause cancers. If you are ill and need medical diagnosis, the small risk from swallowing a radioactive drink is outweighed by the fact that it could help doctors to find out what is wrong with you.

Most activities have some risk – we need to think about whether the risk is worth taking!

A radioactive 'barium meal' (pale blue) shows up on an X-ray photo.

B

?
5. Look at B. For someone having a barium meal,
   a what are the risks
   b what are the benefits?
6. Would doctors give a barium meal to someone who is not ill? Explain your answer.

We are exposed to risks all the time. We can avoid or reduce some risks, but in other cases we think the possible risk is worth the benefit.

C

D

E

? 7 Look at photos C, D and E. For each one:
  a describe the possible risks
  b suggest why the people are willing to accept the risks
  c suggest how the people could reduce the risks.

8 Think of a plus, a minus and an interesting point about this statement: People are exposed to radiation.

9 Francesca has been given a mobile phone. Richard tells her that there are serious risks involved when using it. What should Francesca do? Explain your answer.

Summary

Nothing is _____ safe. Sometimes it is worth accepting the _____ from an activity because of the _____ it will bring. We should try to _____ risks as much as we can.

benefit   completely   risk   reduce

229

P3.8 Fossil fuels and electricity

How is electricity produced from fossil fuels?

A **fuel** is a substance that releases heat energy when it is burned. It is a store of **chemical energy**. The three **fossil fuels** are coal, oil and natural gas. These fuels can be used in power stations to produce electricity. Since electricity is produced from another energy form, it is called a **secondary energy source**.

> **1 a** What is a fuel?
> **b** Name three fossil fuels.
>
> **2** Why is electricity called a *secondary* energy source?

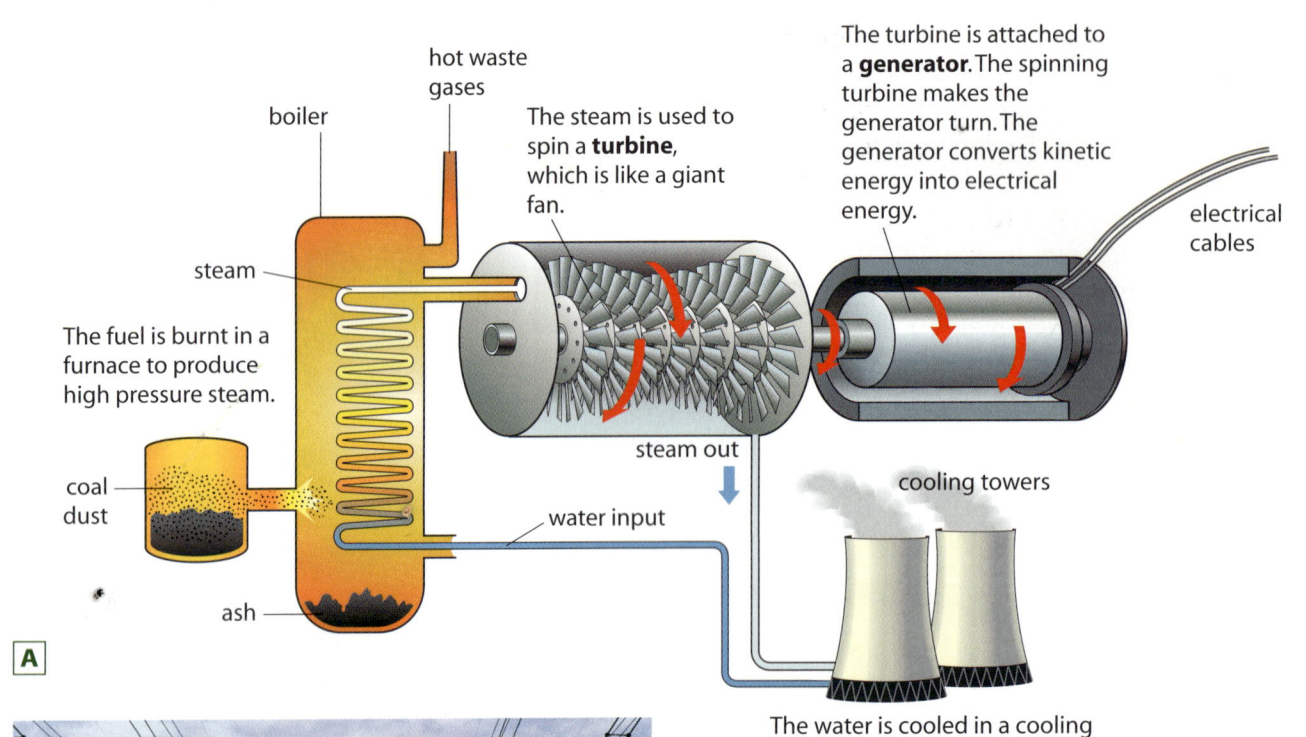

A Diagram of a power station showing: coal dust fed into a furnace/boiler producing high pressure steam; hot waste gases exit the boiler; steam spins a turbine (like a giant fan); the turbine is attached to a generator which converts kinetic energy into electrical energy, sent through electrical cables; steam out goes to cooling towers where water is cooled before being sent back to the furnace as water input; ash collects at the bottom of the boiler.

- The fuel is burnt in a furnace to produce high pressure steam.
- The steam is used to spin a **turbine**, which is like a giant fan.
- The turbine is attached to a **generator**. The spinning turbine makes the generator turn. The generator converts kinetic energy into electrical energy.
- The water is cooled in a cooling tower before being sent back to the furnace.

B Electricity is sent around the country through the National Grid. About 2% of the energy carried by the National Grid is wasted as heat.

> **3** What happens in these parts of a power station?
> **a** furnace and boiler
> **b** turbine
> **c** generator
>
> **4** How is electricity transported across the country?

230

Electricity is a very convenient form of energy because:
- it can be used in many ways, by many different devices
- it can be sent long distances across the country
- it does not produce any polluting gases when it is being used.

Electrical energy is very difficult to store, so it needs to be produced when it is needed. It is important that the supply of electricity matches the country's demand.

Fossil fuels are a convenient source of energy for producing electricity. However:
- they produce large amounts of carbon dioxide gas when they burn, which causes **global warming**
- sulphur in the fuels produces sulphur dioxide gas, which dissolves in water to make **acid rain**
- they are **non-renewable** resources, which means that they will eventually run out.

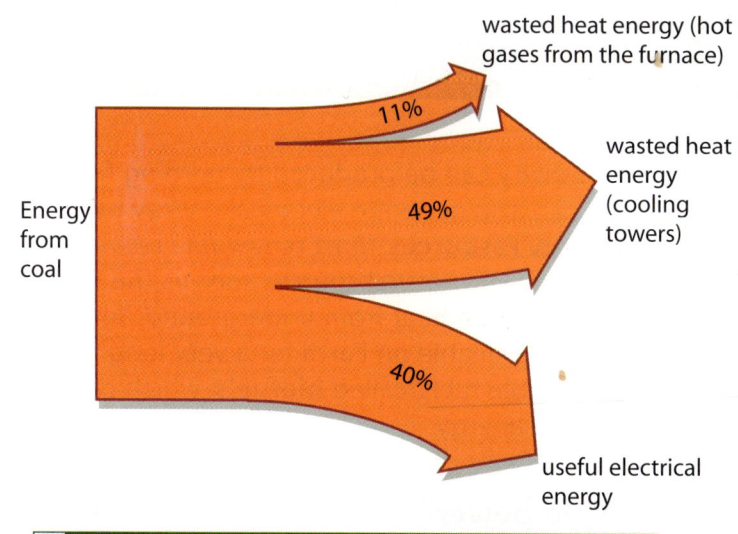

C A power station is not very efficient. Over half of the energy originally in the coal is wasted.

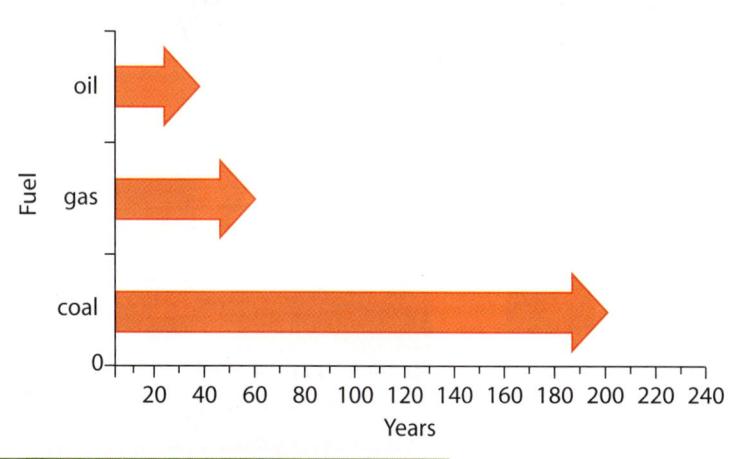

Energy from coal: 11% wasted heat energy (hot gases from the furnace), 49% wasted heat energy (cooling towers), 40% useful electrical energy

D How long different fossil fuels will last.

5 List three ways in which energy is wasted when electricity is generated and sent around the country.

6 Name two polluting gases that are released when coal and oil are burned.

7 What is the main problem with using non-renewable resources?

8 Complete this sentence in as many different ways as you can: Electricity is made from coal…

9 Imagine that you could develop your own 'perfect' fuel for use in a power station.
  a Describe what this fuel would be like.
  b Explain how it would be 'perfect'.

Summary

Fossil fuels are _____ to release energy which is used to produce _____. The steam turns _____ which drive a _____ to produce electricity. Electricity is a _____ energy source because you need to burn fossil fuels first. Fossil fuels are _____ resources because they will eventually run out. Burning fossil fuels produces gases which harm the _____.

burned   generator   non-renewable
environment   secondary   steam
turbines

P3.9 Renewable energy resources

What are renewable energy resources?

Electricity can be produced by burning fossil fuels. However, we can also generate electrical energy using **renewable energy resources**. Most renewable resources convert energy from natural sources such as the Sun, the wind, the tides or even heat from underground. Renewable resources will be available on Earth for a very long time. There are also renewable fuels, called **biofuels**, which can be burned to release energy.

> 1. Name three sources of renewable energy.
> 2. a Do most renewable energy resources require a fuel?
>   b Explain your answer to part a.

Wind power

In a wind turbine the kinetic energy of the wind turns the turbine blades, which drive a generator to produce electricity. Large generators can send electricity to the National Grid so that it can be used in places such as homes and offices. Small generators can be used to generate electricity in isolated places.

> 3. How does a wind turbine produce electricity?
> 4. How is this electricity used?

Geothermal energy

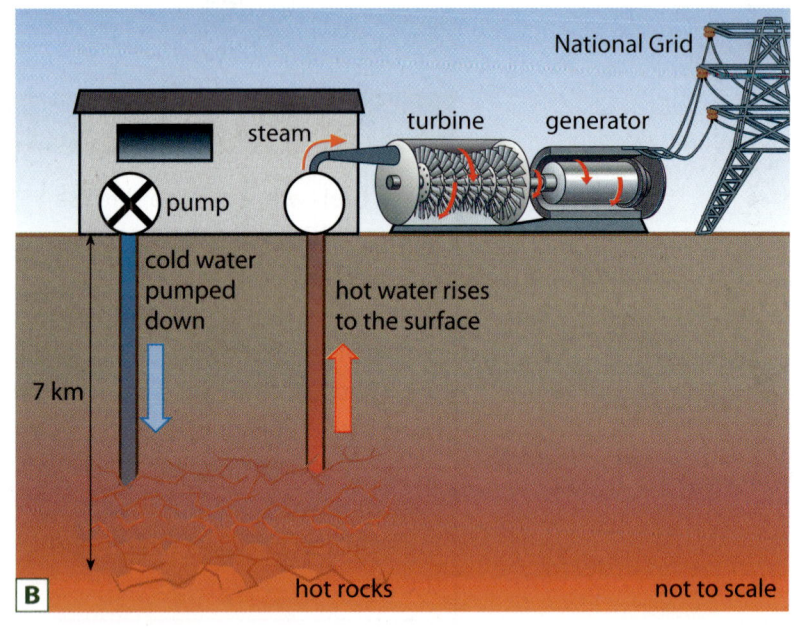

A

In some places such as Iceland, Mexico and New Zealand the rocks beneath the ground are very hot because of natural radioactivity. This heat energy can be used to generate electricity.

B

> 5. Look at diagram B. How does a geothermal power station produce electricity?

232

Hydroelectric power

Hydroelectric power uses water that is stored high up behind a dam. When the valves are opened, water rushes down from the dam at high speed to turn turbines, which drive a generator. Hydroelectric power stations are usually found in hilly areas.

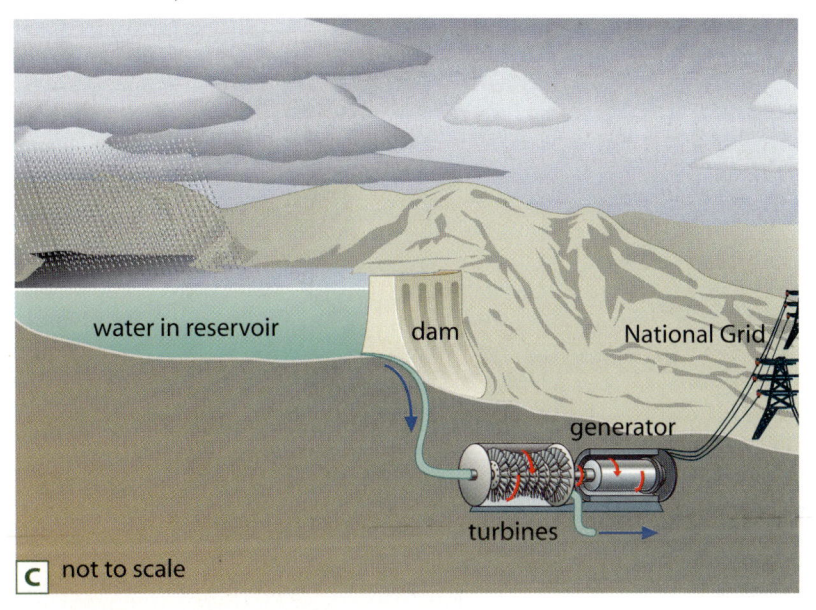

C not to scale

D Solar cells convert the Sun's light energy directly into electricity.

E Tides make water in the sea rise and fall. The movement of the water drives turbines which drive generators.

F Generators are driven by the up and down movement of waves.

6 Why do hydroelectric power stations need to be in hilly areas?

Biofuels

Biofuels include wood, methane, animal dung, cereals such as maize and sorghum and other crops such as cassava and cane sugar. Wood is obtained from forests that are managed for this purpose and methane is obtained from farm waste. Animal dung and cane sugar can be used to produce bio-alcohol. In Brazil, this **biomass** provides a cheap alternative to petrol.

Other renewable energy resources include **solar power**, **tidal power** and **wave power**.

7 When and where might:
 a solar power be very useful
 b solar power be no use at all?

8 Think of a plus, a minus and an interesting point about this statement: All of our electrical energy should come from the wind.

9 Which renewable resource do you think is the best? Write a paragraph explaining your choice.

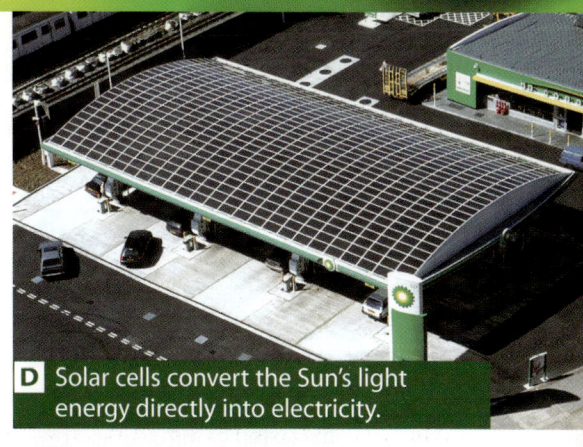

Summary

_____ resources will last for a very long time. Some energy resources make use of the energy from the _____ and the wind. Wind _____ turn the kinetic energy of the wind into _____ energy for use in homes. Biomass (such as _____ or animal dung) can be _____ as a fuel.

| burned | electrical | renewable | Sun |
| turbines | wood |

233

P3.10 Nuclear power

What are the benefits and drawbacks of nuclear power?

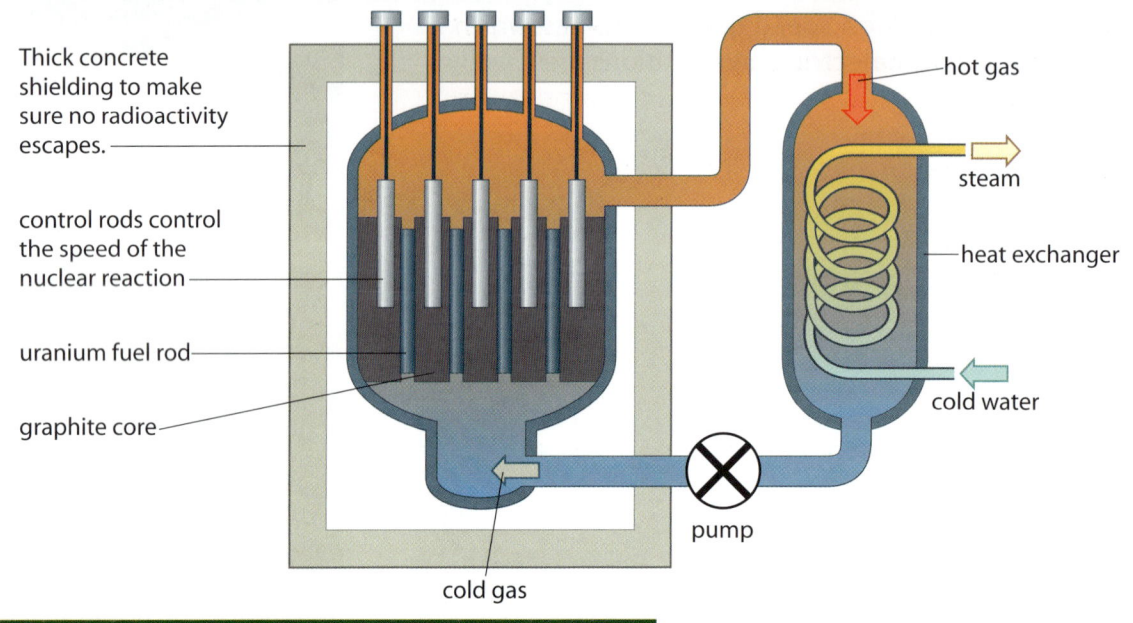

A A nuclear power station has a nuclear reactor instead of a furnace.

Diagram labels: Thick concrete shielding to make sure no radioactivity escapes. Control rods control the speed of the nuclear reaction. Uranium fuel rod. Graphite core. Cold gas. Hot gas. Steam. Heat exchanger. Cold water. Pump.

Nuclear fuel can be used to produce electricity. Unlike fossil fuels the nuclear fuel is not burned. Instead **nuclear fission** releases a huge amount of heat energy because of the changes that take place in the nucleus of the fuel atoms.

? 1 How is a nuclear fuel different from a fossil fuel?

Nuclear power stations do not produce harmful greenhouse gases or cause acid rain. They are designed so that the radiation is contained and controlled so it is not dangerous to workers inside the power station or people who live outside the power station.

? 2 Explain why nuclear power stations are less polluting than those that use fossil fuels.

3 Is a nuclear accident likely in the UK? Explain your answer.

Although nuclear power is 'clean', there are problems associated with it. If a nuclear accident happened, millions of people could be seriously affected by direct irradiation and contamination. The cost of building and **decommissioning** (closing down) nuclear power stations is enormous and they are only useful for about 30 years. In fact, a nuclear power station may cost more money to build and decommission than the amount of money it makes from electricity production.

B The Chernobyl accident in 1986 killed 32 people immediately, and many more in the months that followed the clear-up.

? 4 What are the possible problems linked to nuclear power?

5 What is 'decommissioning'?

Nuclear waste

Used nuclear fuel is often taken to a **reprocessing plant** where the unused fuel is removed so that it can be used again. What is left is called **nuclear waste**. It has a long half-life so it will remain radioactive for many thousands of years. Some materials and parts of the reactor also become radioactive. Nuclear waste is not considered safe until its radioactivity is similar to the level of background radiation. Table C shows the different kinds of nuclear waste. There are strict rules about how the different kinds of radioactive waste must be disposed of.

Waste Category	Examples
Low level waste	• used protective clothing
Intermediate level waste	• reactor components
High level waste	• the parts of used nuclear fuel that cannot be reprocessed

C

D Very strong containers are used when nuclear waste is transported around the country.

?
6 Why does nuclear waste need to be buried deep underground and not just stored in a warehouse?

7 Look at photo D. Why does the container for the nuclear waste have to be very strong?

8 Where do you think would be the best place to build a nuclear power station? Draw a labelled map to explain your answer.

Summary

Radioactive material is used in a _____ reactor to produce _____ energy. Nuclear fuel does not produce _____ gases such as _____ dioxide. Nuclear waste can remain _____ for _____ of years.

carbon   greenhouse   heat   nuclear
radioactive   thousands

235

P3.11 Renewable or non-renewable?

Which resources should we use?

The electrical energy that we use in our homes can come from fossil fuels, from nuclear fuels or from renewable energy resources. Homes, hospitals and factories receive most of their electrical energy from power stations that use fossil fuels or nuclear fuels. The advantages and disadvantages of nuclear and fossil fuels are shown in table A.

Fuel	Advantages	Disadvantages
fossil fuels (coal, oil and natural gas)	• reliable and easy to obtain • do not produce harmful radiation	• produce greenhouse gases • non-renewable
nuclear fuel	• reliable and easy to obtain • does not produce greenhouse gases	• non-renewable • produces radioactive waste • dangerous if accident occurs • nuclear power stations expensive to build and decommission

A The advantages and disadvantages of nuclear and fossil fuels.

?
1. Name three sources of electrical energy used in our homes.
2. What are:
   a the advantages shared by fossil fuels and nuclear fuels
   b the disadvantages shared by fossil fuels and nuclear fuels?
3. a Which do you think is best, nuclear fuel or coal?
   b Explain your answer to part **a**.

B This is the nuclear power station at Three Mile Island in the USA. Many people think it is an eyesore.

Although fossil fuels and nuclear fuels have many advantages, especially because they are so convenient, these fuels will eventually run out and our energy needs will have to be provided by renewable resources. These also have advantages and disadvantages as shown in table C.

Advantages	Disadvantages
• renewable – will not run out • do not produce greenhouse gases • no fuel costs (except biofuels) • low maintenance farms)	• unreliable – e.g. solar power does not work at night, wind power does not work when it is not windy • inefficient – low energy output • can be expensive to set up (geothermal) • can be unsightly and noisy (wind farms) • can take up large areas of land, though you can still farm beneath them (wind farms) • can damage the environment (hydroelectric/tidal)

C Advantages and disadvantages of renewable energy resources.

D Some people are concerned that birds may be killed by wind turbines.

?
5 List three advantages of renewable resources when compared with non-renewable resources.

6 What are the advantages of fossil fuels compared with renewable resources?

7 Why might some people not be in favour of building wind farms, hydroelectric dams and tidal barrages?

8 Why do you think geothermal energy can be so expensive to set up?

9 Which do you prefer – non-renewable or renewable resources? Explain your answer.

Summary

Electrical energy is produced from different resources including _____ fuels, nuclear fuels and _____ resources. Some people think that certain renewable resources are _____ and unsightly. Some think that _____ fuels are unsafe because accidents can release large amounts of _____ into the _____. Some renewable resources are _____ because they don't work all of the time.

fossil   noisy   nuclear   radiation
renewable   unreliable   environment

237

P3.12 Sustainable development
What is sustainable development?

In developed countries electricity is taken for granted. However, over two billion people in the world (which is one person in three) do not have access to electricity. They must rely on fuel sources such as wood or kerosene for cooking.

> **?**
> 1 a How many people in the world do not have access to electricity?
>   b What proportion of the world's population is this?
> 2 Which types of fuel do people in the developing world use for cooking?
> 3 Look at picture B. What does this tell you about the availability of energy in different parts of the world?

A Dried animal dung makes a useful fuel in the developing world.

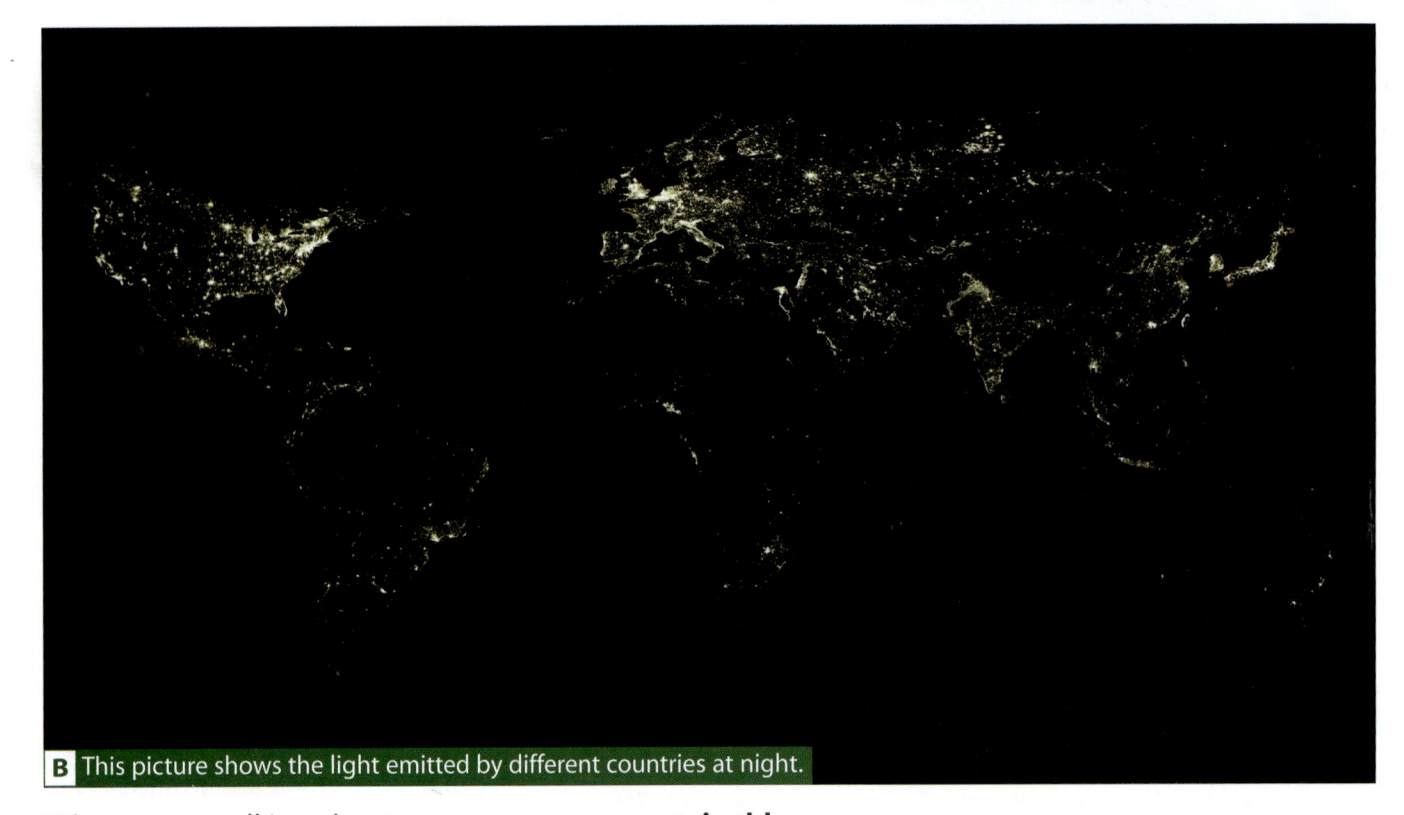

B This picture shows the light emitted by different countries at night.

When we are talking about energy resources, **sustainable development** means finding ways of obtaining enough energy for our needs, without polluting the Earth's atmosphere and water supplies any more than we have done already. There are two issues to consider here:
- what *can* be done, based on the technology that is available
- what *should* be done based on what is morally right for everyone.

> **?**
> 4 What is meant by the term sustainable development?

238

People representing the governments of the world have met to discuss the most important issues surrounding sustainable development. They have agreed that the following things should be done:
- increase the number of renewable energy resources throughout the world
- develop new technologies that will produce electrical energy without releasing greenhouse gases
- stop governments giving **subsidies** (money) to companies that produce electricity from non-renewable energy resources
- produce vehicles that are less polluting
- help more people to use modern biomass and wood technologies
- help poorer countries develop and use new energy technology.

The World Summit on Sustainable Development in 2002 looked at ways to improve people's lives while protecting the environment. Over 100 world leaders addressed the summit. In total, 193 countries were involved in discussions, and over $1000 million was made available to try to solve the world's energy problems.

C

5 a What do governments believe are the most important issues for sustainable development?
  b Which of these do you think is most important? Explain your answer.

6 Why do you think so many countries are involved in discussions such as the World Summit for Sustainable Development?

7 a How *can* rich countries help poorer countries to become more developed?
  b How *should* rich countries help poorer countries to become more developed?

8 Complete this sentence in as many different ways as you can: Sustainable development is needed…

9 Apart from the area of energy development, sustainable development also includes the development of health. What problems might occur here and how should they be addressed and improved?

Summary

Sustainable _____ involves developing new _____ for producing electricity that do not cause more _____. This should be done because we are rapidly running out of _____ fuels. It is important that _____ countries should benefit from these developments.

| development | fossil | pollution |
| poorer | resources | |

239

P3.13 Power for the people
Which energy resources should be used to generate electricity?

The population of Copperwheat City has increased by nearly 250 000 over the last 20 years. The government has decided that a new power station is needed to meet the extra demand for electrical energy. The nuclear power company *Powerfuel* will build a nuclear power station on the outskirts of Copperwheat City.

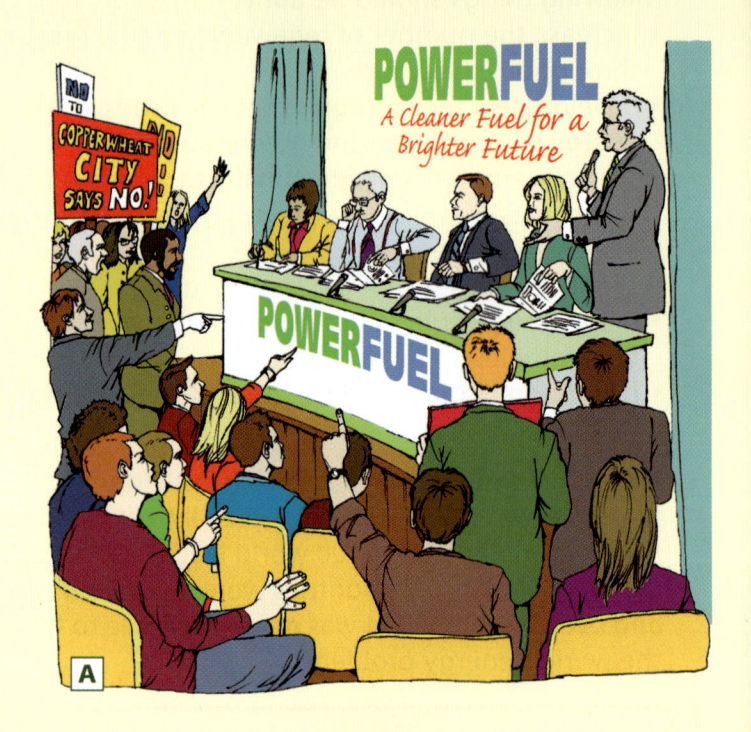

1. **a** What is radioactive decay?
   b What are the three types of radiation that can be produced by radioactive decay?
   c Describe the properties of each kind of radiation.
   d Give one use for each kind of radiation.

2. **a** Describe how nuclear fuels are used to generate electricity.
   b How is a fossil fuel power station different from a nuclear power station?

3. Why does Copperwheat City need another power station?

4. What are the advantages of nuclear power?

A

There are different opinions about whether the new power station should be built.

> The new nuclear power station will provide many jobs and will meet the extra demand for electricity. The power station will be completely safe and nuclear fuel will be transported to the power station from Russia.

B Sir Quentin Jones.

> Nuclear fuel is totally unsuitable! The citizens of Copperwheat do not need another power station at all. If people wasted less energy then we would be fine.

C Bernice Goldberg.

5. Is Sir Quentin correct when he says that the new power station will be completely safe? Explain your answer.

6. Why might Bernice think that nuclear fuel is unsuitable?

> Nuclear power is not suitable for this location. The coastal area is much better suited to a wind farm. The local background radiation levels will not be affected if wind turbines are used.

D Professor Robert Storey.

> Powerfuel has been in trouble in the past for not following the correct safety procedures when storing and transporting radioactive waste. They also do not support schemes of sustainable development in other parts of the world.

E Dave Brookes

7 a Why is wind energy referred to as a renewable resource?
   b Name three other renewable resources.
   c Give one advantage and one disadvantage of each of the resources that you named in part **b**.

8 a List two advantages of wind farms compared to nuclear power.
   b Describe one disadvantage of wind farms compared to nuclear power

9 a What is background radiation?
   b Name three sources of background radiation.

10 Could other renewable resources be used in this location? Explain your answer.

11 a What does 'half-life' mean?
    b How can radiation harm the body?
    c Why do workers in a nuclear power station wear film badges?

12 a Why is it important to transport and store nuclear waste properly?
    b How should nuclear waste be stored?

13 What might the inhabitants of Copperwheat feel when they learn about the problems that *Powerfuel* have had?

14 What is meant by sustainable development?

Glossary

abortion Stopping a pregnancy by removing the fetus.
absorb Take in, such as when infra-red radiation is absorbed by your body and you feel warmer.
acid rain Rainwater which is more acidic than normal (with a pH often as low as 3 or 4). It is produced when sulfur dioxide from burning fuels dissolves in rainwater.
acquired characteristic Characteristic that is developed by use and passed on to offspring, as defined by Lamarck.
acrylamide A chemical produced when starchy foods are cooked at high temperatures.
activity The number of unstable nuclei that decay each second.
adaptation Characteristic which is successful in an environment, which allows the organism to survive and breed.
aflatoxin A poisonous substance produced by certain moulds.
air quality A measure of how free the air is from pollutants.
air A mixture of gases that covers the surface of the Earth.
alleles Different forms of a gene for the same characteristic, e.g. alleles for red flowers and white flowers.
allergic When a food produces an unpleasant reaction in the body.
alpha radiation Radiation consisting of positively charged particles given out by an unstable nucleus.
amino acids The units which make up proteins, and which proteins turn into during digestion.
anaphylaxis A severe reaction to foods that cause an allergy.
ancestor An organism that evolved into a more recent organism.
antibiotic Chemical used to kill or stop the growth of microorganisms inside the body.
antibodies Chemicals made by white blood cells which destroy particular microorganisms.
arteries Blood vessels with thick muscular walls that carry blood away from the heart.
asexual reproduction Reproduction involving only one parent, producing offspring that are genetically identical to each other and to the parent.
asteroid A small rocky body that orbits the Sun.
atmosphere A layer of gases that surrounds the Earth.

atom The smallest part of an element that can exist.
average The average of a set of numbers is found by adding them all together and dividing by the number in the set.
background radiation Naturally occurring radiation that is present all around us. It comes from buildings, rocks, food and cosmic rays from outer space.
bacterium (plural bacteria) A single celled microorganism much smaller than an animal cell. Bacteria were the earliest life forms.
becquerel (Bq) The unit of activity. 1 Bq is one atom decaying every second.
best estimate The mean (average) of a set of data that is presumed to be close to the true value.
beta radiation Radiation consisting of negatively charged particles given out from an unstable nucleus.
Big Bang The idea that the Universe was created in a 'big bang' explosion and has been expanding ever since.
biodiversity Either the number of different plant and animal species within a habitat, or the genetic variety within a species.
biofuel Any fuel that is produced from plants or animal waste.
biomass Plant or animal material that can be burned to release heat.
bisphenol A chemical used to coat the inside of food cans.
booster A top-up dose of a vaccine.
brain damage Damage to the brain.
brain Part of the body which coordinates response to stimuli.
brittle Property of a material that causes it to break rather than change shape when a force acts on it.
cancer A disease where cells in the human body start to divide uncontrollably.
capillaries Smallest blood vessels with very thin walls so blood can exchange dissolved food and gases with cells easily.
carbon cycle How carbon is cycled between living organisms and the air.
carrier A person that has one allele for a disease, but does not have the disease itself. Carriers can pass the faulty gene on to their offspring.
catalytic Using a catalyst to speed up a chemical reaction.

cause A factor that produces a change in another factor.
cell The basic unit which living things are made of.
cell cultures A collection of cells grown in the laboratory that new medicines can be tested on.
cellulose A carbohydrate that makes up plant cell walls that together can form a fibre.
cellulose A polymer containing many glucose units which cannot be digested.
central nervous system The spinal cord and brain which coordinate messages in the nervous system.
characteristics Features that an organism has, e.g. curly hair.
charge A property of a particle that allows it to exert a force on another charged particle. Charges can be positive (+) or negative (−).
chemical energy Energy that is stored in chemical form, such as in coal, oil or food.
chemical reaction A chemical change in which new substances are formed but there is no change in the number of atoms of each element.
chlorophyll The green chemical in plants that absorbs light energy for photosynthesis.
chromosomes Thread-like strands found in the nucleus of a cell. Chromosomes are made of DNA and contain the 'instructions' for a living thing.
clinical trials Trials in which a new drug is tested on humans to find out whether it is safe and whether it works.
clone A clone has exactly the same genes as the organism it was made from.
colours Chemicals added to food to enhance their colour.
coma Being completely unconscious.
combustion Another word for burning. A chemical reaction between a fuel and oxygen that gives out heat.
comet A body made of frozen gases and bits of rock that has a long, elliptical orbit.
common ancestor An ancestor shared by two or more descendants.
community A group of different species living in the same habitat.
competition Fighting for the same resource, such as food, space or a mate.
complex behaviour Behaviour which requires learning or thinking, rather than just responding to the environment.
compound A substance containing two or more elements chemically joined together.
compression A force that tries to squash a material.
conserve Protect from dying out.

contamination The process whereby radioactive materials in the form of gases, solids or liquids get into the human body.
continental crust The type of crust that forms the continents.
continental drift The idea that the continents can move around, as explained by Wegener.
control Part of an experiment where the variable being investigated is not changed.
coordinate Link together or organise, as the brain organises how we respond to stimuli.
coronary arteries Arteries that supply the heart muscles with blood, providing oxygen and nutrients for the muscle cells.
correlation When two factors show a similar pattern of change. For example, when one factor increases the other does as well.
corroborate Agree with, or back up.
crater The hole in the ground made by an asteroid or meteorite hitting the Earth or other body. (Craters also form in volcanoes.)
cross-linking The bond between two polymer molecules.
crude oil A mixture of hydrocarbons formed from dead organisms by heat and pressure over millions of years.
crust The top, solid layer of the Earth.
cuttings Parts cut from a plant that can be grown into new plants.
cystic fibrosis An inherited disease that causes cells to produce sticky mucus. It is caused by a recessive allele.
decommissioning The closing down and safe dismantling of a power station.
decomposers Organisms that break down dead organisms (e.g. bacteria and fungi).
density The mass of a specific volume of a substance, e.g. the mass in kg of 1 m^3 of the substance. Density = mass/volume.
descendant An organism that evolved from an ancestor.
designer babies Babies whose genes have been modified to give them particular characteristics, such as being good looking, or good at sport.
detector Something which can detect radiation of a particular wavelength, such as the eye, skin, or photographic film.
diabetes A condition where the amount of glucose in the blood is higher than normal.
diabetic A person with diabetes.
digestion Breaking down large food molecules into smaller ones that the body can use.

direct irradiation The process where the human body is exposed to an external radioactive source.
DNA The molecule that carries all the instructions for living organisms; can copy itself.
dominant A dominant allele always shows itself in the offspring.
dormant (volcano) A volcano that has not erupted for many years.
dose A measure of the amount of damage radiation does to the body. It depends on the type of radiation and how much of it there is. Dose is measured in sieverts.
ductile Property of a material that allows it to be drawn into a wire or fibre.
durable A durable material will not wear out quickly in use.
earthquake waves Waves that move around or through the Earth after an earthquake.
effector cells Cells which carry out the response to a stimulus, such as muscle cells.
elastic Property of a material that allows it to return to its original shape and size when a force acting on it is removed.
electromagnetic radiation Electromagnetic waves given out by an object, such as light or radio waves.
electromagnetic spectrum The whole range of electromagnetic waves, from gamma rays to radio waves.
electron A particle with a negative charge found outside the nucleus of an atom.
element A substance that cannot be broken down into anything simpler by chemical reactions. An element consists of one type of atom.
embryo The ball of cells that grows from a fertilised egg.
embryonic stem cells Unspecialised cells taken from an embryo. Stem cells can become any other kind of cell.
emissions 'Carbon dioxide emissions' means the amount of carbon dioxide produced by burning fuels or forests.
emit To give out (radiation).
emulsifiers Chemicals that bring about emulsification in food.
endangered At risk of becoming extinct.
endocrine gland Sensors in the hormonal system which secrete hormones into the blood system.
engulf Scientific word for swallowing. It is what white blood cells do to harmful microorganisms.
E-numbers Numbers given to food additives to show that they have been approved.

environmental conditions Physical conditions of a habitat, such as amount of light, water and wind, as well as all the biological conditions, such as food, competition for space with other organisms, etc.
environmental factors Things such as the amount of food or diseases, that can affect the growth and development of an organism.
enzymes Substances made of protein that speed up chemical reactions in living organisms.
epidemic A disease that affects many people in a community.
epidemiological study Study of a large number of people to look for links between a disease and the factors that may cause it.
erosion The movement of bits of broken rock by gravity, wind or water.
error The difference between a measurement and the true value.
ethical decisions Decisions about what is right or wrong.
ethical issues Ideas about whether certain things are right or wrong, and whether they should or should not be done.
eutrophication Bacteria multiply by feeding on dead material and use up all the oxygen in the water.
evolutionary tree A diagram which shows how organisms are related to each other through evolution.
evolve Change characteristics over time, become a new species.
excretion Ridding the body of toxic waste substances.
exposure How much radiation we receive.
extinct A species that no longer exists.
factor A quantity that can be measured, changed or controlled.
fertilise When male and female sex cells join.
fertilisers Substances added to soil to replace lost nutrients and help plant growth.
fibre (materials) A material which has been drawn into a thread or filament.
fibre (plants) A more common word for cellulose.
film badge A badge, containing photographic film, worn by people who work with radioactive materials. The photographic film is used to check whether people have been exposed to harmful levels of radiation.
flavour enhancers Food additives that are used to improve flavour.
flexibility How bendy a material is.
food additives Chemicals added to food during its production.

food chain A diagram which shows how energy is transferred from a producer to the animal that eats it, to the animal that eats that animal and so on.

Food Standards Agency A government organisation that oversees all food standards and safety.

food web A diagram showing how all the food chains within in an environment link together.

formula A short way of showing the atoms in a compound.

fossil fuels Non-renewable fuels such as coal, oil and gas that have formed over millions of years from dead animals and plants.

fossil Preserved remains of organisms, such as bones, found in rocks.

fractional distillation The separation of the components of a mixture which have different boiling points.

fractionating column/tower The tube in which separation of the substances in crude oil takes place.

fractions Parts of crude oil which have boiling points within a certain range.

fuel A material that is used to release energy.

function Job – for instance, the function of red blood cells is to carry oxygen.

fungicides Chemicals used to kill fungi and moulds.

fungus A type of microorganism, some of which grow on skin and make it sore.

fuse Join, as when male and female sex cells fuse.

fusion When hydrogen atoms join together in a nuclear reaction and release energy.

galaxy Millions of stars grouped together.

gametes Sex cells, e.g. sperm cells or egg cells.

gamma radiation Radiation that is given out by an unstable nucleus in the form of photons that travel at the speed of light.

gamma rays A high energy form of electromagnetic radiation with a very short wavelength.

gas A substance that flows and fills any space that it occupies.

Geiger counter A device used to measure radiation.

gender Whether an organism is male or female.

gene therapy Curing an inherited disease by putting correctly working alleles into a person.

gene Part of a chromosome. One gene contains the 'instructions' for a particular feature such as flower colour.

generalist feeder An animal which feeds on many foods.

geohazard A hazard or danger caused by the Earth, such as a volcano or earthquake.

geothermal energy Energy from hot rocks under the Earth's crust.

global warming The gradual warming of the Earth's atmosphere due to the extra carbon dioxide that humans are putting into the atmosphere.

glucose The small unit which makes up cellulose and starch, and which starch turns into during digestion.

greenhouse effect When gases in the atmosphere trap heat energy/ infra-red radiation and keep the Earth warm.

greenhouse gas Gases such as carbon dioxide that trap heat in the atmosphere.

habitat A place where a community of plants and animals lives that has a particular group of environmental conditions.

half-life The time taken for the activity of a material to halve from an original value.

hardness How difficult it is to scratch or cut a material.

hazard A property of something that could cause harm to health or the environment.

hazcards A set of cards that lists the hazards of substances and ways of dealing with them.

heart attack When the heart fails to pump blood properly; often caused by blockage of the coronary arteries

heart disease May be caused by a build up of fatty substances in the arteries leading to the heart.

herbicides Chemicals used to kill weeds and other unwanted plants.

high blood pressure Where the heart is having to work harder than it should.

hominid Human-like organism.

hormonal system The part of the body which carries messages from sensor cells and to effector cells using hormones.

hormone A chemical secreted into the blood by an endocrine gland. Hormones control processes in the body.

Huntington's disease An inherited disease that attacks the nervous system. It is caused by a dominant allele.

hydrocarbon A compound containing only carbon and hydrogen atoms.

hydroelectric power Electrical energy produced when water in a high reservoir is allowed to move quickly downhill and drive a generator.

hydroelectricity Electricity generated by water falling from a reservoir through turbines.

hypothesis An idea or explanation that can be tested scientifically.

identical twins Twins that are born because a fertilised egg cell has split into two separate embryos.

immune system A system in your body which includes white blood cells that protects your body from infections

immune Able to make antibodies to fight a disease quickly so you don't become ill.
immunised Resistant to or protected from disease.
impact A collision, such as when a meteorite hits the Earth.
incineration Burning a material completely.
infectious disease A disease that is caused by microorganisms and can pass from one person to another.
influenza An infectious disease caused by a virus that affects the respiratory system.
infrared Electromagnetic radiation with a longer wavelength than visible light. We can feel this as heat.
inherit Receive from your parents.
inherited disease A disease that is passed on from parents to offspring by a particular allele.
inherited Characteristics that have come from a parent.
inner core The central, solid part of the Earth.
insecticides Chemicals used to kill insect pests.
insulin The hormone that controls the amount of glucose in the blood.
intensity The amount of energy from radiation reaching a certain area. For example, more intense infra-red radiation feels hotter.
ion An atom that has become charged.
ionisation The process by which atoms become charged. Can be caused by radioactive particles or rays.
ionising radiation Radiation that causes atoms to becomes ions.
ions Charged particles.
IVF In Vitro Fertilisation. The technique where an egg cell is fertilised in the laboratory, instead of inside the woman's (or animal's) body.
kidneys Organs that clean the blood and remove urea and other molecules for excretion.
landfill Burying rubbish in holes in the ground.
late onset diabetes Another name for Type 2 diabetes.
lava Molten rock on the surface of the Earth.
Life Cycle Assessment An examination of every stage in the manufacture and use of a material for a particular purpose, comparing its economic and environmental costs with other potential materials.
life cycle The sequence of events that happen to a material from obtaining the raw materials for its manufacture to its disposal as waste.
lifestyle factors Factors that are affected by the way a person lives their life.
light pollution Light from streetlights or other sources that interferes with observations made using telescopes.

light year The distance that light travels during one year.
liquid A substance that flows but has a fixed volume.
liver The organ that makes and destroys chemicals in the body.
magma Molten rock beneath the surface of the Earth.
malleable Property of a material that allows it to change shape when hammered or squeezed.
malnutrition Lacking in essential nutrients.
mantle The layer of the Earth just beneath the crust.
mass extinction When many species become extinct over a short time from a geological point of view (e.g. less than a million years).
mass vaccination When many people in a population are vaccinated against a disease.
mass The amount of matter contained in a body. It is measured in grams (g) or kilograms (kg).
mean Found by adding up a set of figures and dividing the total by the number of figures in the set.
Medical ethics committee A group of doctors who decide whether it is right that something should be done just because it can be done.
melting point The temperature at which a solid changes to a liquid.
memory cells White blood cells left in the blood after infection. They make antibodies quickly if you are infected again by that microorganism.
meteor A small piece of rock that burns up as it passes through the atmosphere.
meteorite A piece of rock that is not burnt up in the atmosphere and hits the Earth.
microorganism Any organism that you can only see clearly with a microscope.
microwaves Electromagnetic waves with a wavelength between infra-red and radio waves. Can be used for mobile phone communication and cooking food.
Milky Way The name of the galaxy that our Sun is part of.
mixture A substance composed of two or more elements or compounds not joined together.
modify change
molecule A particle made up of two or more atoms joined together.
monomer A small molecule which can combine with itself or other monomers to make a polymer.
moon A natural body that orbits a planet.
multicellular organisms Organisms made of many cells, i.e. almost all the plants and animals you see.
naphtha The fraction of crude oil with a boiling range of 100–150 °C; used in chemical manufacture.
natural fertiliser A fertiliser made from animal and plant waste.

natural selection When variations in characteristics are selected by the environment, and only individuals with successful characteristics survive to breed.
natural Occurs in nature.
nebula A cloud of dust and gas thrown off by a red giant star when it
nervous system The part of the body which carries messages from sensor cells and to effector cells along nerves.
neutral Something that has no charge.
neutron A particle with no charge found in the nucleus of an atom.
nitrates Compounds containing nitrogen that plants can absorb and use.
non-renewable A non-renewable fuel cannot be replaced and will eventually run out.
NO$_x$ General term for the oxides of nitrogen, i.e. nitrogen oxide and nitrogen dioxide.
nuclear fission The process of splitting atoms in a nuclear power station to release large amounts of heat energy.
nuclear fuel The fuel used in nuclear power stations, especially uranium.
nuclear power Energy generated by the break up of the nuclei of the atoms of certain elements such as uranium.
nuclear waste The waste materials from a nuclear power station.
nucleus (physics) The central part of an atom, where radiation comes from.
nucleus (biology) The 'control centre' of a cell. It contains the chromosomes.
obesity Being very overweight.
occupational radiation Radiation that people are exposed to in their place of work.
oceanic crust The type of crust that forms the ocean floors.
oceanic ridge A ridge in the middle of an ocean where new oceanic crust is being created.
oceanic trench A deep part of the ocean caused when one plate moves down beneath another.
osteoarthritis When the joints wear away.
outcome The result of an action or change in a factor.
outer core A liquid layer in the Earth, which lies above the solid inner core.
outlier A measurement that is very different from the other readings in a set of data.
ozone layer Part of the atmosphere where ozone is found in a higher concentration.
ozone Three oxygen atoms in one molecule.
pancreas The organ that makes insulin.
parallax A way of finding the distance to stars by measuring the angle of a star at different times of year.

particulate carbon Tiny pieces of solid carbon.
particulates Tiny pieces of solid material.
pesticides Chemicals used to kill pests that destroy crops.
photon A 'packet' of energy carried by electromagnetic radiation.
photosynthesis The chemical reaction that happens in plants. It uses light energy to convert carbon dioxide and water into sugar and oxygen.
planet Something that orbits a star. The Earth is a planet.
planetary nebula A cloud of dust and gas thrown off by a red giant star when it is becoming a white dwarf.
plaque Fatty lumps that can develop on the inside wall of a blood vessel and block it. In a coronary artery, this leads to a heart attack.
plastic Property of a material that allows it to keep its new shape and size when a force acting on it is removed.
plasticiser Small molecules mixed with a polymer to keep the polymer molecules apart.
plastics Commonly used word for polymer materials.
plate tectonics The theory that parts of the surface of the Earth move around.
pollutant A substance present in the environment as a result of human activity that can harm the environment or health.
pollution index A number based on the average amounts of each pollutant present.
polymer A material made up of very long molecules formed when lots of small molecules join together.
polymerisation The process in which monomer molecules join together to form a polymer.
positive In terms of a medical or genetic test, a positive result means that the person has the disease or the allele that could cause the disease.
predict Say what will happen in the future, based on a theory.
prediction Something that a hypothesis or theory says will happen and can be tested.
preservatives Chemicals added to food to prevent the growth of bacteria and fungi.
product The substances formed during a chemical reaction.
properties Features or characteristics of a substance such as its colour, strength or hardness.
protein A polymer made up of amino acids, containing carbon, hydrogen, oxygen and nitrogen. Our genes carry the instructions for making proteins.
proton A positively charged particle found in the nucleus of an atom.
public authorities Governments or local councils who are responsible for people's safety.

public transport e.g. buses, trains, trams.
pyroclastic flow A fast-moving cloud of hot gases, ash, dust and rock caused by a volcanic eruption.
radiation Particles and rays that are given out by radioactive materials.
radio waves Electromagnetic radiation with a long wavelength. Used to transmit TV and radio programmes.
radioactive decay The process whereby an unstable nucleus turns into a more stable nucleus by giving out alpha, beta or gamma radiation.
radioactive Any material that gives out alpha, beta or gamma radiation.
radon A radioactive gas.
range The lowest and highest value between which the true value of a quantity is likely to fall.
reactant The substances present at the start of a reaction
receptor Another word for sensor.
recessive A recessive allele only works when both chromosomes in a pair have the recessive allele.
recycling Reusing a material over and over again.
red giant A star that has used up its hydrogen fuel and expanded.
refining The separation and purification of materials obtained from a natural resource.
reflect Bounce something back from a surface, e.g. when light is reflected by a mirror.
reliable Results that can be trusted because the study was carried out properly.
renewable energy resources Renewable resources will not run out.
renewable Something that is replaced by natural processes, e.g. a source of energy that is not used up such as wind or solar power.
reprocessing plant A building where useful nuclear fuel is recycled or extracted from nuclear waste for reuse in the nuclear reactor.
reproduce When an organism makes offspring.
resistant When microorganisms are no longer affected by an antibiotic.
respiration The chemical reaction that happens in all living cells to release energy by converting sugar and oxygen into carbon dioxide and water.
risk An estimate of how dangerous a hazard is in a particular situation.
rubber A polymer material that is elastic and deforms relatively easily.
satellite A body that orbits a planet. A satellite can be artificial or natural.
seafloor spreading The formation of new crust at oceanic ridges, which causes oceans to become wider.

secondary energy source A source of energy that is produced from another source. For example, electricity is a secondary source because it is produced using other forms of energy (such as by burning fossil fuels).
secrete Release a substance made by a cell, such as a hormone.
sedimentation When sediments are deposited.
sediments Bits of rock formed by weathering.
selective breeding When humans choose which characteristics they want and breed from organisms which show them.
sensor cells Cells which respond to a stimulus, such as cells in the eye that respond to light, also called receptor cells.
sensor An instrument that can detect a change in some property of the environment and give a reading, e.g. a thermometer, carbon monoxide sensor.
sex chromosomes Either of the X or Y chromosomes that determine the sex of an organism. In humans, a female has XX sex chromosomes and a male has XY sex chromosomes.
sexual reproduction Reproduction that involves a male and a female. Sex cells from each parent fuse at fertilisation.
side-effects The unwanted effects on the body caused by a vaccine or medicine.
sievert (Sv) The unit of dose.
solar power Using the energy of the Sun to generate electricity or to heat water.
Solar System The Sun and all the planets, asteroids and comets that are orbiting it.
solid A substance with a rigid shape and fixed volume.
source Something that gives out electromagnetic waves or radiation.
specialised When a cell is adapted to its job. For instance, sperm cells are specialised because they have a tail to help them to swim.
specialist feeder An animal which feeds on only one type of food.
species (in evolution) A group of organisms with the same characteristics, (living) a group of organisms with the same characteristics that can breed with each other.
stabilisers Chemicals that keep foods emulsified.
stable A material that does not change.
star A large ball of gas that produces heat and light energy.
starch A polymer made up of glucose units, which can be digested. It contains carbon, hydrogen and oxygen.
stiffness Property of a material that determines how easily it will bend.

stimulus A change in the environment that an organism responds to.
strain A new form of a microorganism.
strength Property of a material that determines the force required to break it.
structural protein Proteins that make up parts of the body such as muscles, skin or hair.
subsidies Public money that is given to companies to help them. Usually this money is given to companies by the government.
sustainability The ability of a resource to be used and replaced without damage to the environment.
sustainable Can continue for many years.
sustainable development A programme of developing new energy technology that does not harm the environment or use up non-renewable resources.
sweeteners Chemicals added to foods to make them sweeter.
symptoms Effects of disease on the body.
synthetic fertiliser A fertiliser made by a chemical process.
synthetic Manufactured from other substances.
target cell The effector in the hormonal system, where a hormone makes something happen.
tax A sum of money that people have to pay to the government for a service.
tectonic plates Sections of the surface of the Earth that can move around.
tension A force that tries to stretch a material.
terminate To stop – this usually refers to stopping a pregnancy (having an abortion).
theory An idea that is tested and explains a wide range of observations.
tidal power Energy from the tides.
tool An object or idea which is used to make something else happen.
toxic Poisonous.
toxins Poisonous chemicals made by harmful microorganisms.
trace A tiny amount of a substance in a mixture.
transmit Send or allow energy or waves to go through something.
Type 1 diabetes Diabetes that occurs when the pancreas does not make any insulin.
Type 2 diabetes Diabetes when the pancreas does not make enough insulin.
ultraviolet Electromagnetic waves with a shorter wavelength than visible light. It can give us a sun tan or skin cancer.
uncertainty The difference between a reading and the true value.
unstable A material that becomes more stable by giving out radiation.
urea The waste product of the breakdown of unwanted amino acids.
vaccination Giving someone a vaccine.
vaccine Weakened or dead microorganisms which are put into the body to make you immune to a disease.
variation Differences in characteristics, such as colour of eyes, length of neck.
variety A subgroup of a species which has a slightly different set of characteristics.
veins Large blood vessels that carry blood back to the heart.
vent (volcano) The part of a volcano where lava or gases and ash come out.
vertebrates Animals with backbones.
virus Very small type of microorganism that can only reproduce inside the cells of another organism.
volume The amount of space taken up by a body.
wave power Energy from waves on the sea.
weathering The process of breaking up rocks.
white dwarf A small star that forms when a red giant collapses.
wind power The use of wind turbines to generate electricity.
X-rays Short wavelength electromagnetic radiation. Can be used to detect broken bones.
yield The amount of useful substance produced by a crop plant.

Index

abortion 23–5
acid rain 48–9, 231
acrylamide 205
activity (radioactive materials) 222–3
adaptation 170
additives 198–201
aflatoxin 203
AIDS 87
air pollution 34–59
air quality 35, 53, 56–7
alleles 18–19
allergies 203
alpha radiation 220, 224
amino acids 206, 209
anaemia 213
anaphylaxis 203
Andromeda galaxy 82
animal testing 102, 104
antibiotics 100–1
antibodies 92, 94
aphids 12
argon 39
arteries 106, 212
asexual reproduction 12–13
asteroids 74–5, 76–7
asthma 51, 59
atmosphere 38–9, 76, 148–9, 166
atoms 42, 123, 219, 224

background radiation 218
bacteria 12, 88, 100
becquerel (Bq) 222
best estimates 37, 115
beta radiation 220, 224
Big Bang 83
biodiversity 186–7
biofuels 232–3
bisphenol 205
blood vessels 106
boiling 124
bonds 128
breathing 34–5
brittle materials 119
burning 34, 44–7, 152–3

cancer 145–7, 213, 223–5
canned food 205
capillaries 106
carbon cycle 152–3
carbon dioxide
    atmosphere 39
    carbon cycle 152–3
    global warming 158–9
    greenhouse effect 154–5
    molecules 42
    photosynthesis 150–1
    pollution 45, 49

carbon monoxide 41, 46
carriers 21
cars 55
catalytic converters 54, 56, 59
cells
    chromosomes 10, 14–15
    effector cells 174–5
    fossils 166
    memory cells 92–4
    sensor cells 174–5
    specialisation 14–15
    stem cells 28–9
    white blood cells 92
cellulose 121, 206
central nervous system 176
CFCs 149
characteristics 10, 170, 173
chemical reactions 42–3
chlorophyll 150
chromosomes 10, 14–17
climate change 156
clinical trials 103
clones 12–13, 28–9
coal 44, 47, 48, 50
colourings 198
combustion 34, 44–7, 152–3
comets 74
communication systems 176–7
competition 181–2
complex behaviour 178
compounds 42–3, 112
compression 118
concrete 118
condensing 124
conservation 185
contamination 202–5, 226
continental crust 62
continental drift 64–5
control groups 103
cooking 143
cork 127
coronary arteries 106–7
correlations 50–2, 108–9, 158–9
cotton 121
craters 75
crops 157, 195
cross-linking 130
crude oil 122–5
crust 62
cultures 102
cystic fibrosis 21–2

Darwin, Charles 170–3
decomposers 152, 194
defences 90–1
density 117
designer babies 27

250

diabetes **210–11**
diet **211–13**
digestion **206–7**
dinosaurs **77**
diphtheria **89**
diseases
    air pollution **50**
    extinction **182**
    global warming **157**
    inherited diseases **20–3**
    microorganisms **88–9**
DNA **10–11, 167, 169**
dominant alleles **18–20, 22**
ductile materials **119**
durable materials **119**
dust **39**

E-numbers **199**
Eagle Nebula **82**
Earth
    formation **166–7**
    greenhouse effect **154–7**
    Solar System **74**
    structure **62–3**
earthquakes **72–3**
effector cells **174–5**
egg cells **14–15, 17**
elasticity **119**
electricity **52–3, 55, 230–1**
electromagnetic spectrum **140–1**
electrons **219**
elements **42–3, 81, 112, 219**
embryonic stem cells **28–9**
embryos **15, 27, 30–1**
emissions **159**
emulsifiers **198**
endangered species **184**
endocrine glands **177**
energy **128, 142, 208**
environmental factors **10, 13**
enzymes **11, 206–7**
epidemics **97**
epidemiological studies **108**
erosion **62–3**
errors of measurement **37**
ethene **126, 128**
ethical issues
    abortion **24–5**
    embryos **30–1**
    genetic testing **9, 24–5**
    testing treatments **104–5**
    vaccination **87**
Europa **81**
eutrophication **194**
evidence **68–9**
evolution **168–73, 178–9**
evolutionary trees **168, 179**
excretion **209**
extinction **77, 157, 164–5, 167, 182–5**

farming **194–7**
fat **209, 212**
fertilisers **192–3**
fibre (nutrition) **206**

fibres (materials) **120–1**
film badges **227**
flavour enhancers **199**
flexibility **118–19**
food **190–215, 218**
food chains **180**
food webs **180–1, 186**
formulae **42**
fossil fuels **44–7, 52–3, 153, 230–1**
fossils **166, 168, 182, 223**
fractional distillation **124–5**
fuels **44–7, 52–3, 54–5, 125, 152–3, 230–1**
fungi **88, 100, 195**

Galapagos finches **172**
galaxies **60, 82–3**
gametes **10, 14**
gamma radiation **141, 146, 220–1, 224**
gases
    atmosphere **38–9, 166**
    CFCs **149**
    greenhouse gases **154–5, 158–9**
    natural gas **44–5**
Geiger counters **220, 222**
gender **16–17**
gene therapy **26–7**
generalist feeders **181**
generators **230**
genes
    biodiversity **187**
    characteristics **10–11, 173**
    functions **10–11**
    modification **26–7**
    reproduction **8–9, 12–13**
genetic testing **24–5**
geohazards **70–3**
geothermal energy **232**
global warming **139, 155–61, 231**
glucose **177, 206–9, 210**
gold **112**
gravity **80, 83**
greenhouse effect **154–5**
greenhouse gases **154–5, 158–9**

habitats **180, 186**
half-life **222–3**
hardness **118**
hazards **40–1, 70–3**
health **50–1, 212–13**
heart attacks **107–9**
heart disease **106–7, 212**
heat **142–3**
herbicides **195**
high blood pressure **213**
hominid species **178–9**
hormones **177, 210**
hospitals **100–1**
Hubble, Edwin **83**
Huntington's disease **20, 22**
hydrocarbons **45, 122–3**
hydroelectric power **52, 233**
hydrogen sulfide **41**
hypothesis **172**

identical twins **28**
immunity **92–3, 95**
incineration **132**
infection **92–3, 97**
influenza **95**
infrared radiation **141–3, 154–5, 159**
inheritance
    characteristics **170**
    diseases **20–3**
    genes **12, 170**
insects **157, 195**
insulin **177, 210–11**
intensity (heat) **142**
intensive farming **194–5**
ionising radiation **146–7, 224–5**
ions **146, 224**
IVF **8–9, 17**

landfills **132**
lava **70**
laws **53, 55**
Life Cycle Assessment (LCA) **134–5**
life cycles
    polymers **132–3**
    stars **81**
lifestyle **107**
light **140**
light years **78**

magma **67, 70**
malleable materials **119**
malnutrition **190**
mantle **66–7**
manure **196**
mass **83, 117**
materials **112–37**
mean **37, 115**
medical ethics committees **105**
medicines **102–3**
melting points **116, 129**
memory cells **92–4**
meteor(ite)s **75**
microorganisms **87–93, 100**
microwaves **141, 143–5**
Milky Way **60, 82**
mixtures **112**
mobile phones **144–5**
molecules **42–3, 123, 128, 167**
monomers **126**
moons **74**
Mount Pinatubo **71**
mountains **64–5**
mudflows **71**

natural fertilisers **196**
natural gas **44**
natural materials **121–2, 127**
natural selection **170–1**
nervous system **176**
neutrons **219**
nitrates **192, 194**
nitrite **198**

nitrogen **38, 192**
nitrogen oxides **41, 47**
non-renewable resources **231, 236–7**
nuclear power **52, 234–5**
nuclear waste **223, 235**
nuclei **10, 219**
nylon **126–7**

obesity **190, 212**
occupational radiation **226–7**
oceanic crust **62**
oceans **49, 66–7**
oil **44**
organic farming **196–7**
osteoarthritis **213**
outliers **37, 115**
oxygen **34, 38, 45–6, 148**
ozone **148**
ozone layer **148–9**

packaging **204**
Pangaea **65**
parallax **79**
parasites **182, 195**
particles **219**
particulates **46**
pea plants **19**
penicillin **100**
pesticides **195, 197**
pests **195–6**
petrol **44**
photons **140–2**
photosynthesis **34, 49, 150–1, 192**
planetary nebulae **80**
planets **60, 74, 81**
plankton **49, 150**
plants
    alleles **18–19**
    food production **192–3**
    photosynthesis **150**
    reproduction **13**
    respiration **150–1**
plasticisers **131**
plasticity **119**
plastics **120–1**
plate tectonics **66–7**
pollutants **35, 40–3, 52–3**
pollution **34–59**
pollution index **36–7**
polymerisation **126**
polymers **126–35, 206**
polythene **126, 128**
power stations **52–3, 234**
predictions **68–9, 172**
preservatives **199**
proof **69**
properties of materials **112, 116–21**
proteins **11, 206, 208**
protons **219**
Proxima Centauri **78**
pyroclastic flows **71**

radiation 78, 138–63, 218–21, 224–9
radio waves 141
radioactive dating 66
radioactive decay 221
radioactivity 216–29
radon 218
range 37, 115
recessive alleles 18–19, 21–2
recycling 133
red giants 80
refining 124
reliability 109
renewable resources 52, 232–3, 236–7
reproduction 8–9, 12–13
resistance 100
respiration 34, 150, 177, 208
ringworm 89
risks 41, 228
rocks
    fossils 166
    materials 113
    radioactivity 218, 223
    weathering and erosion 62
rubbers 120–1
rubella 89

sea levels 156
seafloor spreading 67
sedimentation 63
selective breeding 171
sensor cells 174–5
sensors (air quality) 36–7
sex chromosomes 16–17
sexual reproduction 12–13
shellfish 49
shooting stars 75
side-effects 87, 95, 97
sieverts (Sv) 225
silk 121
skin cancer 147
smog 50
smoking 109
soil 194
solar power 52
Solar System 60, 74–5
soot 39, 46, 48
specialised cells 14–15
specialist feeders 181
species 167, 182–5
sperm cells 14–15, 17
stabilisers 198
stable elements 219
starch 206–7
stars 60, 78–9
steel 118
stiffness 118
stimuli 174–5
strains 95
strength 118
structural proteins 11
sulfur dioxide 40–1, 47, 54

Sun
    life cycle 80–1
    photosynthesis 150
    radiation 142
    Solar System 74
    Universe 60
sustainability 186, 238–9
sweeteners 199
symptoms 89
synthetic fertilisers 194
synthetic materials 122–3

taxes 55
tectonic plates 66–7, 72
tension 118
testing treatments 102–5
tetanus 93
theories 50, 68–9, 128–30, 172–3
toxic foods 202
toxicity 40–1
toxins 89–90
trace gases 39
transport 54–5
treatments 102–3
twins 28

ultraviolet radiation 141, 146–9
uncertainty of measurement 114
Universe 83
unstable elements 219–21
uranium 219
urea 209

vaccination 86–7, 94–9
variation 170
veins 106
viruses 88, 100
visible radiation 141
volcanoes 39, 70–1
volume 117

waste disposal 132–3
water vapour 38
weathering 62–3
weeds 195
Wegener, Alfred 64–5, 68–9
white blood cells 92
white dwarfs 80
whooping cough 93, 96–7
wind power 232
wool 121

X chromosomes 16–17
X-rays 141, 146

Y chromosomes 16–17

Pearson Education
Edinburgh Gate
Harlow
Essex
CM20 2JE
UK
www.longman.co.uk

© Pearson Education Limited 2006

The right of Penny Johnson, Peter Ellis, Michele Francis, Sue Kearsey, Penny Marshall, Michael O'Neill, Gary Philpott and Steve Woolley to be identified as the authors of this work has been asserted by them in accordance with the Copyright, Designs and Patents Act of 1988.

All rights reserved. No part of this publication may be reproduced, stored in a retrieval system, or transmitted in any form or by any means, electronic, mechanical, photocopying, recording or otherwise without the prior written permission of the Publishers or a licence permitting restricted copying in the United Kingdom issued by the Copyright Licensing Agency Ltd, 90 Tottenham Court Road, London, W1P 9HE.

First published 2006

ISBN-13: 978-0-582-85334-8 / ISBN-10: 0-582-85334-6

Project management and
development editor: Sue Kearsey
Editor: Liz Jones
Design and production: Roarr Design
Illustration: Oxford Designers & Illustrators Ltd
Picture research: Charlotte Lippmann
Indexer: Indexing Specialists (UK) Ltd
Printed In China
GCC/01

The publisher's policy is to use paper manufactured from sustainable forests.

Acknowledgments

The publisher would like to thank Basil Donnelly, Leonie Garratt, Christina Garry, Ben Green, Miles Hudson, Peter Kennett, Alison Knowles, Colin Lever, Alistair Sandiforth and Dorothy Warren, for their help in the production of this book.

We are grateful to the following for permission to reproduce photographs:

Advertising Archives: pg109; **Agripicture**: pg196 (Peter Dean); **Alamy**: pg10 (Photofusion/Liam Bailey), pg18(t) (Imagebroker/Martin Siepmann), pg31(t) (Imagestate/Pictor International), pg31(r) (Network Photographers), pg32(t) (Comstock Images), pg35(l) (Robert Harding), pg36 (Keith Dannemiller), pg44(m) (Carlos Davila), pg46(b) (LGPL/Andrew Lambert), pg48(br) (Phototake Inc./Mauritius,GmbH), pg86(l) (Imagebroker/Harald Theissen), pg86(m) (Phototake Inc./Yoav Levy), pg87(m) (David Young-Wolff), pg101(b) (David Hoffman), pg102(mr) (Agstock USA, Inc /Ed Young), pg103 (Tetra Images), pg108 (John Powell), pg112(tr) (Robert Harding / Glyn Genin), pg112(ml) (1Apix), pg113(b) (Jeff Morgan), pg114(l) (Plainpicture GMbH & Co. KG / Sebastian), pg117(t) (Dominic Burke), pg118(bl) (Adam Muttitt), pg118(br) (Janine Wiedel), pg120(tr) (Network Photographers), pg121(tr) (Holt Studios International Ltd.), pg121(m) (Peter Casolino), pg122 (PhotoStockFile/Tristan Hawke), pg132(t) (Robert Brook), pg142(m) (Bilderlounge/BreBa), pg144(t) (Acestock Ltd.), pg161 (Travel-shots), pg177 (Noel Yates), pg185(ml) (Terry Whittaker), pg194 (Alastair Balderstone), pg212(r) (Denis MacDonald), pg216(t) (Image 100), pg216(m) (John Foxx), pg216(b) (Image Source), pg217(tr) (Image 100), pg217(tl) (Dynamic Graphics Group), pg217(m) (Pictor International), pg221 (Powered by Light RF), pg229(t) (Photofusion/Peter Oliver), pg229(r) (StockShot/Tim Porter), pg229(m) (Mediacolor's), pg230 (LGPL/Jim Gibson), pg232 (Paul Glendell); **Anthony Blake Photo Library**: pg116(l); **Ardea**: pg16(t) (Pat Morris), pg171(tr) (Jean Michael Labet), pg173(mr) (John Mason); **BP**: pg124; **Collections**: pg48(tl) (Brian Shuel), pg55(t) (Brian Shuel), pg57(b), pg137, pg139, pg181(ml), pg218(b); **Corbis**: pg14(t) (Reuters), pg23 (LWA/Dann Tardif), pg29(l) (Reuters), pg30(t) (George Shelley), pg30(m) (George Shelley), pg30(b) (Reuters), pg31(m) (Michael Prince), pg32(b) (Rob Lewine), pg40 (Roger Ressmeyer), pg44(r) (Toby Melville/Reuters), pg48(tr) (WildCountry), pg48(bl) (Ted Spiegel), pg55(b) (Tom Wagner), pg69 (Ralph White), pg70 (Bettmann), pg71(l) (Roger Ressmeyer), pg71(r) (Alberto Garcia), pg73 (Underwood & Underwood), pg86(br) (Karen Kasmauski), pg93 (Jose Luis Pelaez, Inc.), pg96(l) (Steve Raymer), pg112(tl) (Reuters), pg118(t) (Marc Lecureuil), pg130 (Serge Timacheff), pg135(t) (Bettmann), pg142(tr), pg157(tr) (Reuters/Toby Melville), pg158 (Lloyd Cluff), pg192(t) (David Turnley), pg202(bl) (Adam Woofitt), pg202(br) (Wolfgang Kaehler), pg215 (Paul Barton), pg227(l) (Sygma/Bernard Bisson), pg227(r) (Charles O' Rear), pg234 (Igor/Kostin), pg236 (Bettmann); **Crown Copyright**: pg95, pg98, pg212(l); **Custom Medical Stock Photo**: pg20(m), pg20(b) (Jan Leestma); **Ecoscene**: pg34(l) (Amanda Gazidis), pg34(m) (Jon Bower), pg197(t) (Chinch Gryniewicz); **Eduardo Kac**: pg27 (GFP Bunny, 2000. Alba, the fluorescent bunny); **FLPA**: pg157(b) (Peter Davey), pg172(l) (Tui De Roy/ Minden Pictures), pg172(r) (Michael Gore); **Food Features**: pg117(b), pg218(t); **Galaxy**: pg75(mr) (Kipp Teague/David Wood/NASA), pg76(bl) (Andrew Stewart), pg83(r) (Howard Brown-Greaves); **Getty Images**: pg8 (Keystone), pg26(bl) (Time Life Pictures/Ted Thai), pg50 (Keystone), pg100(t) (Time Life/W. Eugene Smith), pg191(tm) (Digital Vision); **GLKS**: pg187 (Klaus Dehmer); **Holt Studios**: pg18(m) (Nigel Cattlin), pg192(b), pg193(m), pg193(b), pg195(t), pg195(b); **Marwell Preservation Trust**: pg185(mr) (Bill Hall); **Mary Evans Picture Library**: pg46(t); **Mickie Gelsinger**: pg26(br); **Missouri State Univeristy**: pg76(t) (Kevin R. Evans); **Mountain Camera**: pg62(br) (John Cleare), pg62(bl) (John Cleare), pg63(tl) (John Cleare), pg63(tr) (John Cleare), pg64(tl) (John Cleare), pg65 (John Cleare), pg84(b) (John Cleare), pg166(t) (John Cleare); **NASA**: pg79, pg80(tr), pg80(br), pg81, pg82(l), pg83(m), pg166(b); **Natural History Museum**: pg68, pg223; **Nature Picture Library**: pg174(tr) (Andrew Cooper), pg174(br) (Jeff Rotman), pg184(mt) (Dave Watts), pg185(tl) (Paul Hobson); **NHPA**: pg12(tr) (George Bernard), pg13(ml) (George Bernard), pg49 (Mark Bowler), pg152 (Jordi Bas Casas), pg154 (Alberto Nardi), pg164(tl) (Daniel Zupanc), pg164(r) (B Jones & M Shimlock), pg164(b) (Martin Harvey), pg167 (A.N.T. Photo Library), pg168 (Daniel Heuclin), pg169 (Christophe Ratier), pg171(l) (David Middleton), pg171(mr) (Yves Lanceau), pg173(ml) (Stephen Dalton), pg174(bl) (Mark Bowler), pg178(tm) (Jonathan and Angela Scott), pg178(tr) (Steve Robinson), pg181(t) (Stephen Dalton), pg181(mr) (Steve Toon), pg183 (Melvin Grey), pg184(mb) (A.N.T. Photo Library), pg184(r) (David Middleton), pg185(tr) (Martin Harvey), pg186(r) (Ernie James), pg191(b) (Ernie James), pg202(tl) (Guy Edwards), pg202(tr) (George Bernard); **Oxford Scientific**: pg13(mr) (Kent Breck); **Panos**: pg238(t) (Mark Henley); **Penny Johnson**: pg133(b); **Photofusion**: pg56(b) (Paul Ridsdale); **Photographers Direct**: pg237 (Anders Carlsson); **R.A. Landheinrich Meteorites**: pg75(t) (Iris Langeinrich/www.nyrockman.com); **Reuters**: pg157(tl) (Utpal Baruah); **Rex Features**: pg235 (Herbie Knott), pg57(t), pg72, pg102(tr) (Hayley Madden), pg114(r) (Matt Baron); **Ronald Grant Archive**: pg61(r) (Christine); **Science Photo Library**: pg9(t) (Bsip, Laurent), pg9(m) (Hank Morgan), pg11 (Michael Donne), pg12(br) (David Scharf), pg14(b) (Eye of Science), pg15 (Steve Allen), pg16(b) (Biophoto Associates), pg21 (Hattie Young), pg28 (Helen Mcardle), pg29(r) (Coneyl Jay), pg35(m) (Ian Boddy), pg35(r) (James King-Holmes), pg42 (Shelia Terry), pg43 (Andrew Lambert), pg44(t) (Steve Allen), pg52 (Alex Bartel), pg56(t) (NASA), pg60(m) (M-sat Ltd), pg60(b) (Planetary Visions Ltd), pg64(tr), pg66 (Dr. Ken Macdonald), pg74 (Jerry Lodriguss), pg75(ml) (John Sanford), pg76(br) (Julian Baum), pg77 (D. Van Ravensswaay), pg78(t) (David Parker), pg78(mr) (Frank Zullo), pg80(ml) (Mark Garlick), pg80(m) (Lynette Cook), pg82(r) (Robert Gendler), pg83(t) (Jean-Charles Cuillandre/Canada-France-Hawaii Telescope), pg87(t) (CDC), pg88(l) (Dr.Linda Stannard, UCT), pg88(m) (Andrew Syred), pg88(r), pg92 (Eye of Science), pg94(l) (Ian Hooton), pg94(r) (Samuel Ashfield), pg96(m), pg96(r) (Dr. M.A. Ansary), pg99 (CC Studio), pg100(m) (Scott Camazine), pg101(m) (Damien Lovegrove), pg102(ml) (BSIP, Laurent H. Americain), pg110 (Mark Clarke), pg113(tl) (Robert Brook), pg113(tr) (Agstock/Harris Barnes Jr.), pg116(b) (Heine Schneebeli), pg120(m) (Alexis Rosenfeld), pg129 (Alex Bartel), pg133(t) (David Nunuk), pg140 (Duncan Shaw), pg141 (Ted Kinsman), pg146(t) (Sinclair Stammers), pg146(b) (Scott Camazine), pg147 (Erika Craddock), pg159 (D.A. Peel), pg165(l) (Jeremy Walker), pg173(t), pg178(b) (Pascal Goetgheluck), pg182(r) (Philippe Plailly), pg184(l) (Pat & Tom Lesson), pg203(t) (Mark Thomas), pg209 (BSIP VEM), pg210 (Cordelia Molloy), pg211(b) (Samuel Ashfield), pg212(b) (Shelia Terry), pg219 (Astrid & Hanns-Frieder Michler), pg225(l) (James King-Holmes), pg225(r) (Cordelia Molloy), pg228 (Dr P. Marazzi), pg233(t) (Martin Bond), pg233(m) (Martin Bond), pg233(b) (Martin Bond), pg238(b) (M-SAT Ltd.); **Skyscan**: pg60(t); **Still Pictures**: pg39 (Jeff & Alexa Henry), pg53(t) (Das Fotoarchiv/Manfred Vollmer), pg53(b) (Jorgen Schytte), pg54 (Das Fotoarchiv/Friedrich Stark), pg61(tl) (Shehzad Noorani), pg61(m) (UNEP/Robert T. Wells), pg85 (Peter Arnold), pg121(b) (Mark Edwards), pg132(b) (Paul Glendell), pg148 (Peter Arnold), pg150 (Martin Bond), pg165(m) (Jean-Luc Ziegler), pg165(r) (Martin Wendler), pg178(tl) (Steve Kaufman), pg191(tr) (Lineair Fotoarchief), pg191(tm) (UNEP), pg203(b) (Das Fotoarchiv); **Topfoto**: pg198(t) (Heritage Image Partners); **Warren Photographic**: pg12(tl) (Jane Burton); **Woodfall Wild Images**: pg182(l) (David Woodfall), pg186(l) (David Woodfall); **www.glofish.com**: pg26(t).

The following photographs were taken on commission © **Pearson Education Ltd** by:
Gareth Boden: pg89; **Rick Chapman**: pg13(mr), pg52(t), pg112(mr), pg120(tl,tm,b), pg125(all), pg134, pg135, pg140, pg143(t,m), pg144(b), pg153, pg191(tl), pg197(b), pg198(b), pg199(t,m), pg203(m), pg204(all), pg205(all), pg210(b), pg213, pg214; **Trevor Clifford**: pg101(t), pg115, pg119, pg125, pg131, pg207.

Front cover photos:
Main image: (c)David Trood / The Image Bank / Getty Images
Inset: (top)(c)Denis Scott / Taxi / Getty Images; (middle) (c)Bryan Peterson / Taxi / Getty Images; (bottom) Punchstock / Digital Vision (royalty-free).

Every effort has been made to trace the copyright holders and we apologise in advance for any unintentional omissions. We would be pleased to insert the appropriate acknowledgement in any subsequent edition of this publication.

Every effort has been made to trace and acknowledge ownership of copyright. If any have been overlooked, the publisher will be pleased to make the necessary changes at the earliest opportunity.

Licence Agreement: *21st Century Science GCSE Foundation CD-ROM*

Warning:
This is a legally binding agreement between You (the school) and Pearson Education Limited of Edinburgh Gate, Harlow, Essex, CM20 2JE, United Kingdom ('PEL').

By retaining this Licence, any software media or accompanying written materials or carrying out any of the permitted activities You are agreeing to be bound by the terms and conditions of this Licence. If You do not agree to the terms and conditions of this Licence, do not continue to use the CD and promptly return the entire publication (this Licence and all software, written materials, packaging and any other component received with it) with Your sales receipt to Your supplier for a full refund.

21st Century Science GCSE Foundation CD-ROM consists of copyright software and data. The copyright is owned by PEL. You only own the disk on which the software is supplied. If You do not continue to do only what You are allowed to do as contained in this Licence you will be in breach of the Licence and PEL shall have the right to terminate this Licence by written notice and take action to recover from you any damages suffered by PEL as a result of your breach.

Yes, You can:
1. use or install *21st Century Science GCSE Foundation CD-ROM* on Your own personal computer as a single individual user:

No, You cannot:
1. copy *21st Century Science GCSE Foundation CD-ROM* (other than making one copy for back-up purposes);

2. alter *21st Century Science GCSE Foundation CD-ROM*, or in any way reverse engineer, decompile or create a derivative product from the contents of the database or any software included in it:

3. include any software data from *21st Century Science GCSE Foundation CD-ROM* in any other product or software materials;

4. rent, hire, lend or sell *21st Century Science GCSE Foundation CD-ROM*;

5. copy any part of the documentation except where specifically indicated otherwise;

6. use the software in any way not specified above without the prior written consent of PEL

Grant of Licence:
PEL grants You, provided You only do what is allowed under the Yes, You can table above, and do nothing under the No, You cannot table above, a non-exclusive, non-transferable Licence to use *21st Century Science GCSE Foundation CD-ROM*..

The above terms and conditions of this Licence become operative when using *21st Century Science GCSE Foundation CD-ROM*.

Limited Warranty:
PEL warrants that the disk or CD-ROM on which the software is supplied is free from defects in material and workmanship in normal use for ninety (90) days from the date You receive it. This warranty is limited to You and is not transferable.

This limited warranty is void if any damage has resulted from accident, abuse, misapplication, service or modification by someone other than PEL. In no event shall PEL be liable for any damages whatsoever arising out of installation of the software, even if advised of the possibility of such damages. PEL will not be liable for any loss or damage of any nature suffered by any party as a result of reliance upon or reproduction of any errors in the content of the publication.

PEL does not warrant that the functions of the software meet Your requirements or that the media is compatible with any computer system on which it is used or that the operation of the software will be unlimited or error free. You assume responsibility for selecting the software to achieve Your intended results and for the installation of, the use of and the results obtained from the software.

PEL shall not be liable for any loss or damage of any kind (except for personal injury or death) arising from the use of *21st Century Science GCSE Foundation CD-ROM* or from errors, deficiencies or faults therein, whether such loss or damage is caused by negligence or otherwise.

The entire liability of PEL and your only remedy shall be replacement free of charge of the components that do not meet this warranty.

No information or advice (oral, written or otherwise) given by PEL or PEL's agents shall create a warranty or in any way increase the scope of this warranty.

To the extent the law permits, PEL disclaims all other warranties, either express or implied, including by way of example and not limitation, warranties of merchantability and fitness for a particular purpose in respect of *21st Century Science GCSE Foundation CD-ROM*.

Governing Law:
This Licence will be governed and construed in accordance with English law.

© Pearson Education Limited 2006